BRITISH AIRCRAFT CORPORATION

British Aircraft Corporation

A HISTORY BY CHARLES GARDNER

BOOK CLUB ASSOCIATES · LONDON

ISBN 0 7134 3815 0

Photoset in 11 on 12pt Bembo by
Servis Filmsetting Ltd, Manchester
and printed in Great Britain by
The Anchor Press Ltd, Tiptree, Essex

This edition published 1981 by
Book Club Associates
by arrangement with
B.T. Batsford Ltd, London.

Contents

List of Illustrations

★ Photographs marked thus are by Arthur Gibson.

* Photographs marked thus are by Arthur Gibson.

Foreword

by Sir George Edwards, OM, CBE, FRS

When the British Aircraft Corporation was first formed, I remember describing it as 'a Great Adventure' and I think this book shows that it was certainly that. Charles Gardner was in a strong position to write about it as he saw it from the inside, which is a somewhat more reliable viewpoint than that adopted by many commentators who have not even got close to their subject from the outside. It was in 1953 that I persuaded him to leave the BBC, where he was their Air Correspondent, and join my team at Weybridge – Vickers-Armstrongs (Aircraft) as it then was – and then BAC, continuing under the chairmanship of Mr Allen Greenwood after my retirement at the end of 1975.

The drawing together of the constituent parts of BAC was not easy. Made up as it was of the Aviation and Guided Weapons interests of Bristol Aircraft, English Electric, Hunting and Vickers, there was an immediate problem of reconciling the four companies who, in various fields, had been highly competitive and had fought one another for a good many orders, both home and away. I have heard it suggested by outside people that the competitive position between the companies for home orders was something of a sham. No one who took part in any of these struggles would subscribe to that view. Retaining the individual dedication of each team to their own product but, at the same time, making sure that the front presented by BAC was a united one required a fair mixture of diplomacy and firmness.

The inspired choice of Lord Portal as BAC's first Chairman – and his selfless acceptance of the invitation to take the Chair (which he regarded as a duty) – was the biggest single unifying factor around which we all gathered. His status was such that every one of us, regardless of our allegiance prior to the formation of BAC, was glad to serve under him as the head of a great new undertaking of which we had each become a part. The process of first drawing authority to the centre and then putting much of it back to the Divisions was made possible under his wise leadership and could almost be the subject of a book of its own.

Not that life was easy for the newly formed company. We had not been going long before the usual pattern of cancellations of military projects and difficult conditions in the civil aircraft world made the going hard. But we fought our way through and ended up with a highly profitable company which made a substantial contribution to both the country's export effort and its defence capability.

We pioneered international collaboration on advanced technical programmes, starting with Concorde, and we had the ability to do almost any job in the aerospace business. I was always adamant that we should keep intact the three basic ingredients, military aircraft, civil aircraft, and guided weapons including Space projects; it cheered me greatly to see this same structure retained when the company was finally nationalised. The interchange of skills and flexibility which the three activities provide are, in my opinion, essential for a large aerospace company that is in the business to stay.

At the time of writing this foreword, the issue of British Aerospace shares has not yet been made to the public. It is interesting, to say the least, that two privately owned companies in the form of BAC and Hawker Siddeley Aviation, both highly profitable, should have to go through the double pain of nationalisation and a merger, only to see their shares go back into private hands again. This foreword is written with knowledge from the inside, as is the book itself. Apart from its historical interest, I hope that the book may help some future executive (or – dare I say it? – Minister or Civil Servant) to see that the path he is intent on following is not necessarily going to end in glory.

The book also gives some idea of the courage and determination of the people with whom I had the honour to work, and it is good that their efforts should be thus recognised. I have always maintained (and it has now become fashionable for others to say the same thing) that Britain's future depends on exploiting her industries based on higher technology, especially engineering, however painful the necessary changes may be. The demands made on the designers of the aerospace industry have always been so great that newer developments were and are continually being called for in order to meet their needs. In showing how BAC was formed and preserved, I think this book will also show that the company played a larger part in preparing British industry for the role it must play in the future than it was ever given credit for during its lifetime.

I am delighted to write the foreword to this book and hope that it will achieve the success which it deserves as it sets out in a broad historical sweep what BAC was all about.

Acknowledgements

This account of BAC (1960–77) is weighted towards affairs at Board-room level and in Whitehall. It therefore may appear to take for granted much of the brilliant and dedicated work which was done during those seventeen years in project and design offices at the Divisional sites, in the administration and direction of complex production lines, and in the efforts of thousands of highly skilled engineers on the factory floors. It pays far too little tribute to, or makes only sparse mention of, men who travelled the world so successfully to sell and to service BAC products, and whose professional skills laid the real foundation for the Corporation's success.

To these former colleagues, many of whom now, fortunately for this country, deservedly hold senior posts in British Aerospace, the author apologises. This book should have said so much more about them.

To the many people who helped with the research and who patiently probed their memories and records to sort out the sequence of the events of yesteryear, I give my thanks. In particular, my gratitude is due to Norman Barfield at Weybridge, and Alec Johnston at Warton, for a lot of material; to Arthur Gibson for his many-sided expertise, and for so many of his beautiful pictures; to Joyce Brixey, who, for all the BAC years, was personal assistant to Sir George Edwards, for her filing system, and especially to Beryl Clavey, the only person in BAC who could ever read my handwriting, and who, in her time, has translated into readable English so many thousands of pages of it.

Finally, no attempt is made here to chronicle the crowded events after nationalisation. Aerospace has for long been a political football but at least there is now only the one British ball – and it is a very strong one.

I
Rationalisation – the
First Steps

It is a matter of somewhat daunting fact that at the end of World War II, there were twenty-seven British airframe design companies, and eight British aircraft engine companies. True, four of the airframe units were nominally members of the Hawker Siddeley Group, but this arrangement was managerially a loose one, and each component ran its own design affairs, and competed vigorously with others in the Group for available work.

Table 1 British aircraft and aero-engine industry, 1946

Airframe manufacturers

Airspeed Ltd
★Sir W.G. Armstrong
   Whitworth Aircraft Ltd
Auster Aircraft Ltd
★Avro (A.V. Roe & Co. Ltd)
Blackburn Aircraft Ltd
Boulton Paul Aircraft Ltd
The Bristol Aeroplane Co. Ltd
Cierva Autogiro Co. Ltd
Cunliffe-Owen Aircraft Ltd
The de Havilland Aircraft Co.
   Ltd
The English Electric Co. Ltd
The Fairey Aviation Co. Ltd
Folland Aircraft Ltd
General Aircraft Ltd
★Gloster Aircraft Co. Ltd
Handley Page Ltd
★Hawker Aircraft Ltd
Martin-Baker Aircraft Ltd
Miles Aircraft Ltd
Percival Aircraft Ltd

Portsmouth Aviation Ltd
Saunders-Roe Ltd
Scottish Aviation Ltd
Short Brothers Ltd
†Vickers-Armstrongs
   (Weybridge)
†Vickers-Armstrongs
   (Supermarine)
Westland Aircraft Ltd
   ★Members of Hawker Siddeley
Group
   †Owned by Vickers Ltd

Aero-engine manufacturers

Alvis Ltd
Armstrong Siddeley Motors Ltd
Blackburn Aircraft Ltd (*Cirrus*)
The Bristol Aeroplane Co. Ltd
The de Havilland Engine Co.
   Ltd
Metropolitan-Vickers Electrical
   Co. Ltd
D. Napier & Son Ltd
Rolls-Royce Ltd

By the late 1940s, therefore, it was the conventional wisdom of observers, especially outside the industry, that there would soon have to be a considerable contraction in the number of aircraft and engine firms, especially so because the complexity of new aircraft at the start of the jet era was rising steeply and, with it, both the development and the unit costs. What are now known as electronics were beginning to come in, supersonic speeds for military aircraft were within grasp, as were whole new families of warlike stores to be carried and aimed, including atom bombs and rocket-powered missiles. The days of knocking up quick, cheap, private-venture prototypes in the experimental hangar were over. The development of a significant new aircraft, military or civil, would, henceforth, have to be backed by resources of the kind which many of the twenty-seven firms did not possess. Further, this expensive complication and sophistication were predictably going to increase, and, correspondingly, the ability of the industry's main customer, the Government, to buy the end-product in quantity was going to decrease.

Even so, though it was now peacetime, and there was a great surplus of wartime equipment to be reduced to scrap, the overall outlook for the aircraft industry was, paradoxically, not at all bad. Many challenging new frontiers had been reached by wartime developments — especially those opened up by the jet engine and rocketry. The commercial aircraft markets were clearly likely to 'explode' in the 1950s, and the performance and efficiency of every kind of airborne vehicle were at the start of very steep upward curves.

There was little doubt that Great Britain had the men who could exploit these fascinating technical opportunities. The industry abounded in brains, foresight, and abilities of all kinds. The men who had produced the Spitfire, Hurricane, Wellington, Lancaster, Mosquito, Meteor, the gas turbine engine, radar, and the weapons to go with them, were mostly still around, and still in their prime. Two key organisational things, however, needed to be looked at right away. The first was the problem of fragmentation of effort spread over so many, and mainly small, concerns; the other was firm guidance in the form of a Government/industry plan. The Government, of course, was in control of both the UK home markets: the military one directly, and the civil one indirectly, through the three newly formed nationalised airlines — BEA, BOAC, and British South American Airways (later merged into BOAC).

In fact, all that happened was that there was a tragic decade of disarray, partially caused by the onset of the Korean War, partially by official technical cowardice, and partially by the obstinacy of the industry itself. Twenty-seven aircraft firms were, by inspection, at least twenty too many, but, in considering the situation, due regard must be paid to the towering personalities who controlled the most important of these firms. Inside Sir Thomas Sopwith's Hawker Siddeley Group there were Sir Roy Dobson at Avro, and Sir Frank Spriggs and Sir Sidney Camm at Hawker. Sir Frederick Handley Page continued to run his own company with an iron rod; the Fairey family was at Fairey; at Vickers, under the chairmanship of that great man, Lord Weeks, were Rex Pierson and a rising young George Edwards, with Joe Smith, the wartime developer of the Spitfire, at Vickers-Supermarine. De Havilland were then, as until the end, a law unto themselves as the 'only true aristocrats' of the business; Bristol, under the White family, were the pride and joy of the West Country; and, coming up over the horizon, was the powerful figure of George Nelson of English Electric with plans for a jet bomber later to be called the Canberra. At Rolls-Royce was the massive figure of Lord Hives. Never had the reputation of the industry stood so high in public esteem, never had it been blessed with so many outstanding men, and never before had it had such opportunities to dominate the world, even including the USA, by its technical brilliance. Equally, never had it been less likely that such personalities would willingly become subservient to each other – certainly not while business remained to be done.

The Government, however, and to give it credit, was willing to knock a number of heads together – if not directly, then indirectly – by the placement, or non-placement, of orders. It envisaged an overall labour force of 150,000 as the desirable norm, and the reduction of fragmentation by maintaining only a selected number of design teams – just enough to meet its national duty to provide the defence of the country. This purely theoretical assessment of the manpower requirement was soon to be shown to be over 65 per cent in error.

As a first step it was decided, as a negative measure, to turn off the taps and to order no major re-equipment of the front-line defence forces until the mid-1950s; to restrict the pursuit of supersonic flying to study of data from air-dropped models; and to abandon, or fail to support, transonic projects. On the civil side, it pinned its faith on the unrealistic Brabazon Committee list of recommended types, on the basis of Government help with development, but the airliner business basically was to be by private enterprise, privately funded. It is only fair to say that the industry agreed heartily with the last part, as it, too, saw commercial aircraft as something it could, should, and would handle on its own.

Finally, the Government, which already had the Ministry of Supply standing in its battalions between the armed forces and their suppliers, created the Ministry of Transport and Civil Aviation to perform a similar function for the national airlines. It was during this period that the head of one manufacturing company complained that he had had a committee of twenty-five people – twenty-two from the Government and three from his company – to consider a proposed modification to a door.

No one will ever know what 'merging' effect the policy of the Attlee Government would have had by its restriction of orders to selected design teams. The Korean War of 1950 caused the plan instantly to be shelved, and a re-armament boom followed under what was seen as the likelihood of the outbreak of World War III. By mid-1955, the industry employed not 150,000, but nearly 250,000 people, and only two airframe firms and one engine firm had gone from the lists. General

Aircraft and Blackburn had merged, and so had Cierva and Saunders-Roe (into the Saunders-Roe helicopter division). Metropolitan-Vickers engines had been bought out by Armstrong Siddeley Motors. There was, however, the first sign of Governmental irritation at the design rivalry between member companies of the Hawker Siddeley Group, which still operated Avro, Armstrong Whitworth, Gloster and Hawker as virtually separate and competing entities.

This book is not intended to be a history of the British aircraft industry but only of the British Aircraft Corporation, which was not formed until 1960. The sad, sad story of the missed opportunities and of the dithering (which led, for example, to the huge purchase of Canadian-built F86 Sabres in 1953 when the RAF could have ordered the Hawker P1052 or P1081) has already been told elsewhere, notably in Derek Wood's carefully researched book *Project Cancelled*. It is, however, germane to see how, in the end, twenty-seven airframe firms came down to two companies (BAC and Hawker Siddeley Aviation) plus Shorts, Westland, and Scottish Aviation. At the same time, the eight engine companies of 1955 eventually became just one − Rolls-Royce.

After Korea, a number of the trends that had been predictable in 1946 had become confirmed as fact. The rapid rate of technological progress and sophistication of the military products, which were the mainstay of the industry, had inevitably led to a malevolent spiral. The gestation period of a major new aircraft from concept to delivery was creeping up towards ten years, whereas the life of any one Government was only half that at a maximum. This put every equipment decision taken by one Government at risk if that Government was replaced by another − a situation which was to climax in 1964/5.

Research and development costs for a 'ten year' aeroplane were also on a steep up-slope, and so, inevitably, were the unit costs of manufacture once the non-recurring expenditure (research and development and tooling) was out of the way. With all costs so much on the increase, the actual number of production aircraft which could be afforded by the defence budgets declined pro rata.

This meant that the UK was always selling, or trying to sell, off what Sir George Edwards has called 'the thick end of the learning curve.' By contrast, the US industry has always exported from the 'thin' end of a production run of at least several hundred aircraft.

This UK problem of trying to operate a high-technology business, with huge research and development and tooling costs charged against a relative handful of initial production aircraft, rapidly became the dominating problem of the industry in both military and civil fields. It still is the major fact of life today. For years, the UK managed to retain a world competitive position because its man-hour costs were very much below − indeed half − those of the USA, while the actual research and development man-hours per project were about the same. The production man-hours story was, however, in the USA's favour for the learning curve reason given, and also because, as a corollary, they were able to put much more horse power into the hands of each factory-floor worker. In recent years, the gap in man-hour costs, once so favourable to the UK, has narrowed considerably, and it was this, as much as anything, which eventually led to the onset of European collaboration aimed at expanding initial order-books while sharing the non-recurring investment monies.

Dr Keith Hartley of York University, writing in a 1965 paper on the industry, pointed out that, in 1954, a total of 155 combat aircraft represented a value of £6.164 millions, while four years later 178 combat aircraft were valued at £29 millions. Since inflation accounted for only a relatively small part of this increase, Dr Hartley comments that these rising unit costs were due to the greater size and complexity of modern aircraft. In the years 1953, 1954 and 1955, the industry produced a rough average of 2000 aircraft a year. By 1957, this was down to 968, but, by airframe weight, a more reliable yardstick, it was still turning out 84 per cent of the weight produced in 1953, which weight had then represented 2287 machines. By 1960, however, numbers were down to 510 aircraft and weight to 41 per cent of that of 1953.

In 1955, however, there was still no sign of a diminution in the number of design firms. Buggins' turn was still, somehow, enabling everyone to survive. The ultimate nonsense of ordering three V-bombers — each with its own development costs but 'split' production numbers — was helping to sustain Vickers, Avro and Handley Page. Gloster had the Javelin and a thin-wing Javelin development, English Electric was still building Canberras and developing what was to become the Lightning, while Hawker were getting into their Hunter stride. De Havilland had the Sea Venom and Sea Vixen, Supermarine the Scimitar, while Blackburn were preparing to follow the Beverley with the Buccaneer. Saunders-Roe were developing a 'rocket-plus-jet' fighter, and Fairey were following up the Gannet anti-submarine aircraft with the FD2 Delta which, in 1956, was to carry the world's air speed record to 1132 m.p.h. The FD2 was seen as the basis for an outstanding supersonic fighter, and, as Derek Wood has pointed out, was almost exactly the same as the Mirage. Armstrong Whitworth were soon to get the Argosy, and there was much helicopter activity affecting Bristol, Fairey, Westland and Saunders-Roe. On the transport side, Vickers had the very successful Viscount, and the V1000; de Havilland were salvaging the original Comet into the Comet IV and building Herons and Doves. Bristol had the Britannia, the Freighter, the Sycamore and Belvedere helicopters, and, more profitably, its Bristol engines and rockets.

But, basically, the situation was unhealthy. The military procurement system was demonstrably wrong, as the ever mounting list of cancellations was to show. Design and development resources were kept

employed on sophisticated projects, some of which went on as far as the
flight stage before being axed. Nothing is more wasteful of the nation's
best brains and expensive facilities than to tie them down for years on
aircraft and weapons which are then aborted. Hawker, in particular,
suffered heavily, having two potentially world-beating supersonic
designs by Camm stillborn, and, in the end, the company was never to
build a supersonic aircraft.

It was at this time (1955) that the first stirrings since 1946 were felt at
Government level that maybe they, as the holders of the purse strings,
should do something positive to reduce the number of aircraft and
engine firms, and to harness the industry's resources to a sensible joint
plan for fighters, bombers, transports, helicopters, trainers, and the
engines to power them. At the Ministry of Supply, Under Secretary
Denis Haviland had written in February 1954 a closely argued paper.
The industry, he said, should no longer rely on Buggins' turn to spread
ever more thinly the work affordable by the nation. It should re-organise
itself into fewer and stronger units, and new contracts should only be
placed with firms, or groups of firms, which had the resources and
strength to handle them. He made the point that the UK had more major
airframe firms than the USA — which was absurd. In short, Haviland was
advocating what amounted to compulsion, perhaps more in hope that
the hint of it would do the trick rather than that a Conservative
Government would actually and actively interfere with the free play of
market forces. This Government was, however, four to five years later,
to take the bull increasingly by the horns and demand rationalisation or
else.

Civil aircraft were still seen by the Government and perforce,
therefore, by the industry, as a domain for private venture (save for
some help on research and development) although the cost-rise story of
big jetliners was every bit as steep as that for combat aircraft. Very few
major airliners were capable of showing an overall profit to their
manufacturers (British or American). The increases in size and efficiency
and utilisation had resulted in world markets, in terms of numbers-off,
getting to be too slender, and especially so for the UK, striving to enter a
field dominated by the Americans. As one leading British manufacturer
put it (but some years later): 'All I know about break-even numbers is
that as soon as you get close, some development or re-design, or stretch,
or modification needs new investment which puts the target out of sight
again.'

A type of transport whose competitive selling price would once cover
amortisation of research and development and tooling on a sale of fifty
or sixty off, soon had this 'break-even' number go through the century
and on to 200. More recently, a foreseeable sale of 300 or more is
required to make the job worth starting, unless it is to be subsidised for
political, currency, or strategic reasons.

Back in 1954/5, however, all this lay in the future, and Denis

Haviland's 1954 paper was simply aimed at a reduction in the number of firms, a severe curtailment of Buggins' turn, and a modicum of sensible Government/industry planning.

His paper was considered and discussed in Whitehall, but, almost predictably, nothing immediately came of it. The arguments were shelved for another four years, and a few more cancellations (and the 1957 Defence White Paper) before Aubrey (later Sir Aubrey) Jones was to refer the subject to the Cabinet (although not a member) and, at the same time to initiate some action, this time publicly, and with a pistol in his holster if not in his hand.

The Duncan Sandys Defence White Paper of 1957 was the biggest shock ever, at that time, to be administered to the aircraft industry. It pointed out that there was a very definite limit to the effort which the UK could afford to devote to defence. Defence would be thermo-nuclear, and so, accordingly, manned combat aircraft were to be phased out, and replaced by missiles – or as Sandys always called them – 'rockets.' When Prime Minister Harold Macmillan had given Duncan Sandys a new brief in January 1957, he had publicly spelt out that he was to secure a substantial reduction in defence expenditure and manpower, and, to achieve it, the Minister was given almost unlimited powers to change the size and shape and organisation of the armed services and their equipment and supply.

By the time Sandys (later Lord Sandys) had responded vigorously to his brief, there was nothing left to the British airframe industry on its dominant military side save the P1 Lightning and the still uncancelled Operational Requirement No. 339 – the famous Canberra replacement – towards which every major design team in the country now turned its attention. Everything else had gone out of the window, including the Mach 2+ bomber (the Avro 730), the Fairey Delta fighter (OR 329), and the Saunders-Roe 177 rocket-plus-jet fighter, which had already flown and in which both Germany and Japan had shown strong interest. Earlier cancellations had included the Hawker P1083 (1953) and then, after the Sandys White Paper, the M=2+ P1121, which was 80 per cent completed early in 1958, and which Sir Sydney Camm was to describe as 'the greatest miss in British Aviation.'

As military work represented some 70 per cent of the industry output and employed 60 per cent of its manpower, the effect of the Sandys decision that all war was atomic war and that manned aircraft should be replaced by missiles was paralysing. Looking back on it, it was almost a laughable hypothesis. Sandys' 'rockets,' however vividly he may have recalled his involvement in the threat of the V2 and the near-panic it produced in some of his fellow politicians, were in no way ready to take over the air offence/defence of the country, as subsequent events were to prove. Nor was his assumption valid that only nuclear-delivery missiles were significant – a US fad of the period, but one which the USA never pursued to the extent of cancellation of conventional war airframes.

What Sandys set down was really a Dan Dare scenario which might conceivably be valid by the turn of the century, but which bore no relation to the state of the art or the practicalities of life for the 1960s.

The brutal fact remained that, at a stroke, Sandys killed all the advanced projects, together with some of the engines (Gyron and RB106) to power them, which were in the 1957 pipeline. He demoralised the Royal Air Force and the industry, and set British military aviation development back by at least several years – and some say by a decade. As Lockspeiser had done something similar with supersonics only eleven years earlier, the industry had had more than its fair share of Government-inflicted wounds.

Looking back on the period 1946–58, it still challenges comprehension that such a mess could be made of such a favourable initial situation. The 1946 decision by Sir Ben Lockspeiser, the Director General of Scientific Research at the then still-surviving Ministry of Aircraft Production, to cancel the Miles M52 supersonic aeroplane and to ban any other supersonic venture, and to use models instead, was made in the same year that the Americans first flew the Bell X1 rocket plane. This was soon to become the world's first manned aircraft to achieve supersonic speed. It was to be eight years before a British-built aircraft was to fly supersonically straight and level. The United States Air Force had supersonic F100 swept-wing fighters in service in early 1954, which was before the RAF even got its first Hunter, and five years before it got its first supersonic P1B Lightning.

During these wasted and wasteful years, the British passed up the opportunity of building what was in effect a more advanced Mirage (the FD2 fighter), and a slightly earlier and superior Phantom F4 (the Hawker P1121). The P1081 fighter, which flew in June 1950, could have prevented the big 1953 import of F86 Sabres, and could have led to the supersonic P1083 which was near completion when cancelled in June 1953.

Marcel Dassault himself publicly raised an eyebrow at the cancellation of the FD2 concept, later acknowledging that its appearance in France (on trials for which no suitable British flying area was available) led him to adopt the same delta configuration for the Mirage. 'If it were not for the clumsy way you tackle things in Britain, you could have made the Mirage yourselves,' Dassault told the Englishman, Jack Gee, author of *Mirage – Warplane of the World.*

Great Britain also passed up the opportunity to produce the world's first trans-Atlantic-range big jet transport, the V1000 (for Transport Command) and its civil version, the VC7. This was cancelled in November 1955 – with first flight scheduled for early 1956, just a month or two away. This aircraft would have upstaged both the long-range Boeing 707 (which first flew in 1959) and the DC8 (first flight, 1958) on non-stop Atlantic services by some two years. 'The biggest blunder of all,' Sir George Edwards was later to write. Indeed, it was effectively to take Britain, and with it, Europe, out of the long-haul big-jet market – a market in which it could have been the pace-setter. Save for a small and belated flurry with the VC10, which only served to emphasise the 'might have been,' this situation still appears to have become virtually irreversible. When it is remembered that the cancellation was made in order to favour the jet-prop Britannia (not delivered to the RAF until April 1959) and to safeguard Northern Ireland sub-contract Britannia employment at Shorts, it seems even more tragic.

Behind all this muddle and disorder lay what Denis Haviland was later to describe as nothing less than a Whitehall civil war between the Treasury, often supported by the Board of Trade, on one hand, and the Royal Air Force and the other aviation interests, on the other. 'From 1954 to the time I left the Civil Service in 1964, and, indeed after,' he wrote in a review of this period, 'the Treasury never missed the opportunity presented by a proposed new programme, or by a variation or an extension of an existing one, or even by the due provisioning of the next slice of funding for a Cabinet-authorised project, to mount a major attack. Its continual objective was to reverse Government aviation policy and decisions on the grounds that the military programme of the day was too large, and that the civil programme was uneconomic.'

In the case of the V1000, however, it was BOAC which became the final arbiter of its fate when it gave, in 1955, as its official view to the Government that 'the only way in which customers will not wish to cross the Atlantic will be by fast jet.' This became translated by the Government spokesman in the V1000 cancellation debate as 'BOAC is satisfied that for the foreseeable future it will be fully competitive on the North Atlantic with Britannias.' The 'foreseeable future' was very short-term – exactly a year later, in November 1956, BOAC was asking Government permission to buy Boeing jets. It was certainly the view, both in Ministerial and industry circles, that Boeing had special friends at the BOAC court, but an unofficial enquiry on these lines concluded that, although there were grounds for suspicion, there was no likelihood of proof.

Another, and certainly comparable, civil disaster was the story of the BEA jet requirement which eventually was met by the de Havilland 121 Trident. Either the proposed VC11, or the 121 in its 'big' format with three Rolls-Royce Medway engines, would have been a world-class aeroplane. The extent to which Boeing feared a big Trident is brought out in Harold Mansfield's *Billion Dollar Battle*. Indeed, firmness of decision and promotion in 1958 for the Medway-engined 121 might even have halted what was still a very uncertain Seattle view of a project later to be the all-time best-selling Boeing 727. As it was, BEA, having deemed the VC11 too big, then emasculated the Trident as submitted, chopping down its seating, shortening its range and so condemning it to the Spey engine of limited development potential. The way to the world markets was opened for Boeing, and the Medway, possibly the most important engine in Britain's armoury, was never to be put into production. The Medway would not only have 'made' the Trident, it would also have allowed the BAC One-Eleven to have had a proper development programme, and have provided a lighter and better engine for TSR2 than the Olympus. Ten years later, Sir George Edwards still saw the Medway cancellation as one of the key bad decisions of his time – ranking with that of the V1000. 'If the Medway had been chosen for the TSR2, then TSR2 might well never have been cancelled,' he said.

The Trident decision, however, provides a useful checkpoint by which to bring this chapter back on to its proper theme of the compacting of the UK airframe effort. There was a new requirement attached to the original 1957 competition for the BEA aeroplane, and that was 'collaboration' between design firms. Whitehall was, for the first time, using the club which it had always had, as it were, up its sleeve to produce the aims first voiced in 1946 and submitted in more detail by Haviland in 1954. The BEA short-haul jet requirement of 1957 had to go not just to one firm, but to a consortium. After Vickers had been ruled out because the required aircraft was, in Sir George Edwards' view, too small for world markets, and in BEA's view his VC11 was too big, Bristol appeared to have the inside track with the Bristol 200, and they immediately teamed up with Hawker to offer a joint company for the project. De Havilland replied with a mix of Saunders-Roe, Hunting, Fairey and possibly Handley Page. This eventually settled out at a consortium of de Havilland ($67\frac{1}{2}$ per cent), Hunting ($22\frac{1}{2}$ per cent) and Fairey (10 per cent) and, in February 1958, the Aircraft Manufacturing Company (Airco) was formed and was the eventual winner of the BEA order. This was yet another example of the UK satisfying its own narrow domestic requirements without regard to what could be sold to the rest of the world. However, with the Trident, the process of Whitehall-supervised shot-gun marriages had begun – even if this particular consortium was, in the end, not to endure, but was to be a victim of a bigger and better marriage bureau presided over by Duncan Sandys.

2

A Whitehall Ultimatum

It is now generally agreed that the Whitehall shot-gun – first used on the BEA contract – was initially laid, naked and loaded, on the table for all present to see, at an historic meeting on 16 September 1957, at Shell Mex House. In the absence of Aubrey Jones on a Ministerial visit to the USA, the Permanent Secretary, Ministry of Supply, Sir Cyril Musgrave, presided, and all the heads of the key companies in the industry were there. Sir Roy Dobson and Sir Frank Spriggs represented Hawker Siddeley; Sir George Edwards, Vickers-Armstrongs and Vickers-Supermarine; Mr (later Sir) Aubrey Burke, de Havilland; Lord Caldecote and Mr H.G. Nelson, English Electric; Captain E.D. Clarke, Saunders-Roe; Sir Frederick Handley Page and Mr R.T. Stafford, Handley Page; Sir Matthew Slattery, Bristol Aircraft and Short Brothers; Sir Reginald Verdon Smith and Mr C.F. Uwins, Bristol; and Mr E. Turner, Blackburn.

Sir Cyril, emphasising that he spoke with the full authority of the absent Minister, got straight to the point which was that only one military aircraft project had (so far) survived the 1957 White Paper, and that was OR 339 – the Canberra replacement. There was no certainty of further military aircraft projects and, assuming OR 339 went ahead, the contract would only be placed with a group of firms, or with two or three companies acting in co-ordination and with one designated as the leader. The Government hoped for eventual rationalisation and amalgamations, and the units or groups so formed had to be strong on both the military and civil sides, have a viable forward programme as a group, and have all-round financial strength. How the industry so grouped itself was its affair, but group itself it must.

The reaction of the heads of industry to this ultimatum was strong and virtually unanimous. For the industry to remain viable at all in any form, there had to be an on-going military programme, not just the rather dubious carrot of a possible Canberra replacement. Further, the airframe industry could not (repeat) *not* possibly exist on civil work alone. Sir Cyril said there was certainly no hope on the military side unless there were major amalgamations or rationalisation on the lines he had sketched out as a condition for submissions for OR 339. He could only repeat that it was, therefore, up to the industry to arrange their own affairs and pick their own partners if they wished to put in a submission.

After the meeting had ended, and the industrialists had departed, more or less in silence, Denis Haviland, who was present as Under Secretary (Air), Ministry of Supply, recalls that Sir Cyril Musgrave turned to him and said two words, 'We've won.'

This Aubrey Jones/Musgrave/Haviland view of the necessity to compact the industry by economic sanctions, expressed privately to industry in September 1957, became open Government policy in May of 1958 when Aubrey Jones stated, 'In the Government's view, it would be fruitless to continue research and development expenditure unless the industry re-organises and strengthens itself to the extent necessary to meet the changed conditions with which it is now faced.' The Government policy was to 'encourage' the industry to re-shape itself into stronger units, and, if this was done, the industry was expected to be able to finance the development of new civil projects without Government assistance.

Dr Hartley, in his 1965 paper to the Royal Aeronautical Society, states that Aubrey Jones considered that the Government, being the industry's major customer, was obliged to use its power of placing contracts to reduce the number of airframe and aero-engine firms and strengthen the survivors. Only by such action could the UK industry compete with the USA. Jones told Parliament that his concept of an ideal standard for an aircraft firm was one that was engaged in both military and civil aircraft and also in industrial non-aircraft activities, so that it could raise its capital on the basis of its entire diversified structure. Such an 'ideal' firm had also to possess the technical ability and the financial strength to undertake aircraft projects with the minimum of delay. To meet this criterion, there would have to be concentration, but (again a main theme) the Government was not saying which firms should merge with which.

The key thinking in this new policy statement was that the Government saw its ideal aviation company as one which was in effect, a diversification or an offshoot of a bigger industrial enterprise based on non-aircraft activities. There were not many which fitted this description. The Hawker Siddeley Group, Vickers and English Electric certainly did and, to a lesser extent, Bristol. These companies, therefore, clearly had a key part to play in any re-organisation, especially if the Hawker Siddeley Group became more closely integrated and less internally competitive for aircraft contracts.

None of these 1958 statements was, of course, news to the industry. They had had it spelt out to them in September 1957, and, ever since that Musgrave meeting, private talks had been going on between all the parties. There were two major considerations to be borne in mind. The first was short term – a submission in response to OR 339 which satisfied the Musgrave collaborative criteria; the second was the formation of permanent mergers or alliances which satisfied the Government policy as initially indicated by Musgrave and clothed in more detail by Aubrey

Jones. The two considerations did not necessarily need to be the same. A satisfactory short-term arrangement for OR 339 might or might not blossom into a marriage, although clearly such a happy event would be pleasing to the Government. Put another way, the Government would be distinctly displeased if nuptials did not follow.

The instrument of OR 339 was, thanks to Sandys, the only one still remaining to the Government with which it could enforce its wishes. It was, in truth, a far from ideal one. It was a critical and an advanced project, and one unlikely to be brought to operation by committee-type control and command structures which the combined work and ideas of two or three hitherto autonomous design teams would make necessary. Examination of these aspects of OR 339 is postponed to the later consideration of the TSR2 story. Suffice it for the purposes of this chapter to say that the criteria for OR 339, plus generalisations on the placing of vague future work, led to a whole spate of talks about alliances, if not of marriage. The rumours of who had been seen talking to whom abounded: Shorts and English Electric; Bristol and Vickers; Bristol and de Havilland; Vickers and English Electric; Hawker and de Havilland; Vickers and de Havilland; all were, at various times, reported to be more than the conventional good friends. The BEA jet airliner order already referred to was a factor in all this, and at one time it looked likely that the Hawker Siddeley Group and Bristol would merge to shut out de Havilland, whose design was preferred by BEA, but of whose financial resources to take on the project the Ministry had doubts. To counter this, de Havilland itself discussed mergers, first with Hawker and then with Bristol, and finally settled with Hunting and Fairey in the Airco consortium, as we have already seen.

It would be both unrewarding and boring to try to trace all the proposals and counter-proposals which were made or discussed in 1958 and 1959. In 1958, there were still – in effect – twenty airframe firms (counting Auster and Miles) and six aero-engine companies. By 1960, there were two major airframe groups, one helicopter group, and two engine groups, with Handley Page, Scottish Aviation, Short Brothers and Beagle 'on the outside.'

The internecine warfare within the Hawker Siddeley Group, which had culminated in Gloster, Avro and Hawker all putting in proposals for OR 339, was finally being taken in hand, and eventually one OR 339 Group submission was belatedly, and unsuccessfully, made in mid-1958. Mr Handel Davies, at that time Director of Scientific Research in the Ministry of Aviation, recalls that the bitterest rivalry in the lobbying and brochure warfare over OR 339 was between Avro and Hawker – member-companies of the same group. 'There were about nine design submissions for OR 339,' Handel Davies recalls, 'and each one had to be evaluated in detail by teams of Government experts. It became ridiculous,' he adds, 'and everyone in Whitehall and most of the senior men in the industry fully realised it.'

In 1959, it so happened there was also a General Election, from which the Conservatives retained power, and promptly themselves played a merger game by bringing together the Ministry of Supply and the civil aviation responsibilities of the Ministry of Transport into a Ministry of Aviation. This was placed under Duncan Sandys as a Cabinet Minister. His appointment, after his sponsorship of the 1957 Defence White Paper, was hardly welcomed by the industry over which he now reigned *in toto*, and to which, in the view of many, he had already administered one crippling blow. Sandys immediately endorsed the previous Ministry of Supply policy. His own ultimate aim was simple and, indeed, sensible. It was for two airframe groups and two engine groups – each strong enough to retain the competitive edge in all fields and so avoid the technological stagnation of monopolies. Each group was also to be financially strong enough to carry the commercial aircraft load with only a minimum of injection of re-payable Government funds as launching aid. This became formal Government policy.

Sandys was not to achieve his ideal – but he came near enough to it. The two groups became three simply because none of the big airframe contenders wanted to have an offshoot speciality of helicopters. So all helicopter interests were eventually put together into Westland Aircraft Limited, which embraced Saunders-Roe (incorporating Cierva), Fairey Helicopters, and the Bristol Helicopter Division. Short Brothers, being almost ($69\frac{1}{2}$ per cent) Government-owned (Bristol held a minority $15\frac{1}{4}$ per cent and so did Harland and Wolff), was a very big economic factor in the politics of Northern Ireland, and was not central to the initial marriage market, while Sir Frederick Handley Page's evaluation of his company's worth failed to coincide with that of any potential buyer. Handley Page remained on the outside until it went into liquidation in 1970. In the light aircraft field, Auster and Miles were re-formed as British Executive and General Aviation in 1960, became Beagle Aircraft in 1962, and were in the receiver's hands in 1970. Scottish Aviation, which managed to survive intact until nationalised in 1977, took on certain ex-Beagle and Handley Page work, but did not take over the companies.

The final outcome of all the 1958 and 1959 wheeling and dealing which went on under the muzzles of the twin Government pistols of the BEA order and OR 339 resulted in the following:

Table 2 Re-organisations within the British aircraft and aero-engine industry

Taking the companies in the order listed in Table 1 (page 13), this was the eventual disposition of the postwar names:

Aircraft manufacturers

Airspeed   Purchased by de Havilland, 1940. Became
                            Airspeed Division of de Havilland, 1951.

Armstrong Whitworth	Part of Hawker Siddeley from 1935, became part of Hawker Siddeley Aviation on its formation in 1963.
Auster	Became Beagle Aircraft, 1962; closed, 1970.
Avro	Part of Hawker Siddeley from 1935, became part of Hawker Siddeley Aviation on its formation in 1963.
Blackburn	Merged with General Aircraft, 1949. Taken over by Hawker Siddeley, 1960. Became part of Hawker Siddeley Aviation, 1963.
Boulton Paul	Leased out designs and became part of Dowty Group, 1961.
Bristol	Became part of BAC on formation in 1960.
Cierva	Taken over by Saunders-Roe, becoming part of Helicopter Division, 1951.
Cunliffe-Owen	Ceased business, 1948.
de Havilland	Taken over by Hawker Siddeley, 1960. Became part of Hawker Siddeley Aviation, 1963.
English Electric	English Electric Aviation Ltd formed 1959. Became part of BAC, 1960.
Fairey	Became part of Westland Aircraft, 1960.
Folland	Taken over by Hawker Siddeley, 1960. Became part of Hawker Siddeley Aviation, 1963.
General Aircraft	Merged with Blackburn Aircraft, 1949.
Gloster	Part of Hawker Siddeley from 1935, became part of Hawker Siddeley Aviation on its formation in 1963.
Handley Page	Liquidated, 1970.
Hawker	Part of Hawker Siddeley from 1935, became part of Hawker Siddeley Aviation on its formation in 1963.
Martin-Baker	Dropped aircraft side to concentrate on ejector seats.
Miles	Miles Aircraft liquidated, 1947. F.G. Miles Ltd formed 1951. Became part of Beagle Aircraft, closed 1970.
Percival	Became part of Hunting Group, 1944. Name

changed to Hunting Percival Aircraft Ltd in
1946, and to Hunting Aircraft Ltd in 1957.
Became part of BAC, 1960.

Portsmouth Aviation	Closed, 1949.
Saunders-Roe	Became part of Westland Aircraft, 1960.
Scottish Aviation	Continued as independent unit until nationalised into British Aerospace, 1977.
Shorts	Has continued as independent unit.
Vickers	Vickers-Armstrongs (Aircraft) Ltd formed 1954 to acquire aircraft business carried on at Weybridge, Supermarine etc. Became part of BAC, 1960.
Westland	Became specialist helicopter manufacturer and has continued as independent group, taking over Saunders-Roe, Bristol and Fairey helicopter interests, 1960.

Aero-engine manufacturers

Alvis	Ceased aero-engine development, late 1950s.
Armstrong Siddeley	Acquired Metropolitan-Vickers, 1949. Merged with Bristol Aero-Engines to form Bristol Siddeley Engines Ltd, 1958. Bristol Siddeley taken over by Rolls-Royce, 1966.
Blackburn	Became part of Bristol Siddeley, 1961.
Bristol	Became Bristol Aero-Engines Ltd, 1955. Merged with Armstrong-Siddeley Motors to form Bristol Siddeley Engines Ltd, 1958. Bristol Siddeley taken over by Rolls-Royce, 1966.
de Havilland	Became part of Bristol Siddeley Engines, 1961.
Metropolitan-Vickers	Acquired by Armstrong-Siddeley Motors, 1949 (see above).
Napier	Joined Rolls-Royce, 1961.
Rolls-Royce	Became sole British aero-engine manufacturer through acquisition of Bristol Siddeley Engines, 1966. Liquidated, 1971. Company re-formed as Rolls-Royce (1971) Ltd and now known as Rolls-Royce Ltd.

3

Vickers, English Electric and the TSR2

Although BAC was not officially formed until 1 July 1960, its basis was firmly set on 1 January 1959, when the Government announced the award of a contract to Vickers-Armstrongs (Aircraft) Limited and English Electric Aviation Limited for a new supersonic military aircraft to be known as TSR2 – the initials standing for Tactical Strike Reconnaissance, the roles required of the Canberra replacement OR 339. Vickers were designated by the Government as the lead firm as per the policy requirement for a lead firm laid down at the Musgrave meeting, and the work was to be shared fifty-fifty. Bristol Siddeley Engines were to be given, subject to negotiation, the contract for the power plant – a reheated version of the Olympus, the 22R. This anti-Medway decision was to affect not only the fate of TSR2 but also the future of two major British airliners – the Trident and the BAC One-Eleven.

From the time that the aircraft subsidiaries of Vickers Limited and the English Electric Company Limited were the chosen bedfellows on the one major aircraft project remaining after the Sandys axe, it was almost inevitable that the two parent companies – Vickers Limited and the English Electric Company Limited – would eventually merge their aircraft and guided weapons offshoots into a powerful new aerospace company. It so happened that these aerospace interests fitted very well together.

English Electric, under the first Lord Nelson of Stafford, with Lord Caldecote as his Aviation Administrator, had a very strong specialised military design office under Freddie Page (later knighted), and this team was, in fact, the only one in England with experience of a production supersonic warplane – the Lightning. Vickers-Armstrongs (Aircraft), now under George Edwards, had a fine commercial aircraft team which had established itself with the Viking and then won worldwide recognition with the turbo-prop Viscount – the world's first turbine-powered airliner, of which it eventually sold 438 to thirty-five different countries, including ninety-one to the USA and fifty-five to Canada. It had also, and at the same time, gained a good name for military production management with the Valiant bomber, which had been delivered to schedule, and had had further transport design experience with the Vanguard, built to an uninspired BEA propeller-driven specification, and with the imaginative and tragically cancelled V1000/VC7. Vickers also had moved to Weybridge key men from the Supermarine design office as the Supermarine Aircraft factory at South Marston near Swindon, after completing the Scimitar order for the Royal Navy, eventually went over to hovercraft, aviation sub-contract and general engineering as part of the Vickers Limited engineering activities.

Lord Nelson had, for some time, been taking a growing interest in the potential of the civil airliner business. There had, in fact, nearly been a civil version of the Canberra with an initial market among some Texas oilmen. A tie-up with Vickers would give English Electric a share in a company which had already made Britain's biggest-ever international breakthrough in the civil field, while, for good measure, both companies had guided weapons interests, of which more anon.

Vickers, however, had not been English Electric's first choice of partner in responding to OR 339. This preference had been given to Shorts, because Freddie Page's Warton design team had been attracted to giving not just a STOL but a vertical take-off ability to their submission, using a VTO platform based on Shorts' experience with their VTOL aircraft, the SC1. Warton had initially submitted for OR 339 a delta-winged two-seater with twin RB142/3 Medway engines with reheat, called the P17A. An interceptor-fighter version was also offered. There was no doubt that the English Electric P17A, with or without the amazing Short P17D VTO platform (which employed no fewer than seventy engines, mostly little RB108 lift motors – with and without 'tilt') was a first-rate design. It was based on a concept of initial simplicity to get the prototype aircraft airborne as quickly as might be, and then for nav-attack and other such equipment already under development – the advanced electronics – to be added later. The Royal Air Force was undoubtedly very impressed by the P17A – understandably so, as English Electric were always likely to be the favourites to replace their own splendidly successful Canberra. English Electric had also given the RAF not only its first supersonic fighter, but one which, in the interceptor role, was probably, in its time, the finest in the world.

The Vickers submission was the product of a team led by George Henson of Supermarine and came in two models – a single-engined twin-seater using blown flaps (as per the Scimitar and the Buccaneer) and a twin-engined version, the Type 571. The 571 was a revolutionary proposal in that it offered the required blind terrain-following, nav-attack and weapons system as a fully integrated package – the complete opposite of the 'add-on-afterwards' school of thought. The argument was that the systems were the heart of the aeroplane and a high performance flying platform should be built around them.

There were many other OR 339 submissions, notably from Bristol, Avro and Hawker, but the Air Staff, by as early as mid-1958, had virtually decided on what amounted to the P17, but incorporating the Vickers integrated systems concept from the 571. This made it what Derek Wood has aptly described as a 'clever' aeroplane with lots of fail-safe protection to cover all aspects of its complexity. It was also an aeroplane which, if it came off, would be a world-beater.

The surprise, perhaps, was that Vickers were chosen to be the lead firm – that is, the contract would be placed with them, and English Electric would be designated as sub-contractors but with a guaranteed half-share of all the airframe work. This gave no pleasure at all to Lord Nelson or Warton who, seeing themselves as playing second fiddle, kept pointing to their record with the Lightning and the Canberra and generally crying 'offside.'

Freddie Page – though, from its formation, one of the strongest advocates of the concept of BAC (all of whose aircraft interests he was one day to control) – still feels that TSR2 was the wrong 'welding flux' for the union. He believes the merger should have come first and not the contract. Further, that the original P17, led by Warton, as part of the new company, and shorn of the 571 complexities of integrated systems, might then have held the day and survived the orchestrated anti-TSR2 campaign, so avoiding the aircraft's ultimate death on the grounds of cost. The Air Staff, however, apart from the operational attractions of the integrated systems, could not wait for the stately dance of a big merger and preferred Vickers to lead because of their track record of production management and on-time deliveries. English Electric, rightly or wrongly, was not highly regarded in this respect. Sir George Edwards subsequently made the point that there was 'a damn sight more to developing and producing a new aeroplane than a brilliant project office, and the Air Staff knew it.' It was the Air Staff which insisted on Vickers being in the saddle.

Undoubtedly, inside English Electric Aviation there was lack of cohesion, and even of mutual respect, between the Warton design team and the main production centre at Preston, which factory belonged to the English Electric Company Limited and not to English Electric Aviation. The 'boss' of the Preston works was Arthur Sheffield, a very strong character, who reported to Lord Nelson and by no means to Freddie Page or, before him, to Teddy Petter. Sheffield had little time for 'designers,' and didn't care who knew it. It was this weakness at English Electric in a key area where Vickers at Weybridge was known to be strong (George Edwards' writ ran to every corner of the plant) which was the deciding factor. Vickers were given the lead, and the integrated systems concept stayed. Any later and hindsight argument as to whether a P17 would have survived the 1964/5 axe is partly subjective, and is a matter on which Warton and Weybridge can never be expected to agree. Many believe no form of OR 339 aeroplane could have withstood the combined assault on it by the Treasury and by the Royal Navy spearheaded by Lord Mountbatten, then Chief of the Defence

Staff, and Lord Zuckerman, his Chief Scientist, plus the advent of the 1964 Labour Government.

Sir George Edwards' own recollection of the 'preliminaries' between Vickers and English Electric is that there was never time to achieve Freddie Page's wish for 'merger first – TSR2 design team second.' The RAF wanted the TSR2 matter settled, and would not have waited while the details of a major merger were hammered out. The Controller (Air), Air Chief Marshal Sir Claud Pelly, is reputed to have said he would not accept an English Electric-led project. Sir George recalls that the details of the joint TSR2 set-up took a lot of sorting out, with English Electric fully set on being given a separate contract direct from the Government and not from Vickers.

This became a sticking point, but was finally resolved in a forty-five minute telephone conversation between Sir George and Lord Caldecote while the latter was standing in the hallway of his home, surrounded by family and luggage, having been caught on the point of departure on holiday. 'I offered Warton the assembly of one of the prototypes,' Sir George said, 'and that finally did the trick.' Much later, however, this Warton prototype ran into problems – 'They weren't used to this kind of work,' said Sir George, 'and got into a tangle. Weybridge was used to prototype construction and in the end I had to move it to Weybridge, though such was never my intention at the time of the deal.'

But, before the TSR2 contract with Vickers/English Electric was signed on the first day of 1959, there were a number of 1958 hurdles still to jump. Much as the Air Staff wanted a 'state of the art' aeroplane to be its main armament through the sixties and into the seventies and beyond, it had to beat off the very determined running attempts by the Royal Navy and the Treasury to make the Royal Air Force accept as a Canberra replacement the Blackburn NA39 (Buccaneer), a pre-production order for twenty of which had been placed as long ago as 1955, to give the Navy a subsonic, twin-engined, carrierborne low-level, strike aeroplane. Blackburn, who had been unlikely winners of the NA39 competition, firmly believed that Lord Mountbatten, then the First Sea Lord, would eventually push the naval Buccaneer through to the Royal Air Force, which would reduce the costs, especially to the Navy.

But the Air Staff would have none of it. Buccaneer, they said, was too slow, had too long a take-off, insufficient range and too limited a nav-attack system for their needs – which was all undeniably true. OR 339 finally weathered that particular storm, at least for the time being, and by June 1958 the Defence Requirements Policy Committee approved the necessary expenditure. This was one month after a controversial seminar had been staged at the Royal Empire Society at which the Assistant Chief of Air Staff (OR), Air Vice Marshal 'Digger' Kyle, had spelt out to a powerful audience of military and civil leaders and politicians the need for an aeroplane of outstanding performance. He had been backed up by the Chief of the Air Staff, Marshal of the Royal

Air Force Sir Dermot Boyle, who strongly challenged the thinking behind the 1957 White Paper, and so fell foul of the Minister, Duncan Sandys. Sir Dermot said: 'We are convinced that we will require manned aircraft for as far as we can see, to supplement the missile in both the offensive and defensive roles.' It was a mini-revolt by the Air Marshals and the Government backed away from an all-out confrontation which they suspected Dermot Boyle was strong enough to lead.

Finally – to get the Vickers/English Electric team which the Air Staff wanted to do their chosen P17/V571 amalgam – Short Brothers had to be cleared from the system. English Electric, as we have seen, had been partnered by Short Brothers in their initial joint OR 339 submission, and there was a written agreement (as required) that they would undertake any contract together. Shorts, therefore, let it be known that if the P17 was chosen they would keep English Electric to the agreement, which did not match up with the plan to have English Electric and Vickers tackle the TSR2 with Vickers in the lead.

In the end, the RAF re-issued OR 339 as a definitive requirement under a new number, OR 343, which Operational Requirement was written round the English Electric/Vickers aeroplane. This Duncan Sandys-inspired ploy made the contest a new ball game, and Shorts were out of it. OR 343, the final specification for TSR2, was very tight, very ambitious, and very advanced. It called for an aeroplane which could do all-weather, long-range, nuclear and non-nuclear strike, and all kinds of reconnaissance, as well as battlefield support, and yet have a performance better than the best jet interceptor and be STOL into the bargain. Vickers and English Electric were ready to tackle it and, as stated, the basic TSR2 contract was signed on 1 January 1959.

In July 1959, the initial contract was placed for the first stage of development, but, throughout all this paper-signing, the anti-TSR2 lobby of the Royal Navy, Zuckerman, the Treasury and a group of powerful civil servants were still united in their determination to kill the project by whatever means came to hand. They were only biding their time.

By December 1959, Bristol Siddeley finally received the engine contract for the Olympus 22R – Sir George Edwards having failed in his attempts to have the lighter and more 'potential' Rolls-Royce Medway instead. When he knew he had lost – which was well before the final formalities with Bristol Siddeley were completed – he remarked: 'This is the first time I have ever been told what engines I must have for an aeroplane and I have taken the precaution of getting the Minister (Aubrey Jones) to give me this order in writing.'

The fuller story of TSR2 comes later in this book – but, with the complication of Short Brothers duly removed, English Electric and Vickers began working together, with a very good relationship established between Lord Nelson and George Edwards. The two men had much in common, held each other in respect and trust and, to use George Edwards' phrase, 'spoke the same language.' The first Lord

Nelson of Stafford did not long survive the mergers, but his able and highly technically qualified heir, the Hon. H.G. Nelson, later the second Lord Nelson of Stafford, remained a pillar of strength in BAC for all its seventeen years of existence.

Once it was clear that English Electric and Vickers would get the TSR2 order, the next question was one of enlarging the consortium by at least one more company to provide the Government with the second of its two 'ideal' fixed-wing airframe groups – Hawker Siddeley clearly being the other. Throughout 1958 and 1959, no one in the industry had lost sight of what they had been told by Musgrave, and no one doubted that the Government was in earnest. After the 1959 General Election, Sandys, whose determined views were well known, was moved to the Ministry of Aviation, but there was some softening at the Ministry of Defence, which was now under Harold Watkinson (later Lord Watkinson), who did not entirely share the Sandys obsession with an all-rocket all-nuclear defence policy. There was, therefore, a glimmer of hope that new manned aircraft would be required after all, and that the military work, on which the industry relied for its bread and butter, would somehow continue.

To round off this point, it was during Watkinson's stay at the Ministry of Defence that the problems of the Blue Streak ballistic missile and of the Blue Steel stand-off missile came to a head. The American Skybolt air-launched weapon was then planned to take over the main nuclear deterrent role for the UK. The cancellation of Skybolt by President Kennedy in 1962 (the UK had ordered 100) left the UK high, dry and angry. It also killed a requirement for a new big long-range Skybolt-carrier aircraft, and transferred the main responsibility for Britain's nuclear deterrent from the Royal Air Force to the Polaris and to the Royal Navy, where it still remains.

In late 1959, however, things were undoubtedly looking a bit brighter for the aircraft industry, provided it voluntarily formed itself into its two airframe, one helicopter and two engine groupings. With Hawker re-organising themselves into a more centralised coherence, and buying up Blackburn and Folland, the second group would clearly now have Vickers and English Electric at its core. That left Bristol, de Havilland, and Handley Page, and some smaller fry such as Hunting and Scottish Aviation to be brought into the system. Short Brothers, as has been said, were seen as a political special case, and, being Government-controlled, sufficient work for them could always be written in as a prerequisite on any future Government-sponsored project – civil or military. In 1960, however, the Government tried hard to sell Shorts to BAC – but without success. The light-aircraft people could be left to look after themselves, no one in Whitehall caring particularly whether they sank or swam. In fact, they were soon to sink.

In 1959, therefore, the final merger interest centred on de Havilland and Bristol – with a sidelong glance at Handley Page.

4
The Birth of the British Aircraft Corporation

The obvious partner for Vickers/English Electric in setting up Britain's second major aerospace group was de Havilland. De Havilland had an all-round capability including weapons, a world-known name, and an appreciation of what effort and spend were required to capture worldwide civil markets. This experience included, after the cut-down of the capacity of the original Trident, a realisation that building airliners to the insular outlook of BEA and BOAC was not the way to get the overseas orders which alone could provide the production runs needed to get to the thin end of Sir George Edwards' 'learning curve.' There were, therefore, a number of high-level discussions involving especially Vickers' Chairman, Lord Knollys, his Managing Director, Sir Charles Dunphie (who took over from Lord Knollys as Chairman in 1962), Sir George Edwards, the Nelsons, father and son, and the de Havilland hierarchy, mainly Sir Aubrey Burke. It was about this time that the Bristol and Hawker engine firms were being merged, and de Havilland, with its own, and now rather isolated, engine company, was talking to Hawker at the same time as it was negotiating with Vickers. It is the generally accepted view that one reason de Havilland backed away from joining with Vickers and English Electric was that Sir Aubrey foresaw the possibility that, in such a merger, he might well find himself playing second fiddle to Sir George Edwards who was clearly likely to head up the aircraft side in the new group, and whose financial mainstay would be the TSR2 rather than the de Havilland Trident. Whatever the reason, the de Havilland talks collapsed, and Sir Roy Dobson clinched a deal whereby Hawker bought all the shares in de Havilland, which then became a wholly owned part of the Hawker Siddeley Group.

The separate negotiations between Bristol and Hawker went on until the very day the Hawker purchase of de Havilland was announced, and indeed Mr W. Masterton and Mr T.B. Pritchard of Bristol were actually at a meeting with Mr J.F. Robertson, Financial Director of Hawker Siddeley, when a note was passed in and Robertson announced that Hawker had just bought de Havilland and were no longer interested in Bristol.

From that rather dramatic moment it was almost inevitable that Bristol would join with Vickers and English Electric. Tom Pritchard tells the story that, when he and Willie Masterton were ushered unceremoniously out of Hawker, and finding themselves with a wait for their train back to Bristol, they adjourned gloomily to the Paddington cocktail bar and ordered themselves large gin and tonics. 'I said to Willie,' Pritchard recalls, 'that we must now open immediate talks with Vickers and English Electric with a view to forming a company on the same lines as the British Motor Corporation (Austin/Morris merger) – that is with no one member having a majority shareholding in the new amalgamation. I even suggested a name – British Aircraft Corporation. This proposal was agreed by the Bristol Aeroplane Company Board, and discussions with Vickers and English Electric were started almost immediately.' Sir George Edwards also recollects receiving a call from Lord Knollys at that time telling him that Vickers' talks with de Havilland were off, and that he should forthwith have a look at Bristol. Lord Caldecote recalls getting a similar directive from Lord Nelson. There is, however, some evidence that there had been preliminary discussions between Vickers and Bristol at top level before the Hawker purchase of de Havilland. Sir Reginald Verdon-Smith remembers some private talks between himself and Lord Knollys earlier in 1959. As the two men were friends and shared banking and insurance interests which often brought them together, it is difficult to imagine that, in the current atmosphere of merger and consortia, the heads of two of the country's large aerospace owning companies did not sound each other out.

The situation at Bristol Aircraft at the time of the talks which eventually led to the formation of BAC was not particularly bright. The overall company was Bristol Aeroplane, which wholly owned Bristol Aircraft Limited, a separate company formed in 1956 with Peter Masefield (now Sir Peter) as Managing Director. Bristol Aeroplane also jointly owned Bristol Siddeley Engines which, in order to get the Olympus order for TSR2, had been formed in April 1959 by the merger of Bristol Aero-Engines with the aero-engine interests of Hawker Siddeley. Blackburn and de Havilland engine companies joined Bristol Siddeley Engines soon afterwards. It was Bristol Aircraft Limited which Bristol Aeroplane were concerned to see taken into the new Vickers/English Electric combine. The main projects of Bristol Aircraft at the time were the Britannia, which had recently come into production, the Sycamore helicopter, in production, and the twin-rotor military Belvedere, in development, the Bloodhound anti-aircraft missile, for which major orders were shortly expected, the experimental Type 188 all-steel research aircraft, and what amounted to a feasibility study on a supersonic transport. Masefield was also having some preliminary work done in the light aircraft field.

It had been Bristol Aeroplane's original intention to sell off the helicopter interests of Bristol Aircraft to Westland (which it successfully did – the deal being completed in 1959) and to merge the rest of the aircraft and weapons activities with Hawker. This, as has been stated, fell through, hence the Vickers/English Electric negotiations. The Blood-hound was the main card in the Bristol hand, and this would have been attractive to the English Electric Guided Weapons side, based at Stevenage, which had produced the rival Thunderbird. The discussions and formalities were accomplished amicably and quickly and, by the end of 1959 the British Aircraft Corporation was poised for formation and was to be jointly owned by three parent companies, Vickers Limited (40 per cent), the English Electric Company Limited (40 per cent) and Bristol Aeroplane Company Limited (20 per cent).

In late December 1959, as Sir Reginald Verdon-Smith revealed in his Barnwell Memorial Lecture in 1972, the Government gave to the prospective parents of BAC a reassuring policy document which was clearly intended to facilitate the mergers. Although it was later whittled down somewhat by Duncan Sandys' officials, the original Government document contained the following paragraphs:

1. The Government believe it to be in the general interest that the aircraft industry should concentrate the bulk of its technical and financial resources into four strong groups, two making air-frames and guided weapons and two making aero-engines. In that event, the Government intend to concentrate their orders, as far as practicable, on these four groups, except where specialised requirements or social policy make it necessary to do otherwise. The Government also propose to encourage the Airline Corporations to follow the same course.

2. Every endeavour will be made to harmonise civil and military requirements for new types of aircraft.

3. The Government will give all suitable support to the industry's efforts to develop markets at home, in the Commonwealth and in foreign countries.

4. In order to provide the industry with a sound foundation, the Government intend to maintain, at public expense, a programme of aeronautical research of about the present size.

5. It is recognised that it will be necessary for the Government to contribute towards the cost of developing promising new types of civil aircraft, subject to suitable arrangements for participation in earnings from sales.

6. Should the proposed merger of the Vickers, English Electric and Bristol companies materialise, the Government have it in mind, subject to the negotiation of detailed contractual arrangements, to provide specific assistance.

There was then set out the basis of launching aid which the Government was prepared to offer for the VC10, Super VC10 and VC11. This, as Sir Reginald has commented, was as positive a statement of Government policy as industry had ever received, although the 'escape clause' in paragraph one – '. . . except where specialised requirements or social policy make it necessary to do otherwise' – did not pass unnoticed.

With the above piece of paper before them, the three parent company Boards accepted the mergers in principle and, on 6 January 1960, what Sir Reginald has called 'the General Arrangement Drawing' for BAC was agreed and submitted to the Minister. Again, to quote from Sir Reginald's Barnwell Memorial Lecture:

> This document, which was accepted by the Government, very clearly defines the structure and intended method of operation of the merged activities and, as it would now seem, betrays the rather grudging extent to which the three principal companies were prepared to join forces. It was to be a 'Joint Aircraft Company'; there was to be an independent Chairman who would also be the Chief Executive. The Company would be owned by the principal Companies in the proportions Vickers 40 per cent, English Electric 40 per cent, and Bristol 20 per cent. The Company would acquire the share capital of the aircraft subsidiaries of the principal companies. The Board would comprise the independent Chairman, representatives of the Companies and outside Directors. The Headquarters would be in London and would in due course require Secretarial, Financial, Contracts and Sales Departments. The Chairman would depend upon the Managing Directors of the subsidiary companies for technical advice, but at a later date a small central technical staff would be formed.
>
> The plants concerned were to be those of the subsidiary companies but, because of the difficulty of separating aircraft work from other engineering activities, a large part of the English Electric aircraft manufacturing capacity at Preston and the whole of the Vickers-Armstrongs works at South Marston had to remain in the hands of the respective principal companies, whilst the Helicopter Division of Bristol Aircraft – in which neither English Electric nor Vickers was interested – was to be hived off and sold by Bristol to Westland. [This was actually happening in parallel with the formation of BAC.]
>
> There was considerable anxiety about the effect that the merger might have upon employees in each unit. Each of the principal companies was proud of its own tradition as a responsible employer, and each had its own esprit de corps and long-established loyalties and practices – for example in such matters as pension schemes. It was therefore declared that the three parties should be able to assure the workpeople concerned that the new organisation would not make their prospects of employment less favourable than if the three groups were to continue to operate separately. It would be the intention that work on projects already in hand should be carried out in their existing locations. Another major hurdle to be overcome concerned the contracts for projects then currently in hand. Were these to be

turned over to the new company or not? Some of them were highly profitable and not lightly to be surrendered, whilst others were quite the reverse and not to be accepted at any price. Nor was it possible to put a reliable value on their future earning capacity. As a result it was agreed that contracts for so-called 'current types' would be accepted by the new company for account of the respective parent companies. This was the origin of a practice which became known as the Old Account/New Account formula which, despite many well-intentioned efforts to get rid of it, still survives to this date [the date of the lecture was 28 March 1972] and only goodwill on all sides has prevented the phrase 'current types' from becoming a sea lawyer's delight.

Complex proposals were then evolved by the companies to deal with problems of valuation of assets, capital structure, taxation, subvention payments and the like, and the details of launching aid for the VC10 and VC11 were settled with the Ministry. Agreement was also reached regarding the division between 'old-account' and 'new-account' projects. In particular the VC10 remained an 'old-account' project and among the 'new-account' projects were to be VC11, TSR2, Blue Water, Thunderbird II, Bloodhound II and the SST 'if this becomes a contract.' In line with the concept of a joint company, it was recognised that, as a matter of policy, 'the parent companies would expect substantially the whole of the annual profits to be distributed to them,' future requirements for working capital and private venture expenditure to be by way of loans or capital investment.

These arrangements were spelt out in a merger agreement between the owners, in which was also included a provision under which none of them could dispose of shares to a third party without first offering them to the others in accordance with an elaborate procedure. In retrospect, this limitation was probably a mistake – it was unnecessary at the beginning and increasingly inappropriate and restrictive as circumstances changed.

Speedy progress was next made in working out the organisation of the Company. An important departure from the original proposal that the independent Chairman should also be Chief Executive was introduced. Lord Portal of Hungerford accepted an invitation to be the independent Chairman, but on a non-executive basis, and it was arranged that he should be supported by an Executive Director, Aircraft (Sir George Edwards), and an Executive Director, Guided Weapons (Lord Caldecote), with William Masterton as Finance Director. The name British Aircraft Corporation was approved by the Board of Trade and the company took over the constituent companies from their parents with effect from 1 July 1960.

In parallel with the formation of BAC, the Hunting Group was prompted by the Minister of Aviation to explore with the three principal companies the possibility of joining them. In view of Hunting's participation in a company known as Airco which de Havilland had formed for the development and production of the DH121 [ultimately the Trident], various difficulties had to be resolved, but these were amicably settled. In May 1960, BAC acquired from the Hunting Group, for £1.3 million, 70 per cent of the share capital of Hunting Aircraft, together with a first refusal on the balance. This acquisition proved to be of an importance to BAC out of all proportion to its size since it brought with it not only the Jet Provost but also the design study for the H107, a 40–50 seat short-haul jet transport project which in due course, and after many metamorphoses, emerged as the BAC One-Eleven.

It is opportune to record at this point that during the next three years or so various other possible mergers or acquisitions came under consideration. These included Handley Page Limited, Short Brothers & Harland Limited, and Boulton & Paul Aircraft Limited, but in no case could the parties find sufficient common ground. In any event, the BAC Board eventually considered that the Corporation was more than fully occupied with its own integration, in executing the projects in hand, and in wrestling with the Government in an unending struggle to prevent the 1959 declaration of policy from being almost entirely eroded by cancellations and delays.

Some of the principals, including Sir George and Lord Caldecote, today agree that the old account/new account arrangement mentioned by Sir Reginald Verdon-Smith was a mistake, although it certainly enabled Vickers to claw back much of its VC10 outlay. Sir George, however, says it would have been easier to have put the whole lot 'into one ball of wax' and then had an arrangement with the parents that there should be cross-compensation and balance for any good profits or heavy losses which followed from investments already made. The system, however, endured despite several attempts to kill it off and was eventually inherited by British Aerospace.

The London headquarters chosen for BAC were at 100 Pall Mall – on the top floors of a new concrete box which had sprung up on the site of the old, historic (and bombed) Carlton Club. It was the view of BAC that small London headquarters were essential, and that it would be wrong in those early, and somewhat touchy days, to use the London offices of any one of the three parents.

It will be seen from the first key appointments that Vickers-Armstrongs had charge of the Aircraft side (Sir George), English Electric the Guided Weapons (Lord Caldecote), and Bristol the finance (Willie Masterton). The Company Secretary, Mr J.O. Charlton, came from English Electric, and the men chosen to run such essential departments as had to be centralised because they were clearly corporate were a fair mixture of Vickers, English Electric and Bristol in their origins. Staff was kept to a minimum because, as Sir George was fond of saying by way of encouragement to the headquarters staff, 'A headquarters never built anything.' Indeed, he himself was seldom there, save for meetings, but preferred to remain close to the design teams at Weybridge, which were then fully occupied with TSR2, VC10 and VC11.

5
Early Shaping . . .

The initial structure of BAC was hammered out during the last days of 1959 and the first half of 1960, mainly by a working party chaired by Mr Ronald Yapp, Director in charge of Administration of Vickers Limited, and consisting of senior Directors from the parents, plus specialists as required. One of the first decisions to be taken was that of the name of the new company, and five proposals were considered:

Amalgamated British Aviation Limited
British Aircraft Company Limited
British Aircraft Manufacturing Company Limited
British United Aviation Limited
UK Aircraft Construction Limited

The working party was strongly in favour of 'Consolidated British Aviation Limited.' By mid-January 1960, all the above suggestions had, mercifully, been ditched, and two new ones substituted – 'British Aircraft Corporation' (this may have come from the Masterton/Pritchard discussion at Paddington but there is evidence that it had been considered at a much earlier stage) and 'British United Aircraft Corporation.'

The two name suggestions were but part of important basic proposals which came from two top-level meetings of Sir Reginald Verdon-Smith and the Hon. H.G. Nelson (later to inherit his father's title of Lord Nelson of Stafford) and Sir Charles Dunphie, Managing Director (later Chairman) of Vickers, on 19 and 22 January 1960. They recommended for the new company a Board which comprised a Chairman (at first Executive, but later changed to non-Executive), two Executive Directors, one for Aircraft and the other for Guided Weapons, and a Finance Director. In addition, they proposed two non-Executive Directors each from Vickers and English Electric, and one from Bristol. The subsidiary companies (Vickers-Armstrongs (Aircraft), English Electric Aviation, and Bristol Aircraft) should continue to be operated day-to-day by their local Boards but reporting to the new main Board.

Sir George Edwards, in scribbled home-written weekend notes on the minutes of the above meetings, commented:

NAME

I, at any rate, have a strong preference for 'British Aircraft Corporation' and so does everyone else I've tried it on. The American United Aircraft Corporation would be certain to protest at the suggested alternative.

STRUCTURE

This could be made to work, providing it was made absolutely clear to the subsidiary company MDs that the Executive Director in charge was, in effect, the boss and what he said went. The Executive Directors would be in a hopeless position if they became involved in interminable arguments over every decision they wished to take. I have some strong feeling over this in view of our experience with English Electric on TSR2 – despite the contract and responsibility resting with Vickers.

HEADQUARTERS

Should, I am sure, be as small as possible and HQ admin. can be very small indeed . . . especially if, as proposed, subsidiary companies handle their own contracts with their own contracts staff . . . which has some merit providing there is unity of approach, especially to M of A.

As has already been seen from the quotations from Sir Reginald's 1972 lecture on the history of BAC, the above was basically how things were finally ordered. A Press release of 18 May 1960 announced the first Directors of British Aircraft Corporation as:

Marshal of the Royal Air Force Viscount Portal of Hungerford, KG, GCB, OM, DSO, MC (Chairman)

Major General Sir Charles A.L. Dunphie, CB, CBE, DSO (Deputy Chairman)

The Hon. George Nelson, MInstCE, MIMechE, MIEE (Deputy Chairman)

Sir Reginald Verdon-Smith, LLD, BCL

The Rt Hon. Viscount Caldecote, DSC, AMIMechE, AMIEE, AFRAeS (Executive Director, Guided Weapons)

Sir George Edwards, CBE, Hon. FRAeS, Hon. FIAS (Executive Director, Aircraft)

Mr William Masterton, CA (Financial Director)

Mr G.A. Riddell, CA

Mr R.P.H. Yapp

(Mr Riddell was from English Electric and Mr Yapp from Vickers.)

The same release announced that it had been agreed that BAC would acquire the controlling interest in Hunting Aircraft Limited which, with Bristol Aircraft Limited, English Electric Aviation Limited, and Vickers-Armstrongs (Aircraft) Limited, would become an operating subsidiary of British Aircraft Corporation.

Another January 1960 decision was to set out which projects were for the 'new account' of BAC as distinct from 'old-account' projects on which BAC would be contractors to the appropriate parent.

'New-account' projects

English Electric

Lightning – Mark V onwards
TSR2
Thunderbird II
Blue Water

Bristol

Britannic (Belfast) wings
   (There was a Bristol-Shorts tie-up on Britannias for the RAF and a *quid pro quo* on Belfast wings)
Bloodhound II
Supersonic Transport (if this became a contract)
or Type 216[1] using equivalent capacity
Miscellaneous research and development contracts

Vickers

VC11
TSR2
Swallow[2]
Guided Weapons other than Vigilant (see below)

'Old-account' products

English Electric

Canberra – all marks
Lightning – Marks I to IV
Thunderbird I
Spares etc. for the above

Bristol

Britannia
Bloodhound I
Type 188 (supersonic development aircraft)
Plastics
Spares etc. for the above

1 The Bristol Type 216 was a proposed development of the Bristol Freighter for Silver City Car Ferries. It was not built.
2 The Swallow was the Dr (later Sir) Barnes Wallis swing-wing experimental aircraft study.

Vickers

Viscount – all marks
Vanguard – all marks
VC10 – all marks
Super VC10
Scimitar
Vigilant anti-tank missile
Spares etc. for the above

As has been stated, all the above 'old-account' products remained entirely the financial and contractual responsibility of the appropriate parent, but the work on them was done by 'sub-contract' on BAC. This meant that, as far as the employees of BAC were concerned, they carried on with the existing programmes for these projects as though there had been no change – the financial sort-out as between the parents being a matter of internal accountancy.

The ex-Hunting Aircraft work, which now became mostly (and soon entirely) for BAC account, was:

Jet Provost
(The RAF's main training aircraft)

Hunting H107
(44/55-seat jetliner study with a possible military application)

Jet flap research aircraft
(An experimental aeroplane designed to fly at a high lift co-efficient of $c_L = 7.0$ in level flight, gliding flight and landing, using the principle of the jet flap)

FD2 development
(A contract to modify a Fairey Delta FD2 supersonic aircraft to incorporate a wing with the 'ogee' planform, such as was favoured for the proposed supersonic transport aircraft)

The manpower which was to be merged into BAC was:

Vickers	11,652
English Electric	8570
Bristol Aircraft	7894
Hunting Aircraft	1914
Total	30,030

There was also, for a time, and in addition, a Supermarine (South Marston) workforce of 1700, which eventually reverted to Vickers Engineering.

The actual state of play of the various projects on the formation of
BAC was:

Vickers

Viscount

Another 13 scheduled to be built.

Vanguard

Eight of 43 Vanguards ordered had flown, but the programme had been,
and was still being, badly held up because of serious faults in the Tyne
engine.

VC10

Thirty-five being built for BOAC and a further order being considered,
either for the standard VC10 or for the Super VC10 – a larger and
longer-range version. First flight of the prototype VC10 was scheduled
for the end of 1961.

VC11

A new jetliner project falling between the de Havilland 121 (Trident)
and the VC10. The VC11 was under detailed discussion with Trans-
Canada Airlines.

TSR 2

Swallow

Variable-geometry project being worked on by Dr Barnes Wallis.

Bristol

Britannia

Production virtually complete.

Bristol Type 188

All-steel supersonic single-seat research aircraft for Ministry of Aviation
(two ordered).

Bristol 216

Car-ferry transport design for Silver City Airways (not proceeded
with).

Supersonic airliner

Feasibility study for a six-engined aircraft to carry 130 people for 3000
miles at $M = 2.2$. This design study was partially covered by Government
contract and partly at company liability. Possible collaboration with
France and/or the USA was being explored.

Britannic wing

Bristol design and manufacture of the wings for ten transport aircraft for the RAF being built by Short Brothers and Harland in Belfast (aircraft later re-named 'Belfast.')

English Electric

Canberra

Main production (over 1400) virtually completed. Of these, 450 were built in the USA by Martin (B57) and 50 in Australia. In addition, Shorts built 23 Canberra PR9 high-altitude reconnaissance aircraft.

Lightning

Twenty-five flying, and contracts already held for substantial numbers of Mk1, Mk1A, Mk2 and Mk4 (2-seater) versions.

TSR2

Hunting

Jet Provost

Contracts for 200 Jet Provost Mk3 trainers, of which 88 had been delivered; production rate, 8 a month, rising to 10. Contracts also anticipated for an improved-performance Mk4 for 100 or 160 aircraft.

H107

Civil jetliner proposal – later to become the BAC One-Eleven.

Jet flap aircraft and FD2 conversion

Under construction.

DH121

Wing work on the DH121 under the Airco agreement.

The above work-in-hand for BAC produced a four-year forecast of profits for the new company, 1960–64, of £10.59 million total – or an average of £2.6 million a year, which, considering the capital and resources employed and the high risk, was, although viable, hardly a bonanza proposition. There was clearly going to be very little scope for any further adventurism in the private-venture civil market.

To complete the project picture, Bristol also had in mind a light aircraft (a twin-engined six-seater executive) called the Bristol 220, and Denis Haviland (now Deputy Secretary (C) at the Ministry of Aviation) asked about its likely fate in March 1960. He was not given a definite answer, but all the implications were that the design effort available at Bristol – which, on the purely aircraft side, was seen as its most important contribution to the merger – would be fully bid for by

Weybridge and Warton, and it would be unwise to get it tied up or fragmented on projects such as the B220. In the event, Peter Masefield, Managing Director of Bristol Aircraft, did not himself join BAC, and he was allowed to take such work as had already been done at Bristol on light aircraft, including the B220, to his new company, Beagle Aircraft, which combined Auster and Miles. Beagle Aircraft did put into production a twin executive and, indeed, BAC bought one and operated it for some years, it being the main commuting vehicle in which Sir George used to pilot himself and members of his staff from Weybridge to the various BAC airfield sites.

One immediate problem after the legal formation date of BAC – which was on 1 July 1960 – was to get the employees of the four subsidiary companies to 'identify' with this new British Aircraft Corporation which, at that time, meant little or nothing to them.

The death of the old names – Vickers, Bristol, English Electric and Hunting – could either be accomplished at the stroke of a pen, or left to a gradual process of decay spread over several years. There were many legal and contractual difficulties which argued against the stroke-of-a-pen solution, which was never really considered. The component or member companies of BAC, therefore, kept their old names and, indeed, their full legal existence, under their own Boards, but were officially described as '. . . a subsidiary company of British Aircraft Corporation' – thus getting the name of the new Corporation, as it were, into the act. To the outside world, however, especially abroad, it was of immediate importance to establish the identity of British Aircraft Corporation and, with it, an image of combined strength and ability which would impress potential customers, principally foreign Governments and airlines. An almost identical problem was, seventeen years later, to face the nationalised British Aerospace.

What BAC did was, from the outset, to feature in all its corporate advertising and sales promotion literature, exhibitions, Press releases and the rest of the outlets of publicity, the three words 'British Aircraft Corporation,' but, with purely product advertising, it also featured the appropriate subsidiary company name, thus linking the old and known name with the new and unknown one of BAC. There was no attempt, as was later to happen with the Hawker Siddeley Group, to put a 'BAC' tag on to a product already long known as a Bristol or Vickers or English Electric design. It was never the 'BAC VC10,' or the 'BAC Lightning' – but the 'VC10 – Vickers-Armstrongs (Aircraft) Limited, a member company of British Aircraft Corporation' or the 'Lightning – English Electric Aviation Limited, a member company . . .' etc.

Lord Portal, who had consented to be the 'neutral' Chairman of BAC, after a unanimous approach from all three parents, forecast that it would be eight years before the BAC sales forces in the field ceased to complain that, in presenting their visiting cards, they would be asked 'BAC? Who and what is BAC?' In fact, the transition probably took only about four

The BAC One-Eleven – first aircraft to bear the 'BAC' prefix – became the best-selling of all British airliners. The photograph shows a Series 500, largest of the production versions, with 'hush-kits' fitted to its Spey engines.

Jaguar taking off from a section of motorway in a demonstration of its ability to use improvised airstrips. This Anglo-French project proved that Europe could secure, through collaborative programmes, the benefits which stem from American-scale production runs. Substantial export orders have been added to the initial Anglo-French orders for 400 aircraft.

A unique photograph of an equally unique occasion: the only known photograph of the only occasion when the two Concorde prototypes (the French-assembled 001 and the British-assembled 002) flew together. This was at the Salon de l'Aéronautique at Le Bourget in June 1969.

The Panavia Tornado swing-wing all-weather combat aircraft (*top*) represents the long-delayed culmination of British research into variable-geometry design dating back to the Barnes Wallis investigations which began as early as 1945 and to Warton's P45 proposal in 1963.

The historic occasion when supersonic passenger travel became a commercial reality: the British Airways and Air France Concordes in Washington, after completing their synchronised double inauguration of the world's first supersonic airline services on 24 May 1976.

Rapier, the ultra-low-level defence system, which did more than any other project to establish the Guided Weapons Division as the European leader in missile engineering.

UK4, on which BAC was prime contractor, was one of a series of satellite projects which established the Electronics and Space Systems Group as a leader in its field.

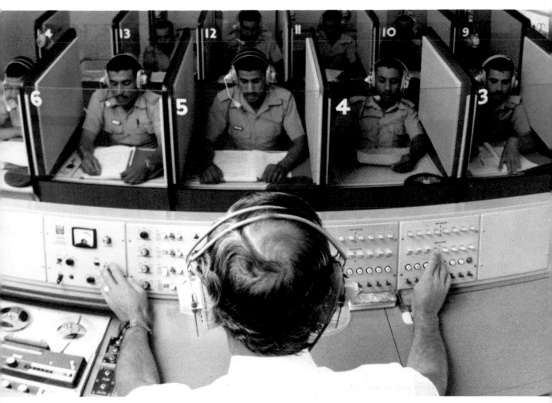

Under the Saudi Arabia Support Contract – described as 'the most important order ever placed with BAC' – the Corporation became responsible for a wide range of tasks, from the teaching of English to new entrants of the Royal Saudi Air Force *(top)*, to flying training on Warton-built Strikemasters *(below)*.

Nose-to-nose meeting of two aircraft which symbolised BAC's combination of civil and military aircraft capability: Concorde 002, carrying out the first overseas demonstration tour in 1972, with a Lightning fighter of the Royal Saudi Air Force at Dhahran in June 1972.

years, mainly thanks to a good decision of the BAC Board to fund a substantial initial publicity budget for 1961 – by far the largest one in real terms which was ever to be approved.

Internally the transition was helped by the happy fact that, alone of all the subsidiary companies, Bristol had a house newspaper called *Airframe*. This was promptly taken over as an overall BAC newspaper and expanded to cover news of the Corporation itself and of all its sites. It was, throughout the lifetime of BAC, to remain a 'straight' newspaper and was never involved in political propaganda as between Trade Unions or management. At first, a small charge was made for it, but later it was distributed free to all employees and pensioners. It still survives, but as *British Aerospace News*, and today covers what used to be all of BAC and Hawker Siddeley plus Scottish Aviation, its circulation having increased from under 8000 to nearer 80,000. A roadshow programme of talks, film shows, exhibitions and special literature was also undertaken to tell the employees on each of the sites in BAC about what the other chap did. Similar films, slide shows, and brochures were prepared to emphasise to overseas customers and agents the overall ability of this great new corporation in every major aspect of aerospace from the Jet Provost to the VC10 and from the supersonic Lightning to the Vigilant anti-tank missile. BAC was described as a 'New Force in World Aviation' and shown as being in the same league as the US giants such as Boeing, Douglas and Lockheed.

The overseas sales organisation was one of the major subjects which had been tackled well before BAC was legally formed. Chief Sales Executives were appointed – Mr Allen Greenwood (Weybridge) being named as Chairman of the BAC Civil and Military Aircraft Sales Committee, and Mr E.L. Beverley (Stevenage) as Sales Manager, Guided Weapons. Two other central headquarters appointments which concerned Sales were Mr G.E. Knight (Filton) as Commercial Manager, BAC, and the author (Weybridge) as Publicity Manager with overall responsibility to Messrs Greenwood and Beverley for all publicity, Press and public relations activities of BAC and its four subsidiaries. The appointments already listed plus those covering Personnel, Accountancy, Insurance and Office Administration completed the BAC headquarters, which certainly met Sir George's insistence that it be kept small ('A headquarters never built anything').

In its early years, BAC had a very centralised command structure. It could not be otherwise while the four subsidiaries and nine major sites (Warton, Preston, Samlesbury, Accrington, Stevenage, Filton (Aircraft and Guided Weapons), Weybridge, Hurn and Luton) were being 'tuned' as to production and design workloads, future projects, spare capacity, and so on. The individual product development and sales teams were left more or less undisturbed, but drawn together at the top by Greenwood and Beverley respectively. The complicated matter of overseas agencies, however, had to be sorted out promptly as, in key countries, there were now up to four agents – one inherited from each subsidiary, and each thus able to claim he represented BAC.

This was a long and sometimes animated process as the Sales Manager of each product tended to insist that his agent in country x was the one BAC should have. But, like all such things, it was finally settled on a give-and-take basis, though, here and there, military or Guided Weapons responsibility was given to one agent and civil or aircraft to another in the same territory. The Aircraft Sales meetings and subsequent organisation were fairly painless, but, until the merger, the Bristol Guided Weapons team with Bloodhound, and the English Electric one with Thunderbird had been very energetic rivals, with Eric Beverley – now the BAC Guided Weapons Sales Manager – at the head of the English Electric effort, and Group Captain 'Taffy' Higginson the chief salesman at Bristol. The early Guided Weapons Sales meetings tended to be very lively affairs, with sparks flying in all directions. Robin Caldecote, as Executive Director Guided Weapons, exercised a calming influence, and social exchange visits between the men of Stevenage and Filton for skittles and beer evenings eventually took some of the heat out of what everyone had known would, initially, be a prickly situation.

To continue this organisational story a bit ahead of the chronology of the book so far, the centralised management through two Executive Directors and a Finance Director continued until September 1961, when BAC's birth pangs were more or less over. By then it was clear that BAC would have to have one overall operational boss ('the Ministry of Aviation must have some one chap whose pants they can kick,' Sir George had written in another context, about a year earlier), and that boss had to be responsible to the BAC Board and through that Board to the parents.

The idea of the original triumvirate (Edwards, Caldecote and Masterton) had been that, with one head man put publicly on parade from each of the three main merging companies, the transition to BAC would be the more easily accomplished, and a minimum of inter-site jealousy aroused. Inevitably, there were rumblings – 'a Vickers take-over' summed up a lot of Warton opinion (especially remembering TSR2); 'an English Electric take-over' was alleged at Bristol Guided Weapons. Weybridge, except for the small Guided Weapons team which had developed the Vigilant man-portable infantry anti-tank missile, was undoubtedly a bit smug. The Guided Weapons people at Weybridge feared, however, and with good and logical cause, that they would either have to remuster to the aircraft side or go to Stevenage, which was a specifically Guided Weapons site, and the centre of the BAC Guided Weapons activity.

The choice of the 'one boss' in day-to-day command of BAC, the wearer of the labelled pants which the Ministry of Aviation could kick, fell, not unexpectedly, on Sir George, who was appointed BAC Managing Director on 1 October 1961. Lord Caldecote became Deputy

Managing Director while remaining Chief Executive (Guided Weapons). On the same date, Marshal of the Royal Air Force Sir Dermot Boyle joined the BAC Board with special responsibility for co-ordinating the administration of personnel and for training and education within the Group. The BAC Board had earlier been expanded to include Mr A.D. Marris, a banker, as a non-Executive Director. (Sir Dermot Boyle, that former Chief of the Air Staff who had publicly criticised the Sandys White Paper, was later appointed Vice Chairman of BAC.)

Two months after Sir George became Managing Director of BAC, he also became Chairman of the three main subsidiaries – Vickers-Armstrongs (Aircraft), English Electric Aviation, and Bristol Aircraft. He already was Chairman of Hunting Aircraft. This corrected, at the earliest opportunity, an upside-down situation created by Sir George's appointment as Managing Director, since the then Chairmen of the three subsidiaries were no less than Major-General Sir Charles Dunphie, the Hon. H.G. Nelson, and Sir Reginald Verdon-Smith. Individually and collectively, they were very heavy metal indeed, each being the senior main Board member from the three parents, and it was, by inspection, impossible to have them, when wearing their subsidiary Board hats, subject to the decisions of Sir George when, as key BAC Board members, they were the main arbiters of overall Corporation policy.

The Aircraft Sales organisation was also tidied up about this time. With both civil and military aircraft in the BAC catalogue, and with English Electric, Vickers, Hunting and Bristol all engaged in making them, centralised control was by no means as straightforward ad-ministratively as with Guided Weapons Sales under Eric Beverley. It was eventually sorted out when Allen Greenwood became Manager, Aircraft Sales and Service, and to help him he had a Civil Aircraft Sales Manager, R.C. Handasyde, a Military Aircraft Sales Manager, J.K. Quill, plus two Technical Sales Managers (J.R. Ewans, Military, and D.J. Lambert, Civil). The responsibilities of the specialist Sales Managers of the individual aircraft products were not changed, i.e., Jeffrey Quill did not get deeply involved in the day-to-day selling of Jet Provosts, nor Bob Handasyde with Britannias. Quill's personal efforts at this time were mainly devoted to TSR2 and Handasyde's to VC10. Allen Greenwood's main function was to co-ordinate the total aircraft sales effort, to avoid duplication of potentially bewildering visits to the same customer from different BAC sites, and to run frequent checks to see that there was not over-concentration on one market to the detriment of another.

At this time, the average BAC routine aircraft sales team consisted of a salesman who had the contacts and knew the politics of the country or the airline concerned, and a technical salesman, who was a highly qualified performance engineer, with a slide-rule at the ready. The industry was at a bridge-passage between the traditional or 'suede shoe' method of selling between old friends over a drink, and the sophisticated and detailed analysis of every phase of an aircraft's performance and economics which had now become dominant. It was not very long before 'tech-sales' became central to every sales presentation. Such presentations required several specialist engineering experts, each to speak on his own aspect of the aircraft, supported by engine and electronics men from supplier companies, and backed by much heavy luggage of colour-slides, film and brochures, all carefully compiled and tailor-made for each potential customer.

Under Greenwood's guidance, BAC devoted much time to the full preparation and rehearsal of its aircraft sales presentations and provision of high-standard literature. BAC quickly gained a reputation for doing at least as thorough a job as any of its American competitors and, indeed, a bit better than most. The accent was very much on coherence of performance at the rostrum, and if, as sometimes happened, the man who knew most about a particular aspect of the aircraft was not the best man to put it over, then the main presentation was left to someone else, and the key expert was held in reserve to field questions and to take part in more private man-to-man sessions with the customer's engineering moguls.

Organisationally, BAC, at least for its first and centralised phase, was more or less complete after eighteen months of Corporate life. Sir George was firmly in the aircraft saddle and was keeping close personal technical watch on TSR2 and VC10, and on the ever more complicated dealings with Whitehall. He had a strong financial team in Masterton, Mr Reg Sawyer and Mr J. Armitage (Weybridge), who had been appointed BAC Comptroller. He also brought in, to be BAC Production Director, Mr A.W. ('Charlie') Houghton, who had been instrumental in sorting out the Viscount and Valiant lines, and keeping them on the rails when both were threatening to fall far short of promised deliveries. Charlie Houghton had started life as a tea-boy at Weybridge, and when, on one occasion, someone described him rather glossily as a 'former apprentice' he bit the man's head off – 'Don't try to dress me up an ex-apprentice. I never was. I was the tea-boy and anything I've learnt I learnt on the factory floor.' Houghton had been with George Edwards' little team during the war when Edwards was 'Experimental Manager' at Weybridge, and later Sir George was to say that there was practically no part of an aeroplane that he and Charlie Houghton hadn't themselves hammered out at a bench at one time or other. They were still at it together as late as 1953, when they took their tool kits down to Wisley for all of one weekend and managed to finish the prototype Valiant B2 for appearance next day at Farnborough. They ended up covered in grease and with spanners all over the place – but the B2 was ready for take-off by the time they were through.

Thus, by the end of 1960 and early 1961, BAC had been formed, with an initial capital of £20 million, its immediate management pattern had been set, and the key personalities chosen and given their terms of reference. The Government requirements for a powerful group with strong interests outside aviation had been met, in that BAC was an aerospace diversification for all three parents, and it was now up to the Government to keep its part of the deal by placing such contracts as it had to offer with either BAC or the other airframe group, Hawker Siddeley. In fact, the only contract it had on offer during the time of the formation was for the new transport for the RAF – which it awarded to Shorts.

6

. . . And Early Problems

An analysis of the workloads set out in the previous chapter will only serve to underline the self-evident fact that TSR2 was central to the whole future of BAC. The Corporation had been formed for the purposes of TSR2, and TSR2 was its intended bread and butter. Meanwhile, Lightning and Jet Provost were enough to look after the Warton/Preston and Luton sites, but Bristol was in a very bad way. Weybridge had work enough with Vanguard and VC10, though both were money-losing civil projects, while Guided Weapons were making but a small contribution to the common weald.

The immediate first-aid needed was to save Bristol, whose airframe side was facing a shut-down. One of Sir George Edwards' first tasks on becoming Chief Executive (Aircraft) was to go to Bristol and make a thorough investigation into the Filton situation. 'I was horrified at what I found,' he was later to say. 'They had virtually nothing. There was some Britannia work, and they were building the first of the two little Type 188 all-steel experimental aircraft – and that was it. The design team was working on the Supersonic Transport study which was a long way from being a contract, and on the Silver City freighter, which came to nothing. The last thing I wanted to do was to start BAC off with a closure or even serious unemployment, so I had to shift some work down to Filton from other sites, and do it right away.' In fact what Sir George did was to move assembly of the two-seat Lightning (the Mark IV) and some VC10 work to Filton; by so doing, he managed to keep it afloat – but only just.

The overall Weybridge future outlook – at least financially – was itself not all that bright, TSR2 excepted. Both the Vanguard and the VC10 were private-venture aeroplanes and the sole account of the Vickers parent. The Vanguard, whose sad commercial fate was virtually settled by the time BAC was formed, was a big four-engined turbo-prop put on to the market at a time when the pure jet was coming into its own and propellers were rapidly going out of fashion as front-line equipment. The Vanguard had its origins back in April 1953 as a 'Viscount Major,' to a specification drawn up by BEA for an aeroplane to cruise at 370 knots carrying 100 passengers over stage-lengths of up to 1000 st. miles with reserves. Coincidentally, Trans-Canada Airlines (now Air Canada) had a requirement for a broadly similar if slightly smaller aeroplane. Some sixty project studies were made at Weybridge to meet the BEA specification, a number of them being pure jets because there was strong feeling in the Project Office that a new aeroplane with propellers coming into service in 1960 would be lacking in sex-appeal. The 'Vanjets,' as they were called, were eventually ruled out, and the Vanguard became a double-bubble fuselage aeroplane, with the lower 'bubble' providing considerable cargo capacity – a feature which was particularly attractive to TCA. The engines were four of the new Rolls-Royce Tyne turbo-props of over 4000 s.h.p. each, driving de Havilland airscrews.

The production Vanguard eventually became capable of carrying a payload of 24,000 lb and had floor room for up to 139 passengers in six-abreast seating, as well as its cargo capacity. The maximum payload range possibility, using integral tanks, had been increased to nearly 2000 st. miles at 412 m.p.h. at 20,000 ft. It was this aeroplane, the Type 952, of which TCA ordered twenty in January 1957 – and later added three more. BEA had ordered their twenty Vanguards in July 1956, but were so impressed by the TCA improvements that they later changed their last fourteen aircraft to be virtually the same, though with 29,000 lb of payload.

The total sales of the Vanguard were, unhappily, to remain at forty-three – due to a combination of adverse circumstances. In the first place, the BEA specification was too specialised to attract a very large market – a point which Sir George was to emphasise to the Select Committee on Nationalised Industries in 1964. Secondly, a lot of time was wasted in finalising the design, and thirdly, the Tyne engine ran into a series of major troubles. It had been hoped that the Tyne would have had the bugs taken out of it by a considerable programme of airborne tests in a couple of Ambassador airframes, but by the time of the Vanguard maiden flight, made by Jock Bryce from Weybridge to nearby Wisley on 20 January 1959, the engine and its chosen airscrew had not even flown together. This combination of a green engine, a green engine/airscrew match, and a green airframe was to prove very costly. A series of HP compressor failures on the Tyne held up the flight test programme for months, and later there were major engine-seal problems. At the same time Lockheeds were selling, with typical vigour, their own big turbo-prop Electra. Had the Vanguard not been delayed by its engine problems, and had it taken some of the Electra sales, it is possible that it might have done quite well as the first cheap-fare airbus. Well enough, perhaps, to have broken even.

The Vanguard's seat-mile direct costs were, indeed, very low (down to 1.35 old pence at 1000 miles) and on the shorter journeys its block-time was virtually the same as that of a pure jet because it didn't have to climb so high for its economy. In fact it could be shown – and was shown – that the Vanguard V953 could operate profitably at 60 per cent passenger load factor between some city pairs in the US A at the same fare as the Greyhound Coach – and that without counting anything for the huge cargo-hold capacity. The 'Airbus' breakthrough, however, was never made, and – although the acroplane did very well for BEA and TCA (who in 1966 started to convert their Vanguards to 42,000 lb carrying cargo-planes) – Vickers lost £18 million on this second-generation turbo-prop, which should almost certainly never have been a turbo-prop at all.

One good thing which did come from the Vanguard was the 'milled from the solid' technique which was developed for the wings, and which was later extensively used in the VC10 and One-Eleven. This gave Weybridge considerable pioneering experience in fail-safe multi-load path techniques, together with the milling machines to cut the metal, and it also enhanced their reputation for rugged and reliable engineering.

With hindsight, it is easy to be wise about the Vanguard, but, in 1956, with the Viscount established and with no military work in sight at Weybridge to succeed the Valiant, Vickers had very little choice but to accept the Vanguard or to contemplate closing the site. As Sir George said at the time, 'It looks as if we will have to keep Weybridge going without a single piece of Government paper in the place. Nobody's ever tried it before, and it is going to be a highly interesting experience.' Certainly initial orders for forty aircraft looked fairly good by UK standards and the gamble, though well seen as one, seemed, on the available information of the day, worth the taking.

The other Weybridge aeroplane at merger time was the new VC10 for BOAC, which is dealt with in a later chapter. This was another potential money-loser for the Vickers parent – in the end it was to lose more money than the Vanguard – but it was, in 1959, in the eyes of the Government, an important stabilising factor in the formation of BAC. The real VC10 political storm clouds were still to come, although even by 1959 the barometer was clearly falling. There were, however, in the mill, two back-up proposals to the VC10 – the VC11, and (after the acquisition of Hunting) the Hunting H107 small jetliner study. Which would be the right aeroplane to build? And could anything be done to turn the VC10, or a VC10 derivative into a Viscount-type success? These were two of the most urgent basic questions on the desk of the new Chief Executive (Aircraft) of BAC.

At the same time as he was pondering these VC10/VC11/H107 problems, Sir George Edwards was very aware of the fact that, since the formation of BAC at, in effect, Government insistence, not one new Government contract had been placed with the Group. The Belfast had been given to Shorts, admittedly only an order for ten, hardly a production run which could justify the research and development expenditure for a Tiger Moth, let alone a major military transport – but there was more to the situation than that. In the offing was a further possible contract for a more important military transport for the Royal Air Force, known as OR 351, and thirty of these were going to be the initial buy. If OR 351 followed the Belfast to Shorts, then the Government was clearly going back on its merger 'carrot,' and its December 1959 policy statement that Government orders, save in special political or economic circumstances, would only be placed with one or other of the two new Groups which Duncan Sandys had set himself to create. It was clear that Shorts, being in Northern Ireland and 69½ per cent Government-owned, looked very likely to be a permanent 'special case.'

BAC also had another, and most fundamental worry, and that was for the safety of their central contract – that for TSR2. Right from the day of signature, TSR2 had a formidable array of adversaries. The Treasury was dead set against it because the Treasury was, and on occasions still seems to be, a determined adversary of the British aerospace industry overall. It saw very large sums of public money being invested to produce military hardware of ever-increasing complexity and cost when, in the Treasury's view, it was much simpler and cheaper to buy what Britain needed from the US shelves. Dollar expenditure could be contained by under-licence build on UK factory floors, and the design capability of the industry could be limited to a few cheap and cheerful projects such as trainers or minor guided weapons. The engines for any new aircraft could, of course, be by Rolls-Royce or Bristol Siddeley. If what was left of the airframe industry wanted to play with airliners, then it was free to do so, providing it didn't involve the Treasury.

The counter-argument to the Treasury's view was that American defence equipment did not always suit the defence problems of the UK; that if the UK had relied on US available and battleworthy equipment to fight the Battle of Britain we would have lost the war; that by killing off British aerospace design ability and making it a sub-contract organis- ation, it would spread ruin throughout all of the country's high- technology and electronics industry and light engineering, most of which relied on aerospace to be its spur to progress; and that the Treasury policy would make the UK for ever subservient to whatever future policies, however unpalatable, the US chose to adopt.

Further, Britain was an exporting country and it had to export – not import – to live. There was an almost unlimited future potential in aerospace exports, and the UK and the USA were the only two western countries with the self-contained skills, resources, and establishments to design and produce aircraft at any level of sophistication the state of the art permitted. To abandon this ability, built up over fifty years, at a time when world markets were bound to soar, would be an act of national insanity. It was also predictable that once the USA had gained, by British defection, a western monopoly of new aerospace projects, they could charge the UK anything they liked for aircraft and for spares or withhold sales entirely, unless the UK conformed to some US policy of the day. The alternative, of course, would be for the UK to turn to the USSR, and oddly enough this long-term danger, arising from a crushing of the British industry, was foreseen in the USA itself. There were then (and are today) a number of Americans – albeit in the minority – who do not want to see British and European design ability, competitive though it may be, steam-rollered, and who were genuinely dismayed years later when the UK virtually opted out of a share in the Space Shuttle. Their view was that the Shuttle was likely to open up whole new areas of fundamental knowledge and technology which could well become the property of the USA (and, in parallel, of the USSR), giving those two giants enormous 'blackmail' leverage, industrially, and politically.

The Treasury, however, lives on short-term judgement, in effect from Financial Year to Financial Year, and it was, from the start, opposed to TSR2, which it regarded as an open-ended drain. Ranged alongside the Treasury, as has been stated, were the Royal Navy, the Chief of the Defence Staff, Admiral of the Fleet Lord Mountbatten, and his scientific ally, Sir Solly Zuckerman.

'Right from the start,' said Sir George Edwards in later years, 'I heard the hoofbeats of this united opposition to TSR2. I knew it would have a struggle to survive, especially as we were not allowed to have the Medway engine. While there was a Conservative Government, I reckoned the project would go through, but I did not think it would last more than a month or so if there was a Labour Administration, and I also reckoned that Labour was set to win the next election.'

It was, therefore, with the possibility of the loss of TSR2 at the back of their minds, and with no prospect in sight of any other Government business except maybe OR 351, that the BAC Board decided, in the summer of 1961, to have a face-out with the Minister of Aviation (then Peter Thorneycroft, later Lord Thorneycroft). At the same time, and for many of the same reasons, Sir Roy Dobson, head of the Hawker Siddeley Group, was also working up to a similar face-out. As a result, BAC and Hawker Siddeley agreed to meet to discuss an industry/Government situation which affected them both, and to discover what common ground they had in joint or separate confrontations with the Minister.

7
Increasing Anxieties

The first BAC-Hawker Siddeley Aviation 'protest' meeting was held at BAC's Pall Mall offices on 25 July 1961. Lord Portal, Sir George Edwards, Lord Caldecote and Mr Masterton represented BAC, and Sir Roy Dobson (Chairman), Sir Aubrey Burke (Deputy Chairman), and Mr (later Sir) John Lidbury (Director and Chief Executive) represented HSA.

Lord Portal opened by saying that although the two Groups were in direct competition in all fields, there were, nevertheless, a number of points on which there was an identity of interest and the meeting therefore had been proposed to explore such points informally.

This meeting had, in fact, first been mooted in early June, and both teams, therefore, had been able to collect full briefs from all their sites. One of the main themes running through these reports, which covered all Ministry of Aviation aircraft and weapon contracts, was the slowness of the Ministry of Aviation Contracts Department in feeding out, in dribs and drabs, contractual cover for authorised projects on which work was in hand. This forced the contractor – BAC or HSA – to continue on its own, using company money, on the verbal promise that contractual cover was 'on the way' – and with no guarantee that the Government would not change its mind and subsequently repudiate all responsibility for the monies spent on its behalf without written authorisation. On the other hand, to wait for such written authorisation would often involve complete cessation of activity on major projects, involving employment stand-offs and considerable extra costs and programme delays, while the Whitehall game of 'stop – start' was played out by the bureaucrats.

Instance after instance of this was tabled by both Groups, and it was pointed out that, from time to time, the uncovered sums at risk, and the resulting non-recoverable interest charges, were too heavy for industry to continue to bear. Further, large sums of money were spent at the start of a verbally promised contract which were then disallowed by the Government on the grounds that this work was prior to the eventual written contract starting date. Some £350,000 was so spent on TSR2 and not 'recognised' by the Ministry of Aviation. BAC pointed out that its Lightning Mk3 took three years to gain a production contract, and work on it was continued by fifteen interim development contracts, each of which needed an average of six months' negotiation. During these three years, the Ministry did not set in hand the parallel accessory equipment from outside suppliers and, as a result, much of the equipment was in an undeveloped state when the production order was actually placed, leading to yet more delays and more costs.

Lord Portal accordingly told the Government that BAC had resolved that, in future, and as a matter of principle, it would not authorise private-venture expenditure on defence items beyond the feasibility study stage. If the Government was not then prepared to provide appropriate contract cover and finance, work on that project would cease and, if necessary, technical teams would be disbanded. This was, he said, an extreme step, but BAC was quite determined. The companies were being verbally encouraged by technical departments of the Government to continue work after the feasibility stage, but written contract cover was then either not awarded at all or was unduly delayed and all interim expenditure before the contract date was then dis-allowed. Sir Roy Dobson said HSA had met exactly the same treatment and he agreed that his company would now also act in the way proposed by BAC.

The next, and even more fundamental, item was what both BAC and HSA saw as the Government's failure to adhere to the spirit of the Aide Memoire on the Aircraft Industry dated 8 January 1960. This, it will be recalled, was the statement which said that the Government intended to concentrate its future aviation requirements as far as practicable on the new Groups (BAC and HSA) except where specialised requirements or public policy made it necessary to do otherwise.

Sir George Edwards said there was considerable evidence that the Government was not keeping to the spirit of this Aide Memoire. For example, the Government was now prepared to place a contract for the refurbishing of BAC-built aircraft with one of the independent com-panies. It might, Sir George added, be politically necessary from time to time to sub-contract work to independent companies, but the channel through which such work should reach them was via the main Groups. Sir Roy Dobson agreed and added that certainly no design work should be placed with the independent companies (which companies were mainly Shorts and Handley Page) because it was precisely in order to create the necessary strength and maintain the teams to handle such design work that BAC and HSA had been formed by Government action in the first place. Lord Caldecote added that weapons were being developed with the independent companies under the cloak that they were merely developments of existing products originally designed by a particular company, when, in fact, they were entirely new weapons. Sir Roy again agreed and said that Government delays were now such that final production could not be undertaken in the right timescale, and this fact was then used by the Ministry as an excuse for buying foreign products.

Sir George Edwards, referring to the lack of long-term planning of Government expenditure, said the Ministry should now be pressed for some indication of the forward level of work so that the size of the technical teams maintained by the companies could be kept in line. Lord Caldecote observed that the Ministry had promised to place holding contracts to assist industry when there were full contract hold-ups, but so far no one had succeeded in getting such a contract.

Finally, there was a long discussion on the profit rates allowed by the Government, which were based on an artifically low rate of interest prevailing just after the war, and had not since been adjusted.

The basic worry underlying this BAC/HSA discussion was the complete failure of the Government to come forward with any statement as to its future intentions for the aircraft industry, and the fear in both main Groups that, having been formed by the Sandys shot-gun marriage bureau, they were now going to be left with no new work, while such official encouragement as there was available seemed to be directed towards Shorts. It was left to each Group to make its views known to the Minister independently, while still keeping in close touch on basic matters.

BAC certainly had several meetings with the Minister of Aviation in the subsequent months, and so did HSA, but to no real avail, in that no long-term plan for its aerospace requirements was ever tabled by the Ministry of Aviation.

Sir Reginald Verdon-Smith says of this period, 'There was increasing anxiety about the future for both the aircraft and guided weapon design teams. Month after month, frequent representations were made to Ministers and even directly to the Treasury; these were made both separately and through the Society of British Aerospace Companies, and with the Hawker Siddeley Group, all in an endeavour to establish a realistic five-year plan within the framework of a ten-year forecast which was necessary to implement the declared policy of support for the industry. At the same time, increasing emphasis was also being placed by the manufacturers on the need to have regard to export potential. But these representations met with very little success and a mood of growing frustration developed.'

There were, at this time, various distractions and complications which wasted a lot of time at both BAC and HSA. First of all there was the nonsensical stately dance round the so-called NATO aeroplanes, given the nomenclatures of NBMR (NATO Basic Military Requirement) 3 and 4. NBMR3 was a supersonic VTO light strike fighter and NBMR4 was a transport to support the fighter. The idea of standardisation in NATO aircraft was as praiseworthy and necessary in 1961 as it is today, but this particular exercise was never going to amount to anything. NATO, as such, had (and has) no funds of its own – the money and forces coming from the individual member countries of the alliance. This meant that, to get a NATO aeroplane, all the countries concerned, most of which had aircraft factories, had to agree to buy a committee-chosen design as submitted by one design-leading firm but with manufacture spread among other European partners. What then happened was predictable. The arguments and proposals were developed on nationalistic lines according to who was the design leader. The French (Dassault) – with BAC in support – put forward a Mirage IIIV with Rolls-Royce direct-lift engines for NBMR3, and BAC also had its own 'saver,' with Italian support, in a variable-geometry solution. HSA, first with Germany, and then on its own, tabled the supersonic VTOL P1154, which became the most generally favoured entry – but it was all a great waste of time and led to nothing. The NBMR3 contest, however, did give the Ministry of Aviation a reason for delaying a decision on a similar Royal Air Force requirement for which HSA had entered the subsonic VTOL P1127 (Kestrel/Harrier), and this drew from Sir Roy Dobson the rebuke that the Air Staff seemed to prefer the shadow to the substance.

There was also the affair of Shorts. The Government had let it be known in July 1960 to both BAC and HSA that it would be more than happy to sell its $69\frac{1}{2}$ per cent controlling interest to either Group. The discussions and analysis of this proposed new merger occupied many BAC man-hours. In March 1961, BAC had informed the Ministry of Aviation that if the Bristol submission for OR 351 – the 35,000 lb payload STOL transport – was accepted, they would place 40 per cent of the work on Shorts, and that, if a developed Belfast got the order, then Shorts would equally place 40 per cent of the work on Bristol. By November 1961, the Ministry was asking whether BAC would relieve them of Shorts if thirty modified Belfasts were ordered to OR 351. The whole proposition was examined in depth – especially Shorts' very high overheads – and was rejected unless the Government could give BAC a much firmer idea of its long-range plans for the industry and of the workload likely to be called for. Without such basic information, BAC could not see its way clear to add to its existing capacity, especially at a time when it was still very much occupied in consolidating the recent mergers made in anticipation of work which had not been forthcoming. HSA also expressed nil interest, and Shorts are still an 'independent company' and outside the nationalised British Aerospace – even though the Government owns nearly 70 per cent of it.

Prior to the examination of the Shorts situation, BAC had received feelers, if not a formal approach, from Handley Page and had decided that there was nothing Handley Page had to offer which was of interest to BAC.

By late 1961, the Government aircraft work which was up for competition was OR 351 – the Beverley/Hastings replacement already described – and OR 346, which was for a Mach 2+ high-altitude fighter-bomber-reconnaissance multi-role aeroplane of considerable sophistication, and a multi-role maritime reconnaissance aircraft. BAC had also proposed a variable-sweep research aircraft, including the conversion of two Lightning aircraft to get actual flight-test experience of swing-wings. This proposal fell on stony ground.

For OR 351, BAC had put forward a Bristol design – the B208 – which had deflected-thrust engines, and also a BAC 222, which was a Tyne-engined, short take-off version of the Lockheed C130 Hercules, but with boundary layer control.

The argument and delays about OR 351 dragged on and on, with no decision. The requirement was subsequently radically revised to be a VSTOL aeroplane, thus wiping out thousands of project office man-hours in almost every design centre in the country. Eventually, the HS681 was selected neatly in time to be cancelled in the Labour Government's massive 1964/5 sweep-away of all new RAF projects. In the end, the RAF's new transport aircraft turned out to be a straight dollar purchase of sixty-six Lockheed Hercules, already a veteran American design. The ambitious OR 346 aeroplane was shelved, and attention was switched to a naval requirement for a Sea Vixen replacement, ER206. A BAC team under Alan Clifton (ex-Supermarine) produced a Type 583 design, a variable-geometry-wing interceptor with two reheated Medways. This requirement was also shelved and a later BAC variable-geometry design, the P45, was to emerge only to die amid the general 1964/5 slaughter.

This potted and gloomy story of Governmental indecision, delay, wasted effort, and cancellation is inserted here to show that, despite the many promises of a long-term plan, despite the undertaking in the 1959 policy statement and despite the pleas and warnings from industry, nothing happened in BAC on the military aircraft front, except some orders for more Jet Provosts, between the merger and the present European collaborative aircraft, the Jaguar (May 1965) and the MRCA Tornado (December 1968). Nothing, that is, save that, after the US cancellation of Skybolt and with it the proposed Skybolt-carrying VC10, the RAF did take fourteen VC10s for the (then) Transport Command. There was also, eventually, the award of what became the Concorde.

What BAC did get in return for its compliance with the wishes of its political masters was the cancellation of its central contract, TSR2, the cancellation of the Anglo-French AFVG which replaced it (not the fault of the Government), the cancellation of two of its key guided weapons, PT428 and Blue Water, and the failure to award it the OR 351 contract – once the carrot for the BAC purchase of Shorts.

Even as early as 1961, while TSR2 was still a going concern, Sir George Edwards told the Minister of Aviation (Thorneycroft) that 42 per cent of BAC's labour force was employed on work that had begun as private venture (VC10 and Vanguard) and that, on the contracts it then held, the labour force would be down to 21,500 by the end of 1964 and BAC would be out of business by 1966.

Contrasting the British attitude to the industry with President

Kennedy's clarion call of Project Horizon (full planning details requested on 3 March and ready for him to announce on 5 September), Sir George commented, 'From what we have heard, there is not going to be nearly enough work for one of your two airframe Groups – let alone the two.'

Looking back, it is remarkable that BAC ever survived the mid-late 1960s. That it did do so was largely due to a very brave decision in May 1961 to go ahead with a new jetliner called the BAC One-Eleven on the back of an initial order for ten from Freddie Laker, then the head of British United Airways. Considering what had happened with the Vanguard and seemed likely to re-happen with the VC10, there was no obvious reason why the parents should put their feet into the cold waters of civil aviation again. Yet they did so, probably because Laker, unlike the two national airline Corporations, did not demand his own special aeroplane to a specification which had little chance of export sales (e.g., the Vanguard, the original smaller Trident, in many ways the first Viscounts, and, of course, the VC10). In contrast, Laker was willing to encourage and actively help with an aircraft which was designed from the start for the world market.

8

VC11 or
BAC One-Eleven

At the time of the formation of BAC, Weybridge was pinning much of its hope for the future, as far as civil aircraft were concerned, on an aeroplane designated the VC11. This transport was a medium-range, scaled-down version of the VC10, with four RB163 engines.

A lot of effort had been put into the VC11 project, originally an entrant in the BEA competition which went to the Trident, and some £300,000 of company money had been sanctioned, of which over £200,000 had been spent by the end of January 1961. One of the most significant Government undertakings which had been included in the policy statement of December 1959 was a willingness by the Government to contribute (up to a maximum of 50 per cent) towards the launching costs of new airliners. This was a milestone, because hitherto the official view was that airliners were the private affair of the industry – a view which industry itself had held until development costs began to escalate out of reach of private finance. The VC11 had secured such a Government contribution (subject to a go-ahead) of £9.75 million – half of the total estimated launching cost of £19.50 million. At a purchase price of £1.18 million, the calculated number of aircraft against which all the launching costs would be covered was seventy-two. The VC11 also had a customer – Trans-Canada Airlines – which had signed a letter of intent for fourteen aircraft. A number of other airlines were also showing interest, notably Continental Airlines – one of the US Viscount operators. The VC11 was about the right size for the world market but, like the original Trident, was adjudged too big for BEA.

In addition to the VC11, however, and as a result of the merger, there appeared the Hunting 107 project for a small twin-jet airliner for about fifty passengers, using Bristol Siddeley BS75 engines of some 7000 lb thrust each. Considerable internal BAC debate ensued. It was clear quite early on that BAC could not do both aircraft, not if Filton was to keep its options open on the B208 military transport as well as the chance of the talked of SST. The argument therefore boiled down to VC11 versus H107, and their respective prospects in world markets. Heavily on the side of the VC11 was that it had Government launching aid agreed, and it had a customer. Furthermore, that customer was an important overseas airline – the same airline that had made such a key contribution to the professional development of the Viscount, and also to the up-grading of the potential of the Vanguard.

Sir George Edwards often stated that the Viscount did not become an internationally competitive aircraft until Group Captain Gordon McGregor's TCA team got their teeth into it, and, in so doing, educated the Weybridge design office until it could stand comparison with those of the USA. McGregor, the President of TCA, and Edwards were also personal friends, and Sir George was initially very wishful to do the VCII. On the other hand, there was some pretty heavy competition in the broad field covered by the VCII – notably the Boeing 727, and the potential stretch still left in the Trident. It was also not going to be easy to look after and develop an aeroplane whose first customer was the other side of the Atlantic from the manufacturing base. The delays inherent in making the VCII decision were also reacting against the aircraft because, lacking a firm statement that it was going to be built and that deliveries would begin by a stated date, some potential customers slipped away to the B727.

Meanwhile, support for a twin-jet was growing in BAC. Sir George ordered a major evaluation of the world market to be made, and some eighty-nine airlines – later extended to a hundred – were visited in what was, at that time, the most thorough market research exercise ever undertaken for a British civil project. The reports were most favourable and led to the conclusion that the H107 could be very successful if it could be made bigger and given more powerful engines than the BS75.

The upshot of this was that the H107 was redesigned into the BAC 107, and then the BAC One-Eleven, with two Rolls-Royce RB163 engines – the engine which was later to become the Spey.

Sir Reginald Verdon-Smith has since confessed that he was dismayed at this conclusion. Choice of the RB163s was a considerable set-back to Bristol Siddeley's hopes of penetrating the civil market with the BS75 (Bristol Aeroplane, a BAC parent, was a 50 per cent owner of Bristol Siddeley Engines). Furthermore he thought that the BAC One-Eleven, to get its required sales, would be tackling the difficult US market, and such a challenge on their own doorstep would stimulate a fierce counter-attack from the US manufacturers. It did, of course, do just that, and the DC9 and Boeing 737 were a direct result of the early sales in the USA of the BAC One-Eleven. For a time there was an alternative 'little One-Eleven' with BS75 engines on offer, but it had no takers.

The die having been cast, the search for a first customer began in earnest. At the same time, discussions were opened with the Ministry of Aviation to transfer the £9.75 million of launching aid agreed for the VCII to the new BAC One-Eleven. The first customer was Freddie Laker (later knighted), then the head of the British independent airline, British United Airways, who ordered ten One-Elevens, with options on five more. The aeroplane was in business, the VCII was abandoned, and the Government launching aid was duly granted. The sales teams could now go out with firm proposals. They were no longer talking about a brochure, but a real aircraft which was being built and for which real delivery dates could be quoted.

If Sir George was disappointed about losing TCA, he was delighted at getting an order from BUA, because, for the first time, a British independent was strong enough to become an initial customer for a new aeroplane. This broke the UK 'monopoly' situation of BEA and BOAC, it having hitherto been regarded as impossible to get into business without a first order from one or the other. Past experience with the Vanguard and then the Trident, as well as the pre-TCA Viscount, had shown that aircraft tailor-made for BEA had little appeal elsewhere. Laker, however, looked at life through a wider angled lens and, like Sir George, he was devoted to the ultimate world success of British aviation – a dedication the existence of which was certainly open to qualifications, if not doubt, among some of the senior decision-makers in the nationalised Corporations.

The BAC Board decision of May 1961 to go ahead with the BAC One-Eleven, to put a first batch of twenty on the line, and to drop the VCII was, in the end, vital to the well-being of the Corporation, for it was the One-Eleven which was to be its mainstay in the otherwise bleak years after the death of TSR2. It was a decision not easily arrived at in the light of Vanguard and Britannia experience. A visit to the USA by Sir George at the end of February 1961 was probably the deciding factor. He returned from it convinced that there was genuine interest in a twin-jet with a larger, more sophisticated specification than the original H107, and that it would probably be attractive to Braniff, American, and Continental. These three operators, and others, reported Sir George, were quite happy with a twin-engined configuration, the performance of the Caravelle with United Airlines having been shown to be satisfactory in service and acceptable to the passengers. There were, he said, nebulous paper aeroplanes floating about from Douglas and Boeing, but if BAC went firm quickly with a short-range twin-jet they could get in ahead of the competition, though they would undoubtedly encounter it in the end. The separate and more general market survey already mentioned also led Allen Greenwood, head of the Civil Sales Committee, to come out in favour of doing what was to become the One-Eleven.

Parallel with these assessments, hard bargaining was in process with Freddie Laker. Geoffrey Knight, who, when at Filton, had sold Britannias to Laker and was, at that time, engaged in trying (in the event, successfully) to sell him VC10s, was the man chosen to spearhead the BAC attack. Laker had, as had most airlines, already rejected the little H107, but was egging BAC on to the bigger RB163-engined proposal. The Weybridge and Hurn design teams under Basil Stephenson, Weybridge Director of Engineering in overall charge of the project, and the Luton one under Fred Pollicutt (Technical Director) and A.J.K. Carline (Chief Designer), the originators of the H107, worked closely with Laker, and the upshot was an aircraft of 74,500 lb all-up weight, with a payload of 13,800 lb (up to seventy-nine passengers), a cruising speed of 540 m.p.h., and optimised round-stage-lengths of 200–500 miles.

Geoffrey Knight recalls that once the specification had been agreed, there was prolonged 'horse trading' about the price, with side-issues such as paying for pilot and engineer training costs and publicity support being moved around the board like chessmen. 'Horse-trading' was, in the event, a reasonable description of what went on, because Knight remembers that the deal (at nearly £709,000 per aeroplane) was finally settled with Laker between races at Sandown Park.

So, for the second successive generation of short-haul transports, the British had spotted a gap in the American coverage and had jumped in to fill it. BAC had done this at a risk which no American manufacturer would ever have taken – a starting order for only ten aeroplanes. Sir George, however, said at the time, 'This is an area where we do have an advantage. We are used to organising ourselves round very small initial production runs – the Americans aren't. They want to see a run of a hundred of a new airliner before they commit themselves. We can never have such a luxury and have to make do on what we can get.'

The BAC Board decision to put the One-Eleven into production with only a contract for ten was, however, not quite as foolhardy as might appear in retrospect. It had before it this world survey, airline by airline, which showed that, once the project was a runner, one US airline (Braniff) was very likely to buy, and there was a chance of a considerable order from American Airlines. It was envisaged that thirty-five more aircraft were highly likely to be sold quickly with 134–44 as a 'probable' total, and up to 600 aircraft as 'possible' – depending upon what competition emerged and when.

In fact, 222 One-Elevens had been sold by the time BAC was nationalised and yet a further batch of aircraft was being laid down at Hurn. Had it not been for the tragic accident to the prototype, followed by a second 'headline' accident which was not due to any failure of the aeroplane at all, and had more engine power been available for development, that sales total might well have been close to the 600 mark distantly seen in 1961.

As it was, the One-Eleven stayed in production from the start of manufacture in 1961 for the whole lifetime of BAC and beyond. This success was despite the fact that the full potential of the aircraft was never able to be exploited for lack of engine development. The Rolls-Royce Medway engine was never built, and its cut-down version, the Spey, even with water injection, never had enough in reserve to enable the One-Eleven to be 'stretched' in the way that it should have been, and in the way that was envisaged when the project was undertaken.

Great pressures were put on Rolls-Royce to take the Spey well beyond the 12,550 lb static thrust which it eventually achieved for the One-Eleven 500, an aircraft which, as will be shown later, also became of the utmost importance to BAC. But, by then, Rolls had bigger fish to fry in the RB211 – the engine which was eventually to bankrupt them. The relationship between the airframe makers and Rolls-Royce has something of a history of disharmony, especially after the death of Lord Hives. Derek Wood in his book *Project Cancelled* has gone as far as stating that Rolls-Royce had no great love for the British airframe industry and worshipped at the American shrine. There is undoubtedly a lot of truth in what he says, and the aircraft side often found it fitting to remind Derby that all their most successful engines – the Dart, the Avon, the Conway, the Tyne even, and the Spey itself – owed their initial existence to a specific British requirement for a British aeroplane. It was (and is) also true that Rolls-Royce were, perhaps because of 'the magic of the name,' the blue-eyed boys in Whitehall, and this was later very apparent when collaborative projects became the order of the day, and British official emphasis was always on engine leadership at the sacrifice of the airframe side. Geoffrey Knight once, at a Press conference, in answer to a question, spoke his mind about Spey engine deliveries and development for the One-Eleven, and found himself in the national headlines for his temerity. Sir George himself also publicly commented that, whenever he wondered what he had been put on this earth for, he quickly found that the answer was to bend bits of tin to put round Rolls-Royce engines. The truth probably is that, once the RB211 was started and ran into all its teething troubles, Rolls-Royce had no top-level technical effort to spare for anything else – including aft-fan Spey proposals for the One-Eleven, or, for that matter, the needs of the Adour for the Jaguar, or, for a time, RB199s for the MRCA. Ronnie Harker, a servant of Rolls for forty years, effectively says as much in his book *From the Wings*.

9
The One-Eleven

It would seem logical, at this point, to carry through with the story of the One-Eleven. In writing a history of such a large company as BAC, which never had fewer than eight sites (counting airframe Filton and Guided Weapons Filton as separate) and at one time had as many as eleven, it is only too easy to become tangled in a cat's cradle of events and products and projects, each with its own chronology, and each with its repercussion on doings and decisions elsewhere. The details of the products, and their success and their failure, inevitably had their effect on the organisational and financial development of BAC, and on its relations with Whitehall, Rolls-Royce and BOAC. To write a history of BAC year by year would, therefore, be to write the first chapters of a dozen or more concurrent serial stories starting in 1960, and then, perforce, to mark them all as 'continued in our next instalment,' bewildering author and reader alike in the process. With so many balls in the air at the same time, it becomes necessary, now and then, to focus on them one by one.

The One-Eleven played a considerable and a continuing part in the whole of BAC's story, as it was one of the three products which remained in being throughout the Corporation's life – Concorde and the Jet Provost/Strikemaster being the other two. It was also the only aeroplane wholly designed and built by BAC, and above all, it came to its sales peak at a time when the other fortunes of the Corporation were at a low ebb.

It had always been the contention of Sir George, from the very start, that BAC's strength lay in the fact that its abilities and resources covered all three main fields of aerospace – civil aircraft, military aircraft, and guided weapons and space. 'Our three-legged stool,' he called it – adding that, if one of the legs was ever sawn off, the obvious result could scarce be avoided.

As events turned out it was a commercial aircraft – the One-Eleven – which was the main leg of BAC in its earlier years, then came the turn of Guided Weapons – or rather a combination of Guided Weapons with a big resurgence from the Military Aircraft Division. Each of the three basic activities of BAC, by natural evolution, eventually became Divisionalised – Commercial Aircraft Division, Military Aircraft Division, and Guided Weapons and Space Division, and each, in its turn, bore the major load of the BAC stool. Conversely, had each of these three Divisions been a separate, self-contained commercial enterprise, then each, at some time during BAC's seventeen years of life, would probably have had to close its doors. This was a point which Sir George made strongly to politicians who, in the 1970s, were advocating the complete separation of British (and indeed European) aerospace into watertight compartments labelled, Civil, Military and Weapons. BAC's Military Aircraft Division could hardly have survived, on its own, the cancellation of TSR2 and AFVG, or Guided Weapons Division the cancellations of PT428 and Blue Water. Commercial Aircraft Division entered a bad patch after the tail-off of Concorde and One-Eleven, hopes of any new airliner being inextricably mixed with the interminable Government-controlled political discussions with Europe on who should build what. These discussions had still made no visible progress a year after BAC had been nationalised. In other words, the elements of BAC were, at all times, interdependent in structure, and it was this interdependence which made the company not only viable, but successful.

To return to the One-Eleven, this was a private-venture product based on a worldwide market survey, ordered by a private-venture independent airline, BUA, but in receipt of the promised 50 per cent Government launching aid which kept the initial risk within the bounds of BAC contemplation.

The first model of the One-Eleven was the '200 Series,' with a seating capacity up to seventy-nine and a take-off weight of 78,500 lb, built round two rear-mounted Rolls-Royce Spey Mk506 engines rated at 10,400 lb static thrust. The whole aeroplane was uncompromisingly designed for the heavily travelled short-haul routes of the world. This meant it was engineered for quick turn-round, high utilisation, and low costs and break-even loads, with the objective of bringing, for the first time, jet comfort and speeds to routes which hitherto had been, and seemed likely to continue to be, served by propeller aircraft. It was in short, a genuine jet replacement for the Viscount.

Further, it had built into it the then world-unrivalled BAC Viscount and Vanguard experience of five million hours of turbine-powered airline flight experience and the hard-won knowledge of what operators – especially in the USA – required and expected from a major-league supplier in the way of service support, spares and guarantees.

The One-Eleven also had the advantage of Vanguard and VC10 experience in using 'milled from the solid' or 'sculptured' components in place of fabricated parts built up by riveting or bonding. The use of machined skins, milled from solid alloy planks, was first introduced on the Vanguard wings. Then, on the VC10 and One-Eleven, this advanced process was extended to many fuselage components, giving increased fatigue life and ease of inspection.

The One-Eleven aircraft systems were split into continuously operating halves, either of which could keep the aircraft working normally without loss of performance, and fail-safe engineering concepts were used throughout.

Warranties were demanded of all equipment suppliers, and as much choice as possible was given to individual operators for key equipment to match that in the rest of their fleet. This tough line on equipment brought some protests from British suppliers, who were uncompromisingly told, 'It is up to you to sell yourselves to the airlines. If you can convince them that your product is better than the one they have chosen, then BAC will be delighted to fit it. What BAC will not do is to risk losing a customer for British aircraft and British engines by telling the buyer that he also has to have your particular piece of electrical or other ancillary equipment instead of the one he wants on a take-it-or-leave-it basis.' There is little doubt that this attitude, resented at the time, led to improved and more competitive British equipment engineering and after-sales service. In the past, Vickers had had some poor experiences with insufficiently developed or tested British 'bits and pieces,' and Sir George once told the Institute of Electrical Engineers, in a downright speech, that he was tired of hearing that a quarter of a million pounds' worth of Viscount was on the ground because of the failure of some £15 bought-out component with 'salt across the terminals.'

Everything conceivable was done to make the One-Eleven an 'operator's aeroplane,' and this was quickly evident to airline engineering teams. The first sale of ten aircraft to BUA was quickly followed, in October 1961, by an order for six (plus six more on option) from Braniff International Airways, whose routes were mostly 250 miles or less. This was the first time a US operator had ordered a British airliner 'from the drawing board,' and six months later the Braniff order was duly increased to twelve, and later to fourteen.

The second American carrier to order the One-Eleven was Mohawk Airlines, which carried a million passengers annually on an inter-city system over ten States. Mohawk's choice was challenged by the American Civil Aeronautics Board, which gives a subsidy to local carriers. CAB queried the need for jets on local service routes, and doubted the ability of the One-Eleven to operate economically for Mohawk. The airline President, Mr Robert Peach, replied: 'Our planned operation of four One-Elevens on 200-mile stage-lengths shows a break-even load factor of 46.5 per cent — a load factor which has historically been achieved by Mohawk. The seat-mile costs are substantially below those of the most efficient short-haul transport now operational over the actual flight stage length proposed.' The CAB revised its view, and agreed to the purchase because the One-Eleven would not increase, but rather contribute to a reduction of subsidy while, at the same time, improving services to the travelling public. Eventually Mohawk operated twenty One-Elevens.

During the time the first Braniff and Mohawk sales had been under negotiation, a major follow-up was being made of the initial interest expressed by American Airlines – one of the 'big four' US carriers. The first BAC One-Eleven 200s were now being built at Weybridge and Hurn, with Hurn as the final assembly factory, as it had been for most of the Viscounts. The Spey engine, however, was now developed in a more powerful version, the Mk511 of 11,400lb static thrust instead of the 10,410 lb of the Mk506. This enabled BAC to offer the One-Eleven 300/400 Series with a seating capacity of eighty-nine, and with take-off weight increased to 92,000 lb and a consequent increase in range.

The One-Eleven Series 400 was a very suitable aeroplane for American Airlines, and a big sales effort was launched. The importance of a One-Eleven order from such a world-famous carrier as American Airlines could hardly be over-stated, and from 1962 to 1963 Geoffrey Knight and Derek Lambert virtually lived in New York, commuting home at weekends. Sir George also was a frequent visitor to the American Airlines headquarters, the airline president, the legendary C.R. Smith, being an old friend. The bargaining was hard, tough and long drawn out, especially as American Airlines was proud to bear that flag name and was apprehensive about the effect on its image of buying British, however good the product. But, eventually, the breakthrough was made, and on 17 July 1963, they ordered fifteen One-Eleven 400 Series (operated rather anonymously as 'Astrojets') – an order which was subsequently increased to twenty-five and then to thirty. The initial order for fifteen aircraft was, at that time, the biggest single dollar export contract ever won by the UK – totalling with spares, £14 million ($40 million). For this, and for subsequent sales efforts on behalf of the One-Eleven, Geoffrey Knight was later awarded the CBE for services to export.

One of the factors which aided these US sales of a new British aircraft was the existence at Arlington (Virginia), on the outskirts of Washington National Airport, of a considerable BAC after-sales servicing and spares organisation operated by BAC (USA) Incorporated, headed by an ex-Supermarine engineer, Murry White. Arlington had been established, at considerable Vickers' investment, to support, as a contract requirement, the initial US sales of the Viscount. As a result, an American operator could get what amounted to 'over the counter' service of airframe spares from a nut and bolt to a whole wing. The British car manufacturers had in the 1950s done this country's reputation no good at all by selling cars into the USA with an inadequate spares organisation. This did not happen with the Viscount. It became the Arlington boast, publicly supported by the operators, that they got better spares and service support from Britain than they did from their own West Coast giants. The Rolls-Royce engine was supported from Rolls-Royce Canada, which was established near Montreal.

Arlington saw to it that its Viscount reputation was fully maintained on the One-Eleven, and it expanded its business to cover those equipment suppliers who were unrepresented directly in the USA and, indeed, to act as US agents for a variety of British light engineering firms. In 1977/8, BAC – now British Aerospace Inc. – joined with Rolls-Royce, and moved to impressive new headquarters hard by Washington (Dulles) International Airport. There, they 'look after' all former BAC and HSA aircraft based in the USA and also cover Concorde spares requirements.

One month after the American Airlines order had been announced, the prototype One-Eleven flew at Hurn on 26 August 1963, in the hands of Jock Bryce. There was a large, even unwieldy, audience of Press, TV and general public who saw Bryce bring the aeroplane in for a beautiful landing right on the border-line of dusk. By that time, the One-Eleven had been ordered not only by BUA, Braniff, Mohawk and American Airlines, but by Kuwait (three), Central African Airways (two) and Aer Lingus (four) – a total of fifty aircraft, thirty-one of them being to the USA. Among those present at the first flight was Freddie Laker who was asked rather aggressively by a BBC current affairs interviewer, 'Just why have you ordered this aeroplane, Mr Laker?' Freddie gazed benignly at the camera for a couple of seconds and then replied, 'Because I'm as nutty as a fruit cake.' To give the BBC its due, the 'interview' was used.

The production plans for the One-Eleven, which had started with the laying down of an initial batch of twenty Series 200, had been most carefully made. The front and centre sections of the fuselage were built at Hurn, the factory of final assembly, and there mated with rear fuselage and fin (from Filton) and the wing torsion-box structures (from Luton). Weybridge provided the landing gear and the sculpture-milled skins for wing and fuselage. By April 1964 – eight months after the first flight – components for all ten BUA aircraft had been completed, five fuselages had been produced for Braniff, and the first American Airlines model 400 was in final assembly. Weybridge had completed more than forty sets of wing skins. By mid-1964, One-Elevens were coming off the line at two a month, increasing to four a month by 1965. A 'double line' had been introduced which gave scope for further expansion and, at peak, up to six One-Elevens were built in one month. In charge of One-Eleven production expansion was Arthur Summers, formerly Managing Director of Hunting Aircraft at Luton.

The One-Eleven programme control was exercised through a Project Controller, in whose chart room was monitored all the 'milestones' for each aircraft. The Controller was provided with the best computer support available, covering new design development, stock control, re-ordering procedures, spares inventories and all the other basics to keep the line flowing by spotting potential hold-ups before they occurred. Taking assembly man-hours as a primary yardstick of efficiency, these were reduced to less than one-fifth of the figure for the initial production aircraft, and BAC was able to sell off the thin end of Sir George's 'learning curve.' This efficiency encouraged the BAC Board to keep the production flow going by the progressive laying down of batches of 'stock orders.' The Board's courage paid off, because it led to competitive delivery lead-times, and to a constant flow of sales.

BAC, in close consultation with the operators, also introduced what was known as the 'on condition' maintenance philosophy. This was made possible by the split-systems concept, which could accept the in-flight failure of a component – said component being able to be checked *in situ* and changed if showing a malfunction. Eventually, over 82 per cent of the One-Eleven's rotable components were 'on condition,' and less than 0.5 per cent of the remainder had an overhaul life of less than 5000 hours. The aircraft structure was also extensively fatigue-tested – indeed, up to 115,000 simulated flight cycles, or forty-six years of operation at 2500 hours a year on typical regional stage-lengths.

The whole of the One-Eleven programme – inception, design, sales production, after-sales service, and customer training schemes – was something to be proud of, and it was certainly as good as anything offered on the other side of the Atlantic. The aircraft's performance, too, was most satisfactory – as was demonstrated on many sales tours and by the operating airlines. Its despatch reliability rate was 98 to 99 per cent – indeed, in 1969 it had a worldwide average of 98.15 per cent while, on short stages in the USA, it was breaking even, on all costs, with only twenty-two passengers when the average passenger load factor was 60 per cent – which meant fifty-three people. This despite a 10 per cent sales tariff barrier which added over 3 per cent to the costs. The One-Eleven was consistently cheaper to operate than its nearest competitor, and consistently had higher load factors than either the DC9 or the B737. It was achieving turn-round times at *en route* stops of as low as six minutes – with only twenty minutes per termini. Its fuel costs were some 20 per cent lower per block-hour than the competition.

By the time BAC was nationalised, 222 One-Elevens, in various marks, had been sold to sixty operators in sixty-three countries, and the value of the sales was £383 million, over two-thirds of it for export. These overseas One-Elevens will long continue to earn money for this country, because, in a lifetime of operation, each aircraft, with spares, financing and servicing, brings in, at the end of the day, at least the value of its original purchase price. When a British civil aeroplane is sold abroad for, say, £3 million, this will eventually become at least £6 million, or probably £7 million – not allowing for escalation.

The One-Eleven became, in fact, Britain's biggest-ever export-earning civil aircraft, and its contribution to the balance of payments is still by no means over. Despite this success – a success which meant so much to BAC's finances in the mid and late 1960s – there are many who, and with good reason, still sigh over what might have been if only the airframe had been matched by a British engine development or an engine availability to enable it to grow in size when the market was ripe for the stretched One-Eleven which BAC was never able to offer.

IO

The Set-Backs

From a 1963 viewpoint, the One-Eleven future looked rosy indeed. The Spey 'dead end' was still some years ahead and, in the meanwhile, the engine was developing well. One-Eleven sales were healthy and the lead-time of a year over the DC9, which had been announced as a starter in 1962, was as competitive as could be hoped for, considering the size of the world market and the fact that BAC had already bearded the Americans in their own den. This valuable lead-time, however, was to be seriously cut back, when, on 22 October 1963, tragedy struck at the One-Eleven.

On that morning, the prototype took off from Wisley with test pilots Mike Lithgow (a former Supermarine Chief Test Pilot and world speed record holder in the Swift) and Dickie Rymer, who had been BEA's chief Viscount pilot before joining the Viscount test team at Wisley, and who was one of the most experienced commercial pilots and instructors in the country. They had aboard a test crew of five.

The object of the flight – the fifty-third in the prototype – was to measure stability on approaches to the stall, up to the very aft position of the aircraft's centre of gravity – forty-two such approaches and recoveries having previously successfully been made at other centre of gravity settings and covering all flap-angles. On this fifty-third flight, four approaches to the stall had been made with the aircraft 'clean,' and it was on the fifth test, with eight degrees of flap, on full aft centre of gravity that the accident happened, and all aboard were killed.

The information from the two flight recorders and inspection of the wreckage showed that the aeroplane hit the ground in more or less a flat, horizontal attitude, with little forward speed but very high vertical descent. The stall had been at a high angle of incidence, but had not been accompanied by the usual nose-down and self-recovering change of attitude. The aircraft started to go very sharply downwards but still with the nose up, thus making the relative air-flow come at the wings from below and so increasing the angle of incidence while also forcing the elevators to trail up. Nothing could be done as the pilots did not have sufficient control power to do more than momentarily check the 'up' elevator, which eventually reached the up-stop despite a large push force on the control column. There was no spin and the aeroplane fell flat to the ground.

The instrumentation later revealed exactly what had happened, and the cure was quite quickly worked out. The wing leading edge shape was modified to give a more definite nose-down pitch at the stall, the pilot's power over the elevators was increased, and automatic stall warning with stick-shaker and stick-pusher was incorporated. These modifications were fully tested and approved by the certification authorities in the UK and the USA. As soon as the cause of the accident was identified, BAC passed on all technical information about it, and about the cure, to the rest of the world's aircraft industry, including (and especially) to Douglas, whose DC9 had a similar T-tail configuration.

The extreme nature of the fatal stall test – high incidence at full aft centre of gravity and with flap – was, although required for certification, something which was never likely to be encountered in normal airline flying. It was, however, a remote corner of the flight envelope which had to be probed, and the crash, and the subsequent search for and testing of the cure, not unnaturally gave worry to customer and potential customer airlines. This situation was made worse not long after when a second One-Eleven force-landed in a field.

This aircraft had been continuing stalling tests and, because of the first accident, a tail parachute had now been fitted as a safety measure. The circumstances in which the tail parachute came to be deployed on this flight are not easy to disentangle – save that there was later full agreement, backed up by the instruments, that it was not ever necessary, as the aircraft had already recovered from its stall in a normal manner. The parachute, however, was, in fact, deployed and the aircraft was then flown round, under control but dragging this parachute behind it until the pilot put it down in a field. As the flight recorder showed, and the pilot later agreed, all he had to do was to release the parachute and fly home to Wisley in the usual way as the aeroplane was completely normal, save for the fact it had its parachute out. To the outside world, however, here was another One-Eleven 'stalling' accident, and there was considerable coverage for it in the UK and US media, which did a deal of temporary harm to the One-Eleven.

BAC teams were sent out right away to all customers and potential customers, taking with them the flight records, and, as they were talking to professionals, they were soon able to demonstrate the truth of what had happened. Nonetheless the two accidents, coming close together and both connected with stall tests, undoubtedly undermined confidence in the One-Eleven at a critical time, and gave Douglas a market advantage, even though their DC9 was also T-tailed.

By the time the One-Eleven 200 came into simultaneous service with BUA and Braniff in April 1965, doubts about the aeroplane had been removed, but the One-Eleven, from then on, had to face competition on every sale not only from the DC9, but from the Boeing 737 which had also entered the lists. The Boeing decision to become a third aeroplane in this short-range jet field was made when it seemed that the aeroplane could hardly become, at least not for a long time, a commercial success.

The market of the day, it was argued, could not sustain or justify the development programmes of three competing aeroplanes. The 737 was thus initially a 'spoiler' for both the One-Eleven and the DC9.

Despite the set-backs, the basic One-Eleven development programme began very well. The Spey was taken from its 10,410 lb static thrust of the 200 Series (1965), to the 11,400 lb static thrust of the 300/400 Series (in service, 1966) to the 12,550 lb static thrust of the 500 Series (in service, 1968).

The 300/400 Series, as has been said, was evolved for American Airlines, who contributed a number of valuable suggestions for design refinements. The 400 Series was the Americanised aeroplane and the 300 Series the British equivalent.

The availability of the Spey 512, with initially over 1500 lb more static thrust than the original Spey 506, enabled BAC to evolve the One-Eleven 500, which had 13 feet 6 inches added to the fuselage and a 5 feet increase in wing span, leading to a take-off weight of 92,453 lb and, eventually 104,500 lb and increasing the seating capacity to ninety-seven and then to 119.

The 500 Series was first developed for the short-range needs of BEA's German and UK domestic routes. BEA put in ninety-nine seats, and had the underfloor hold volume increased by 29 per cent. A number of aerodynamic refinements were incorporated and there was an all-round improvement in mission performance.

For the dramatically increasing Inclusive Tour holiday market, a longer-range One-Eleven 500 was needed to cover the many European and Near East resorts which lie within a 1000 mile to 1500 mile radius from the airport of origin. The Spey came up with another 550 lb of static thrust, and the One-Eleven was able to cover the ranges needed with 119 passengers.

But that was the end of the Spey development and, when the major market called for a further stretch in the One-Eleven up to 130 or more seats, the One-Eleven could not respond to the challenge of the four stretches of the DC9 and the JT8 engine up to 137 seats and eventually 160.

Baulked at the top end of the scale, BAC branched out into a new version of the One-Eleven – the 475 Series, aimed at bringing jet travel to the secondary airfields, mostly those serving remote places in thinly populated areas. This called for an ability to use unmetalled and gravel runways, short take-off and landing, and above-average descent and climb-away paths.

To achieve this, the 475 used the 400 Series fuselage with seventy-nine seats combined with the 500 Series wings and the 12,550 lb static thrust Spey Mk512-14DW (Designed Wet) engines. The underneath of the aircraft and the flaps were protected against flying gravel, and deflectors were fitted to the nose and main gear. A large cargo door was also available, to give a mixed freight/passenger ability. This aeroplane gave some remarkable demonstrations on all kinds of grass and other natural-surface airfields in South and Central America, making sales to several airlines with difficult local routes to serve.

In 1975, the possibilities were belatedly explored of a re-fanned version of the Spey giving nearly 17,000 lb of thrust, and a study was made of an up-to-134-seat One-Eleven 700 – but by then the large-capacity end of the market had passed both engine and airframe by.

One result of the One-Eleven success story – for, despite the later limitations on development and the fierceness of the competition, success story it undoubtedly was – was the interesting relationship it brought about between BAC and Romania.

In 1968, Tarom, the Romanian national airline, and the Romanian Government did a deal with BAC whereby they bought six One-Eleven 400s, and entered into a joint arrangement with BAC and Britten-Norman for the local assembly (and then local build) of 212 Britten-Norman Islander light transports. In doing this, Romania acted with considerable political independence, which they followed up in 1975 by ordering five One-Eleven 500s – a contract which included certain One-Eleven and Rolls-Royce engine work to be done locally – and also another batch of Islanders. At the time of nationalisation, Romania was discussing with BAC a deal on One-Eleven 475s for over eighty aircraft – some to be built in the UK and then gradually transferring to Romanian manufacture and a joint marketing programme, which deal was duly announced in 1978.

Thus the story of BAC's only purely BAC aeroplane lived on after BAC was itself taken over. In all its marks, it received a total of £19 million in Government launching aid (the company contributing the same sum), in return for which the Government had received at nationalisation under £4 million in direct levies, but well over £250 million in export sales, while at the same time providing British equipment for eight British operators, including BEA (later British Airways).

First Report

To go back from the full story of the One-Eleven to the time of its beginning, the Chairman's first report on the new Corporation was issued in April 1962 and covered, in general, events from 1 July 1960 onwards. It showed that sales (i.e., goods delivered), in the first full financial year of BAC amounted to nearly £75 million, of which £28 million was on 'new account' projects whose profits were for the benefit of BAC, and £47 million on work done for the parents on pre-merger 'old account.' BAC's profit on its own £28 million amounted to £1.577 million, from which were deducted provisions in respect of private venture development on a range of products (including the One-Eleven) totalling just over £1 million. After providing £237,000 for interest on loans from the parents and on bank overdraft, there remained a balance before tax of £330,000 and after tax £90,000.

It will thus be seen that BAC, as such, and on its own account, was making only $5\frac{1}{2}$ per cent gross profit on its turnover, and was ploughing back all that was left after tax. The future order book at the end of 1961 stood at £238 million (old and new accounts), but Lord Portal emphasised in his report that a large part of the Corporation's activity was the fruit of heavy private expenditure in the past (Vanguard, VC10, the Vigilant missile, and BAC One-Eleven). The future depended on a sequence of new projects being initiated to take the place of those which had passed through the design and development stages and were now in production. Above all, therefore, what was needed was a firm long-term programme planned with Government backing.

Lord Portal was here drawing attention to one of the in-built problems of any aerospace company. The moment a new project has passed its design peak in terms of design man-hours and is moving on to the factory floor, there becomes spare (and expensive) capacity in the design office. Yet the design team, which progressively becomes more and more unemployed as its latest aircraft comes into quantity and money-earning production, is one of the key assets of the business. It is in its designers that great experience and very high skills reside, and the team has to be kept together. If it is not, then the company is not in a position to tackle the next project, and so comes to a dead end.

One part of a design office can be kept at work developing and refining the product in build, but unless there is something new coming in at the starting end, the company is in danger of losing, or having to stand off, some of its best brains. Keeping a balance, therefore, between the work-loading of the design office, and that of the production line (which is the source of actual income) is extremely difficult. The peaks and troughs are severe. As with production, the worst of them can be softened to some extent by transfer of work within a multi-activity company such as BAC, but this is only a short-term aspirin for what is a perpetual headache. Government work was, in 1962, as it still is, the real bread and butter of any aerospace industry, and planning that work is a long-term business. The service lifetime of aircraft is always extending, and the interval before replacements correspondingly becomes longer. But, to match that, the gestation period gets longer too and, as BAC was to find out, the longer the gestation period, the greater the chance of political cancellations.

BAC and its parents, as Lord Portal was pointing out, had already done all they could in the way of private-venture risk on the Vanguard, VC10, Vigilant and One-Eleven, and they were in no position to gamble further. Only the Government could supplement that work with long-term plans and firm contracts (such as for TSR2 production) and so enable the company to calculate the design and production staff needed to meet future national demands. This plea to the Government for a firm, coherent, long-term programme for the British aerospace industry was doomed to remain largely unanswered for all of BAC's life. Perhaps, with the British political system, with a potential change in all policies, and especially in defence spending, every five years at most, the question is unanswerable – at least by the British Government on its own.

Even without a change of the colour of the Government, the Treasury will always attack a British project on its peak year of spend because that spend, such as on TSR2, stands out like a sore thumb and tends, for that reason, to get chopped off in whatever is the latest economy drive. In this annual pruning, no account is taken of the money already spent on the project – that is water under last year's bridge – and one of the great advantages of European collaborative projects is that the British Treasury can no longer, on its own, spell death to a programme. Sir George summed this up by saying that the hardest thing about a collaborative project is getting it started. Once two or three Defence Staffs or Governments have agreed on a common specification for a common need – which can take quite a time – it is then virtually impossible to cancel it. All partners have to be of the same mind at the same time to do that, and the chances of them all agreeing to cancel are even less than the chances of them agreeing to do the job in the first place.

In the 1961 report, the first glimmers of European collaboration were showing through – talks with Sud Aviation of France about a joint

Supersonic Transport, and work with Dassault on the NBMR3. There was also the formation of an organisation called 'Inertial Guidance – Europe.' This was a collaborative enterprise between the Stevenage instrument wing and the well-known American precision instrument and inertial guidance company of Honeywell. Guided Weapons at Stevenage had built a very modern precision instrument and gyroscope facility with super-clean areas and all the shock-protection and expensive equipment which goes with such work. It had close links with Honeywell, and both companies saw the chance of landing a lot of inertial guidance equipment orders from Europe. A jointly staffed office was opened in Paris, but for some reason it did not catch on, and after about a year it languished and died. The Stevenage facility, at that time easily the best of its kind in Europe, survived, and still goes on from strength to strength with many ingenious applications of inertial quality gyros for weapon guidance and aircraft systems, for naval use, and for commercial instruments.

Also announced in the 1961 report was the formation of British Aircraft Corporation (AT) Limited – the 'AT' standing for Anti-Tank. This company took over what were described at the time as 'certain projects' developed by Fairey Engineering Limited. In fact, this was a cover for the vehicle-mounted anti-tank missile started by Fairey under the code name of 'Orange William,' which, under BAC, became the successful 'Swingfire.'

About the time of this first Chairman's report, in April 1962, BAC had opened negotiations for a loan from the Finance Corporation for Industry (FCI). Eventually, after much discussion, BAC was granted a ten-year, £15 million loan (guaranteed by the parents) at the rather high non-risk interest rate of $1\frac{1}{2}$ per cent above bank-rate, increasing to $2\frac{1}{4}$ per cent after 1969. This was reinforced by overdraft facilities from Lloyds Bank of up to £5 million, with other banks joining in to take any excess of this. At that time BAC's share capital was £20 million, of which £13.6 million had been paid by the parents. There was a further £$3\frac{1}{2}$ million in advances from the parents, and an overdraft facility of £5 million – the actual overdraft being just over £2 million.

The total finance required by BAC at the end of 1962 was estimated at £31 million, reaching a peak of £50 million by the end of 1964 and reducing to £45 million by the end of 1965. The 'peak' was caused by One-Eleven launching costs and work in hand. The parents would be making up the full capital of £20 million and had the intention of building up their investment in BAC to £30 million. The gap between that £30 million and the £45 million needed at the end of 1965 would be met by the FCI loan and the extra 'peak' by bank borrowing. The BAC sales forecast (shown as 'new' and 'old' account and expressed in £ millions) was estimated as: 1962, £37 and £38; 1963, £46 and £47; 1964, £70 and £46; and 1965, £101 and £31. It will be seen that, reasonably enough, the 'old account' work was to be gradually overtaken by 'new account,' until a big jump (One-Eleven) took 'new account' sales over the £100 million mark in 1965.

The FCI loan was granted and was fully drawn on over the years, being repaid in 1972.

Thus BAC – as it moved towards its 'new account' era – financed itself to face the 1960s by a mixture of parent company money, FCI loan, and overdraft facilities.

12

VC10

By the time the BAC merger discussions started, there was already a question mark over the future of the VC10. This project was seen both by English Electric and Bristol Aeroplane as a potential loser, and they wanted no financial part of it. It was a Vickers' 'old account' enterprise, and was part of the clumsy 'old account – new account' arrangement on which BAC was eventually formed.

Most historians of the industry have seen the VC10 as reflecting little credit on the way BOAC and the Ministry of Transport and Civil Aviation handled a major procurement decision which, coming on top of the losses caused by BEA's tailor-made requirement for the Vanguard, could well have put Vickers, had it still been on its own, out of the aircraft business.

In any VC10 chronicle, it has to be remembered that this was not an aircraft foisted on BOAC by some industry/Government machination. It was an aircraft actively sought and specified in detail by BOAC as a free agent, and for the design and manufacture of which BOAC approached several firms before Vickers, notably de Havilland and Handley Page.

The 1964 Report from the Select Committee on Nationalised Industries records that, in 1956 BOAC had come to the conclusion that the design of neither of the then proposed American jets (Boeing 707 and DC8) was suitable for BOAC's eastern or African routes. The proposed Boeing carried too many passengers and the runways at a number of airfields on those routes were too short for, or otherwise limited, the performance of the American aircraft. BOAC therefore needed another aeroplane, and they were instructed by the Government to order it from de Havilland (the Comet V) providing that (a) the aircraft was suitable and that (b) BOAC were not to be required to order a particular number of aircraft.

This latter proviso was purely inward-looking, wasteful of assets, and unrealistic. It was likely to result in the build of a handful of specialised UK-only aeroplanes and de Havilland, not unexpectedly, said they would not proceed unless at least fifty aircraft were ordered, as anything less would be uneconomic and unprofitable. BOAC, were, therefore, released from their obligation to buy from Hatfield as they did not want fifty Comet Vs. Meanwhile, BOAC, which only a year before had turned down the V1000 because the jet-prop Britannia would keep the airline competitive in the North Atlantic 'for the foreseeable future,' had already applied for and been given permission, at a time of great dollar shortage, to buy fifteen B707s specifically for the Atlantic routes 'in order to hold' their competitive position (BOAC, in fact, had asked for seventeen Boeings). To get permission for the big dollar spend, BOAC agreed to buy twenty aircraft from British manufacturers – and this meant twenty aircraft of a new design as there was nothing suitable for the Empire routes in production in the UK or, indeed, anywhere else. All these matters were fully reported at the time, especially so because the rumpus about cancelling the British V1000 just before its maiden flight, and the cynical reasons given for so doing, were still fresh in the public mind when the Boeing application was made just a year later.

To get its special southern and eastern aeroplane, BOAC eventually came to Vickers, and the airline's Requirements Committee described the VC10, in April 1957, as 'the most promising conception of which we have had details, and as attractive an aeroplane as we can hope to obtain for our eastern hemisphere operations for service in 1963–4.' (The VC10 began operations in April 1964.) BOAC's Chairman, Sir Gerard D'Erlanger, wrote to the Minister that the VC10 'fulfils technically and operationally all the requirements of the Corporation on these routes.' He also said that the project was 'tailored to our requirements.' There was no question, therefore, of BOAC being coerced into the purchase of an aircraft it did not like or did not want. The nub was really how many aircraft *did* BOAC want, because to set up a line for twenty-off of a big but limited-market aeroplane was a short cut to disaster.

The negotiations on numbers required and price were conducted in the knowledge that the Government was not prepared to contribute in any way to the cost of the project, but nonetheless both the Ministry of Transport and Civil Aviation and the Ministry of Supply attended a meeting between BOAC and Vickers in April 1957. BOAC then spoke of a firm order for twenty-five, with ten more on option. Vickers – who were taking all the financial risk – wanted an order for all thirty-five and at a higher price, because the initial trend-setting price for Boeing 707s had already proved uneconomically low for Boeing themselves, and Vickers had vivid memories of their losses on the Vanguard, which Sir George reminded the meeting had been another aeroplane tailored to the requirements of a national carrier. The VC10 break-even figure was then quoted as forty-five aircraft (in the event, a considerable under-estimate).

Vickers, however, were, at the time, privately hopeful of further substantial sales to BOAC because they had seen a detailed BOAC forecast, sent to the Minister, which showed an eventual need, by 1966–7, not of thirty-five aircraft, but of sixty-two, and, by Vickers' reckoning, a sale of sixty-two VC10s could prove profitable and Weybridge badly needed the work. So, in May 1957, the order was announced for thirty-five VC10s for use on the southern and eastern routes but the aircraft was to have the important new capability of development to serve the North Atlantic. This later proviso was made to cover the further twenty-seven of the sixty-two aircraft mentioned in the BOAC statement to the Minister, and the contract, when signed for thirty-five aircraft in January 1958, included an option on twenty more. Sir George was later to tell the Select Committee that he had no recollection of any ultimatum by Vickers on the question of numbers to be ordered, but it has to be said that Vickers had good reason to believe that the final number would be sixty or more.

In January 1960, just as BAC was being formed, Vickers ran into financial trouble over the VC10. The cost estimates had been discovered to be under-estimated by 'quite a lot' (as Sir George told the Select Committee) and, unless orders for ten of the twenty on option were made firm, the whole VC10 production was in jeopardy. These ten aircraft were to be of the developed type (Super VC10), stretched and improved to be suitable for the North Atlantic, with maximum seating for 212 people.

In June 1960, the contract for the extra ten Super VC10s was signed, making forty-five aircraft in all. Undoubtedly there was an element of duress about this extra order because the Minister had now added his pressure to that of Vickers, the VC10 prospects being part of the Minister's own plans for the formation of BAC. Certainly the incoming Chairman of BOAC, Sir Matthew Slattery, tried, unsuccessfully, to stop the contract being signed before he took office in July but was told that, because of Ministry pressure, it was too late.

During the next year, BOAC wanted the specification of the Super VC10 altered downwards to 163 seats, and this was done, giving the aeroplane a smaller capacity but a greater suitability for its deployment on all BOAC routes, North Atlantic included. Both parties seemed happy with the new specification, and the overall contract was freely altered to fifteen Standard VC10s and thirty Super VC10s. Later, the fifteen Standards were reduced to twelve to keep the mounting cost of the whole order within the Treasury's capital authority. BOAC paid £600,000 compensation to Vickers.

The Royal Air Force was now interested in the VC10, and five of a military adaptation of it were ordered for the then RAF Transport Command. The military VC10 used the Standard VC10 fuselage, but the more powerful Rolls-Royce Conway Mk550 turbo-fan engines (22,500 lb static thrust) of the Super VC10. It had the fuel capacity of the Super, and incorporated a side-loading freight door already developed for BUA. The wings also incorporated various improvements arising from the VC10 development programme.

The military order was probably placed, at least in part, to give help to Vickers who, as has been said, were running into deep water in the project. They twice, in 1961 and 1963, had to apply to the Government for some launching aid money for what had hitherto been a private venture. In the end, a total of £10.2 million of such aid was given towards a launching cost which eventually reached £50 million. Nonetheless, there was military need for the RAF VC10, which was for so many years to give splendid service to the nation.

The prototype Standard VC10 first flew on 29 June 1962 from Brooklands to Wisley. The VC10 was the last complete aeroplane to be built and assembled at Weybridge, and this, therefore, was the last prototype flight from an airfield whose aviation history goes back to 1909 but whose runway was now at its limit of 1300 yards. The VC10 also marked the last of a fifty years' line of Vickers aircraft.

The VC10, with the rear-engined high-lift wing configuration made necessary by the BOAC requirement for outstanding airfield performance to meet the 'hots and highs' case, then ran into stall and drag problems. These were cured by improvements to the slats on the 'clean' wings, by the addition of wing fences, and by the alteration of the angle of the engine nacelles. But something like an extra £1½ million had to be spent by Vickers to sort the teething problems out.

In January 1964, Sir Giles Guthrie became Chairman of BOAC (three months before the first Standard VC10 services were introduced) and Guthrie immediately began drastically to re-organise BOAC and its route structure. He first decided to cut the order for thirty Super VC10s to seven, and then to cancel the lot and buy six Boeing 707-320Cs instead. Prior to publication of this decision, there had begun what appeared to be a BOAC-orchestrated campaign against the VC10 in certain parts of the media, and this campaign did undoubted harm to sales prospects. It is hard to sell an aircraft whose own home customer is proclaiming its lack of faith in it from the housetops.

The Government, however, refused (July 1964) to accept the Guthrie all-American plan, and told him to take seventeen of the thirty Super VC10s to meet his new estimated requirements up to 1967, and to keep ten more on option – production for BOAC to be 'suspended' after the seventeenth aircraft. At the same time, the remaining three BOAC Super VC10 positions were allocated to the Royal Air Force, which had already increased its VC10 order to eleven, this new decision thus bringing the RAF total to fourteen. All fourteen of the RAF aircraft were made to the 'mixture' specification already described.

Finally, in March 1966 – a year after the Super VC10 had entered service on the North Atlantic – BOAC cancelled its 'suspended' option for ten aircraft and paid £7½ million in cancellation charges. The total production of the VC10 – including the prototype which was refurbished and sold – ended as under:

BOAC	12 Standard VC10
	17 Super VC10
RAF	14 Military VC10

British United Airways	3 Standard VC10
Ghana Airways	3 Standard VC10
East African Airways	5 Super VC10
TOTAL	54 (18 Standard VC10)
	(22 Super VC10)
	(14 RAF VC10)

Vickers Limited's loss on the VC10 was some £20 million.

The Select Committee of 1964 found, not surprisingly, that there was considerable confusion over the role of BOAC. Was it to operate solely to make profits, or had it some grander design which gave it an active duty to support the home aircraft industry? Successive Chairmen interpreted the priority of their duties differently, but it was not until Guthrie that there was a directive in writing from the Minister (Julian Amery) that BOAC was to be run on a commercial basis.

It appeared to be suggested by BOAC to the Committee that it had been forced from the start to order an unrealistically large number of VC10s, but Sir George replied by asking why was it – if BOAC felt they had been bullied into buying too many VC10s – that they had completely and freely re-negotiated the contract in 1961 to fifteen Standard and thirty Super VC10s – representing far more capacity than they had previously commissioned?

Some very odd statements were made to this Committee: Sir Basil Smallpeice (Managing Director of BOAC) complained that Vickers in their design and engine disposition departed from the Boeing optimum, when he must have known that the whole point of such departure (rear engines and clean wings) was precisely to enable the VC10 to do what the Boeings then could not do – i.e., operate from the 'hots and highs.' Roy Jenkins, in the House of Commons, also complained that Vickers had not put their engines in the same 'highly successful' position as the Americans, despite the clear fact (as *Flight International* pointed out) that the reason for the VC10 being the way it was, was one of necessity and not of national vanity.

In the event, as the aviation world knows, the VC10's success in service was immediate and sustained. The passengers loved it, and, at the end of July 1964, the passenger load factors on the West African routes were averaging 80 per cent, and for Central and South Africa the figures were at one stage up to 98 per cent. There were many authenticated cases of passengers, unable to book on a desired VC10 service, waiting days for a seat rather than fly in any other aeroplane. In 1967, BOAC was still reporting in Sydney that the VC10 was more than balancing its slightly higher operating costs than the 707 by its consistently higher load-factors.

The success story of the Super VC10 on the North Atlantic was equally dramatic. In its first year, 1965, the Super achieved a load factor nearly 20 per cent higher than the average of fourteen other IATA operators on the North Atlantic. The figures were:

Super VC10	71.6 per cent
Average BOAC	60.8 per cent
Average for fourteen airlines (excluding BOAC)	52.14 per cent

BOAC's B707 figures were inflated by spill-over from fully booked Super VC10s, and it also now emerged that the Super VC10 needed only an extra one or two passengers over the 707 to break even.

In the next year, the Super VC10 average passenger payload was 69.7 per cent and that of the fourteen other IATA airlines was 53.4 per cent. Each percentage point of passenger load-factor was worth in a year about £1.58 million to BOAC, and this made the much criticised Super VC10 a bigger profit-earner than the 'optimum' Boeing 707.

Technically, all VC10s gave an excellent account of themselves, and BOAC reported (1972–3) that the Super VC10s were averaging 11.09 hours per day against the 707's 8.7 hours – and that the operating costs per revenue flying hour were: Super VC10, £486, and B707, £510.

So the Super VC10 – denigrated in advance by BOAC as 'too expensive to operate economically' and for which reason they obtained some £30 million in subsidy as recompense – turned out to be actually cheaper to fly than the 707 and also to attract many more passengers.

With a 60,000-hour airframe life, the rugged VC10 was still firmly holding its place in the affection of the travelling public when BAC was nationalised, thirteen years after the VC10's first introduction into service.

The saddest part of this story is that, when the VC10 had good chances of export sales, notably to Middle East Airlines, BOAC were most reluctant to produce serious operating data to support the BAC sales case. Indeed, they gave foreign operators the distinct impression that the aircraft was a money-loser when the contrary was the case. Nor did BOAC reveal the large sums they had had to pay for structural modifications to their fleet of Boeing 707s. It is unwise to impute motives, but undoubtedly BOAC had, as they say, 'egg on their face' over the anti-VC10 campaign, and they also had obtained a £30 million 'operating loss' subsidy whose validity could, perhaps, be called into question if the full truth became officially known.

It is, however, only fair to say that BOAC had for years been under much attack for its losses, yet, until the directive given by Amery to Guthrie, it was also expected to support British industry, in which, after the Comet and the Britannia, it had lost faith. The safe thing to do, by BOAC's book, was to standardise on Boeing – and that is more or less what Guthrie set out to do. The VC10 stood in his way, and when he could not get rid of it, he demanded, and got, compensation for being 'forced' to operate what, in the event, became the most popular and profitable aeroplane in his fleet.

It was true that, at the start, the Standard and the Super VC10s were a little more expensive to operate than the 707s – but this was more than offset by the passenger attraction of the aircraft. As *Aircraft Engineering* pointed out, such attraction 'cannot be reflected in conventional technical evaluation methods and cost formulae . . . comparisons with other jets are incongruous unless full account is taken of such [passenger appeal] factors.'

Thus the VC10 came to a sad end as far as Vickers and BAC were concerned, and with it went Britain's and Europe's last chance of staying in the subsonic long-haul aircraft business, presenting the USA with a monopoly which may never now be challenged. Had some of the potential airline orders for the VC10 been encouraged rather than otherwise by BOAC, the line might still have been in operation to take advantage of a very active Chinese interest in the aeroplane in 1973, an interest so great that, at one time, they wanted BAC to re-start the aircraft. Unfortunately this was economically impossible, and a big export opportunity had, perforce, to go a-begging.

13
Guided Weapons – the Initial Problems

Mention has already been made of the damage done to the Guided Weapons side of BAC by the 1962 cancellations of PT428 and then of Blue Water. But not much else has yet been said in this book about BAC's Guided Weapons efforts, and many of the 'Guided Weaponeers' would regard that as par for the course, and as the story of their lives.

It can hardly be contested that, at the start of BAC, Guided Weapons had some reason to think it was the poor relation of the merger. The first organisational chart showed that Lord Caldecote, as Chief Executive (Guided Weapons), stood side by side with George Edwards (Chief Executive, Aircraft) under Lord Portal's chairmanship. The truth is that both Lord Portal and Sir George were basically aeroplane men and, knowing little of guided weapons, they tended to steer clear of them. In Denis Richards' biography of Lord Portal, Lord Caldecote makes it clear that, as a result, he felt somewhat isolated. He points to the regular meetings and conversations between Edwards and Portal and, to redress what he saw as an imbalance of consultation, he asked to have a weekly meeting with Lord Portal to keep him in the Guided Weapons picture. 'But it just petered out – he seemed totally uninterested. I was sad and disappointed. My chaps were doing a terrific job and their efforts were not being properly appreciated.'

This 'poor relation' complex was further accentuated when Sir George became Managing Director of BAC and Robin Caldecote, Deputy Managing Director. The move was inevitable – there was much more aircraft work in BAC than there was guided weapons, and Edwards was a man of stature and world reputation even before BAC was formed. Lord Caldecote has since made it clear that he in no way resented Sir George's promotion and that, when BAC was formed, he himself saw Edwards as the natural leader of it. He clearly was, however, disappointed that what was a most exciting and challenging new technology evoked no apparent answering spark from either of his two seniors. Richards, in his book, says that Portal probably, at first, regarded guided weapons as a kind of battlefield, and near-battlefield, artillery, but later admitted that he had, for some time, under-estimated the potentialities of guided weapons. Edwards had his own defined field as Chief Executive (Aircraft) and had more than enough on his plate. His view was at the time, and it has remained his view, that running Guided Weapons was a job for a specialist, and that he, Edwards, knowing little of weapons, could not make much of a personal contribution. He certainly could not enter into detailed controversy with Whitehall as he could over aeroplanes. As Managing Director, and later Chairman, he saw his responsibility to be that of getting the best man he could to head up the Guided Weapons team and then leaving him to run his show.

Mr G.R. Jefferson, formerly Manager (Guided Weapons) to Lord Caldecote, and later to be Chairman and Managing Director of BAC Guided Weapons Division, held the same view. In Pat Adams' racy story of BAC Guided Weapons Division, *Good Company*, he records Jefferson as saying, 'Throughout the period of his incumbency, he [Sir George] has been under the most enormous pressure on the aircraft side – maintaining Concorde afloat; TSR2 cancelled round his neck; trying to get Jaguar and MRCA established; ups and downs with BAC One-Eleven, and I think he's been reasonably content to allow something which seemed to be going along fairly well to carry on without adding to his burden that was already pretty heavy. He's been a good supporter of ours, but a supporter rather than an involver.'

In many ways, Jefferson and Edwards were akin – much more so, perhaps, than Edwards and Caldecote. Jefferson (who, in 1980, left British Aerospace to become Chairman of British Telecom) is a tough, practical engineer, but also a master of the detail of his subject, an astute salesman with a considerable awareness of what is or is not likely to be profitable, and, like Edwards, capable of making his writ run. Caldecote – with his academic background and, at times, almost youthful enthusiasm for what was still, for him, a relatively new business – was more inclined to wear his heart and emotions on his sleeve than the down-to-earth Jefferson. Caldecote, however, was just the man to try to hold the initial balance between Bristol and Stevenage while maintaining the pioneering zeal of both.

There were, indeed, some quite remarkable characters to be brought together when the BAC merger threw the hitherto warring factions of Bristol Guided Weapons and English Electric Guided Weapons together. English Electric had a revered, distinguished, and at times impish father-figure in Leslie Bedford, one of the country's true pioneers of guided weapons. He had worked with Cossors on television before the war, then with Watson Watt on radar, and initially joined English Electric after the war as Chief Television Engineer at Marconi. One of Bedford's team was Dr E.K. Sandeman, a radio expert, another brilliant innovator and 'a true eccentric' – the description given to him by Adams. A combination of Bedford and Sandeman, plus Jim Cattanach and Dr R.W. Williams, gave English Electric the nucleus of formidable and original talent. Bristol had David Farrar – described by his professor (reports Adams) as 'one of the most brilliant graduates in Mechanical Sciences at Cambridge within living memory,' and Farrar had the talented Don Rowley as his No. 2. BAC Guided Weapons was a bit of a Cambridge enclave — Bedford, Lord Caldecote, Tom Slator (later Vice Chairman of the Division) and 'H.G.' Nelson himself were all from King's, where Caldecote had also been a Fellow and Lecturer. Farrar and Don Rowley were also Cambridge.

At merger-time, the Bristol Guided Weapons team had devised Bloodhound I — a Bristol ramjet — powered ground-to-air missile to defend the RAF's V-Bomber bases — which became operational in 1956. Ferranti were partners in the project (which was managed overall by Bristol) and provided the radars. From Bloodhound I, after the cancellation of its first development (Blue Envoy) — described by Rowley as 'a sort of a baby Concorde with a delta wing, and quite hefty' — Bloodhound II was evolved. Adams reports that Bloodhound II was invented in a taxi outside Ferranti's by Farrar, Taffy Higginson and Rowley as a result of a remark by Higginson — 'Why don't you do what the engine people do and modify Bloodhound I slightly.' As a result, models were produced showing how the Bloodhound I homing head could be taken off and another one put in its place for half a million pounds. The idea worked, and a second-generation Bloodhound for the RAF was ordered. Had it not been, Bristol, with nothing else to fall back on, would have been out of guided weapons.

Farrar gives much credit to Ferranti for this rescue operation, and particularly to the efforts of their Guided Weapons Manager, Norman Searby, at Ministry meetings. As soon as Bristol and Ferranti began to develop Bloodhound II, they kept one eye on the export market. They had already sold Bloodhound I to Sweden and Australia, and had their appetite whetted for overseas sales. Bloodhound II had four times the range, 35 per cent increase in speed and a greater operational altitude than Bloodhound I. This was a pretty fair jump between a first- and second-generation version of the same weapon and underlines the pace of early guided weapons development in this new department of the aviation business. At the merger in 1960, Bloodhound II was on trials and clearly had a promising future.

English Electric's Thunderbird I ground-to-air system was for the Army. An important Thunderbird requirement, therefore, was that it had to be mobile, whereas Bloodhound I was for static defence of fixed bases. Thunderbird had been evolved in the early 1950s at Luton, which was the original English Electric Guided Weapons headquarters (Stevenage main factory was not opened until 1955), and initially had a liquid-fuel motor, later changed (1955) to solid.

Adams reports that the idea of a liquid-fuel motor almost dissuaded Jefferson from joining the company in 1953. He had come to Luton to be interviewed for a job by Air Vice Marshal Sir Conrad Collier, who was English Electric's Chief Guided Weapons Executive, and to whose founding work the whole of Guided Weapons owes much. (Sir Conrad, who was nearly at retiring age when BAC was formed, decided to take his retirement. He didn't like the merger and he saw the great work of consolidation which lay ahead as being for a younger man – in fact, Lord Caldecote.)

Jefferson had been an apprentice at the Royal Ordnance Factory from 1937–42, held a first-class honours degree in Engineering and obtained that at the age of nineteen the hard way – externally (another point in common with Sir George). He served in the RAOC, then REME, and Anti-Aircraft Command, and later became a member of the Ministry of Supply Technical Staff working on low-level anti-aircraft gunnery. It was this work that convinced him that missiles, not guns, were the answer – hence his appearance at Luton.

Jefferson's application came when Sir Conrad was looking for a potential future Chief Engineer, a job then filled by Leslie Bedford, whose strength lay in creative areas more than engineering control. Sir Conrad, on meeting Jefferson, decided he had now found the man he was looking for and, as a start, appointed him Chief Research Engineer. Within a few years, Bedford became Director of Engineering, and Jefferson became, as Collier had foreseen, Chief Engineer. Meanwhile, Jefferson's distrust of a liquid-fuel motor had been confirmed and his belief that the then Thunderbird would never make an operational system had been amply justified. This had led to a series of new starts on Thunderbird, which undoubtedly had a very difficult birth.

Like Bloodhound I for the RAF, Thunderbird I for the Army moved on to Thunderbird II with longer range, greater altitude and a capability for intercepting higher speed targets. The complete Thunderbird II missile homing head and guidance receiver was developed by English Electric Guided Weapons, using continuous-wave in place of the earlier pulse radar. This new continuous-wave radar, called in the odd colour-code jargon used by the Ministry, 'Indigo Corkscrew,' was developed by Ferranti and used for both Thunderbird II and Bloodhound II trials at Woomera, Australia. Like the Bloodhound II trials, those of Thunderbird II were also just starting off when BAC was formed, and both became operational in 1964. Bloodhound II, which had been given some mobility, though never as much as that required of Thunderbird II, did gain export sales to Sweden, Switzerland and Australia, to a value of £50 million.

In 1960, English Electric Guided Weapons, now in BAC, had two other projects on the go – Blue Water and PT428. Blue Water (originally called Red Rose) was a tactical mobile ground-to-ground system with a nuclear warhead and a range of up to seventy miles. The development contract placed for it by the Ministry in 1958 specified that it had to be air-transportable, have the off-the-road mobility of a three-ton truck, and have a rapid action time – known as 'shoot and scoot.' PT428 was a low-level anti-aircraft system of the kind envisaged by Jefferson when he decided that 'guns were not the answer.' It was a sophisticated weapon and, according to Pat Adams, was seen at the time as being too ambitious for the state of the art. Its rival was the American Mauler, and, says Adams, no one was very surprised when PT428 was cancelled in February 1962 by Defence Minister Harold Watkinson (later Lord Watkinson), who was reportedly also concerned to save money in the interests of TSR2. PT428 did, however, lay the foundations at Stevenage of another weapon destined for outstanding success – Rapier.

The Blue Water cancellation in August 1962 was a much heavier affair. The weapon was making splendid technical progress, and two fully guided rounds had been successfully flown at Aberporth. Harold Watkinson had described it to Lord Caldecote in May 1962 as the most important current guided weapons development and had said 'put all your effort into getting it going as quickly as you can.' In July, Peter Thorneycroft succeeded Watkinson at the Ministry of Defence and, within a month, this 'most important' project was cancelled – again to save money. The death of Blue Water was a terrific blow to BAC Guided Weapons. The weapon had already been 'tipped for stardom' – including by specialist technical writers in the USA, some of whom saw it as the best ground-to-ground tactical missile system on the Allied development list. Great efforts were made by Slator, Caldecote and Jefferson to save it – but to no avail.

At this time, Blue Water was the main new project in the English Electric part of the BAC Guided Weapons, and it was clear that one of the English Electric Guided Weapons factories – the original one at Luton or the newer one at Stevenage – would have to close. Stevenage was the most complete Guided Weapons outfit in the country, so it was Luton which had to go. Only 150 redundancies had been caused by PT428 – but Blue Water caused 1000 (with 500 more to be covered by so-called natural wastage, which means not replacing people who leave, die, or retire). Not surprisingly, a lot of able engineers, whom English Electric wanted to retain, decided to get out of such uncertain employment, and a number of them went to the USA. The effect on morale was considerable, even though 90 per cent of the redundant 1000 got other jobs within six weeks. Some of the key Luton people were found work at Stevenage – but the upset of Blue Water, and the threat it propounded to the existence of the whole of the English Electric Guided Weapons activity, hung like a pall over Stevenage for years afterwards. Meanwhile, BAC Guided Weapons activity was reduced to Bloodhound II and Thunderbird II, and two Stevenage anti-tank projects, Vigilant (ex-Weybridge) and Swingfire (ex-Fairey). There was not much left of the 1960 'wedding feast.'

As has already been indicated, that wedding feast had, in reality, been somewhat of a punch-up. On the English Electric side, Sir Conrad had gone – he had not seen exactly eye to eye with Lord Caldecote, who was overall Managing Director of all English Electric Aviation (including Guided Weapons), and Collier was also unhappy about the merger with

Bristol. To assist Caldecote, three senior Guided Weapons people became Directors of English Electric Aviation: Bedford, Jefferson and Slator. At Bristol, the key figures were James Harper, General Manager of Bristol Aircraft, and David Farrar, Chief Engineer, Guided Weapons. James Harper was a man of considerable ability, much admired by Sir George, and he would undoubtedly have achieved great eminence in BAC had he not been stricken by a tragic and crippling illness which led to his untimely death.

The first meetings between Bristol and English Electric weaponeers were all in an atmosphere of tension – heightened by constant rumours that the Ministry was going to cancel either Bloodhound or Thunderbird. Bristol had two Guided Weapons factories – one at Filton and the other at Cardiff – to match English Electric's Luton and Stevenage and, oddly enough, at various times each company had done sub-contract work for the other. The Bloodhound and Thunderbird rivalry culminated in the Penley Committee to examine the relative merits of the two systems. The Committee found in favour of Bloodhound, which resulted in charges and counter-charges of fiddling the evidence but, in the end, none of it mattered as both weapons went ahead.

Jefferson has described those days for Pat Adams: 'Once the Corporation was formed, it was obvious that, sooner or later, there had got to be some rationalisation of the GW side. Both teams were locked in mortal combat for the market, both home and overseas, and neither of them saw a great future except in terms of Blue Water, with Bristol busily trying to establish a future beyond Bloodhound. No clear lead was being given on what ought to be done. This provided all the ingredients for a period of growing suspicion and antipathy. There was no clear nomination of a top executive responsible for GW with real authority.'

Jefferson then went on to explain that Lord Caldecote was largely hamstrung in trying to exert that real authority, in contrast to Sir George Edwards on the Aircraft side – 'for the first two or three years it was really a question of internal politics in the Corporation. Whenever you have a situation in which nobody is really the boss, then it naturally leads, particularly with a struggle for survival going on, to your being wide open to gamesmanship, political pressure, and increasing acrimony. This undoubtedly happened in those three years.'

On the face of it, Bristol were in the weaker position. They were a minority shareholder in BAC and were a lodger unit on the aircraft site at Filton, whereas Stevenage was a modern, new, purpose-built factory. Bristol and their partners Ferranti, however, had a strong influence in Whitehall and, by reason of their names and historical continuity, were well regarded overseas. Sir Reginald Verdon-Smith, Chairman of the parent Bristol Aeroplane Company, also put a lot of his undoubted weight behind his Guided Weapons people and so did James Harper. Those factors undoubtedly helped Bristol to their trump card – which was export sales achieved against powerful American opposition.

Another important Bristol personality at this time was Jack Jefferies, Guided Weapons Production Manager and later General Manager of Guided Weapons at Filton until both he and Farrar returned to the Aircraft side in 1966 – Farrar later leaving BAC, but Jefferies staying on to become Chief Executive of the Commercial Aircraft Division (Filton).

During those first three years of BAC Guided Weapons, Lord Caldecote worked hard, against considerable odds, to preside over what was then, in essence, a sort of heaven-and-hell amalgamation league, and to contain the acrimony. Then, in March 1963, the semi-autonomous nature of Bristol and English Electric was terminated – and, in the view of many, none too soon. Instead, the Guided Weapons Division of BAC was formed (a Commercial Aircraft Division and a Military Aircraft Division were eventually to follow) and a subsidiary company, British Aircraft Corporation (Guided Weapons) Limited, was created to run it. Sir George became Chairman (as he did of all BAC Divisions), Caldecote was Managing Director, and Jefferson, Chief Executive. Farrar became Technical Director, Bedford, Director of Engineering, and James Harper completed the Board. Jefferies continued to be General Manager at Bristol, and Slator at Stevenage, with Eric Beverley as Sales Manager and Taffy Higginson as his Deputy.

Caldecote and Jefferson could then really set about organising a united enterprise, and, in April 1964, Jefferson moved half of the new Rapier development contract down to Bristol (the launcher and the fire unit) and this one act, more than any words, poured some real cement into the cracks. After that, any outbreaks of the 'them and us' mentality were sat on hard by Jefferson, who also fought the Ministry for the retention of the Filton capability (which success came in very handy when Space began to develop). There were also some senior cross-postings, and by 1964 the barriers were down, and the Guided Weapons Division was at last organised for the greater success which eventually was to come.

14
TSR2 – Tenacious Opposition

For the first four years of its life, BAC and its owners, particularly its Vickers parent, not only had an unhealthy over-investment in the notoriously uncertain civil side of the business, but also had growing doubts about the political future of its military centre-piece, TSR2. It also faced, as has just been recounted, severe problems with its Guided Weapons programme, and it had raised its indebtedness to the prudent limit by borrowings from the parents and from the FCI – the latter load at a relatively high rate of interest.

At the time of the TSR2 cancellation (1965), the VC10 and BAC One-Eleven launching costs were £50 million and £32 million respectively, towards which there was Government aid of £10.2 million and £9.8 million. The ratio of BAC work – not counting the Concorde – was 60 per cent civil to 40 per cent military, but the Board was looking to TSR2 to reverse that position, which was potentially a perilous one, the VC10 being a likely loser, and the One-Eleven not yet a clear winner. The American industry ratio was 70 per cent military and 30 per cent civil.

Over-dependence on the civil market was hardly encouraged by the fact that, despite their advantageous ratio of Government work to civil, Boeing had not brought the 707/720 position to one of profit until late 1963, when well over 1000 had been sold – including the original military tanker version whose development costs had been Government-borne. General Dynamics, by 1961, had lost $143 million on the Convair 880/990; Lockheed had had to write off $50 million development on the Electra; and Douglas, after heavy losses on the DC8, were forecasting $148 million of expenditure on the DC9 up to the end of 1965. The great name of Douglas was already heading for disaster and take-over.

If the civil waters were uninviting, the UK military ones were hardly less chilling. Sir George frequently commented that the placing by the British Government of a military order was merely the necessary prelude to them cancelling it. A rhetorical exaggeration perhaps, but one with sufficient truth in it to make his point. It is certainly true that very few, if any, post-war British military contracts survived unscathed. They were either cut back, killed after tying down lots of valuable project and design office man-hours, or in some other way made the victim of stop-go or plain indecision. 'Turning taps on just in order to turn them off again' was Edwards' description. The victory of the Labour Party in the October General Election of 1964 was about to see virtually all the taps turned off.

The first and almost immediate casualties caused by the new administration were the two Hawker Siddeley projects for the Royal Air Force, the P1154 (the supersonic Harrier), and the V/STOL Transport which was to support it, the HS681. The decision on TSR2 was 'postponed.' The Air Staff concept of a mobile small-field tactical air force was heavily modified and its 'below the radar' all-weather strike strategy placed in jeopardy.

Two books and several learned papers have already been written about the eventual cancellation of TSR2, and it is not the author's intention to turn this history of BAC into yet another full-scale analysis of that sad and far-reaching event. Nonetheless, it has to be covered in some detail because TSR2 had been the catalyst for the BAC merger and its cancellation left such a trail of havoc that, at one time, BAC seemed likely to go out of business.

The background to the award of the contract, and of the development of the Operational Requirement into that of a most sophisticated multi-purpose, multi-systems, low-level, supersonic aeroplane has already been covered. The implacable opposition to TSR2 of the Royal Navy, the Chief of the Defence Staff (Mountbatten) and his Chief Scientific Adviser (Zuckerman), and the Treasury has also been described. With hindsight, it is easy to recognise that the hand of premature death was on the project from the moment of its birth.

The final TSR2 requirement had everything built into it that military imagination could devise, and quite a lot of it was not strictly essential. The aircraft had to be capable of very low-level all-weather penetration of the most sophisticated defences, with a target-dash speed of Mach 1 and a high-level speed in its definitive sortie of at least Mach 1.7. It had to have a radius of action of 1000 n.m. on internal tankage, with a 2000 lb bomb load for a sortie envelope which included a sea-level dash to the target, in and out, of 200 n.m. each way. It had to be STOL to the extent of using 3000 to 4000 feet rough-ground strips, which virtually selected the Olympus 22R because of its absolute thrust — at least, according to one school of thought. The ferry range had to be nearly 3000 n.m. rising to nearly 4000 n.m. with underwing tanks. The aircraft had to have an automatic flight control system, with terrain-following, and be equipped with forward-looking radar, Doppler, inertial platform, Q-band sideways-looking radar, active optical Linescan (which could be transmitted back to base), and computers to handle all the data. Store-carrying provision had to be made for a mix of 2000 lb bomb internally and a great array of external bombs or missiles — a total load of up to 12,000 lb, with a big overload potential from proper runways. Provision also had to be made for two jettisonable under-wing tanks, a ferry tank in place of bombs in the weapons bay, and a 1000 gallon jettisonable ventral tank under the fuselage.

The nav/attack and reconnaissance systems of TSR2 are still worth dwelling on, even twenty years after their conception. For all weather navigation, the pilot had an inertial platform based on high-quality gyroscopes, which picked up any deviation of the aeroplane from its pre-computed track and relayed corrective action, through an air-data computer, to the auto-pilot. The inertial platform by itself was intended to produce an accuracy of two miles in 700 or so, though it never quite met that performance on its own. To help it, however, it had a Doppler radar which measured speed and drift very accurately indeed. A further, and important, addition was a sideways-looking radar which produced pictures of the ground either side of the aircraft, and this could be used to give up to forty fixes per sortie, each fix being virtually a new starting point for the flight. Any correction necessary was fed to the automatic flight control system (AFCS). This combination of the inertial platform, the Doppler, and the sideways radar, gave to TSR2, via a digital computer, an automatic all-weather navigational ability of great accuracy. The flight plan was pre-fed into the computer, and the information of ground speed and drift from the Doppler, of heading and velocity from the inertial platform, and ground fixes from the sideways radar, enabled a presentation to be made to the navigator as an exact position in latitude and longitude, with distance-to-go. If there was any in-flight deviation from the sortie plan as initially fed into the computer, this immediately showed up and was adjusted.

On top of all this, there was the terrain-following forward radar which looked some twenty miles ahead and registered and reported to the auto-pilot (and the human pilot) the shape of the land before it, and enabled the auto-pilot to keep a height of 200 to 300 feet above the obstacle contour of the terrain. For reconnaissance, the TSR2 had cameras, the sideways radar (which could picture moving vehicles and much detail) and also Linescan, which was a kind of day-night TV device painting a picture of the ground beneath and around the aeroplane — which picture could be continuously transmitted to the field commanders during flight.

Bomb aiming was coped with by another computer, which was basically controlled by the forward radar which measured target-distance and, in conjunction with all the other information in the AFCS, triggered an automatic bomb release. Nuclear bombing would be either by a free-fall low-altitude bombing system called LABS (that is 'lobbing' the bomb forward, with the aircraft then doing a wing-over back towards base and safety) or by 'lay-down' (which used a parachute-retarded delivery). These bombing methods could be used 'blind' — but if there was a visual gathering of the target, so much the better. The accuracies called for, especially for ordinary iron-bombs, were of a very high order indeed.

The anti-TSR2 lobby was to make much play of the 'huge' cost of providing systems for 'nuclear horror' weapons, but it will easily be seen that the really expensive part of the bombing system was for the delivery of ordinary HE, which had to be a very accurate operation. Tactical nuclear weapons had a much greater tolerance, for obvious reasons.

The inertial platform was the responsibility of Ferranti, which used much preliminary work done at Farnborough, the sideways radar was developed by EMI, and the digital computer was an Elliott adaptation of the American VERDAN, but with a very much increased demand placed on it. The pilot and navigator both had a moving-map display, and the pilot had a head-up display projected on his windscreen for low-level flight. The displays were produced by Rank Cintel (now part of Elliott Automation) and by Smiths Instruments and Ferranti. Linescan was developed by EMI, the Doppler by Decca, and the nose radar by Ferranti.

Aerodynamically, TSR2 had to have the lowest possible gust-response, flying — as it had to — at low altitude, in very turbulent conditions. The delta wing provided this low response ability, with a wing loading and high lift capability which met the stringent take-off and landing requirements. Structurally, the aircraft had to be very strong and stiff, and the fuselage as well as the wing had, in effect, to be an integral fuel tank. The windscreen had to withstand the impact of a large bird at transonic speed. The undercarriage, a twin bogey design, had to accept an emergency landing at maximum weight, and the rough-field requirement dictated low-pressure tyres. For short take-off the nose could be raised by extending the nose-leg shock absorber strut, although flight testing later showed this not to be necessary. In the structure, there was as much use as possible of machined panels (as with the VC10) and of chemically etched skins.

As TSR2 was designed to be able to use any one of over one hundred small flying fields dotted over Europe, it had to have a mobile support system. BAC, therefore, produced plans for an air-transportable general servicing vehicle which, in conjunction with an automatic test equipment trailer, would maintain TSR2 in the field for a month.

There can be no doubt that the whole TSR2 concept was a terrific challenge, incorporating many features, both in the basic aeroplane and in its systems, that were at, or even just beyond, the then frontiers of the state of the art. There can also be no doubt that technically the British industry responded wonderfully to that challenge and, in the end, produced probably the finest of all its warplanes. What, however, was beyond the British ability (or anyone else's for that matter) at the time, was to evolve a project management system which ever looked like being able to control such a vast and complex undertaking and keep the costs within bounds. For this, some blame must lie at the door of industry, including BAC which had to handle the difficulties inherent in the Vickers–English Electric forced marriage. A large share of it, however, belongs to Whitehall with its proliferation of committees, its buck-passing, and the costly time-wasting, which latter, in the end, was to be TSR2's undoing in that it played into the Treasury's hands.

Vickers, it is true, had been labelled prime contractor back in 1959, and carried that responsibility on into BAC. But it was only prime contractor for the airframe, which never represented more than 35 to 40 per cent of the project. The engines – the Olympus 22Rs – had been selected by the Minister (Aubrey Jones) against the wishes of Sir George, who wanted the then RB131, later developed by Rolls-Royce into the 'Medway' family which could have been so important to British aviation but which was eventually abandoned for lack of sales.

The engine contract was placed direct with Bristol Siddeley, so BAC had practically no knowledge of, or control of, the engine costs throughout. The inertial navigation platform, the forward radar, and reconnaissance system were also on separate direct or 'Category One' contracts – i.e., equipment purchased direct by the Ministry of Aviation to their own specification. The 'Category Two' equipment could be specified and purchased by BAC, but only with Ministry approval. The automatic flight control system, the computers, and the sideways radar were 'Category Two.' 'Category Three' equipment could be purchased directly by BAC, providing it met the supplementary specifications laid down by the Ministry and was within a maximum cost limit.

BAC – or rather Vickers – from the word 'go' had appointed a Project Director for the TSR2 airframe – Henry Gardner, who had as his Project Engineer, George Henson. In March 1963, after a meeting with Sir Henry Hardman, Permanent Secretary to the Minister of Defence, Sir George gave Mr Houghton, who was the Managing Director at both Weybridge and Preston, overall responsibility, under Sir George, for all TSR2 matters.

In some of the writings on the subject, BAC is blamed for not having one man in charge of TSR2 engineering – but it is an allegation without foundation. Furthermore, Henry Gardner had a splendid working collaboration with Freddie Page at Warton. Gardner remembers that one of the biggest difficulties he encountered was getting the equipment for the airframe. The sub-contractors, he recalls, had been convinced by the vociferous anti-TSR2 lobby that the project would never survive, and that, therefore, any research and development or other such work on the components would be wasted and not lead to production orders. As a result, all prices quoted were extremely high and deliveries were extremely late. 'Up till then,' says Gardner, 'aircraft equipment research and development had been amortised by equipment suppliers over the needs of several different types of aircraft, and therefore over reasonable production runs – but with TSR2 they charged the whole lot to us. Furthermore, the Government Research Establishments such as Farnborough were doing a lot of TSR2 work at the time – so some of their costs and overheads got charged to the project as well. All these were costs over which I had no control whatever, but they were all used against us in the end.'

There·is no doubt that, from the start (and BAC is far from blameless here) some ridiculously low estimates for the research and development of TSR2 were made. At one time, a figure (officially approved by a Defence Policy Committee) of £35 million held sway, which supposedly covered the three separate and roughly equal costing sections of TSR2 − the airframe, the equipment, and the power plant. The first estimate for the research and development of the Olympus put in by Bristol Siddeley Engines was £7.3 million − although it has since been suggested that this was on Whitehall advice when the estimated (then) figure was actually about £15 million. In the event, £30 million would have been nearer the final mark.

Apart from a national tendency to estimate low to encourage the project, the truth is that industry overall, including Vickers, and later BAC, had only the slightest idea of the magnitude of the technical task ahead and of the costly snags they would hit. The same story was encountered with Concorde. Such escalation of aerospace estimates was not limited just to the UK, but was a worldwide experience. Boeing, Douglas, Lockheed and Convair had already hit it with their first jetliners and, since the miscalculations were on their own private-venture account, at one time or another it was to bring all four of them to their knees.

Many other similar advanced-technology examples could be quoted outside aerospace: motorways, bridges, big buildings, river schemes, and nuclear projects − many of these started with modest cost estimates, fully documented, examined in detail and accepted by outside experts − yet, in the event, proving to be lacking a nought or two. It was an international teething trouble of high technology − a deadly mixture of optimism and ignorance, based on previous experience which was irrelevant to the size of the new problems.

One of the factors most fatal to TSR2 was that of delay to which the Gibb-Zuckerman procurement system (discussed later) contributed greatly. Had the aeroplane kept to a schedule of first flight in March 1963 and in-service 1965, it would not have been possible to cancel it in April 1965. Yet, having announced the order for TSR2 on 1 January 1959, no holding contract was given by the Ministry of Aviation for six months, and this only covered expenditure up to the September − when it lapsed. This left Vickers and English Electric on their own and uncovered until January 1960 − by which time the 'delay contingency' of three months had already been more than consumed, and the costs had consequently risen.

By June 1960, the Ministry had set up a bewilderment of committees − a Steering Committee under the Permanent Secretary, Ministry of Aviation (Sir Cyril Musgrave) and the Controller (Air), Ministry of Aviation (George Gardner), with BAC (Sir George) and the engine company represented. Then there was a Management Committee, and a whole host of other official committees and panels (thirteen in all) concerned with production, systems integration, cockpit layout, weapons carriage, and so on. There was a Development Progress Committee of sixty members which was Treasury-dominated and on which the contractors were not represented.

There was also, beyond doubt, some time lost inside BAC in ironing out rivalries between Warton and Weybridge.

It was not long, however, before both Sir George and Henry Gardner realised that, although they were nominally responsible for the prime contract, in fact they had virtually no control at all. Henry Gardner was later so say that he could do nothing of any significance without Whitehall's approval – assuming he could discover who in Whitehall was the proper person with whom to raise the matter. It was small wonder that the equipment people were unwilling to risk pressing on with research and development, and charged hugely for what work they did do. Often their prices had been agreed directly with Whitehall behind BAC's back, even though it was BAC's clear function to negotiate for that particular equipment. It was not until October 1960 that a contract was received for £90 million for the first nine development aircraft, and Sir George used this occasion to get the Controller (Air) to meet at Weybridge all the major firms involved, to try to put some feeling of reality and confidence into the project. But it was not until June 1963 that the eleven pre-production aircraft were authorised, and not until the following March was permission granted to order long-dated materials for a further batch of thirty. This was the last contract awarded to TSR2 and, again, Henry Gardner recalls that, when the first nine development aircraft were approved, he was horrified to discover that the cost of the electronics for each aeroplane exceeded the entire cost of a Lightning – which then stood at £750,000.

A major source of TSR2 delay, and therefore of much rising cost, was the engine. Contrary to popular belief, the supersonic Olympus 22R was not the same engine at all as the subsonic Olympus which had been developed for the Vulcan bomber. Its thrust had been increased from 20,000 lb to over 30,000 lb by the addition of reheat, and there were many consequent internal changes needed, mainly because of temperature rises of some 150°C. First of all (autumn 1962), the turbine blades broke on the test-bed and had to be changed for forgings. Then there was reheat trouble, and finally, in December 1962, the 22R, which was to be air-tested installed below a Vulcan, blew up on taxi trials, and the aircraft and engine were burnt out. There were no casualties, but all further testing was on the ground, and was moved to the National Gas Turbine Establishment at Farnborough.

Nearly two years later, and after re-design of the low-pressure shaft (whose fracture had caused the first blow-up), the engine failed again on the test-bed – just before first flight was scheduled. The trouble –

vibration of the shaft at certain speeds — was not eventually fully diagnosed until September 1964 (after first flight) though the dangerous resonance frequency had been identified before then.

The actual TSR2 airframe, which was all that BAC had the responsibility for, had a relatively straightforward history. The wing position was altered by three inches relative to the fuselage in March 1960, but no other major design modification was necessary. There was trouble with the fuel tanks and undercarriage, which was sorted out, and, at cancellation, there were three aircraft practically ready to fly (including the prototype which had, of course, already flown), and seventeen more on the assembly lines at Weybridge and Samlesbury.

By introducing PERT (Programme Evaluation and Review Technique) to production control, and also by applying Value Engineering, BAC made a good job of the TSR2 airframe, at least as far as the muddled decision-making procedures allowed. PERT, by use of computer forecasting, highlighted future bottlenecks, programme slippages, and cost escalations, while Value Engineering was aimed at ensuring cost-efficiency by examining any over-elaborate design details with a view to arriving at simpler and cheaper solutions.

PERT and Value Engineering were but two of the good things to be developed in the TSR2 programme. The electronic nav-attack and computer techniques were greatly enhanced for future use, and over 1000 sub-contracting firms advanced their technology.

As a piece of total, self-contained and almost all-embracing military aviation equipment, the TSR2 was without world rival in its time, and there are many who argue that there has been nothing since which can better it in the long-range, low-level, all-weather strike role. The nearest approach is probably the swing-wing Tornado MRCA.

15
TSR2 – the Blow Falls

The Treasury's opposition to TSR2 was undisguised all through the project's six years and four months of official life. Sir Harold Wilson in his *History of the Labour Government 1964–1970* says as much. Prior to the October 1964 General Election, which gave Labour a working majority of only four (later cut to three), the Conservatives had been forced to make major defence savings in order, or so it was assumed at the time, to continue to finance the 'mobile air-force' concept based on the STOL TSR2, and the VSTOL P1154 and HS681 projects. Two of those savings were made at the expense of BAC Guided Weapons – first, PT428, the ambitious anti-aircraft system, and then Blue Water, that very promising mobile surface-to-surface tactical ballistic missile. Both were cancelled by the Ministry of Defence, and the effect of those set-backs to BAC's Guided Weapons factories at Stevenage and Luton has been seen. The tragedy is that, if these sacrifices were made on behalf of TSR2, they were unavailing and, it can be argued with hindsight, unnecessary.

The effect of the Mountbatten/Zuckerman opposition to TSR2 was continuous, and probably, in the extra time granted them by the delays, decisive. Lord Zuckerman's espousal of the American cause was open and emphatic. A South African Professor of Zoology, his views on scientific disciplines and technologies completely outside his field were, nonetheless, accepted by many senior civil servants of classical education who were equally in no position to take a well-informed technical view. His opinions were also embraced wholeheartedly, at least as far as cancellations were concerned, by the Left, for whom they made excellent political ammunition. Mountbatten's opposition seemed to stem from his desire to get the Royal Air Force to share the Royal Navy's costs on developing and buying the Buccaneer, and not to increase the Air Force vote at the expense of that of the Navy and its carriers.

Whatever his reasons for opposing TSR2, it was Mountbatten who was to deliver the really mortal blow, and he did it 24,000 miles away from London, in Australia. The Royal Australian Air Force had been interested in TSR2 from the start and had been given their first full briefing on the aircraft and its potential by Jeffrey Quill as early as

November 1959. Quill gave three more such presentations at yearly intervals and was also supported by an Australian visit by Sir George. The TSR2 was almost tailor-made for the RAAF bomber requirement, and there is little doubt that, but for Mountbatten, they would probably have ordered it. Had they done so, TSR2 would then have survived. Conversely, had the RAF ordered TSR2, the RAAF would also have done so. In the event, Mountbatten, then Chief of the Defence Staff, so hammered away about the cost-effective superiority of the Buccaneer (which was of nil interest to the Australians) that the Australian Defence Chiefs, and then the politicians, became completely convinced (as they were meant to be) that TSR2 would never be built. The *Sunday Times* in November 1963 reported that Mountbatten had had special cards made – five showing a Buccaneer and one showing a TSR2 – and had the habit of slapping them down and saying, 'Five of these for the price of one of these.' The Australians, who were just re-equipping their fighter squadrons with Mirage IIIs, could not afford new bombers until 1966 at the earliest, and probably not until 1967/8, but they were in no mood to order an aeroplane which might never get delivered. Mountbatten's protracted anti-TSR2 campaign, which, in such a man, could only have sprung from sincere beliefs, convinced them that TSR2, which otherwise suited the RAAF schedule very well, was a doomed project, and the Americans leaped into the breach.

An offer of F111s was made direct by US Defence Secretary MacNamara, together with a free loan of B47 bombers to tide the Australians over, as, at the time, there was a distinct military threat caused by the Indonesian challenge to Malaysia on Australia's doorstep. As a counter-move, Julian Amery agreed to consider the posting to Australia of some V-bombers, though these would have been RAF-manned and not Australian-commanded, which, as Sir Robert Menzies, the Australian Prime Minister, later said, was not the same thing. Lord Portal persuaded Duncan Sandys to persuade Sir Alec Douglas-Home to cable Menzies with a view to re-opening all the options on the TSR2/V-bomber issue, but it was too late, and the F111 deal was closed for twenty-four aircraft at a price of $140 million. In the end, nothing came of the B47 offer – the cost of modifications was too much – but the Australians did finally get delivery of their F111s. This was not in 1967 or 1968, or 1969, but in 1973, ten years after the order, and the cost was not $140 million but $344 million. At one time, they could have had twenty-four TSR2s on a fixed-price offer of £2.1 million each, including engines etc.

Lack of Australian support left TSR2 wide open for a final political blow after the October General Election of 1964. Zuckerman – who, it is reported, had once said that there is more technology in the little finger of one professor from the Massachusetts Institute of Technology than in the whole of British Industry, and whose comment on TSR2 was 'What a pity people should be bothering themselves with such a scandalous waste of public money' – undoubtedly played his part in the closing chapters. He was very close to the new Labour administration and had many opportunities to convince Harold Wilson, Healey (Minister of Defence) and Jenkins (Minister of Aviation) that Britain's proper course was to scrap all its own projects and buy American.

The Zuck–Batten axis, as it was known, did not lack for journalistic support, and both Concorde and TSR2 were under continual attack in the protest media throughout the election period and after it. In an election speech, Harold Wilson made a statement which, in its wording, appeared to reassure the Preston voters that TSR2 would not be cancelled. It is beyond doubt that his words were so interpreted locally. A leaflet was also circulated in Preston (South) stating categorically that a Labour Government would not cancel TSR2, but later the successful Labour candidate said the leaflet was not printed with either his, or his agent's, knowledge. If Wilson meant what he appeared to say at election time, it is clear from his own book that he changed his mind very quickly afterwards. Within weeks of taking office, he had come to the conclusion that Concorde and the three RAF projects – the mainstays of the British industry – would have to go, and that the Royal Air Force would have to accept F111s, Phantoms and the C130 Hercules from the USA. In the event, Concorde survived because it was covered by an International Treaty and not by mere contract and because the French, especially de Gaulle, were determined to go ahead. The rest of the aviation programme was duly scrapped.

Sir George had been fearing the possible demise of TSR2 since the summer of 1964, and Denis Richards, in Lord Portal's biography, states that Sir George wrote to Lord Portal in the August, pointing out that the costs were mounting and giving as a prime cause the splitting of a job of such complexity ('bigger and more difficult than we or the Ministry of Aviation thought') between Vickers and English Electric. The main purpose of the letter was to underline that BAC was too dependent on one contract and to say that the Company should 'not leave itself at the mercy of Government policy,' but must acquire a sufficient hard core of non-Government work.

Sir Harold Wilson writes that he held a defence conference at Chequers on 21/22 November 1964, 'to cover a review of the whole range of defence questions which I, with the Foreign and Defence Secretaries, was due to have in Washington three weeks later.' The Prime Minister's report of that Chequers conference says that Healey was 'moving towards' replacing the P1154 with Phantoms, and that the TSR2 'which would carry the airborne nuclear weapon' was 'clearly marked for stringent review,' as its costs 'were escalating out of all relation to earlier estimates and it was a favourite Treasury target for cancellation.'

There can be little doubt that, at the Washington talks, Wilson had, at least, said he was considering scrapping all three British military aircraft in favour of a direct purchase from the USA, and also that he would do all he could to stop the Concorde. That such an undertaking – which meant handing over the British aviation market to the USA – was an American political and industrial target has since been freely stated by many of President Johnson's then aviation advisers and industrial lobbyists. Whether or not there was an American *quid pro quo* – or even precondition – on support for the current crisis of Sterling, as has so often been alleged, may never be known. Sir Harold has always denied it, and there is no mention in his book of any discussions with the President on the subject, although there had been much crisis-type communication on the UK's currency position the previous month. It is probable that the British did not need any arm twisting to 'buy American'; both the Treasury and Zuckerman had been advocating it long enough.

On 15 January 1965, Sir Harold invited the leaders of the aircraft industry to Chequers for dinner, because, to quote him, 'It had become increasingly clear that all three of the controversial aircraft, HS681, P1154 and TSR2, would go and be replaced in the main by American purchases, the first two by Hercules and Phantoms and supplemented by an increased order for British Buccaneers.' For 'increasingly clear,' it would be fair to read 'already decided.'

Sir George Edwards represented BAC at the dinner, which was also attended by Sir Reginald Verdon-Smith, who was there more on behalf of Bristol Siddeley Engines than BAC. Sir Harold records, 'Roy Jenkins, Minister of Aviation, was with me. The industrialists were utterly frank about the position and we were warned that in addition to the problems they foresaw (disbandment of airframe design teams, and grave repercussions on the development of jet engines) there was a danger that the major company in the industry, the British Aircraft Corporation, might break up, since some of its joint owners were anxious to pull out and apply their investment elsewhere.' Sir Harold adds: 'While we were able to encourage our guests on Anglo-French joint projects and to press them to go wholeheartedly for the proposed European Airbus, we were not able to give them any reassurance on the question of HS681, P1154 or TSR2.'

On 2 February 1965, Sir Harold announced the cancellation of the Hawker projects, but was still officially 'considering' the TSR2. Although it can now be seen that the die was already cast, there was much last-minute activity at BAC to try to salvage some kind of TSR2 production for the RAF.

As early as mid-December 1964, Sir George had written to Roy Jenkins underlining the dominant part which TSR2 played in the future of BAC. He pointed out that the total capital currently employed was £58 million (£32.5 million provided by the parents, and £25.5 million borrowed money). The parents also employed a further £34 million in financing 'old account' projects. Including TSR2, the profits on this capital were at a low level and were expected to average not more than £3.45 million a year for the next four years, of which £1.75 million was from TSR2. Sir George added that cancellation of TSR2 would not only delete about 50 per cent of BAC's forecast profitability, but its removal would so increase the share of the overheads borne by the civil projects (whose sales prices were more or less fixed by the international market) that the other half of the forecast profits would now have to go to covering fixed overheads to keep the civil prices competitive. It would then be impossible to service borrowed capital (£2 million interest in 1965), and so the removal of TSR2 would make BAC unable to earn any return on capital and 'put us out of business.'

This letter was followed up, also in December 1964, by detailed manning forecasts for 1965–8, which showed that the withdrawal of TSR2 would lead to the virtual collapse of the (then) Preston Division. In an attempt to soften the employment position, Sir George told Jenkins, BAC had now committed over £48 million on laying down forty-two more One-Elevens over and above the seventy-four already sold, but those forty-two aircraft could only make a very small profit, provided there was no increase in the overhead charges upon them.

On 16 January 1965, Sir George wrote to Jenkins again, as a result of the Prime Minister's Chequers dinner, setting out (at the request of the Prime Minister) the export situation as affected by TSR2. He made the point that the BAC One-Eleven was, in effect, providing the hard-won export dollars ($200 million) to help finance any purchase of F111s and so to support the rival US industry. He reminded the Minister that the One-Eleven launching costs were £28 million but that his Department had refused to increase its contribution above £9.75 million. He added an appendix showing that the export record of the BAC companies from 1955 to date showed a grand total of £411.5 million, of which £300 million came from civil aircraft.

The arguments were, however, unavailing, and BAC was fighting a lone battle against the Government, the media, and many of the senior officials.

In his book *Inside Story*, Harry Chapman Pincher, famed for his well-informed revelations on defence matters in *The Daily Express*, maintains that the Labour Party leadership had firmly decided to scrap TSR2 while it was still in opposition. A key figure in this was, Pincher claims, George Wigg (later Lord Wigg) who seemed to be Harold Wilson's private adviser on defence matters both before and after he came to power. It was also widely stated at the time that Wigg got some of his technical information from a freelance aviation consultant-cum-journalist, Richard Worcester. Pincher also says in his book that TSR2's fate was finally sealed at a Defence Committee meeting when Denis Healey remarked, 'By the way, Prime Minister, we think you should know that the wing of TSR2 broke under test at Farnborough yesterday.' In fact, such a structural test to destruction is part of the

normal research and development of any new aircraft, and the TSR2
wing had already withstood many times the loading it could ever be
expected to encounter in flight. Apparently no one at this meeting knew
the details of overload tests designed to discover ultimate strength and,
says Pincher, Healey's 'throw-away' line created a damning sensation.

The attitude of the RAF at this critical time was distinctly odd. When
TSR2 research and development costs were mounting, several pleas had
been put in by BAC for relaxation of some of the more fanciful and
expensive of the requirements. There was no need, for example, for
forty computerised *en route* check-points in the nav-attack system — half
that number would have been quite adequate and large savings could
have been made. But virtually no concessions could be obtained, even
when it must have been clear to the Air Staff that the mainstay of their
offensive arm was in dire danger of being ruled too expensive for the
country to afford. All through the destruction of the whole of their
planned Air Force — the two HSA projects and TSR2 — there was never a
hint of a service resignation on the issue. Most commentators have
deduced from this that the Air Staff had already been 'bought off' by the
promise of all the wonderful things that were going to be the F111. Had
they known the truth about the F111 (and the truth about the F111 *was*
already known to some Government advisers) and that the RAF was
going to end up with subsonic Buccaneers — albeit improved and much
re-designed — there would doubtless have been a major confrontation,
which, considering the precarious voting situation of the Government,
Harold Wilson might well not have been able to withstand. It is also fair
comment that if all the media pundits, who now so regularly describe
the TSR2 cancellation as 'disastrous,' had supported rather than attacked
it at the time, there might have been a change in Harold Wilson's heart.

On the question of the RAF's attitude, Chapman Pincher says in his
book that the Air Marshals at one time were prepared to do battle for the
TSR2 to the point of resignation and that he was encouraged by them to
support the project in the *Express* and to make the point that, in the view
of the RAF, the F111 just would not do. There was, however, a sudden
reversal of this guidance which Pincher maintains dated from a private
meeting between Wigg and the Chief of the Air Staff at Abingdon.
After that meeting, he was asked to soft-pedal any criticism of the F111.

The actual Cabinet decision on TSR2 was taken on 31 March — with,
Sir Harold recalls, the Cabinet split three ways, some favouring
continuing with TSR2, some favouring its outright cancellation with
no replacement, and the third group supporting the Defence Secretary's
view that TSR2 should go, but that its military role should be taken
over by an order for American Phantoms, together with one for a
number of F111As. 'I summed up, and this was accepted, that a clear
majority was for cancelling TSR2 and the question of a replacement, if
any, should be further examined in the Defence Committee, subject to
final Cabinet approval. It was further agreed, on my suggestion, that the

decision on TSR2 should be announced in the Budget Speech.'

By the time of its cancellation, TSR2 had flown — and flown very successfully. It had been shipped in major lumps to Boscombe Down as early as March 1964, and there re-assembled for flight. Unhappily, the engine problem was then a major crisis, and there were also some problems with the undercarriage. Julian Amery, with an election due in the autumn, was naturally pressing for action, but it was not until Sunday, 30 September, that the aircraft became airborne. Even at that, the test pilot, Roland Beamont, and his navigator, Don Bowen, had to decide to accept limitations on engine power for this first flight because of the shaft resonance problem, and their decision that they could mainly dodge the critical engine speeds was a brave one. The fitting of partially modified engines incorporating a strengthened shaft, a warning system, and a modified cooling duct, prevented a second flight until the last day of 1964. Beamont knew that reheat fuel–pump oscillation (it was due to the change of a spring) was causing an airframe vibration, and that this was at a frequency very close to that of the human eyeball. As prototype XR219 climbed away on its second flight, this vibration happened, and 'Bee,' to avoid blurred eye-sight, had to throttle back the port engine and continue on starboard engine only. This he did successfully and achieved a single-engined performance test, albeit unscheduled, on flight number two.

The main problems were more or less sorted out early in the new year, and XR219 made a number of highly encouraging flights but at reduced weight and range to avoid full-power strain on the shafts. Some of them were in turbulence which upset the pilot of the chase plane (a Lightning) but were completely unnoticed in the stable, delta-winged TSR2. On the fourteenth flight, the prototype flew supersonic and, on 12 March, Beamont and his other test pilots completed the first part of the test schedule on the twentieth flight. An enormous amount of encouraging data had been accumulated, and it was already clear that TSR2, as an aeroplane, was able to do at least all that had been asked of her. There had also been extensive flight testing, in other aircraft, of TSR2's electronics which were 80 per cent developed on the day of cancellation.

The reason given for cancelling the TSR2 was cost, and the actual announcement was made, as stated, by Mr Callaghan in his Budget statement on 6 April, a political stratagem which caused much controversy. Lord Portal and Sir George from BAC, and Sir Reginald Verdon-Smith representing the engine firm as well as BAC, were asked to the House of Commons and were there informed of the decision. Naturally, they asked to be allowed to telephone the news to the factories so that the workforce could be told by the management what had happened before they heard it direct on the radio or from the Press. BAC had always made a point of trying to tell employees of any important news before they heard it from outside, and had built up a

Marshal of the Royal Air Force Viscount Portal of Hungerford, KG, GCB, OM, DSO, MC, Chairman of BAC from its formation in 1960 until his retirement in 1968.

The Vickers Viscount, one of the number of 'old account' products in BAC's early years, was nearing the end of a long production career when the Corporation was formed.

Production of the Bristol Britannia, another 'old account' aircraft, was virtually at an end when BAC came into being, and work was swiftly moved to Filton from other sites.

Although production of over 1400 English Electric Canberras was drawing to a close in 1960, the aircraft is still in RAF squadron service today and continued to contribute to export earnings all through BAC's life.

Vickers eventually lost £18 million on the Vanguard, which began life as a 'Viscount Major' project, but this 'old account' aircraft gave Weybridge valuable engineering experience later used on the VC10 and BAC One-Eleven.

The two versions of the VC10 – (*above*) the Standard VC10 and (*below*) Super VC10. Much loved by passengers, these elegant aircraft never won for their manufacturers the success which their comfort and flying qualities deserved. Ironically, although their 'sad story' seemed to have ended in a £10 million loss to Vickers, the VC10 is providing valuable work to British Aerospace which is converting a number of aircraft into flight refuelling tankers for the RAF.

Vigilant, the infantry anti-tank weapon project which Vickers brought to the BAC merger. In July 1961, all doubts about its effectiveness were eliminated by a demonstration on Salisbury Plain when – as shown in the illustration above from a contemporary publicity mail-out – tank after tank was hit from all angles and over ranges from 340 to 1100 metres. Vigilant went on to win big export orders and to equip British Army units.

Problems encountered in building the tiny Bristol Type 188 stainless steel experimental aircraft eventually led Sir George Edwards to say: 'It confirms how right we were to build Concorde in light alloy....'

The BAC 221 first flown at Filton on 1 May 1964 was designed to obtain data on the high-speed properties of the slender delta wingform adopted for Concorde and was a rebuild of the Fairey FD2 which captured the world air-speed record in 1956.

Heart of Hunting Aircraft's production programme when BAC was formed was the RAF's Jet Provost trainer, 88 having been delivered of the 200 then on order. In addition to further RAF orders, the Jet Provost achieved considerable export success.

A Soviet 'Bison' reconnaissance aircraft being shepherded out of UK airspace by Lightnings of No. 74 Squadron, RAF. Production of the Lightning – still the only Mach 2 + fighter to be designed and built wholly in Britain – was well established when BAC was formed and continued until 1968.

Sir George Edwards, OM, CBE, FRS, BSC (Eng), HON. LLD, HON. DSC, CEng, HON. FRAeS, HON. FAIAA, HON. FIMechE, successively Executive Director (Aircraft) of BAC, then Managing Director, and ultimately Chairman and Managing Director.

good machinery for doing so. Permission in this case, however, was refused as the announcement was part of the 'still secret' Budget proposals, and the BAC party was virtually imprisoned in the House until after the Budget statement.

As soon as the decision was promulgated, BAC was instructed immediately to reduce to scrap all the aircraft on the line, and soon after the jigs also had to be destroyed. BAC wanted to continue – at a cost of £2 million – some test flying with one of the three completed aircraft – partly to check some TSR2 calculations which would greatly benefit UK, partly in the interests of Concorde, which was also to use a supersonic Olympus. This was turned down unless BAC was willing for all the costs to be debited against the cancellation dues. BAC was in no financial position to agree to this, and the completed aircraft were shipped away – one to Cranfield (and later Duxford), one to be a target on Shoeburyness gunnery range (later reported to be rescued and the shell put together again by enthusiasts), and another to RAF Cosford via Boscombe Down.

Jeffrey Quill, who, as head of Military Sales, was very close to every phase of the TSR2 story, has since said that a huge potential technical return was lost by the failure to continue TSR2 flight trials. He shares the view of most people in BAC at the time that the Government attitude sprang from its desire to see TSR2 dead and with no chance of revival.

16
TSR2 – the Inquest

The inquest on TSR2, in the form of a Commons Debate, was held on 13 April 1965, and in it, the Minister of Defence, Mr Healey, deployed some cost figures for TSR2 which caused much controversy. He quoted (reasonably) £750 million for the research and development and production of 150 aircraft, or £5 million per aircraft on 150 off or £6 million per aircraft if only 110 were ordered. He also claimed that the purchase of an equal number of F111s would save the taxpayer £300 million at least, including the write-off of the money already spent on TSR2 and also its cancellation costs. It became apparent during the debate (and on later occasions) that, in some cases, Mr Healey was using what are now called 'programme costs' – that is, not only the cost of research and development and aircraft purchase – but the total cost of spares, training and maintaining and operating over varying periods of front-line service. It was, however, never quite clear to many MPs when like was being compared with like.

At the time of the debate Mr Healey was aware of, and made passing reference to, an attempt, which arose from the Chequers meeting, to obtain a fixed maximum price for a hundred TSR2s. A proposal to reduce the order from a hundred to fifty aircraft had been vetoed by Sir Charles Ellworthy, the Chief of the Air Staff (later Lord Ellworthy).

Sir Richard Way, Permanent Secretary to the Minister of Aviation, had indeed indicated to Sir George Edwards and Sir Reginald Verdon-Smith on 26 January that the maximum overall cost of a hundred aircraft had to be brought down to £604 million (with a later suggestion of £620 million). The best BAC could then offer (having been given by the Ministry of Aviation the engine costs as £130 million, and the other Category 1 equipment as £65 million) was £670 million – which meant that £475 million was BAC's requirement to cover the research and development of the airframe and payment for the construction of a hundred production aircraft, including the Category 2 and 3 bought-out parts. This left £66 million difference between BAC and the Government which might be negotiated to about £50 million. After much serious discussion on the risks BAC would run on any maximum price agreement, an offer was finally made by BAC to the Ministry of Aviation of £430 million fixed price for BAC's part in building a hundred TSR2s (a reduction of £45 million). This was providing that any profit up to 10 per cent remained with the Company, losses of up to 5 per cent and profits between 10 per cent and 15 per cent were shared fifty-fifty with the Ministry of Aviation, and losses over 5 per cent and profits above 15 per cent were all to go to the Ministry of Aviation.

Sir George pointed out that BAC was thus prepared, if costs exceeded expectations, to contribute to any such excess not only the whole of their hoped-for profit of around £46 million, but also an actual loss of £9 million, making £55 million in all – 'An enormous incentive,' Sir George added, 'to contain the costs.' The Government, however, rejected the offer, because, the Minister told the House, the Government was unwilling to accept open-ended responsibility for all the excess costs above 5 per cent. In fact, with the flight development programme going well, much of the high-risk period was already past.

A breakdown of the final BAC cost figures for a hundred TSR2s shows a research and development and development batch cost of £210 million, and a unit cost per production aircraft of £2.1 million for a hundred off. To this must be added, using the Ministry of Aviation's own figures, with which they said they were satisfied, about £200 million for Category 1 stores – i.e., the engines and some of the electronics – this £200 million including both research and development and production for a hundred aircraft.

It is now possible, by putting all the bits together, to arrive at somewhere very near the truth of what would have been the costs of TSR2.

Non-recurring costs	*£ million*
Airframe research and development, including the nine development aircraft	210
Engine and electronics research and development (approx.)	60
Total launching cost	270
(The figure later quoted by Mr Healey)	
Production costs (100 aircraft)	
Airframe at £2.1 million each	210
Engine and electronics (Category 1)	130
	340

The combined total cost of research and development and production of a hundred production TSR2s (109 aircraft all told) would, therefore, have been £610 million. For 150 production aircraft (really 159), it would have been, allowing for the longer run, some £750 million – the figure much quoted by the Prime Minister and Mr Healey.

Parliamentary and public arguments about the relative costs of 150 TSR2s and of the fifty F111s plus a hundred AFVG aircraft which were eventually chosen to replace them, went on until the cancellation of the F111 order (January 1968) and the death of the AFVG project (July 1967) eventually halted them.

Using the final Healey figures, the total cost of fifty F111s and a hundred AFVGs to replace TSR2 would have been:

	£ million	
50 F111s	125	(which by 1968 had escalated to £425 million)
UK share of AFVG research and development	150	(Both costs escalating at cancellation)
100 AFVG at £1.7 million each	170	
Total	445	

There would also have been extra training and ground equipment costs of some £50 million for using two types of aircraft instead of one, giving a total of £495 million, an apparent saving over the TSR2 150-aircraft programme (£750 million) of £255 million – an impressive if theoretical amount. But, the costs of the divorce from TSR2, viz., the money already spent and the cancellation costs, must also come into this reckoning. These were revealed in 1968 as being £200 million, so that all that was ever, and most optimistically, going to be saved by cancelling TSR2 for an F111 and AFVG mix was £55 million. Much of this looked like disappearing in 1966 as AFVG estimates mounted in the months before it was killed.

It is interesting that when the Prime Minister announced, in January 1968, that the F111 purchase was not going ahead, he claimed this would mean a saving in foreign currency of £425 million – a sum which contrasted dramatically with the £125 million the F111s were supposed to have cost in 1965. The escalation was a matter of 200 per cent. The F111 'lost money' was £46.4 million, and the AFVG 'lost money' was £2.5 million – £49 million all told and not as much as an altimeter to show for it.

To have carried on with 150 TSR2s in April 1965 would have cost, at most, another £580 million. To avoid this spend, the alternative F111 and AFVG programmes would, in truth, have cost well over £800 million had they gone ahead – much of this sum being in dollars. In 1965, however, a 'saving' of up to £700 million by 1980 was claimed.

One thing Mr Healey did not reveal in the TSR2 debate, nor in subsequent debates involving FI11, was that he already knew — and knew as early as February 1965 — that the FI11 as an aeroplane was in deep trouble which would cost a lost of money and a lot of time to cure. A team of technical experts from the Government had visited the General Dynamics plant at Fort Worth officially to 'look at' the FI11, and had come back with very gloomy reports. The high-lift system, notably the leading edge slats, was highly complex and had to be manufactured to extreme tolerances and, even so, was unsuitable for low-level flying because of the risk of damage. Even more serious was the fact that the engine intakes were all wrong, and there was an engine surge problem.

British Government representatives made these and other major technical criticisms in detail to Harold Brown, then Assistant Secretary for the US Air Force and later President Carter's Defense Secretary, and did so in the presence of senior men from General Dynamics. It is reported by those present that Mr Brown, to whom these details were news, rounded angrily on manufacturers and USAF generals alike. In the end, General Dynamics asked the British for help on the intake problem and at least one senior Royal Aircraft Establishment scientist, Dr Seddon, was loaned to the Fort Worth team. The sad story of the initial FI11 problems is now history (it was ten years after order that the RAAF got their delivery — and at two and a half times the cost) but it is a fact that much of what eventually happened was responsibly forecast to Mr Healey by March 1965 — before TSR2 was cancelled.

To round the story off, TSR2 was the first aircraft to be procured under a new system initiated by the late Sir Claud Gibb and developed by Solly Zuckerman. This system laid down that research was an affair for the universities and Government establishments, and applied research was also mainly a Government affair, but with some industrial participation. Then came feasibility studies for a new project, followed by a project study, and a long list of subsequent check-points before a production order was placed. At any one of these check-points, the validity of the whole concept could be referred back to square one, giving almost endless opportunities for delay, and for subsequent inevitable escalation of costs. In the history of TSR2, most of these opportunities were exploited, including an internal Ministry of Defence debate each six months with the Royal Navy trying to sell the RAF the Buccaneer instead.

The damage done to BAC by the TSR2 decision was immense. Sir Reginald Verdon-Smith has written, 'It meant severe redundancies, long and difficult negotiation of the cancellation claim, and the loss of many able and experienced aeronautical engineers, many of whom went to work for our competitors on the west coast of the USA. It also meant a complete dislocation of the carefully evolved balance between military and commercial work. The damage to morale within the Corporation was only matched by the damage to confidence overseas. The contraction of capacity involved closing the Luton plant which was sold to Vauxhall Motors, and transfer of the Jet Provost line to Preston. It became necessary to transfer part of the BAC One-Eleven line from Hurn to Weybridge, thus increasing production costs, and it ultimately led to the decision to concentrate military work in the northern factories and commercial work in the south.'

Tom Pritchard has also described this TSR2 cancellation period as one of the most traumatic periods in the history of BAC. It led to a long series of anxious meetings chaired by Sir George, at which Pritchard and J.E. Armitage covered the financial aspects. The primary problem, Pritchard recalls, was the resultant under-utilisation of the military aircraft production capacity at Preston and Weybridge, and it was clearly necessary to redress this both by closure of facilities and by redundancy.

The decision to close Luton was made only after much heart-searching, and the announcement of the closure by Arthur Summers over the factory loudspeakers must have been one of the most agonising moments of his life. Summers had made Luton into a very efficient and profitable unit, and the transfer of Jet Provost manufacture to Preston (and the wings to Hurn) both led to a significant increase in costs. The alternative, however, was the almost certain closure of Preston, which was unacceptable. The transfer of part of the One-Eleven line from Hurn to Weybridge also led to increased costs. ·

Very strong efforts had to be made to obtain more export sales for the military aircraft already in production, and the important contracts eventually completed with Saudi Arabia and Kuwait in 1966 for Lightnings and Strikemasters were the first major result of this effort.

The redundancies caused to the industry by the TSR2 cancellation were over 8000, of which some 5000 were at BAC. The Government, however, had taken serious note of what had been said to the Prime Minister at Chequers and by Sir George in his letters to Roy Jenkins, about the doubt now cast on the whole viability of BAC and the shift of the overheads to civil products which could not stand them. This same doubt was also expressed strongly by BAC to the Plowden Committee (discussed later) which had been created to look into the aircraft industry at the same time as the cancellations were under way.

As a result, even before the official pronouncement on TSR2 was made, the Government – true to its concepts of European collaboration – had made overtures to the French on the feasibility of two joint projects: one, an advanced trainer and the other, a small swing-wing multi-role aircraft with accent – at least initially – on the fighter end of the scale rather than the bomber. This was known as the AFVG (the Anglo-French Variable Geometry) aircraft, and the two projects were suggested as a package deal. As will be subsequently described, the specification of the advanced trainer on which the French firm of Breguet had the airframe lead and Rolls-Royce the engine lead, was progressively altered until it became the Jaguar, and the AFVG, on which BAC was to have the airframe lead and the French nationalised engine firm of SNECMA the engine lead, died when the French unilaterally withdrew in July 1967.

It is interesting that, by the end of the day, the cancellation of TSR2 on the grounds of economy in favour of the F111 (order withdrawn) and AFVG (cancelled) cost the British taxpayer at least £250 million, and that all there was to show in hardware for that £250 million – know-how apart – was one airframe in a museum. In the meantime, the Canberra replacement, so urgent in 1959, settled out as being the Canberra until October 1969, when the first Buccaneers were delivered to the Royal Air Force. The Canberra was still in service well after BAC had been nationalised in 1977. In 1979, there were still fifty Canberras being refurbished at Warton for the RAF and Venezuela.

The Comptroller and Auditor-General's Report covering 1964 sets out the various total cost-estimates for the development of TSR2 covering all work up to full CA (Controller Aircraft) release for the Royal Air Force (the military equivalent of a Certificate of Airworthiness) as under:

December 1959	£80–90 million	Release in 1966
March 1962	£137 million	Release in 1967
January 1963	£175–200 million	Release end-1968
January 1964	£240–270 million	Release mid-1969

The engine development cost components of the above are given as:

December 1959	£7.3 million
January 1962	£15 million
January 1963	£20 million (destruction of test aircraft)
October 1963	£30.3 million
March 1964	£32.5 million (maximum price)

In their very full 1969 paper – *Crisis in Procurement: A Case Study of the TSR2* – to the Royal United Service Institution, Dr Geoffrey Williams, Frank Gregory and John Simpson wondered if the new 'batch system' of pre-production aircraft built on production jigs instead of a quickly knocked-up flying prototype had not contributed to the cancellation. The argument here is that if some ironmongery had been seen flying early on this might have acted as a deterrent to cancellation, whereas the long period of cost escalation with no actual aeroplane to show for it, inherent in the batch and jigs system, could well have given the Treasury its elbow room for the axe. Another point made in this paper was whether it would not have paid to have ordered the original English Electric P17 for release in late 1963 and have added the Shorts VTOL platform for use from 1965 onwards. Both these questions are, however, academic, because a 'knife and fork' prototype, whether of TSR2 or of P17, would have required engines, and the pre-chosen engine, the

Olympus 22R, was not ready to fly in any aeroplane until September 1964 — and, indeed, it was not really ready then.

As a footnote to this chapter, it came out in 1968 that the first estimate of the cost for modifying the US 'off the shelf' Phantoms for the RAF and the Navy to take the Spey engine and some UK electronics was £25.3 million (February 1964), and by May 1965 it had risen to £45.5 million, the engine development costs having more than doubled from £12.4 million to £28.7 million. The 1964/5 cancellations of British products and their replacement by USA ones can, in retrospect, hardly be claimed as either a financial or an operational success.

17

Plowden

At the time when BAC's Guided Weapons Division was trying to pick itself off the ground after the killing of Blue Water and PT428, and when the fate of the two HSA military aircraft and of TSR2 had, de facto, already been decided, the Wilson Government announced, on 9 December 1964, the Plowden Committee of Enquiry into the Aircraft Industry. Its (? cosmetic) terms of reference were to consider the future place and organisation of the aircraft industry in relation to the country's general economy, taking into account the demands of national defence, export prospects, the comparable industries of other countries, and the relationship of the industry with Government activities in the aviation field.

As someone remarked at the time, this was akin to the setting up, by a team of successful housebreakers, of a committee to advise the householders how they might have stopped themselves being robbed. Sir Reginald Verdon-Smith preferred the analogy of the 'direction of the funeral.'

Lord Plowden, the Committee's Chairman, was Chairman of Tube Investments, and he had with him Mr David Barron (Managing Director of Shell International), Admiral of the Fleet Sir Caspar John (then Chairman of the Housing Association), Aubrey Jones (from March 1965, Chairman of the Prices and Incomes Board), Mr Fred Hayday (an officer of the Union of General and Municipal Workers), Mr Christopher McMahon (Advisor, Bank of England) and Sir William (later Lord) Penney (Chairman of the Atomic Energy Authority). Mr Austen Albu, MP, was a member for a very short time, but resigned and his place was taken by Dr John Cronin, MP. At the same time, Mr St John Elstub, Managing Director of Imperial Metals, was added, with Mr Walter Tye of the Air Registration Board to act as Technical Assessor.

It will be seen that Bill Penney was the only member who was burdened by any professional knowledge of the detailed problems of advanced technology, and that Walter Tye, the Assessor, was unique in that he knew about aircraft. Aubrey Jones had been a Conservative Aviation Minister, and initially responsible for the merger policy of his successor, Duncan Sandys. A big lack in the Committee's terms of reference was that the electronics industry was specifically excluded from its investigations, although electronics were, by now, about one-third in value of a modern warplane. Some on-the-side evidence on electronics was, however, eventually taken.

Once again an enormous number of man-hours was spent by the industry, and by SBAC, in preparing submissions to Plowden. Much of the work had to be done twice – before and after the official cancellations. In mid-June 1965, BAC was able to draw up a Memorandum for Plowden, which Lord Portal also sent to Roy Jenkins, the Minister of Aviation. In it Lord Portal said it was clear that the Government intended to reduce the size of the industry to bring about the transfer of its technological strength into other fields. This paragraph may, or may not, have been a dig at Jenkins who, when asked in the House at one stage of the TSR2 controversy, 'What other fields?' had given an irrelevant list which included the design of modern cutlery and Swedish-type furniture – an answer which drew from Sir George the comment that they would have to export a hell of a lot of three-piece suites to get in the foreign currency value of one VC10.

Lord Portal moved on to refer approvingly to recent positive moves – the proposed Anglo-French ECAT trainer (later the Jaguar) and the Variable Geometry aircraft. He then reminded the Minister that BAC had been formed specifically, and with Government encouragement, to provide a balanced aircraft unit with the right mixture of civil and military work. As a result, it was involved in major commitments in civil aviation, undertaken against the background of the large military programme of TSR2 – raising for the purpose large sums of borrowed money which could be outstanding for many years. The cancellation of TSR2 had come when the BAC One-Eleven was just entering airline service, and the resulting uncertainty of BAC's future was affecting orders and prospects. Lord Portal then referred to the worldwide evidence that modern civil aviation projects had not been commercially viable on their own account, and the fact that all BAC's competitors operated from an extensive background of military work.

'For these reasons,' Lord Portal went on, 'BAC does not share the confidence of the Government that the company can continue successfully on civil work with little support by way of military work . . . if further design and development is expected to be carried on by BAC in the civil field, Government support on a scale much greater than anything previously contemplated will be required.'

Lord Portal's important document – which was an expansion of Sir George's earlier letters to Jenkins – then emphasised the increasing and inevitable committee structure which accompanied Government investment, and more recently – with the 'interdependence' (i.e., international collaboration) policies (emphasised at the Chequers dinner) – a whole new range of international official Steering Committees which had further reduced the authority and scope of industrial management.

The question has to be faced:
'The Portal Memorandum went on whether it is possible to regard aircraft' design, development and manufacture any longer as a practical sphere of activity for commercial enterprise. It should be noted for example:

1. Decision-making is no longer within the more or less exclusive control of the constructor.

2. The cost of most developments can no longer be financed by ordinary risk capital and commercial borrowings. Development contracts and launching aid are therefore essential and bring with them all the inevitable consequences, by way of detailed control, of financial involvement by the Government.

3. Changes in Defence requirements . . . appear to be inevitable and the resulting probability of cancellations makes nonsense of the idea that Defence contracts are commercial ventures. The stage by stage procedure advocated by the Zuckerman Committee leads to long delays and virtually creates a cost-plus contract situation.

Lord Portal made other hard-hitting points and concluded by saying that, but for the independence and initiative of competitive private enterprise, and the technical advances which had been the result, it was doubtful if the industry could have survived. Nonetheless, the industry now stood, an island of commercial activity, surrounded by public authorities and dominated by issues of public policy outside its control.

'Considerations such as these,' the Memorandum ended, 'seem to point to a new alignment in which the industry is recognised as being essentially a national enterprise, is brought under one unified direction, and is established, preferably by voluntary negotiation, on a basis more suited than at present to the essentially international pattern which aviation is assuming for the future.'

The above Memorandum, which Sir Reginald Verdon-Smith later stated represented the views of the parent companies more than of the BAC Executive, was the subject of a meeting on 13 July 1965, between the Plowden Committee and a BAC delegation headed by Lord Portal and including the senior representatives of the owners, plus Sir George.

Lord Portal was asked point-blank what was meant by 'a national enterprise under one unified direction' – and how such could be secured. He replied that he and his colleagues had not concerned themselves with the form in which the industry might work in the future, but rather had attempted to bring to the notice of the Committee the impossibility of continuing as a private enterprise in the conditions which had developed since the Plowden Committee was set up. Sir Reginald amplified the answer by saying the industry was so surrounded by Government influence that initiative and decision-taking on commercial grounds were no longer possible. It was impossible for the industry to continue on these terms. There were numerous official bodies, all of which had a profound effect on the industry's decisions (for example the Transport Aircraft Requirements Committee), and also various advisers on whom Ministers now depended, yet there was no commercial participation in these bodies.

Sir Charles Dunphie and Lord Nelson both emphasised strongly that the corner-stone of the formation of BAC had been the inter-relationship between the existing and substantial military and civil programmes. These conditions had now been totally changed, and a whole stratum of military work had been removed. There were consequently severe financial difficulties because the ability to go on with the hazardous civil programme had depended on the short-term military profits. In spite of the Government statement that it was their policy to have a strong and viable aircraft industry, it was now, as a direct result of Government policy, no longer possible to have secure earnings. If buying in the cheapest market without taking into account other factors was Government policy, as it appeared to be, there was no alternative but for the Government to be totally responsible for the financial outcome of the British industry.

Sir Reginald and Lord Nelson made it clear that BAC had never used the word 'nationalised,' but insisted that a 'national unified plan' was essential whoever owned the industry. Without such unified direction, it was totally impossible sensibly to load the design and productive capacity at whatever level it was decided the economy could support. TSR2 had not been cancelled because of a change in Government policy – the defence requirement was still there and still valid – but it was cancelled because of a change in Government *procurement* policy, which was a different thing. Sir George amplified this by saying that the TSR2 was made to supply a market of possibly 110 aircraft whereas the TFX (F111) production from General Dynamics was to be of the order of 1500 aircraft. There was no way of closing such a gap, and price alone must always favour the Americans. He contrasted (and envied) the French sense of national unity on aviation, and the way the French Government and all its agencies supported sales – such as of the Caravelle. This was in marked contrast to the fate of the VC10 at the hands of BOAC and the Government. The Government had condoned BOAC's action in breaching their contract after seven years, during which BOAC's requirements had changed three times. It was a harrowing experience when potential overseas customers asked why they should buy British when the British Government and airlines did not do so. Sir George added that the position between the British industry and the American industry was like David and Goliath. He had hitherto been comforted by the outcome of that particular conflict, but now the Government had removed his pile of stones and given them to Goliath.

On the defence issue, Lord Portal reminded the Committee that it was a cardinal defence principle that, if the Services depended to any significant extent on foreign equipment or designs, the country would very quickly lose the capacity to produce weapons for its own defence. Finally, Sir George agreed entirely with the concept of Anglo-French collaboration, but did not regard Anglo-US collaboration as practicable. Recent statements by Defence Secretary MacNamara had made him highly suspicious of American intentions.

There was a great deal of high-level plain speaking at this BAC/Plowden encounter, and the Committee was left in no doubt that the industry could not finance itself or survive without military work – any more than the American industry could – and that, if the new Government continued its procurement policy of buying its military equipment in the cheapest (and therefore probably American) market, with no regard for the wider issues, then, in effect, they could have the industry, but they wouldn't have it for very long – or any of the other advanced technology which went along with it.

The Plowden Report, when it was published in December 1965, was, however, an overall disappointment. It was very strong on its analysis of past mistakes, and of the difficulties of the British industry vis à vis the long production runs of its US counterpart, but weak on what ought to be done. Most of the 'inquest' half of a 100-page report could indeed have been written by any informed student of aviation matters inside a week.

The main burden of the Plowden recommendations was that Government support for the industry should be reduced until it needed no more support than was given to comparable industries in Britain ('What other industries were comparable?' was the immediate rejoinder to that). The Committee saw little prospect of substantially increasing sales of purely British products and declared that the industry must turn to collaboration with other countries in Europe. Future requirements for the largest and most complex types of military aircraft and guided weapons, it believed, would in future all have to be met by purchases from the USA, or possibly manufactured under licence, but hopefully there could be some UK-designed content. Civil aircraft should also be a European matter, not just a British one, and manufacturers should normally contribute at least half of the launching costs. There should be fewer delays in decision-making, the Government should set up a single central Governmental organisation to promote aircraft exports, and (about the only positively helpful point) ten years should be made the standard period of the Export Credits Guarantee Department credit cover for all major aircraft types, including the BAC One-Eleven (hitherto only given seven years' cover). Further, the premium charge should be reduced (the US official credit terms had been significantly cheaper than those of the UK).

As to the organisation of the industry, Plowden came to no firm conclusion as to whether there should be one or two main airframe groups or one or two main engine groups. That decision should be made when the future workload, and therefore size of the industry, could be better estimated, although the Committee foresaw a substantial reduction in employment, especially on airframes. As to ownership, the Plowden recommendation was that the Government might take a shareholding (amount unspecified) in BAC and Hawker Siddeley – including the Guided Weapons interests.

The Plowden Report was almost entirely negative and defeatist, and was widely attacked as such. Most people agreed on collaborative (not necessarily always European) enterprises to widen the market and reduce purely national investment risk – but this policy had been accepted pre-Plowden, and was actually being implemented. There was considerable industry distrust of a Government Central Sales Agency – it being strongly held that sales were the affair of the constructor. What was needed was for all Government agencies, overseas missions, and senior serving officers, etc., to support and help the constructor, as was the case in the USA and France and was very emphatically not the case in the UK.

Nothing in particular came of Plowden, save the ECGD improvements, but it did keep the industry and its shortcomings, alleged and real, in world headlines. This heightened the feelings of uncertainty abroad and gave the Americans a splendid chance to go round saying 'Don't buy from Britain, they're getting out of the business and you'll be left high and dry with no spares or technical backing.' After the cancellations and the Plowden report, it was difficult to counter this – or at least to do so with any conviction.

18
Progress 1962–4

The stories of the VC10, One-Eleven and TSR2 have swept the BAC history on beyond the strict chronology of this book – at least as far as the progress and development of the Corporation are concerned. The author's dilemma in this respect has already been explained; the alternative being so to fragment product histories year by year as to make the continual picking up of the pieces too confusing.

To retrace steps, therefore, back to 1962, the Chairman's report for that year spoke of the widespread disappointment at the Blue Water cancellation, but also the confirmation of development and production of Thunderbird II, and further work on Bloodhound II, to facilitate the eventual development of a large, third-generation, surface-to-air weapon which might be needed by all three Services (it wasn't). The Minister of Defence had also announced that Swingfire would proceed for the Army and that an order would be placed for the six additional VC10s for the Royal Air Force.

Other Guided Weapons news was that a family of smaller weapons would be needed by any modern army, including Vigilant, reconnaissance drones, and a light and portable field defence against low-flying aircraft (the first mention of the project which was one day to become Rapier). Export orders for Vigilant had been received from Kuwait and Finland, and, to facilitate anti-tank work, British Aircraft Corporation (Anti-Tank) Limited had, as already noted, been formed with Fairey Aviation. British Aircraft Corporation (Guided Weapons) Limited had been formed to unify the English Electric and Bristol effort.

The Type 188 all-steel supersonic research aircraft had flown on 14 April 1962; the Hunting 126 jet flap research aircraft had also flown. The Bristol 221 (the Fairey Delta modified to a Concorde wing-shape) was being worked on to help the Concorde design programme.

The main burden of the report, however, was recording the Concorde agreement, signed on 29 November 1962, and progress reports on the VC10, which had made its first flight on 29 June 1962, and TSR2. There were additional Jet Provost orders, and BAC was financing a Mark 5 (pressurised) version as such an aircraft might be required from 1965 onwards. The first mention of 'Space' occurs in this report, it being stated that BAC was actively engaged on a number of Space vehicle studies, while a project for the first all-British satellite was being considered by the Government.

The Type 188 all-steel experimental aircraft, to which Lord Portal referred, had a wing shape derived from the original (and cancelled) Avro supersonic bomber. Two 188s had been ordered by the Government but only the one was completed. A complex operations room was also built at Filton to monitor and record the oversea supersonic flights of the aircraft and the automatically transmitted data from them. The 188 had been a terrible aeroplane to build, and it did very little flying, there being considerable problems of maintainability in so dense a structure, packed as its small spaces were with virtually inaccessible wiring and electrics. Its original purpose (the Avro wing) had passed by, but, as Sir George was to say, 'At least we have unique actual experience of building an aeroplane in steel. It confirms how right we were to decide to build the Concorde in light alloy. When the Americans talk about building their SST in steel for Mach 3, I face the outcome with monastic calm.'

The jet flap aircraft made a lot of successful flights in a long programme which greatly enhanced British technical knowledge of this method of increasing lift.

Lord Portal's report for 1963 was published at the end of April 1964. It spoke of the impending introduction into service of the Standard VC10 with BOAC, BUA, Ghana Airways and RAF Transport Command and of the reaction of all who had so far flown in it, that it set new standards of quiet, comfort and airfield performance. The report also covered the initial success of the One-Eleven, its certification, and its forty-four US orders, and paid tribute to 'the seven fine men' who were lost in the prototype, and to the great and unselfish contribution to the safety of air transport made by all who had to subject new airliners to the great extremes of performance and manoeuvre during the test period.

There was again prominent mention of the Concorde – 'This inevitable next step in air travel' – and of the approaching maiden flight of TSR2 (this of course was prior to the engine problems). Lord Portal added, 'That these four major projects, each a notable advance on its predecessors, should be under development at the same time within one manufacturing group gives a measure of the strength of BAC. It is also a confirmation of the fact that British engineering genius continues to lead in those areas in which it has the resources to compete.'

The report also emphasised two points which were to be made many times over the next few troubled years: that the aircraft industry, by its skills, converted relatively small quantities of raw materials into exportable products of great worth, and so made a truly significant contribution to the balance of payments, and that, by pioneering new frontiers, the industry conferred considerable benefits on much of British engineering as a whole.

Total BAC sales for 1963 amounted to £104.5 million (£83.6 million in 1962), of which £42.2 million was 'new account' and £62.3 million 'old account'. The trading profit was £2.411 million but, after providing £722,000 for interest, the net profit was £1.973 million (£1.46 million in 1962). A dividend of 5 per cent was declared on the share capital (the same as in 1962) and the balance of £1.88 million was carried forward to make the unappropriated profits up to £2.07 million. During 1963, a further £5.5 million was drawn on the FCI loan, making a total of £9 million. The value of the order book at the end of December 1963 was £302 million (£190 million on new projects and £112 million on 'old account'). This was an increase of £12 million on 1962.

The report recorded the acquisition of the remaining part of Hunting Aircraft, and it then dealt with the next major step in the development of the organisation of BAC. Lord Portal said that overall integration of BAC had gone ahead so well that the four subsidiary companies (Bristol Aircraft, English Electric Aviation, Hunting Aircraft, Vickers-Armstrongs (Aircraft) and Guided Weapons) had, from 1 January 1964, all become Divisions of one new wholly owned subsidiary company, British Aircraft Corporation (Operating) Limited. There were thus a Weybridge Division, a Preston Division, a Luton Division, a Filton Division and a Guided Weapons Division of BAC (Operating) – each Division (actually a management company) being administered by its own management Board, and represented on the main Board of BAC (Operating). The overall BAC (Holdings) Board became, in effect, a Board representing the combined interests of the parents and of BAC (Operating).

The BAC (Operating) Board consisted of Sir George, as Chairman and Managing Director, the Chairmen/Managing Directors of the Guided Weapons Division (Lord Caldecote), Filton Division (James Harper), Weybridge Division (A.W.E. Houghton), Preston Division (A.W.E. Houghton) and Luton Division (W.A. Summers – who was also responsible for the Hurn factory). Also on the Operating Board were F.W. Page (Chief Executive, Preston), W. Masterton (Financial Director), G.E. Knight (Civil Aircraft Sales Director), A.H.C. Greenwood (Military Aircraft Sales Director and Assistant to the Chairman, also responsible for all aircraft after-sales service) and J.E. Armitage (Financial Controller). Charlie Houghton held overall responsibility for production and for TSR2.

Sir George thus gave up his chairmanship of all the subsidiary companies, putting much more emphasis on decentralisation now that the initial 'drawing together' period of BAC was over. Each Division had a large amount of autonomy and therefore of responsibility to be profitable. It will be noticed that Geoffrey Knight, formerly Commercial Manager of BAC, took over de jure all civil sales and contracts – the job which he had been doing de facto for some time. Allen Greenwood concentrated on military sales and all aircraft after-sales service, in addition to assisting the Chairman on matters concerning international collaborative projects.

The BAC (Holdings) Board under Lord Portal still had Sir George as Managing Director, plus Sir Dermot Boyle, Lord Caldecote, Charlie Houghton, Willie Masterton, Lord Nelson, Sir Reginald Verdon-Smith (Bristol), Sir Leslie Rowan (Vickers), A.D. Marris, G.A. Riddell (English Electric) and Ronald Yapp (Vickers).

Lord Portal noted that the above decision meant the disappearance from the industry of four well-known and honoured company names: Bristol, Vickers, English Electric and Hunting – 'an event we all regret, but an inevitable step towards integrating all our resources.'

Other items of interest in the 1963 report were a further order for twenty-five Jet Provosts for overseas customers – more than 400 being in service with the Royal Air Force and in Ceylon, Kuwait, Sudan and Venezuela – the completion of deliveries of new Canberras to India and South Africa, and the completion of deliveries of Mk2 Lightnings to the RAF. The first Lightning Mk3 deliveries were imminent and ahead of programme. 'The Mk3, with its more advanced weapons system and other performance improvements,' commented Lord Portal, 'is probably the most efficient interceptor-fighter ever built, but it still has considerable development potential.'

The report for 1964, headed *A Critical Year for the Aircraft Industry*, was written with the background of the impending TSR2 disaster; the threats of the BOAC cancellation of all its Super VC10s, and the initial UK attempt to withdraw from Concorde. 'These,' said Lord Portal, with some understatement, 'are not the conditions in which any industry can make forward plans and proceed to carry them out with any certainty. The continuing uncertainty for the last nine months has naturally caused widespread anxiety and unrest among employees whom the nation cannot afford to lose if we are to remain technically a first-class industry.'

The 1964 sales were £116.68 million (£104.5 million), of which £55 million were for 'new account,' and £61.67 million for 'old account.' The trading profit was £2.87 million (£2.41 million) but, after £1.8 million interest and £36,000 tax, the net profit, allowing for a minority interest, was only £981,000 (£1.91 million). No dividend was paid, and the net profit was carried forward to safeguard against possible under-recoveries in development. The total BAC undistributed profit thus became £3.05 million. The order book at the end of 1964 was £361.25 million – £216.8 million for 'new' and £144.4 million for 'old account.' This was virtually the same total order book as that of a year earlier. A further £4.5 million had been drawn from the FCI loan, making £13.5 million of the £15 million available.

The One-Eleven continued to be a bright feature – seventy-three sold and seventeen more on option by the end of 1964, sixty-seven for export. The 200-hour programme of airline route flying had been completed in February 1964 in 23 days, seven days ahead of schedule, by just one aircraft averaging between eight and nine hours a day.

All was still ahead of programme on Lightning Mk3 deliveries, and eleven air forces were operating Canberras, deliveries of new or refurbished aircraft being made to five countries. The pressurised Jet Provost Mk5 had received a Ministry of Aviation development contract, and the H126 had passed its century of flights.

On the Guided Weapons front, the sky was brightening. Bloodhound II was being deployed in Singapore, and delivered to Sweden and Switzerland; there were export enquiries for both Thunderbird and Bloodhound; Vigilant was being exported, and Swingfire was creating overseas interest. The new low-level anti-aircraft system had now been given a title, 'ET316' – and, more importantly, was under full development. Space activities had been expanded, the UK3 all-British satellite was being built, and BAC were now prime contractors for the Skylark sounding rockets for ESRO and the Government. The Guided Weapons Division was also providing specialised services on a number of overseas products such as Polaris, Corporal, AS30 and Jindivik. It was in production, for the Services and civil engineering, with a very ingenious North-finding instrument known as PIM (Precision Indicator of the Meridian) and with inertial navigation systems for aircraft and ships. The value of the Guided Weapons Division's exports in 1964 had been £9.6 million.

In 1963 and 1964, there were a number of important appointments and postings within BAC and its Divisions. Men who were later to play key roles in the Corporation began to come to the fore. Tom Pritchard became Deputy Financial Director as well as Treasurer of BAC (Operating) and gained a seat on the Operating Board. On the TSR2 front, Freddie Page, Chief Executive at Preston, became in May 1964 responsible to Houghton for the TSR2 project as a whole, the responsibilities of Henry Gardner as 'Chief of Staff' for TSR2 being unchanged.

A decision (April 1964) to assemble the production TSR2s at Preston rather than Weybridge, including some of the pre-production aircraft, put more TSR2 emphasis up north. With Mr B.O. Heath as Project Manager (Development), Mr T.O. Williams responsible, as Manager (Aircraft), for all Preston-assembled TSR2s, and Harry Baxendale responsible, as Commercial Director, to Page on all TSR2 contractual matters, the TSR2 centre of gravity was moving to Preston. This shift was triggered by the increasing One-Eleven load plus VC10 at Weybridge, and BAC was moving – though probably not at that time as the deliberate plan it later became – to a military complex in the north and a civil one in the south. Reg Sawyer (ex-Vickers) moved from Pall Mall, where he was Chief Accountant, to be Financial Director at Preston. In the south, the civil sales team was being built up. Eric Beverley came across from Guided Weapons to be Civil Aircraft Overseas Contracts Manager to Geoffrey Knight (Taffy Higginson taking over Guided Weapons Sales), and Knight also strengthened his technical Sales and Commercial staff overall, including two former Chief Test Pilots, Jock Bryce and Walter Gibb.

Overseas direct representation was also built up by the appointment of Henry Sharp to the Far East, Pett-Ridge to South and Central America, D.B. Fowden to the Middle East, and Bob Gladwell to the USA (where he became Sales Director of British Aircraft Corporation (USA) Inc. − the former Vickers-Armstrongs Aircraft (USA) Inc. at Arlington). The Military Sales Office was given some more staff, and there was a general deployment of muscle to bring in more, and much needed, One-Eleven, Concorde, VC10, Lightning, Provost, Canberra and (hopefully) TSR2 orders. At Weybridge, there were technical changes because Basil Stephenson, the respected Chief Engineer who had borne the brunt of the Viscount development, fell ill and later retired, leaving Hugh Hemsley to succeed him, with Ernie Marshall and E.S. Allwright as Deputies. Arthur Summers, Chairman and Managing Director at Luton, was spending more and more of his time organising the One-Eleven build at Hurn, with Bill Coomber as his number two and, after TSR2 cancellation had forced the closure of Luton, Summers became 'king' of the One-Eleven building effort. At Weybridge, Air Marshal Sir Geoffrey Tuttle, who had been General Manager, became Vice-Chairman, with overall Board responsibility for the flying programmes.

19
Problems with the French

The aftermath of TSR2, coinciding as it did with Sir Giles Guthrie's well publicised and damaging attempts to cancel all the Super VC10s, the Concorde doubts, plus the Plowden recommendations that Britain should, in effect, become only a minor aviation power, and that the size and scope of the industry should be reduced, nearly proved fatal to BAC. Only the future hopes for a still financially struggling One-Eleven, and the steady work on Lightnings, export Canberras and Jet Provosts, gave any encouragement to the parents to stay in aviation. Even that resolution was, at the time, far from wholehearted, as can be gathered from the BAC evidence given to Plowden, and the various statements made to the Prime Minister and Roy Jenkins.

It is now clear, looking back to the documents and correspondence of 1966 and 1967, and the Government's actions in 1965 (while Plowden was still deliberating), that neither the Ministry of Defence (Healey) nor the Ministry of Aviation (Jenkins and later Fred Mulley) wanted to lose for the nation the military design capabilities of Warton (Preston) or the established world civil aircraft position held by Weybridge. Nor did they want to see their main guided weapons team disbanded.

Whether the Treasury (Callaghan) shared that view is open to doubt, as the death of BAC and the consequent slashing of the troublesome aerospace industry did not seem likely to bring a tear to the eye of the Chancellor and certainly not to those of his officials. It was their belief – reflected again in Plowden – that the industry absorbed too much of the nation's resources not only of investment, but of skilled and qualified engineers, scientists and technologists. The latter, it was felt – and felt by the Government as a whole – could well be re-deployed to better advantage, though into doing what was never clear. As was pointed out at the time, the aircraft employees, even in 1965, were earning the nation £750 per head in exports, and if re-deployed to other manufacturing industries they would then only be earning the average £400 in exports a head at a time when exporting was the main exhortation of all politicians. BAC employees in 1965 were actually earning £1500 per head in exports – twice the aircraft industry (including BAC) average. Furthermore, all aerospace exports had a conversion ratio of just over 90 per cent – the raw material content being low, but the value of the end-product very high indeed. In short, aerospace exported mainly British technical skills and man-hours, which made it the perfect industry for the balance of payments crisis, as its import content was almost negligible. Further, Britain was the only western nation, other than USA, which had a complete, self-contained and proven aviation ability across the board – research and development establishments, airframe, engines, electronics, metallurgy, radars, tyres, brakes, instruments, etc., and the educational organisations to back them up. France certainly did not have such an ability – and nor, of course, did Germany. The British industry was, in fact, bigger and more powerful than that of all the rest of Europe put together.

To counter this case, the Treasury added up all the public monies spent on aircraft and weapons postwar, and presented the total as though it had been a charitable bequest to a feather-bedded system. It was left to others to point out that most of the monies were straight payment for defence equipment supplied, which would otherwise have had to have been bought for dollars. Much of the rest had gone on cancelled projects whose starting and stopping had been no fault of the industry, but had been done entirely by successive Governments, both Conservative and Labour. It was true that the industry depended largely on Government work – but then so did many others.

It was, however, the defence argument rather than the economic one which prompted the first and immediate official attempts to do something to offset the TSR2 damage. Even before TSR2 was cancelled, Healey, presumably with Jenkins' knowledge and approval, had sent officials and technical experts to France to propose collaborative ventures on what became Jaguar (discussed later) and the AFVG. The intention was to put both projects, if successfully negotiated, into Preston via BAC. This was at the same time that Healey had committed £800 million to the purchase of American Phantoms (to be fitted with Rolls-Royce Spey engines) and of C130 Hercules transports, and was discussing a further £280 million spend on trouble-stricken F111s. He had, indeed, some reason to have an uneasy conscience. All these US purchases could have been avoided by sensible forward planning and by procurement, from British factories, of better aircraft into which a great deal of work had already been put.

BAC promptly, and on a self-help basis, did all it could to provide a rapid alternative to the F111 purchase, while naturally welcoming the Jaguar and AFVG proposals. These would load the design offices, but would not replace the TSR2 on the factory floors for some years. What was urgently needed was some production and consequent payment for hardware. Hence the affair of the Spey-Mirage.

The idea was to get the Government to take jointly made Dassault Mirage IV airframes fitted with Spey engines instead of buying the F111. This, BAC argued, could provide a highly efficient TSR2 replacement aircraft, fully capable of performing the TSR2 essential tasks, at a total cost, for seventy-five aircraft, including development, of under £2 million each. Production assembly would be from two lines, one in France and one at BAC, and production deliveries could start in February 1969.

The proposal was exactly in accord with the announced Government policy of Anglo-French collaboration, would use an existing engine in an existing airframe, and incorporate already expensively developed avionics and nav-attack systems. It would also be complementary to the AFVG, which was also to be a Dassault/BAC collaboration, and, furthermore, there were signs that the French Air Force might be very interested in buying some. Allen Greenwood for BAC and Ronnie Harker of Rolls-Royce became very active in promoting this solution.

Mr Healey has since said that he only loses his temper about once in three years, but, when he does, it is an awesome experience. By all accounts he lost his temper over the BAC/Rolls-Royce Spey-Mirage proposals and referred to BAC in quite unprintable terms. In one outburst he said he would divert his two Anglo-French proposals to Hawker and leave BAC to ponder its sins. It is difficult to understand why he should have taken such a view, as he had not yet ordered any F111s, and the F111, to his certain and detailed knowledge, was already a very dubious proposition indeed. For some reason, however, he believed BAC was trying to roll stones in the way of his AFVG project, which was absurd. BAC wanted both the AFVG for the future and the Spey-Mirage for more immediate reasons. The Spey-Mirage was aimed specifically at the F111 and not the AFVG, and there can be no doubt that it would have filled this bill very well indeed. It would certainly have been an incomparably better aircraft than the subsonic Buccaneers which the RAF eventually was forced to take when the AFVG fell through. An American General said of the Buccaneer proposal in 1965, 'It will give its opponents hysterics, and earn the pity of its friends. The USAF discarded aircraft of the Buccaneer performance a decade ago.'

The better the Spey-Mirage looked, the angrier grew the Minister and Ministry of Defence, while the Air Staff even went to the extent of interfering with RAF flight test reports, as one of the pilots has subsequently admitted. In the end, Sir Henry Hardman, Ministry of Defence Permanent Secretary, spelt it out to Lord Portal personally that, if BAC expected any more Ministry of Defence work, it (and Rolls-Royce) had better lay off Spey-Mirage as the RAF was determined to have F111s.

Healey and Jenkins, working hard to get Jaguar and AFVG launched, saw the Spey-Mirage as a boat-rocking exercise (why?), and Ministry of Defence officials privately told BAC that they were 'barmy.'

Dassault, who would have done very well out of the deal, were understandably angry, and there was much reference to the perfidy of Albion and of her lip service to a European concept while actually being a vassal of the USA. The French were shortly to have their revenge, if for different reasons and motives.

Mr Healey and his officials successfully and quickly negotiated the

Jaguar/AFVG package with the French Government and a Memo-randum of Understanding was announced on 17 May 1965. Its basis was that the French firm, Breguet, would have the airframe design lead on the ECAT[1] trainer/ground attack aircraft (as the Jaguar was then known) and BAC would have the airframe design lead on the AFVG. Conversely, Rolls-Royce would lead in the Adour engine for the ECAT, and SNECMA of France on the engine for the AFVG.

Basically, this was a fair arrangement though, truth to tell, the business of 'leading' was overplayed both politically and in the national media of both countries. Modern aircraft are designed and produced by team-work and by allocation of areas of responsibility, and the days when one man, however talented and strong, thumped the table and said, 'That's the way it's going to be,' were already past. Sir George was often to say, as a result of his collaborative experience, that, when it came to it, sensible and professional engineers were much more concerned with defeating Isaac Newton than with defeating each other. When there was a genuine technical difference as to the best solution of a problem, there would usually be two Frenchmen and three Englishmen advocating one answer and three Frenchmen and two Englishmen against them. Nationalism was secondary to professional judgement and debate, and Sir George has often publicly stated that the extraordinary success of the Concorde flight development programme owed much to such prolonged debate when an old-time Chief Designer might well have ruled one way or the other in an afternoon – and have got it wrong.

At the time of the AFVG, however, nationalism was at a peak in de Gaulle's France, and the British tended to over-react to it. The UK media were already alleging that Concorde was a 'French' aeroplane, or that the French were pretending it was, and that, with ECAT and AFVG, the French would be 'leading' on two out of three collaborative projects. It was all an artificial nonsense really (as both Concorde and ECAT/Jaguar were eventually to show), but de Gaulle's famous 'Non' about the EEC to Harold Macmillan still rankled in Britain, and, again to quote Sir George, 'At that time about the only Englishmen who were still speaking to the French were the engineers on the Concorde.'

The atmosphere, therefore, was not good; the French had the UK attempt to cancel Concorde fresh in mind, as well as the British refusal even properly to evaluate the Spey-Mirage. They did not see the British as reliable partners in anything, and certainly in nothing which might impede the Americans in their objective of reducing European aerospace to a sub-contract status to a US monopoly. The £1000 million pounds' worth of Healey's proposed purchases from the USA for the Royal Air Force had not given the French any reason to believe that the British Government was serious in its statements about preserving a strong aircraft industry, and, it must be said, there were many Britons who agreed with them.

[1] ECAT – Ecole de Combat et d'Appui Tactique (Combat Training and Tactical Strike).

As was later to be discovered, the French Government, after TSR2, had consciously decided that it could now wrest European leadership in aerospace from the UK within a decade, and that a sensible basis for Anglo-French collaboration was that France would be responsible for all airframes and Britain could, through Rolls-Royce, have engine leadership, although SNECMA would (of course) remain in being.

This, argued the French, would reduce the size of the British industry by a good half, and with both countries employing about 100,000 people each, collaboration would be on a 'proper' basis. Such a proposal was, indeed, actually tabled and considered, but there was a 100 per cent revolt against it, not so much by the politicians as by the Services and the senior officials. Had it been accepted, there would be very little advanced technology left in Britain today, and Rolls-Royce would have only continued to exist by courtesy of the French, which, in the view of many, would not have been for very long.

The AFVG itself was quite a good multi-role strike-fighter. Its concept covered French and British naval requirements for carrier work, and various weights and general arrangement layouts were discussed. A radius of action for strike and reconnaissance of 500 n.m., a speed of well over Mach 2 at 60,000 feet, and a take-off and landing distance of 2500 feet to 50 feet were specified. The two engines were to be SNECMA/Bristol Siddeley M45Gs. The initial French requirement was weighted towards strike and the British towards the fighter role, the timescale being 1974/5. Early in 1966, however, something of a reversal of emphasis occurred. The British buy of Phantoms for use as fighters threw more of the UK accent on to strike, and French withdrawal from NATO led them towards the home-defence fighter aspect.

The AFVG lived, even for the relatively short time that it did, on a tightrope, with costs predictably mounting, and in an atmosphere of official and political distrust. The BAC and Dassault engineers, however, and by contrast, worked well together ('more interested in defeating Newton, etc.'). In the view of Ollie Heath at Warton, they could have sorted out the practical problems of the aeroplane and its swing-wing hinge fairly happily. 'Either firm on its own,' he said, 'could have eaten the project, and we had great respect for each other.'

By the end of 1965, the British officials were beginning to be doubtful about the French attitude to the AFVG. Sir George was already worried, and had been so since he made an early special visit to remind Marcel Dassault personally that the terms of the agreement vested technical leadership of the AFVG in the nominated UK firm, which was BAC. The Technical Director, therefore, would be British. 'I wanted no mis-understanding on this score,' he said later, 'otherwise I could foresee endless arguments. There had to be someone who eventually took the decisions and those decisions had to be able to be made to stick. I saw the old man, and it became quite clear to me that he was never going to accept this. Considering the power he held in France, I read the eventual doom of the AFVG in that one conversation.' Before 1965 was over the

French Minister (Pierre Messmer) was already telling Healey that there were problems over costs, but indicated they would be overcome. During 1966, the British Ministry team detected a change in the atmosphere and what appeared to be a lack of candour, or at least signs of unease, in their French colleagues, who were headed by René Bloch and Robert Lecamus.

Eventually, as a result of 'information received,' the British discovered that Dassault was going ahead with a swing-wing project of his own (the Mirage 3G) and that a prototype was well on the way towards completion. (Nothing, incidentally, was ever revealed to the UK about the F1.) Meanwhile, this sense of disquiet had been conveyed to Healey along with a forecast that the French were preparing to pull out – a forecast which the British Minister refused to accept. In the end, the UK officials and some Embassy staff faced Bloch and Lecamus with a question as to what was this all-French prototype of Dassault's and why. At first, all knowledge of it was denied but – after a conversation in French in which Lecamus said, 'It's no good, René, they know' – the Mirage 3G (but not the F1) was admitted. After that, it was little surprise – at least not to the officials – when Messmer told Healey at a meeting in London on 29 June 1967, that the French were withdrawing from the project 'on financial grounds.' The British Minister was furious, because the aircraft, which he himself had said 'lay at the heart' of all plans for the future of the Royal Air Force, was now dead after just over two years of troubled life, and a further 'official' £2½ million was down the drain (although Warton would still challenge the accuracy of that figure). At the same time the troubles with the F111 had intensified, and were now common knowledge. So, in Derek Wood's words, 'Healey was back at square one.'

To give Healey his due, he reacted as quickly as he had done in 1965. The very next day after the blow had been administered to him by Messmer, he was sending an RAF team to Canada to talk to the RCAF about the chances of Britain (a non-F104 user) joining the big F104-G replacement discussions then going on between Canada, Belgium, the Netherlands, Germany and Italy. Officials were also despatched to Europe to talk to the other participants, and eventually it was agreed to admit the UK, initially on an 'observer' basis. This concession was to be a very far-reaching one, because, as a result, the relatively cheap and cheerful fighter concept which the five-nation consortium was examining in 1967, finished up in 1969 as the much more sophisticated MRCA. Canada and Belgium had, as a result, withdrawn, and not in the best of tempers either. The Netherlands (and Fokker) stayed in for about a year longer and a Dutch General, Stockler, became General Manager of NAMMA (see chapter 29, The MRCA), but eventually they, too, pulled out.

Meanwhile, to maintain a fall-back position, but mainly to keep the talented Warton design team together, a new all-British Variable

Geometry study was put in hand – the UK VG.

With the 20/20 vision of hindsight, it was later argued by Ministry of Defence officials of the day that the TSR2/AF VG collapses eventually led Britain and BAC into the most important military project the UK industry has ever been involved in – the MRCA. While this is true, it can hardly be claimed that the great achievement which is now the Tornado came about as a result of coherent UK planning.

20

Jaguar

In contrast to the suspicion and politics of the AFVG, the ECAT/Jaguar programme with Breguet was amicable at all levels, painless, successful, and therefore undramatic and un-newsworthy. When BAC and Breguet began to work on the Jaguar, both firms needed the job. Henri Ziegler was then the boss of Breguet, and he was a very different personality from Vallières at Dassault, and especially from the great Marcel himself. Ziegler had, in Viscount days, been the head of Air France, an early purchaser, and therefore knew many Weybridge people as old friends. He was international in outlook rather than insular, was used to dealing with foreign interests, and had a bubbling sense of fun and enthusiasm. His first instruction to the Breguet (and BAC) staff was that the firms must set the pace and give a good example to the officials – which was a pretty good beginning.

The history of the French ECAT (Ecole de Combat et d'Appui Tactique) was that the French Air Force needed an advanced fighter/trainer with a ground attack capability to replace their F84F and F100s in the early 1970s, and the French ran a design competition for the job. The competition was won by Breguet with the transonic Breguet 121, its main competitor being Dassault. Dassault, not accustomed to losing in France, were predictably very anti-ECAT and therefore anti-Jaguar. They were constantly beavering away to upset the decision, even (and especially) after it became an Anglo-French project and part of the package deal with the AFVG. This was to have an important impact later on when Dassault took over the majority of Breguet shares in 1967, leading to a complete merger in 1971.

The Royal Air Force also had, or was talked into having, a requirement (ASR 362 of 1964) for a supersonic replacement of the Gnat advanced jet trainer, and for a Hunter replacement in the ground attack role, both in the mid-1970s. The British proposed that the Breguet 121 be up-graded to have a more formidable ground attack capability, and that it should also be moderately supersonic and able to protect itself.

This represented quite a change in the French plans but, as the British would be paying half of all the costs and as it would give substantial production work to an ailing Breguet and also advance Breguet technology while strengthening the French Air Force's battlefield hitting power, the changes were agreed within a remarkably short time. There was also — at least for a time — a French naval carrier-borne requirement. The outline of the project was embodied in the Memorandum of Understanding, which was signed on 17 May 1965, and to have hammered out the specification for what, in many ways, was a new aeroplane, by November of that year, was a remarkable achievement.

There were to be five variants: British and French versions of the two-seat advanced trainer (Types B and E), British and French versions of the single-seat tactical strike model (Types S and A), and the French single-seat strike aircraft for their Navy (Type M). There were to be eight prototypes or, more accurately, development aircraft — two French single-seat, two French two-seat, and one French Naval single-seat; two British single-seat and one British two-seat.

Ollie Heath later recalled that BAC-Breguet work on refining and developing the Breguet 121 began with a will, and, in contrast with the AFVG, discussion on the General Arrangement drawings and performance soon expanded into discussions on standards and detail design. There were parallel moves towards the setting up of a full management structure over the whole range of design, planning, costing, sales and so on. The engines for the new aeroplane were to be two RB172/T260 Adours, a Rolls-Royce led design, with Turboméca as their partners. The Adour was then a two-shaft turbo-fan of 4600 lb of dry thrust, boosted to 6900 lb with reheat.

One of the lessons that had already been learned from Concorde was that a separate management company was necessary to control a large collaborative project. There was no such structure for Concorde, which was being run by a series of bi-national and national Governmental and industrial committees, and, administratively, was suffering heavily therefrom. In the case of Jaguar, as the new aeroplane was promptly named, the two airframe manufacturers formed a new joint company known as SEPECAT (Société Européenne de Production d'Ecole de Combat et d'Appui Tactique) to co-ordinate engineering design, manufacture, finance and sales. It was to be established in Paris, and the engine companies did the same, only their joint company was registered in London.

First of all the agreed and up-graded joint BAC/Breguet design proposal and specification had to be brought forward and accepted by the Governments and Defence Forces of both countries, and this, as stated, was done by as early as November 1965. SEPECAT was then set up (May 1966), and it was SEPECAT which received and handled the main contracts placed by the Governments, and also put out the sub-contract work. Its Board was drawn from BAC and Breguet, with alternating chairmen.

This was a much tidier and more businesslike arrangement than the nebulosity of Concorde. SEPECAT — though it had no staff of its own — was a proper company and exercised proper industrial control. BAC and

Breguet thus became legally sub-contractors to SEPECAT, who allocated the work to an agreed fifty-fifty breakdown. It also had the advantage that any future export customers could deal contractually with one separate company established in one country and subject to the known commercial laws of that country. The experience gained from SEPECAT was, some years later, to be used in the formation of the three-nation Panavia, the company established (and, in that case, fully staffed) for the handling of the MRCA Tornado.

Jeffrey Quill and Paul Jaillard of Breguet were responsible for Jaguar sales, and immediately set up a small sales/publicity committee on which Rolls-Royce/Turboméca were represented. Brochures, literature, advertisements and progress bulletins were budgeted for on SEPECAT, and, from the very start, this project had an air of reality and permanence, and successfully so presented itself to the outside world despite the steady undermining which was still coming from Dassault. It was typical of the 'get up and go' atmosphere which marked the launching of Jaguar that its name – usually the subject of protracted discussion – was settled by one telephone call. Henri Ziegler rang BAC and said, 'We need a name and it has to be the same in both languages: I suggest "Jaguar".' Sir George immediately agreed. It was cleared with Jaguar Cars the same day, and within twenty-four hours 'Jaguar' publicity was being prepared for the 1965 Paris Air Show which opened a day or two later. Neither Air Force was consulted, a process which can take literally years. They were presented with a *fait accompli*, about which, as far as the author knows, they never complained.

The initial planning for Jaguar was that each nation would take 150 aircraft, but the 'split' as between two-seat and single-seat varied somewhat in the early years. In 1967, the order was increased to 200 for each country – the Royal Air Force requirement finally settling down, with the demise of the AFVG, at 165 single-seat strike aircraft and thirty-five two-seaters. The French had the initial complication of a requirement for forty 'M' Type for the French Navy, but this order, in particular, was under constant attack by Dassault, and after looking rocky for some time, it was killed in 1972 and replaced with an up-dated version of the Dassault Etendard. This was not before the Naval prototype M05 had carried out a series of successful trials on the carrier simulator rig, and then, in 1970, from the French carrier *Clemenceau*.

With production orders first for 300 and then for 400 off, plus any exports that could be obtained, the Jaguar was the first example of how Europe could combine to get American-type production runs and the competitive costs which flow from such an arrangement. No one European nation could order anything like such a run of a modern warplane on its own. True, there were two assembly lines, one at Warton and the other at Toulouse, but final assembly was the only duplicated manufacturing process. This added something to the cost but, even so, the Jaguar was, and remained, a better buy for an aircraft of its performance and capabilities than anything else on the market. BAC had about 4000 people involved on its Jaguar programme, for which Mr T.O. Williams was the Production Manager and Ivan Yates the Project Manager. Breguet – later Breguet-Dassault, and finally (and inevitably) Dassault-Breguet – employed about the same numbers. There was no duplication in the fifty-fifty manufacturing programme, BAC making the rear fuselage, wings and tail, and Breguet the cockpit and centre section, each shipping completed parts to the other's assembly line.

The main problem which Jaguar had to face throughout all its early life was that the Adour engine was not coming on as well as it should. It was down on thrust, up on consumption and there were reheat problems.

The great Lord Hives is credited with the early remark that he suspected there was much more to reheat than just piddling fuel down the jet pipe, and so, in the Adour, it was to be. From time to time, angry words were spoken because the airframe manufacturers suspected that the Adour was very much secondary in Rolls-Royce minds to the big RB211 which was then on the go. Eventually a part-throttle reheat system, by which the pilot increased reheat percentage as he opened the taps, was successfully introduced. Brilliant though the Jaguar performance has proved to be in squadron service in both the French Air Force and the Royal Air Force, there is no doubt that, for certain battlefield close-support air-combat situations, it could, on delivery, have well done with a bit more power. Such extra power became available in the export version, the Jaguar International, which has two Adour 804 dash 26 engines of 5200 lb of dry thrust each, with a further Adour development to 6300 lb under way. The RAF later decided to take advantage of the dash 26 Adour to improve the Jaguar's agility in the combat role, and the existing Adour 102 engines were modified to provide the extra power.

As the French Air Force was to take first deliveries because its requirement timescale was earlier than that of the RAF, the first four of the eight development aircraft flew in France. The prototype aeroplane E (Ecole) 01 – the first French two-seater – was rolled out at Breguet's Villacoublay plant on 17 April 1968, for ground tests, and it was then taken by road to the Flight Test Centre at Istres, near Marseille. There, on 8 September of the same year, it flew, and by October it had been flown supersonically both by BAC's Jimmy Dell and Breguet's Bernard Witt. The next three aeroplanes, another French two-seater and two French single-seat strike aircraft, were all in the air early in 1969, and the first British Jaguar, the single-seat S06, flew on 12 October 1969.

This was a rapid programme by any standards for a sophisticated modern supersonic aeroplane; for one which had been the product of a two-nation collaborative enterprise, it was outstanding. There were some set-backs, including an engine fire warning in one aircraft, from which the pilot safely ejected, having 'lost' his controls when the emergency hydraulic system was not selected. But this apart, Jaguar sailed through its 3600-hour flight and service trials, and on 19 June 1973, the first French squadron, No. 1 of the 7th Wing, was officially formed, with much ceremony, at St Dizier. About the same time, the first RAF aircraft was delivered to Lossiemouth for engineering familiarisation. The nucleus of the first RAF squadron, No. 54, was formed also at Lossiemouth, in March 1974, and the squadron moved to its base at Coltishall in the July. Four weeks later, it was on overseas detachment in Denmark.

The main difference between the French and British versions of the Jaguar is that the RAF Jaguar has a more sophisticated nav-attack system. The Jaguar's main role in the Royal Air Force is low-level, high-speed interdiction and reconnaissance, and it is capable of carrying 10,000 lb of external stores for a radius of action which varies according to whether it is low level all the way or not, from 450 to 750 nautical miles. It can operate from grass fields, and has landed on and taken off from the M55 motorway.

The British nav-attack system, including laser ranging, although basically a daylight one, is extremely accurate at very low level. It is also designed for a 'one-pass' attack, so that the aircraft can come in fast and low and yet bomb accurately on the one run, hopefully before (should it be a point-defended target with surface-to-air missiles deployed around it) the SAM operators have realised that the Jaguars are among those present. The Jaguar's digital navigation and weapon aiming system (NAVWASS), produced by Marconi-Elliott, is designed to prevent the defenders getting the chance of a second shot.

The basic *en route* navigation system is also designed for minimum error. The safest path (or paths) to a target is pre-computed, allowing for terrain risks and enemy defences. A projected moving map display centred on the aircraft's present position enables the pilot to identify fixes and, if necessary, to update the sortie. For a target whose geographical position is already known (e.g., a bridge), the pilot can acquire it early and accurately, as Jaguar has an inertial navigation system giving both ground speed and position information even when the aircraft is banking or pitching. Once the target has been acquired, the automatic weapon aiming and release system, including Ferranti laser ranging, takes over, and the digital computer provides the pilot with head-up display instructions. If he follows the indicated flight path, the system will do the rest, including weapon-release. For targets of opportunity, the attack system can take over as soon as a target has been seen, but after that the weapon delivery is just as accurate as with a pre-computed objective. After the 'one-pass' attack for which the Jaguar is intended, the navigation system can also be set to provide the best 'escape and return' route to base.

The accuracy achieved by Jaguars since they entered service has been described as 'remarkable' by both the Royal Air Force and the French

Air Force, and there is little doubt that Jaguar is the most potent tactical strike weapon the RAF has ever had. All eight RAF Jaguar squadrons are assigned to NATO, where part of their task is to hit at the preponderance of Warsaw Pact tanks, and to make interdiction raids behind the enemy front. RAF Jaguars are mainly single-seaters, the pilot relying on the Head-Up Display (HUD) which puts all his required information on to the windscreen in his normal line of vision. The two-seat trainer Jaguars are fully operational, but have all the displays available on the screens of both cockpits.

One other of the Jaguar requirements not so far mentioned, but laid down from the very beginning, was for ease and speed of field maintenance so as to cut back substantially on engineering man-hours. Considerable design ingenuity was shown to achieve this, provision being made for rapid engine changes and almost instant access to any part of the aircraft. There are, for example, nearly 400 quick-release panels comprising some 30 per cent of the aircraft's surface. To back this up, there is a most comprehensive Anglo-French spares supply organisation based in Europe.

At the time of nationalisation, a number of development improvements were already in hand for the Jaguar International model, apart from the more powerful Adours. These included giving the aircraft an improved low-visibility capability and provision for overwing air-to-air missiles such as the Matra Magic or the Sidewinder without interfering with the underwing attack stores. The Agave radar can be fitted, and this is optimised for anti-ship operations. Jaguar with Agave can thus launch weapons such as Exocet, Harpoon and Martel. Jaguar exports had already begun at nationalisation, with sales worth £80 million to Oman and one other foreign air force, later named as Ecuador. Before very long, these were followed by the painstakingly negotiated order from India.

One of the favourite questions at BAC Press conferences on Jaguar used to be how it would fare against BAC's own remarkable Rapier low-level anti-aircraft missile system which has a very rapid reaction time and a formidable kill rate. There was, of course, no practical answer to this save to say that, in designing for Jaguar's low-level performance, the aircraft side of BAC had full access to the Guided Weapons data on Rapier and vice-versa. What is for certain is that strike aircraft which attack at medium and high altitude are easy meat for any modern defence, and this was clearly shown in the Middle East wars when fighter-bombers pulling up from low level in order to acquire their targets prior to a dive on them were shot down by SAMs with great regularity. Low level – and the lower the better – is the only way to tackle defended territory, be it by manned aircraft or drones. The sudden tree-top arrival on any scene of a formation of Jaguars at near transonic speed must tax the resources of any defence. Further, not even the major powers can afford to deploy modern SAMs to surround every target, and especially not so in a mobile situation. The development of downward-looking radar aircraft to warn against ground-hugging attackers is the latest move in the never-ending struggle between the technologies of attack and defence, but such an aircraft would be very vulnerable if placed over the battlefield and, if high and distant, would also attract opposition. The developing science of electronic counter-measures also has to be taken into account, but the general low-level tactical situation could well require a new generation of high perform-ance, low-altitude, battlefield fighters armed with downward-firing missiles. Meanwhile, Jaguar has a high survival capability, even in a SAM environment, and it also has the ability, especially in the International model, to take on any pursuers either with its standard cannon or air-to-air missiles. It is not, however, and never was intended to be, an interceptor-fighter in the World War I or World War II sense.

As indicated earlier in this chapter, there were acute problems on the Sales side from the time Dassault took control of Breguet and therefore of the French half of Jaguar. Paul Jaillard, who was very much liked by all his British colleagues, was placed in an almost impossible position as quite often the French were trying to sell the Dassault F1 fighter (in the guise of a fighter-bomber) against the Jaguar. To help them in this they had, of course, all Jaguar performance and cost data, and were able to highlight any development problem of the day, while keeping silent on any hitches with the F1. The French were, by various stratagems, also able at one time, to keep the cost quotation of possible export Jaguars high and to delay deliveries. Especially was this so in India long after the Indian Air Force had announced that its technical evaluation was in favour of Jaguar. Dassault was, in the end, unable to stop the Indian Jaguars, but it certainly delayed them considerably.

It was not until 6 October 1978, that the Indian Government finally announced that it had chosen the Jaguar International to replace the IAF's Canberras and Hunters. The announcement stated that the Mirage F1 and the Swedish Viggen had also been fully evaluated, but the Jaguar had been chosen because it was the most economic of the three options, and had the most favourable delivery dates. It also 'had an edge over the other two aircraft in the important characteristic of survival capability.' Under the agreement, signed for what was by now British Aerospace by Freddie Page, British Aerospace was to make the first few aircraft while helping to set up licensed manufacture in India at Hindustan Aero-nautics, where some three-quarters of the unspecified total number of Jaguars would be built. Ivan Yates, who had done so much to make the Jaguar a technical success, and who was by 1978 Divisional Managing Director, Warton, sent Alan Keys, who with Quill, had worked hard on the sale from the outset, to New Delhi as Executive Director India, co-operating with the Indian Government and with a support organisation at Warton under its Commercial Director, Mr R.H. Evans, who also became Director-in-Charge (India).

The Dassault public argument was that the F1 and the Jaguar were 'complementary' aircraft and that the French Air Force, for this reason, was equipped with both. If a foreign air force needed fighters, they said, they pushed the FI, and if they needed strike aircraft, then they advocated Jaguar. This was not the case. If the main requirement was for strike, Dassault still, as in India, offered the FI, but with a specially developed attack 'fit' which had nothing like the low-level specialised nav-attack system of the UK's Jaguar S model.

At one time in the early 1970s, the Dassault denigration of the Jaguar in favour of the FI became so bad that Sir George publicly spoke out against it and queried the French interpretation of the meaning of the word 'partnership.'

This Dassault determination to sell French at all costs eventually led to a further domination of the European military market by the Americans when, in 1975, in the so-called 'Sale of the Century,' Belgium, Holland, Denmark and Norway all chose to re-equip with, collectively, some 350 of the General Dynamics F16, thus creating another F104 situation which the consortium of European NATO powers, Eurogroup, including all the customer nations, had been formed, among other things, to avoid if possible.

The two main air forces concerned were those of Belgium and the Netherlands, whose key task for NATO was specifically one of ground attack, with a squadron or two of interceptor fighters understandably held back to defend national air space. A decision was made to buy just one type of aircraft to fill both the main task of strike and to re-equip the purely fighter squadrons. This was a very challengeable concept as strike sorties against the sophisticated defences of the Warsaw Pact powers are no job for a fighter-bomber, but require a specialist design such as the Jaguar. This indeed was France's own procurement philosophy, which is why she herself is equipped with Jaguars as well as FIs. Dassault, however, was convinced, because of its very close association with the Belgian Government and by the fact that it had a Belgian factory, that if a 'one aircraft' philosophy was adopted it would win the entire order with the FI.

BAC, which also had good contacts in Europe, believed otherwise, with, as it turned out, very good reason. BAC, therefore, suggested to Dassault that a two-nation approach be made initially to Belgium and Holland, querying the soundness of trying to fill two different air defence roles with one aircraft, and suggesting instead a two-aeroplane solution – Jaguars for strike and FIs for defence. 'In that way,' said BAC, 'you, Dassault, get all the fighter and half the strike work, and this considerable order in Europe can then be filled by Europe and not by the Americans, and furthermore NATO strike ability will be the more credible as a result.'

'No,' replied Dassault. 'We are confident the FI will get the whole order and there is no reason why we should support a scheme which would give any part of it to Britain.'

All attempts, including at high level, to forewarn Dassault of the mounting evidence that either the American F16 or F17 would win over the F1 on sheer high-altitude fighter performance grounds fell on deaf ears, and so BAC mounted its own campaign in all four countries concerned for the 'two-aircraft' solution. Full documentation was issued to show that it was not only much more efficient militarily, but also cheaper and that BAC could match any local manufacture 'package deal' which the USA could offer.

At this stage it was BAC's researched belief that a combined Dassault/BAC offer of F1 and Jaguar would be acceptable, and it turned to the Government for support for the two-aircraft proposal, and also for UK diplomatic support. Unfortunately, Mr Roy Mason, the then Minister of Defence and, as it happened, the Chairman of Eurogroup, said the decision to buy just one type of aeroplane to fill both tasks was one which was for the countries concerned alone, and that British Government support for the two-aeroplane solution would not be fitting. No official help, therefore, was given to BAC; in fact exactly the opposite and, as a result, the USA established the F16 in Europe – and so repeated their earlier F104 domination. This was a success which Dassault almost certainly and the Government most probably could at one time have prevented. By contrast, the combined US industry and diplomatic 'offensive' to sell the F16 was an object lesson. Even high-ranking USAF officers in NATO weighed in with support for the F16, even though the clever but by no means Jaguar-equalling ground attack fit for it meant that NATO would not have the best aeroplane for its main air task of hitting the Russian tanks while reducing, by airfield attacks, the enemy's own air sortie rate.

The whole sad story left BAC, not for the first time, disillusioned, not only by lack of support at home, but by the fact that France, a non-NATO country – or, as someone said, only 'NATO *à la carte*' – should have had so much initially to do with the shaping of a key part of NATO's preparedness. As a result, the whole steamroller weight of American united salesmanship then succeeded in placing a compromise aeroplane at the forefront of allied defence.

21

Take-Over Threats

The success of the One-Eleven and Jaguar programmes and the collapse of the AF VG were all in the future when, in 1965/6, BAC faced its biggest-yet crisis, and indeed the biggest crisis it was ever to face until it was nationalised.

The cancellation of TSR2 had, in Sir George's words, 'knocked the stuffing out of BAC,' and he had so warned the Government, long before the event. On top of that, BOAC were attempting to cancel as many as they could of the Super VC10s, while the development costs of the One-Eleven 200 and 300/400 Series were mounting to over the £30 million mark, with only a £9.75 million launching-cost grant from the Ministry of Aviation. TSR2 cancellation 'hardship' costs were being haggled over, and, because of all the adverse publicity over TSR2 and the VC10, there was a collapse of confidence among potential customers abroad in the future viability of BAC.

Sir George was (June 1965) spending nearly all his time in Whitehall ('Pedalling up and down so fast that my feet are a blur') making sure that the Minister of Aviation (Jenkins), the Permanent Secretary (Sir Richard Way), the Junior Minister (John Stonehouse), and a whole host of officials were in no doubt about the seriousness of BAC's financial situation. His own private analysis of the position was that the company could barely keep its head above water. Roy Jenkins, for his part, was also having a fight with Sir Giles Guthrie over the VC10s, and told him that the seventeen Super VC10s were regarded as sacred by the Government and that he must take them. The Minister also supported a drive in favour of a proposed 'stretched' VC10 (the DB265) with a double-bubble fuselage and a 265-seat capacity. This aeroplane, which had Anglo-French potential (with Sud), and whose development costs were put at £40 million, flitted in and out of the 1965/6 picture, but in the end was not pursued.

About this time (mid-1965), Sir Richard Way told Sir George that the Government's interpretation of BAC's evidence to Plowden was that BAC's parents were not prepared to go on, and he (Sir Richard) asked what BAC needed in order to stay in business. Sir Richard also said he had taxed Sir Giles Guthrie with denigrating the VC10 (which was denied), but added that BAC could assume that the Ministry would ensure that, in future, Guthrie would not criticise the aircraft in such a way as to prejudice future sales. (There was, however, no noticeable abatement in the campaign.)

The short answer to Sir Richard Way's question as to what did BAC need to stay in business was 'money.' This, in turn, amounted to a quick settlement of BAC's claims for cancellation of the TSR2, and the resultant increased overhead costs which had now fallen on the civil work, for which fixed-price contracts had already been signed, plus a 50 per cent Government contribution to the actual launching costs of the One-Eleven 200, 300 and 400 Series. There was also the question of a then proposed One-Eleven 500 for BEA, which, if it went ahead, would require further Government launching cost aid as the 500 Series represented a considerable re-work of the 300/400 model. It would, however, stop BEA buying American at considerable dollar cost.

As seen in mid-1965, BAC needed something like £20 million to continue in reasonable shape, even at the reduced post-TSR2 scale of effort. The parents had already invested all they could prudently afford in BAC, and the company also carried a heavy burden of interest on loans from the FCI and the banks.

It should be stated here that, all through the protracted negotiations which went on week in and week out through 1965 and 1966, the question mark over the future of the British aircraft industry in general and BAC in particular, after the 1965 cancellations, was scarcely ever out of the newspaper headlines. BOAC were continually leaking anti-VC10 'guidance,' and the opponents of Concorde both inside and outside the Government worked hard to create the impression that the SST programme would soon come to a sticky end. From France, there were later to come the first rumours that Dassault would, somehow or other, manage to overturn the Anglo-French military package in favour of an all-French programme. Plowden, too, was already holding its enquiry, and this gave rise to further speculative stories, mostly to the detriment of the industry.

In this context, it has to be remembered that Britain was, and is, in a unique position as far as media coverage of aviation is concerned. In the first place, it has a truly national Press in that the national dailies and Sundays cover the whole country, as do the news and current affairs services of BBC Radio and TV, and of ITV. This is not so at all in the USA, whose public is served by local media, and what is 'front page' in New York may not even get a mention in Chicago or Los Angeles. To a great extent, this is also true in France and Germany.

Furthermore, in Britain there is great competitive rivalry among the nationals, and the search for national exclusive news and 'revelations' is intense. Traditionally, each major weekday and Sunday newspaper and the BBC and ITN employs a specialist air correspondent, sometimes 'doubling' on defence, and each of these correspondents is properly expected to show great energy in bringing to the country's attention every aspect of the doings and news of the aircraft industry and of the ups and downs of its products and projects. This emphasis on day-to-day reporting and comment on aviation is also unique to Britain. In the USA, very few newspapers employ an aviation specialist. There are three or four in Paris and one or two in Germany, but only in Britain is there this highly competitive media concentration on aviation, the results of which can be served up nationwide in the course of one day. This is something which the British industry has always had to live with, and, to be fair, has sometimes gained advantage from.

In 1965 and 1966, however, the picture presented to the country, and to the outside world, was one of almost continuous gloom and doom when even a burst tyre on a development aeroplane could win banner headlines or be the occasion of a TV debate as to whether the project should be scrapped. The net result of all this was, inevitably, that potential overseas customers began to doubt the wisdom of having anything to do with British aircraft. It did not seem to them that BAC, in particular, was likely to continue in business, and the huge orders placed by the Wilson Government in the USA seemed to them to be preparatory to the British Government withdrawing any support whatever from the British aircraft industry. Ministerial statements of Government belief in the vital nature of a strong industry were openly described as eyewash, and it is a remarkable tribute to the BAC Civil Sales team that it managed to get such One-Eleven orders as it did during those controversial years. The Americans had a field-day merely by circulating copies of UK media reports, and, in one case, undoubtedly killed a VC10 sale by this method.

BAC's own appreciation of its immediate post-TSR2 position was that, from 1966 to 1968, Filton would be dependent upon developing Concorde, but from 1968 onwards further employment would rest on Concorde production, which was far from assured. In the absence of this, Filton would probably have to be reduced to little more than a flight test and service department. Preston, however, was in better shape with Lightning and Canberra work, the introduction of the two Anglo-French military projects, and the movement from Luton (to be closed in 1966) of the Jet Provost. These programmes seemed to promise a settled position into the 1970s, with reasonable profits. The Guided Weapons Division also had a reasonable turnover and profits.

Weybridge and the civil projects, however, were another story. The deficit on the One-Eleven, caused by the costs of new developments swallowing up the narrow profit margin on the earlier aeroplanes, was already £16 million, with little indication that the limit had been reached. Weybridge (including Hurn), now minus TSR2, and with all overheads descending on the One-Eleven, was the nub of BAC's problem.

What was urgently needed was for the Government to take half the launching costs of existing One-Eleven versions, which had now reached £32 million, but towards which the Ministry had contributed less than £10 million. The 500 Series would be a separate issue, and at least a 50 per cent grant would be needed towards that as well. Alternatively, and in the special circumstances, the Government might be persuaded to provide 75 per cent of launching aid for the existing One-Eleven models, that sum also to include the Mark 500. If this happened, Weybridge could become solvent, based on deliveries of a further sixty aircraft from 1967 to 1969, on top of the seventy-seven aircraft already due for completion by 1966. Other forecasts, made on a pessimistic basis of sales and of Government aid, however, showed such losses as to make the closure of Hurn, the Wisley test centre, and probably Weybridge, to be likely by 1969.

It would be wearisome to catalogue all the meetings, proposals, and counter-proposals which went on during 1965 and 1966 on this broad issue. The Ministry kept promising quick settlement of TSR2 claims, but settlement-day never seemed to arrive. With each delay, BAC's cash position became worse, and the disappearance of the civil side of the company the more likely. Sir George had repeatedly to remind the Ministry that TSR2 was not cancelled because of a change of defence policy, for which a proper break-closure procedure existed, but because of a change of procurement policy (the F111) and that was a different thing. There was disagreement on profit rates to be allowed, and on the civil overheads case, and, at one time, Counsel's opinion was sought. On the Government side, there was a brief suggestion of a £20 million interest-free loan as a BAC 'rescue act,' although the sales danger of BAC being publicly seen to be in need of 'rescue' to survive, was fully appreciated by both sides.

At one time, it seemed to be agreed by the Ministry of Aviation that a 50 per cent contribution to the actual launching costs of the One-Eleven, plus something like £10 million TSR2 compensation, would be forthcoming, the Ministry being satisfied that BAC needed this cash injection to stay in business. In October 1965, Sir George told Sir Richard Way that the situation boiled down to an immediate need by BAC of £20 million – whether it came from One-Eleven launching aid contributions, or TSR2 compensation, or a bit of both. The position, he said, was desperate.

By 3 November, Lord Portal was writing to Jenkins, reminding him of assurances that decisions would be made by the end of September on the total amount which would be paid in respect of claims arising from the TSR2, whether directly under the contract or consequentially, including the effect on the One-Eleven. These claims had been submitted and examined by the Ministry accountants, yet decisions had now been further delayed for an indefinite period. At best, BAC could expect a minor payment on account.

'It is,' concluded Lord Portal, 'financially impracticable to go on in this way, and, in the absence of substantial payments . . . we must take immediate drastic action to reduce our activities to the level that the present and prospective financial resources will permit. The effect of action on these lines is so far-reaching, affecting customers and potential customers, suppliers, employees, bankers and shareholders, that a proper statement of the reasons giving rise to it must be made . . . we cannot further delay implementing our intention beyond another week or ten days at the outside.'

Roy Jenkins replied on 9 November, suggesting a meeting at the earliest possible moment, and asking what was meant by 'immediate drastic action.' To this query, Lord Portal replied that it meant running down production and design teams, disposing of sales teams which would no longer be required, and thus rapidly arriving at the point at which there would be no civil business. The Chairman then reminded the Minister that, in the last ten years, the companies in BAC had sold for export £300 million worth of civil aircraft and spares, and home sales of the same aircraft had amounted to a further £300 million – a total contribution to the balance of payments of £600 million. BAC had already reduced its manpower by approximately 8000 in the past twelve months, was selling Luton, and, on present indications, would close Hurn, Samlesbury and the Cardiff Guided Weapons facility before the end of 1967.

The Jenkins meeting took place on 16 November, and the Minister promised to support 50 per cent of the actual cost to date of the One-Eleven 200, 300 and 400 Series and 50 per cent of the estimated cost to complete. This would be £6.75 million additional to the £9.75 million already paid – a sum disputed by BAC as an under-estimate. In return, BAC was to withdraw its hardship claim on TSR2, but other TSR2 issues, such as the rate of profit and the excess overheads, were to remain open. Any further steps would have to await the recommendations of the Plowden Committee. The Ministry of Aviation put the latest proposals, notably the grant towards the One-Eleven, to the Treasury, who were expected to approve. In a bombshell decision, the Chancellor turned the Ministry of Aviation down – this, it was later alleged, being part of a ploy to soften BAC for easy nationalisation and merger with Hawker Siddeley.

At this critical stage, Roy Jenkins was translated from Aviation to the Home Office, and he was succeeded by Fred Mulley. The new Minister formally wrote to Lord Portal in a letter dated 11 February 1966, but not posted until 14 February, setting out the decision that there was to be no further Government contribution to the One-Eleven, or payment for the TSR2 'hardship' claim, and no payment for the loss of profit other than that on work done to the time of cancellation. He was, however, prepared to consider a substantial loan to meet BAC's needs for working capital – interest payable at Bank Rate and repayable from 1 January 1967.

This decision, which went in face of all the Government promises and

half-promises which had been so painstakingly discussed and documented throughout most of 1965, was clearly written in the light of the
December Plowden report. This report, as has been seen, recommended
the Government take shares in the two airframe companies, BAC and
Hawker Siddeley, and, while coming to no firm conclusion as to
whether the two firms should be merged, added that the Government
should not seek artificially to maintain the present two-group structure.

The facts of the letter were already known to BAC, and there had been
a meeting with the new Minister on 4 January 1966, on the Plowden
issue before the 14 February communication. From then on, the
question of support for the One-Eleven and the TSR2 claims became
'leverage' in what amounted to take-over proposals by the Government
of BAC.

At this 4 January meeting, which was a bitter one, Lord Portal, Sir
George Edwards, and William Masterton represented BAC. Lord Portal
emphasised that the BAC parents would not enter into any discussions on
Government shareholding until confidence had been re-established.
Payment of an £8.25 million BAC outstanding claim on TSR2
cancellation had been supported by the Ministry and, if it was paid, BAC
would be co-operative in discussing Plowden. Mulley recognised that
BAC had a proper claim, but if they would only talk if their claim was
settled then an element of duress would be introduced which would not
please the Cabinet and could react to the company's disadvantage. Lord
Portal thought the duress was the other way. There were many who
thought and said that the Government had set out to ruin BAC and get a
cheap take-over. While these feelings were in people's minds, there
could be no friendly negotiations. He was not talking about the Ministry
of Aviation, who had been helpful, but about the Government as a
whole.

Sir George emphasised the damage that was already being done by
Plowden, especially in France, who were having misgivings about co-
operating with the UK on simple projects if the Government accepted
the Plowden view that the UK would turn to the USA for big projects.
The UK had the basic ingenuity and ingredients to do any aeronautical
job, and the real problem affecting the industry was the frequency of
cancellations. His most important job was the preservation of the
structure of a balanced company. The last three years had been difficult,
but the last twelve months had been impossible. He moved on to the
absurd position with BOAC and the VC10, and the delay on the One-
Eleven 500 Series decision, as a result of which Aer Lingus had already
bought Boeing 737s. The Minister made it plain that the Government
was considering a majority shareholding in BAC, not a minority one, and
Lord Portal said, if that was the case, he thought the Government would
be obliged to take 100 per cent. In the end, it became clear that BAC
would not discuss the take-over or shareholding issue unless the TSR2
claims were paid, while the Government put the emphasis the other way

round. The Minister observed that, in view of BAC's attitude on the claims, he thought the Government would go ahead with its plans without the benefit of BAC's views or advice.

For much of 1966, BAC – spearheaded by its parents – fought off what was in effect an attempt by the Government to get BAC to agree to surrender itself to the Government. Had this been done, the Government proposed to merge BAC into Hawker Siddeley with the BAC interests very much in the minority. There was a General Election in April, from which Harold Wilson turned his slender majority into an overall one of ninety-seven, and Ministers were now more inclined to flex their muscles. There were also some important changes in the Government line-up. John Stonehouse, who had been a successful and friendly Junior Minister at the Ministry of Aviation, moved to the Colonial Office, and it was noted with considerable interest that Anthony Wedgwood Benn soon replaced Frank Cousins at the Ministry of Technology which took responsibility for all engineering, including shipbuilding, but not yet for aviation. In the view of most people, however, responsibility for what Wilson described as 'the monster' of the aircraft industry would shortly fall into the 'white heat' of Benn's Technology Ministry.

After the discussions on the purchase of BAC by the Government had started – which was before the election – Sir George fastened on one key point, namely, that the Government was completely wrong in its initial estimate of the low value of BAC, and the longer the negotiations were kept going, the more wrong the Government would get their sums.

There were full-scale post-election meetings between BAC and the Ministerial team in May, July and October of 1966, during which time Rolls-Royce had taken over Bristol Aeroplane and Bristol Siddeley Engines and was now in an engine monopoly situation. Rolls-Royce also, as a result of this merger, held the Bristol 20 per cent share of BAC, which suited neither company. Rolls-Royce simply wanted to get rid of their BAC shares, with first refusal, as required, to Vickers and English Electric, but, failing them, to the Government or Hawker or almost anyone. The two major BAC parents wanted none of the Hawker merger, as they would have important money still locked into BAC, but would then have no control over it whatever. Further, all BAC thinking would be opened up to its main UK competitor. If the Government was going to acquire BAC, then it would have to take over the lot, and do so at a proper valuation of the company and not a below-par one arrived at by the Government's continued failure to settle the TSR2 compensation, or to come in fifty-fifty, as promised, on the One-Eleven development costs.

BAC had no confidence in the Government's good faith, and Lord Portal told them so. A further ploy to make BAC seem of little worth stemmed from a very shaky and ill-found estimate of BAC's share price, based on what Rolls-Royce had paid for Bristol, including the 20 per cent of BAC. Both Masterton and Sir Reginald stressed that such a method of 'pricing' BAC was, to put it politely, unsound. As to the merger with Hawker, no one in BAC or the parents wanted anything to do with it. The Operating Board and the BAC Divisional Management also made it quite clear that they were unwilling to work with Hawker and surrender control of projects which they had brought to fruition to people who knew nothing of these projects.

Sir James MacKay of the Ministry of Aviation tried hard to win Sir George round to the idea of a merged company and hinted heavily that Sir George would be the 'big wheel' in the new combine. Sir George replied with all the emphasis at his command that he would have nothing to do with it. Such a merger was wrong in principle, it would upset all the project management teams at a time when they were just getting over the upheavals of the 1960 merger into BAC, and it was not relevant to the situation in the industry.

Lord Portal failed to see what would be accomplished by forcing a merger upon people who didn't want it and who, consequently, would be unhappy, unsettled and discouraged. Lord Nelson made it clear that, if the Government did take over BAC, English Electric would wish to retain the Guided Weapons Division. It was several times suggested to the Government that, if they only settled BAC's outstanding cash claims, BAC was quite prepared to carry on as a private company and felt it could do so profitably.

About this time (summer 1966), Sir George was also warning the Ministry of Defence that he doubted French intention to stay in the AFVG programme. If the Ministry of Defence and the Government wanted to preserve any British ability to design supersonic military aircraft for its own Forces (BAC being the only company with supersonic experience), then the Ministry of Defence should think in terms of a back-up to the AFVG. This could take the form of a British go-it-alone, variable-geometry, multi-role aircraft which could be activated if (in Sir George's view 'when') the French pulled out.

Towards the end of 1966, it became clear to the Government that BAC was genuinely holding the position it had held all along: that settlement of its claims was a necessary prelude to any free discussions as to the sale of its shares to the Government, and that BAC would take no part in any merger talks with Hawker. The Minister then decided to make a pre-emptive statement in the House of Commons, which he did on 21 November, saying that the Government had come to the conclusion that the national interest would best be served by a merger of the airframe interests of BAC and Hawker Siddeley into a single company. It was the Government's intention to take a substantial minority interest in the new company. (The 'minority' interest would come from its total ownership of BAC.)

Soon after this statement, Lord Portal issued a notice to BAC employees saying that the Board had undertaken to co-operate with the

Government and examine the Minister's proposal, but the discussions were likely to be prolonged and the conclusions difficult to foresee. The Chairman assured all employees that their personal welfare was very much in the Board's mind, and advised them to treat with caution any Press speculation or reports which did not come either from BAC or the Minister. He then reminded them that there was a great deal of work to do in meeting BAC's firm order book, and it was in everyone's best interests just to press on vigorously with the work in hand. As far as possible the Board would keep them informed.

The BAC parents were, of course, the shareholders with whom the Government would have to negotiate, and on 7 December, Lord Nelson (English Electric) and Sir Charles Dunphie (Vickers), together with Sir Reginald Verdon-Smith, met Fred Mulley who was accompanied by Sir James MacKay, Mr Snow, the Junior Minister, and other officials. It was explained to the Minister that the position of Rolls-Royce was different from that of Vickers and English Electric because Rolls-Royce were willing sellers of their inherited 20 per cent interest in BAC. Under the terms of the setting up of BAC, Vickers and English Electric had first option on buying the Rolls-Royce-held shares and had been asked if they wanted to exercise that option. This was being considered by Vickers and English Electric.

The parents stressed the long period of uncertainty which had already followed Plowden, and the dangers of losing key staff. In their view, the Government should proceed in two stages – first, purchasing the shares in BAC, and second, negotiating a merger between the then Government-owned BAC and Hawker. To try to do the two stages together would be wrong, and, in any event, BAC would not participate in, or associate themselves with, the problems of merging with Hawker Siddeley. The BAC parents confirmed that they would not wish to participate in any way in the new merged company, nor would they engage in tripartite Government/BAC/Hawker negotiations.

The Minister observed that, while a merged company was the Government objective, this was dependent on arriving at an agreed valuation for BAC shares and assets, and the plan could not go through if such an agreement proved to be unobtainable. The political difficulty of two steps was that he could not seek Parliamentary approval of the purchase of BAC without knowing that this could form a satisfactory basis for a merger with Hawker. To this, the parents replied that that was his problem. English Electric asked for a separate valuation for the Guided Weapons interests which it wanted to retain as part-payment for its share of BAC. The Minister would not undertake to leave Guided Weapons out of the merger, and Lord Nelson said in that case it would be difficult for them to agree to negotiations going forward. The Minister was also reminded of the 'old account/new account' situation in BAC, in which the parents had retained a considerable direct investment.

This was an important meeting because the Government did not have a mandate to take over BAC, and, with Parliamentary time at a premium, Mulley's main practicable way of bringing about his desired one-company objective, was to negotiate a proper purchase of BAC as between willing sellers and a willing buyer at an agreed valuation for the company. Teams were established on both sides for this purpose, the two main parents still being willing to sell – but only at a proper price. Behind the scenes, however, Vickers were beginning to have second thoughts as they (and the Minister) knew that many senior BAC people would refuse to work under Hawker Siddeley who would control the new company with a proposed 70 per cent holding to the Government's (ex-BAC) 30 per cent. In arriving at this percentage, the Government were clearly undervaluing BAC whose parents believed their company was at least as well-found and valuable as the Hawker Siddeley Aviation interests, if not more so. English Electric were also making their retention of Guided Weapons a condition of sale, and it was a condition the Government might well not meet.

Sir George had believed for some time that the proposed 'rationalisation' was wrong for the country. Key BAC men were already under recruiting pressure to join Lockheed, General Dynamics, and other US firms, and, if they did so, then BAC's main projects, including Concorde, would collapse, as Hawker, in his view, did not have the technical strength to take the work over and bring it to fruition. A Hawker take-over, as proposed by Mulley, would lead to most of the top men in BAC, himself included, getting out of the British industry. Lord Portal shared Sir George's views, and was very worried about the Defence aspect.

As Sir George was to say later, the clear way to meet the situation was to play it as slowly as possible. Sooner or later, the Government would have to settle on TSR2 and take its once promised fifty-fifty share of One-Eleven launching costs. The proposed One-Eleven 500 for BEA was looking promising (1966) and the alternative to it was a big dollar spend which, after the VC10 rumpus, would not be popular in the country. This would be especially so as the One-Eleven had already been deemed good enough by leading US operators. 'Time,' said Sir George, 'was on our side for a change. I could see that BAC's value would go up and up, especially as we had recently strengthened our contacts with Saudi Arabia (discussed later). On the other hand, Hawker were not all that well placed, and if the parents just hung on, the valuation position between us and Hawker would reverse itself. In any event, the BEA One-Eleven 500 decision could not hang around any longer. If BEA was to buy British as per the Government edict, then the Government had got to fund the 500, and this would give us a new lease of One-Eleven life and make BAC a pretty valuable property.'

Sir George was soon proved right about the One-Eleven 500: BEA accepted the aeroplane at the end of 1966 and the Government agreed – they had little option – to fund its development costs to the 100 per cent extent of £9 million.

As things turned out, the Government itself dillied and dallied throughout most of 1967 on the so-called 'merger' issue. At first, it was calling for a clear decision and an agreement on valuations by May 1967 at the latest. A variety of different proposals were looked at by BAC and by the financial advisors on both sides (Cooper Brothers for BAC and Binder Hamlyn for the Government). These included – if only briefly – the setting up of a Government Aircraft Investment Company to hold a third of BAC and of Hawker, plus the Government's $69\frac{1}{2}$ per cent of Shorts and possibly all of Beagle. But the stumbling block each time was the price to be paid for BAC or any part of same. BAC's own valuation of itself was around the £75 million mark, and the Government sum was, at one time, as low as £25 million.

The May deadline came and went, and by July BAC was complaining bitterly through Lord Nelson to Wedgwood Benn (the Ministry of Technology was now, as forecast, responsible for the aircraft industry) about the effect on morale and credibility which all the uncertainty was creating. Reports began to filter from the Ministry of Technology from August 1967 that maybe the Minister was thinking that the Plowden proposals of December 1965 and the 1966 Mulley policy of buying BAC and then merging it into Hawker were not all that good. In August, the Permanent Secretary at the Ministry of Technology, Sir Ronald Melville, was writing to Lord Portal to say that the Minister needed more time to consider, and would examine the matter further after the holiday period. Meanwhile, the Ministry of Technology was not in a position to pursue negotiations. There was, in Melville's letter, an inference that the BAC Board actually wanted the Government to purchase BAC – an inference which Sandy Riddell, joint Managing Director of English Electric, was quick to jump on.

There were, thus, two important changes in outlook between December 1965 (Plowden), November 1966 (the Mulley policy statement) and August 1967. The BAC parents, who were, in 1966, content – on reasonable terms – to sell the company outright to the Government (but not content to any Governmental shareholding which meant that the parents had money tied down over which they had no control), were, by August 1967, not anxious to sell at all. This shift probably reflected the continuing steady export sales of the One-Eleven; the sale for £32 million (eighteen plus six optional) of One-Eleven 500s to BEA (January 1967), which launched another and bigger (99-seat) One-Eleven model on to the market; the growth of the Saudi business (discussed later); and the continuation of the Jaguar project at Preston, plus the injection at Preston of work on the RAF buy of Phantoms. As the prospects for BAC improved, so did its value, and, with no mandate for the outright nationalisation of BAC, and with little hope now of getting away with a bargain buy, the Government's enthusiasm for its November 1966 policy waned. In September 1967, BAC's position was further strengthened when, after over two years of unrelenting labour,

Jimmy Armitage was able to announce the final settlement of TSR2 claims, to bring the total sum to £13.25 million, with a further maximum sum of £750,000 for suppliers and sub-contractors.

In November 1967, the BAC parents, visibly strengthened in their resolve, sent what can only be described as a 'very tough' letter to Wedgwood Benn about the delays in deciding policy and their effect on BAC staff and on the company's ability to conduct its business. If no decision was reached by the end of the month, BAC would regard itself as relieved of the obligation (to co-operate with the Government) which it entered into in 1966 and would make this clear to the employees. The devaluation of the pound that month, and all its implications on public expenditure, virtually settled the matter, and the last enclosure in BAC's file on this whole long, drawn-out affair is a telex of a written answer by the Minister on 15 December 1967: 'Following devaluation, the Government are conducting a re-examination of their existing policies in a number of fields. It will, therefore, not be possible for the time being to proceed with the negotiations to implement the policy announced last year [on aircraft mergers]. I have so informed BAC and the Hawker Siddeley Group. I should like to reiterate that, in the Government's view, a merger of the aviation interests of these two companies is desirable.'

So, after two years of upset and upheaval and a year of detailed work and countless meetings which had tied down the efforts of the top executives and especially of the Financial Director, Willie Masterton, the whole of this first merger attempt ended – 'Not,' as Sir Reginald Verdon-Smith commented, 'with a bang, but with a whimper.'

22

Riding the Storm

Because of all the uncertainties, the arguments over TSR2 claims, and the nature of the merger negotiations, Lord Portal made no public statement of BAC's financial position and prospects between 1965 (*A Critical Year for the Aircraft Industry*) and his review of the year 1967, which also incorporated references to 1966.

Heading it *Two Encouraging Years*, the Chairman referred to the Government's decision of December 1967 not, for the time being, to proceed with the merger policy, and BAC's consequent intention to proceed as a private company. He said that BAC had made a remarkable recovery from the shattering blow of the TSR2 which, because of over-dependence on one key project, had threatened the stability and even the viability of the whole Corporation.

The report went on to say that the success of the BAC Sales teams, notably those engaged on Lightning and One-Eleven, had played a major part in re-establishing a balanced position. By the end of 1967, the workload in the four Divisions of BAC (Weybridge, Filton, Preston and Guided Weapons) was at a level which could hardly have been hoped for in mid-1965. BAC was able to pay dividends of 6 per cent in 1966 and $7\frac{1}{2}$ per cent in 1967. In the three years ending June 1967, BAC had exported products to a value of £152 million, and the export order book then stood at another £113 million, which, by December 1967, had expanded to £200 million.

The Corporation (continued the Chairman) had gained two Queen's Awards for Export – one for £58.9 million in the year ended June 1966, and another for £68 million in the year ended June 1967. Lord Portal pointed out that in 1965/6 and 1966/7, BAC, with 16 per cent of the industry's employees, contributed 32 per cent and 34 per cent respectively of the industry's record total of exports. In both those years, BAC had exported more than half of its total output and this proportion was increasing. The exports per employee were nearly £2000, compared with the £500 per employee average of UK manufacturing industries, and the £750 per employee of total UK aerospace – including BAC.

The report showed a 1967 total turnover for BAC of £158 million, on which a trading profit of £7,058,000 was made before interest and taxation. Of this, £3,199,000 was 'old account,' and £3,850,000 'new account.' After interest of £1,700,000, and tax, the net profit was £1,533,000. The balance from 1966, after the transfer of £750,000 to the Deferred Taxation Account, was £1,401,000 – giving an available total of £2,930,000. Dividends of £1,500,000 having been paid, the balance of £1,434,000 had been carried forward. The order book at 30 December 1969, stood at over £239.5 million, and orders already received in 1968 were £150 million – excluding Concorde options and Jaguar.

Lord Portal laid particular stress on two themes which BAC sought all through its existence to hammer home to successive Governments and to the British people; first, that Great Britain had the most complete and experienced aerospace industry in Europe in all fields – airframes, engines, weapons, equipment and facilities; second, that BAC favoured collaborative projects, but such projects could only be a commercial success if the end-product was marketable. He quoted John Stonehouse (now back again as Minister of Aviation under Wedgwood Benn at the Ministry of Technology) as estimating the western world civil-aircraft business in the second half of the 1970s as being worth up to £1700 million a year and the military aircraft market in the 1970s in Europe alone as up to £3000 million. 'BAC,' added Lord Portal, 'is probably the best qualified of all European aircraft companies to play the leading part in obtaining for Great Britain and Europe an increasing share of these huge markets.' He noted that products of BAC factories were already in service in, or on order for, over half of all the countries in the world.

Lord Portal had very good reason for stressing these points. It had already come out in Plowden and in subsequent thinking, duly reflected in the media, that, broadly speaking, in Whitehall's view, there was not all that much future in the aircraft industry. The mandarins, it appeared, were quite prepared to sacrifice the airframe side to promote the Rolls-Royce engine company, and the Government had, in apparent pursuit of an anti-airframe posture, just killed three major British military projects in favour of financially disastrous purchases from the USA. The 160 Phantoms alone had cost £415 million. France, on the other hand, was busy seizing every opportunity to take over the British position in airframes in the hope, as has been said before, that, in the long-term, Rolls-Royce would become virtually dependent on them for the ordering and development of any new engines required for what would be French-dominated aircraft projects. France would then have the option of keeping the UK airframe firms alive as sub-contractors, or of teaming up with the USA on engines to kill off Rolls-Royce, or of going in with Germany to the exclusion of the UK altogether. It must be remembered that, at this time, the UK was not in the EEC, and that de Gaulle had already rebuffed both Macmillan and Harold Wilson on the issue of joining. The people in the British industry did not blame the French for their single-minded nationalism – they merely envied it.

Although 1967 was overshadowed by the merger business and by the efforts made to launch the BAC Two-Eleven (described in the next chapter), a number of other important things were going on in BAC which led to the good workload referred to in the Chairman's report. Weybridge/Hurn were busy on the One-Eleven programme, and the last deliveries of VC10; Filton had rolled out its prototype Concorde 002 in December and the SST now represented a substantial programme. Preston had delivered its last Lightning to the Royal Air Force (August 1967) but private-venture development work initiated by Freddie Page to produce a ground-attack version of the Lightning had paid off handsomely with export orders from Saudi Arabia (as part of a big overall Saudi Defence package, fully described in chapter 33) and from Kuwait. The Jet Provost and its variants were still going strong with the development for export of the BAC 145 and BAC 167 versions (later named the Strikemaster) and of the pressurised Jet Provost for the Royal Air Force. There was also a valuable and continuing export trade in refurbished Canberras, already in service in fourteen Air Forces, plus, of course, Jaguar and the sub-contract work on the British Phantoms. At this stage, Preston could already boast of having obtained export orders worth some £160 million. The AFVG had, however, been cancelled, but the Government had funded studies for a purely British combat aircraft, locally known as the UKVG, more perhaps to keep together what was generally regarded as probably the best military design team in Europe, than with any serious intent of funding a new go-it-alone project. Sir George had, in fact, already received some heavy hints from Whitehall that a British go-it-alone aircraft was not on, and that a collaborative venture had to be found – hence all the UK activity to get into the European F104 replacement consortium out of which was eventually to emerge the MRCA.

The Guided Weapons Division had advanced the Rapier to firing trials, and the Swingfire was approaching delivery to the Royal Armoured Corps. The Division was doing steady business on the Space side as main contractor for the Skylark sounding rocket, and had, in May 1967, seen the successful launching of its Ariel 3, the first all-British satellite. There was also just coming into the mill a new Naval Defence weapon called Seawolf. Guided Weapons, however, had made one enormous export breakthrough, only to see it dashed away – a very big defence scheme contract with Libya, built round Thunderbird and Rapier. This very valuable order was negotiated throughout 1967 and formally signed on 30 April 1968, only to be terminated by the Libya *coup* in September 1969 (discussed later).

All in all, however, BAC, because it was a 'three-legged stool,' had survived and picked itself up off the ground by the end of 1967, thanks to the concerted efforts of Civil, Military and Guided Weapons. Its main shortages were a new civil project to supplement and then follow on the One-Eleven, and a replacement for the AFVG. The latter it was to get; the former was not to eventuate in BAC's lifetime.

There were some important personnel changes at BAC in 1967. Lord Caldecote decided to return to English Electric (though remaining on the BAC Board), and Charlie Houghton retired. As a result, G.R. Jefferson became, on 1 January 1968, Chairman as well as Managing Director of the Guided Weapons Division. Sir George became Managing Director as well as Executive Chairman of BAC (Operating), with Allen Greenwood as Assistant Managing Director. The sum total of this and other re-shuffles saw Freddie Page as Chairman and Managing Director at Preston, Geoffrey Knight as Chairman and Managing Director at Weybridge, and Dr A.E. Russell as Chairman at Filton, with George Gedge as his Managing Director – Gedge having a seat on the Operating Board. Jim Charlton, the BAC Secretary from the merger, relinquished his post to join another company and was succeeded by Brian Cookson, his No. 2 and head of the Legal Department. At Weybridge, Henry Gardner, at his own request, gave up his technical directorship to concentrate on long-term programmes and on education, in which he had always taken a great interest, and Ernie Marshall, who had had much to do with the VC10 programme, especially after the sad early death of Hugh Hemsley, became Technical Director.

During the end of 1967 and early 1968, a new BAC administrative block which had been built at Weybridge became, in effect, the operational headquarters of BAC (Operating), and a lot of the expensive Pall Mall space was relinquished, Lloyds Bank occupying more and more of the concrete box which had been erected on the site of the old Carlton Club and of which BAC were the first tenants. The Chairman, Financial Director, Sir Dermot Boyle and the Secretariat remained London-based, but Sir George's main office was at Weybridge, with a second office at Pall Mall. The drift to Weybridge continued through the succeeding years, especially so when Sir George became Chairman and had all his key staff within buzzing distance.

Allen Greenwood, in his new job as Assistant Managing Director, gave up his Sales responsibilities, Quill becoming, in effect, Chief Military Salesman, with Knight, though Chairman and Managing Director at Weybridge, remaining *de facto* head of the Civil Sales teams, with strong technical support from Derek Lambert, John Prothero-Thomas, Chris Hamshaw-Thomas and Roy Proctor at Weybridge and Pat Burgess from Filton on Concorde.

At this time, BAC possessed, and indeed continued to possess to the end, one of the finest civil aircraft technical sales and performance, and marketing analysis organisations in the world. It could produce, at the press of a computer button, information about the traffic, growth rates, frequencies, freight business, and airfield limitations of any city pairs on any airline, as well as its current equipment, predicted future needs, financial state, and so on. It could also produce, within days, and in-house, a printed brochure examining in the greatest detail the suitability of a One-Eleven or a Two-Eleven on an airline's network, and back up the brochure by what were admitted to be among the most coherent 'presentation' methods in the business. It was a tragedy that such a brilliant and innovative team of young engineers at both Weybridge and Filton was never to have another real, rather than paper, aeroplane to sell after the One-Eleven.

23

One-Eleven –
Two-Eleven – Airbus

Of enormous importance to BAC in this 1966/7 period was which
aircraft BEA would order for its fleet for the 1970s. The BEA procurement
position – already touched on in previous chapters – was that in the
summer of 1966 it had asked permission of the Minister of Aviation to
purchase a new all-Boeing fleet of B727s and B737s because its older
aircraft, Viscounts, Vanguards and Comets, were at a competitive
disadvantage. In August 1966, permission for this heavy American
purchase by BEA – hitherto an all-British airline, and a profitable one –
was refused by Fred Mulley who, in effect, told BEA to buy British again,
but gave an undertaking that the Government would see BEA would not
suffer financially as a result.

BAC offered instead of the B737 the 'stretched' BAC One-Eleven 500
Series aircraft, which offer, as has already been described, was successful.
Sir Reginald Verdon-Smith was later to say that obtaining this BEA
order was a 'turning point' for BAC. It certainly played a big part in
convincing the two main parents that retention of BAC was worth
fighting for, which was not noticeably the view they had – understandably – held in 1965.

On 27 January 1967, Sir George and Sir Anthony Milward,
Chairman of BEA, signed the £32 million order for eighteen One-
Eleven 500 aircraft. The BEA 500 had seating for ninety-nine passengers
on 950-mile stages (sixty passengers for over 1650 miles), and had 15 per
cent lower seat-mile costs than the earlier One-Elevens, and a cheaper
aircraft-mile cost than its competitors in the USA. This larger aircraft
($13\frac{1}{2}$ feet longer fuselage, extended wing tips, and maximum take-off
weight up to 91,000 lb from 87,000 lb), had been made possible by the
up-rating of the Spey from 11,400 lb static thrust to 12,000 lb. The
aircraft was to be used by BEA on its German network and some of its UK
domestics, and, for this purpose, had an enlarged freight hold.

BAC had also (as soon as an engine proposal was available, i.e., 1966)
come up with a proposed aeroplane to take the place of the BEA initial
choice of the Boeing 727–200 – the BAC Two-Eleven. Its British
competitor was the Trident 3B. BEA was very enthusiastic about the
Two-Eleven – so much so that Milward publicly stated it was the
aircraft he wanted, and that, had it been on offer in early 1966 (before

there was an engine), BEA would have selected it over the B727 in the first place. BEA was willing to place an order for thirty, plus ten on option, right away. The BAC Two-Eleven was based on two rear-mounted RB211 engines – a new Rolls-Royce proposal of, then, some 30,000 lb thrust. The aircraft carried more people than the B727 (203 as against 160) and it carried them further, more cheaply, and much more quietly. Both BAC and, later, Rolls-Royce were very keen to see that it was built. World market surveys showed that it had excellent export sales prospects and a success at least equal to that of the One-Eleven was confidently predicted for it and, beyond all doubt, would have been achieved.

Unfortunately, BAC's financial position in 1966/7 was such that it had nearly all the civil money it was capable of investing tied up in the earlier One-Elevens; to build the 500 Series and/or the Two-Eleven, the Government would have to meet most of the launching costs – not just a maximum of 50 per cent. In the case of the One-Eleven 500, the Government agreed to pay the development, to the extent of £9 million. The BAC Two-Eleven was, however, not a development of an existing aircraft, but a new aeroplane using a new engine, running the risks, it has to be admitted, of the green airframe and green engine combination which Sir George had disliked in the Vanguard. The launching costs were around £50 million for the airframe and the same for the engine, which was a lot of money, although the 30,000 lb engine and developments of it would have other very important markets, and the Two-Eleven also could expect substantial sales abroad.

The situation was overshadowed by the European Airbus which had started life as an Anglo-French discussion in 1964 and in which Germany began to take part in 1966.

The first BAC-Sud Aviation meeting to discuss a 'high-density short-range aircraft' was held, at Sud's request, in Paris on 24 July 1964, the Sud team being headed by Pierre Satre and that of BAC by Basil Stephenson and Ernie Marshall, thus involving the top civil design men from both companies. Consideration then centred on a 180–200 seater aircraft, initially for BEA and Air France, with a maximum range with maximum payload of 1000 n.m. to be in service in the mid-1970s. A twin-engined design was envisaged using unspecified engines of a new design and of 30,000–35,000 lb thrust.

This Anglo-French initiative soon had the blessing of both Sir George and of André Puget, and Allen Greenwood did all he could to help it along.

A project team was set up with M. Servanty of Sud and Ernie Marshall responsible for the engineering under the joint technical directorship of Satre and Stephenson. The project was given the French working name of 'Galion,' and regular meetings were held to define it and to examine the marketing side throughout much of 1965. Later the 'Galion' began to be slanted by the French towards the much bigger

Airbus, while BAC, with BEA in mind, wanted to stick to the 200-seater.

At Government level in the UK, France and Germany, it was the Airbus which finally gained support, and Wedgwood Benn also decided that the British participation in it should be given to Hawker, BAC being specifically excluded. The Airbus became a firm three-nation venture in the latter part of 1967, using a big proposed 50,000 lb Rolls-Royce engine, the RB207.

By this time, BAC, which had seen which way the 'Galion' was going, was already working in close relationship with BEA on the twin-engined BAC Two-Eleven, based, as already stated, on a new 30,000 lb Rolls-Royce engine, the RB211.

BAC's conviction in 1966 that the 200-seater was the right aeroplane to back was still being vindicated by airline sales in 1979, and by the UK's eventual (1979) decision to become a partner in the new cut-down version of the Airbus, the A310. In 1967, however, Britain was firmly committed to the 300-seater Airbus A300, but with the important firm proviso that a final decision to go ahead would depend upon the aircraft receiving total orders for seventy-five aircraft from the three national carriers concerned − those of the UK, France and Germany. As a 300-seater was too big for BEA, BAC pushed hard with the Two-Eleven, although there were doubts whether Rolls-Royce could handle both the 50,000 lb engine for the Airbus (the RB207) and its then smaller brother, the 30,000 lb RB211, for the Two-Eleven and maybe for a new Lockheed aeroplane. Rolls said they could, but clearly priority would have to be given to the Airbus engine, which now had Government backing.

The fight for the funds for the BAC Two-Eleven became, in effect, a fight against the Airbus (discussed later). On the side of the Two-Eleven were BEA, the Board of Trade, BAC, and Rolls, plus two further intending Two-Eleven customers, Laker and Autair. Against it were Wedgwood Benn and Stonehouse at the Ministry of Technology, who were insistent upon a European collaborative enterprise, i.e., the big Airbus, which had no firm customers.

The struggle became a very public one, and from the summer of 1967 onward the media was full of debate on whether the UK should back the Airbus or the BAC Two-Eleven, the latter for delivery to BEA (twelve aircraft) by the summer of 1972. All the professional market surveys were on the side of the 200-seater British aircraft with a range of 1500 miles. No airline in Europe then wanted a 300-seater, nor did those airlines which had ordered Boeing 747 Jumbos (i.e., most of them) want a second 50,000 lb engine, the RB207, to maintain, as well as the JT9Ds of the Jumbos. The 300-seater market lay mainly in the USA for the trunk carriers wanting a coast-to-coast range (which the Airbus did not have), and there were already US proposals to meet that market − the Lockheed TriStar and the Douglas DC10. In that competition a 'Euro-Bus' with RB207s would come a bad third.

On the other hand the world market for a 200-seater was put by BAC at 1500 to 1700, and Mr Stephen Wheatcroft estimated the demand in Europe alone as 300–400 aircraft. The only rival to the Two-Eleven was the 727–200 with 160 seats, which was too small, and very noisy at a time when aircraft noise had become a limiting factor on night movements. The BAC Two-Eleven would have been the quietest aeroplane then in use, and would also have had much better economics than the 727 and a better range. The main criticism of it was that it was not wide-bodied, but, thirteen years later, British Airways was to buy a fleet of the new and narrow-bodied Boeing 757s.

Looking back, and with the now knowledge of the subsequent 727 and 757 sales which the Two-Eleven might well have got, it is difficult to follow the logic which led the Government to support a 300-seater French-led 'Eurobus' powered by Rolls-Royce 50,000 lb thrust engines – a formula for which there was no identifiable demand – rather than the BAC Two-Eleven and the RB211 engine, for which there was a worldwide need.

On 15 August 1967, Sir George wrote to Milward:

Dear Sir Anthony,

British Aircraft Corporation are confident that the BAC Two-Eleven will capture a worthwhile share of the overseas market. Their increasing success in selling One-Elevens provides a natural outlet for the aeroplane, and the new specification made possible by the higher-powered engine undoubtedly increases its attractiveness world-wide.

In order to ensure that BEA, who have consistently supported the project since its inception, have a fleet of BAC Two-Elevens for operation in the Summer of 1972, BAC are, pending a final decision, continuing to work on the whole programme at their own expense.

It is hoped that this will go some way towards answering any comment that BAC is not, in fact, behind the aeroplane. Also, it has been suggested that the company is reluctant to carry a share of the development cost, and wishes the Government to take it all. This, in fact, is an academic issue until such time as there is a firm engine programme to which the airframe programme can be joined. When BAC know that the Rolls-Royce RB211 engine is to be available, then they will be prepared to discuss with the Government the best method by which the project can proceed and BEA can have the aeroplane they want.

Yours sincerely,
George Edwards

The text of the letter was released and published in most of the newspapers.

BAC also took full-page advertisements setting out the detail of its £530 million of exports and its home sales (frustrated imports) of a further £635 million, and stressing its hard-won acceptability all over the world as a builder of first-class airliners. The Ministry of Technology, however, had a completely closed mind on the subject, despite BEA making statement after statement that it wanted the BAC Two-Eleven, and that if it couldn't have it, it would stick out for 727s rather than Trident 3s.

All to no avail. The Airbus A300 and the RB207 were voted the available monies, and the Government regretted it could make no cash available for the BAC Two-Eleven.

What then followed was high comedy or tragedy, according to one's viewpoint. Predictably there was no interest from BEA, Air France or Lufthansa in the 300-seat Airbus with RB207s, but a lot of Lockheed interest in the RB211. Faced with the hard facts of life the UK eventually withdrew from the Airbus, while the RB207 was dropped at a cost of £2 million and the RB211 was funded after all. In the intense technical competition to get the Lockheed TriStar order, Rolls-Royce then over-reached themselves both technically and contractually and went bankrupt. Had they been doing the comparatively straightforward 30,000 lb RB211 for BAC in 1967, it is doubtful if they would have been pushed on initial performance or on contract into the tragedy of 1971.

Sir George discussed the 200-seater situation direct with the Prime Minister as early as July 1967 when he found himself seated opposite Mr Wilson at a National Gas Turbine Establishment luncheon. Sir George, in reply to a question from the Prime Minister, forecast total One-Eleven sales of 200 if there was no further Spey development and of 400 if there was. He also told him that the Airbus would be competing head on with US projects, but BAC could sell a lot of Two-Elevens. If money was available for only one project it should be the Two-Eleven. The Prime Minister was, Sir George later noted, fully aware of the Two-Eleven position, and he also indicated to Sir George that the Cabinet attitude to the industry was very anti. They thought the UK was just no good at aircraft (!).

In October of 1967, the Select Committee on Nationalised Industries issued its report on BEA, and underlined the new problems which arose from the manufacturers dealing with the Ministry of Technology and the airlines dealing with the Board of Trade − key information thus being exchanged at second-hand. It also queried the usefulness of the Transport Aircraft Requirements Committee, which no one seemed to consult. The report was based on evidence given in the summer of 1967, and underlined the solidarity of airline support for the BAC Two-Eleven, which only re-opened old wounds as the die was now cast for the Trident 3, though the actual purchase was not made until early 1968.

In his 1968 New Year's message to his staff at BEA, Sir Anthony Milward wrote, 'The Two-Eleven was, in my view, the finest and most advanced aircraft which this country could produce and incorporated the very latest in engine design, both as regards economy and, above all, quietness. It therefore grieves me very much that the Government should shy away from this project like a startled horse because "we cannot afford it." If we cannot afford the best, can we afford the second-best?'

So the Trident 3 it was, and the Two-Eleven died, to be succeeded in the BAC Project Office by the BAC Three-Eleven. The BEA claim for 'compensation,' as promised by Mulley, was not long in coming, and, perhaps more surprisingly, there was also a compensation claim for buying the One-Eleven 500s instead of B737s. The claims were mainly based on delvery dates, it being argued that, had BEA bought American, they would have had 727s and 737s much earlier than One-Eleven 500s (re-named Super One-Eleven) and Trident 3s, and that, because of the delay, they were losing money on their older equipment. Also, they would get the One-Elevens first − which, in their planning, was the wrong way round; they had wanted the bigger aeroplane first.

The Board of Trade eventually gave BEA £25 million by agreeing to write off about a quarter of the airline's capital debt. The announcement to this effect was made by Anthony Crosland, President of the Board of Trade, on 10 July 1968.

The decision was closely parallel to that when BOAC were told by Roy Jenkins that they could not back out of their Super VC10 order in favour of Boeing − the VC10, of course, having been tailor-made to BOAC's own specification. In that instance, in the capital re-structuring, BOAC were given £30 million for operating what later proved to be the most economical aircraft of their fleet.

The One-Eleven 500, having been put into production for BEA, went on to achieve sixty-one further sales by 1977, most of them for export. It is interesting that in the Nationalised Industries Report on BEA, Mr L. Williams, Under Secretary (Air) at the Ministry of Technology, is quoted as saying to the Committee that, in return for Government Sterling launching aid for a civil project, the Ministry would expect each £1 to produce between £5 and £10 gain to the balance of payments in actual exports or frustrated imports.

The application of this formula to all marks of the One-Eleven (£19 million total launching cost, minus £3 million direct re-payment = £16 million Government investment) shows a handsome overall national profit − inflation notwithstanding. On Mr Williams' evidence, a sales value of £160 million for One-Elevens would have been good value to the country on the £16 million launching aid. In fact the total sales of One-Elevens up to nationalisation had produced over £260 million in exports plus the home sales, or frustrated imports, worth over another £120 million, to eight UK operators, including BEA, who would otherwise have had to buy American. Even the VC10, with £9 million of unrecovered launching aid, certainly met this £10 for £1 Government criterion, as it produced much more than £90 million across the balance of payments. The engines used on the VC10 and the One-Eleven (the Conway and the Spey), practically cleared all their launching-aid money by direct re-payment levies, leaving all sales income as a benefit.

At this point, because UK financial commitment to it scuppered the BAC Two-Eleven and because the Rolls-Royce financial problems which arose from the RB207/RB211 programme left no monies for the later BAC Three-Eleven proposal, a fuller account of the origins of the European Airbus should be given. This was a French-dominated proposal which was pressed hard in various guises from 1966 as part of the overall plan to make France the centre of European airframe manufacture and the natural focus of European aerospace activity. It culminated in September 1967 when a Memorandum of Understanding was signed by the British, French and German Governments.

This provided for Britain and France each to contribute 37.5 per cent and Germany 25 per cent of the development costs of an airframe, and for Britain to provide 75 per cent of the development costs of an engine, with Germany and France dividing the rest of the engine money equally. The launching costs were estimated at £130 million for the airframe and £60 million for the engine, the Airbus project definition to be completed by June 1968 and the in-service date to be 1973.

There was a 'milestone' at project definition when the three Governments would (or would not) agree to prototype construction, and such approval would only be given (at British insistence) if orders for seventy-five of the aircraft, known as the A300 (300 seats), had been received from the airlines of the three participating nations by that date. The British Government had agreed to French leadership on the airframe, providing that Rolls-Royce RB207 engines were used, and, in effect, the requirement became one for the best aeroplane which could be built round two of these engines which had a proposed initial thrust of 47,500 lb — Rolls-Royce having said they needed to have a 50,000 lb engine to offer in order to face future US competition.

To use this kind of thrust efficiently, the A300 became a big-capacity aeroplane, and eventually it grew to over 300 seats — far too big for the airlines, which stood well clear of it. The result was that even though the project definition milestone was moved back from June 1968 to the autumn, there was still not a single airline order in sight, let alone the seventy-five specified in the Memorandum.

While the A300 project was struggling along, the Americans were getting on with the McDonnell-Douglas DC10 and the Lockheed L1011 TriStar, thus giving Rolls-Royce a chance to get in on a much more promising market for a 40,000 lb thrust engine (with potential up to 50,000 lb), which was an uprated RB211. On 12 December 1968, the Minister of Technology (Benn) told the House of Commons,

> The House will recall that at the meeting in Paris in August with my French and German colleagues we agreed to give the consortium of firms a further period to complete the design stage of the A300 aircraft with a view to improving its technical performance, reducing price, and testing the market.

The response of world airlines to the revised proposals has not been encouraging and the prospects of an economic return both to the firms and to the Government were not sufficiently good. The consortium of firms have, therefore, withdrawn the present A300 design and have said they now wish to put forward proposals for a scaled-down version. In these circumstances, the costs involved in the development of the RB207 engine for the European Airbus can be saved and Rolls-Royce are stopping work on the engine in this application.

The withdrawal of the A300 design presents the three Governments with a new situation which they will have to consider. As far as Her Majesty's Government is concerned, I must make it absolutely clear that I cannot in any way commit the Government to give financial support to any new proposals which may be brought forward by the consortium. In this new situation, we shall judge these or any other proposals on their merits against the stringent economic criteria which we apply when Government launching aid is sought, including the assurance of a firm market, and against the need to control the aggregate level of public expenditure.

By the end of 1969, the A300 – mainly under pressure from Henri Ziegler, who had now become President of the French nationalised company, Aérospatiale – had been scaled down to 250 passengers and could be powered by two RB211–28 engines or by American JT9D–15 or CF6–50 engines in the 45,000 lb to 50,000 lb class. The General Electric CF6 had been chosen for the DC10 and the RB211 for the Lockheed TriStar – so all the Rolls-Royce effort was now on the RB211, whose forward projection to 50,000 lb thrust for a long-range TriStar made the RB207 look unnecessary anyway.

The new 250/270-seat European Airbus named the A300B, was of more interest to the airlines than the 300-seat A300, but none seemed close to placing an order so, in March 1969, the UK decided to go no further in financing the project and pulled out.

By now, the European Airbus had been turned into something very like BAC's own BAC Three-Eleven (see the next chapter) in performance specification, and BAC maintained to the Government that there was a strong preference among the airlines to deal with a proven company like BAC, with a good track-record in the field, rather than with a politically created consortium. It was generally believed at the time that Wedgwood Benn's words '-these, *or any other* proposals . . .' were selected to give room for launching aid support for the new Three-Eleven.

British interest in the A300B was, however, maintained by Hawker Siddeley, who designed and supplied the wings as a private venture, and the first aircraft were sold to Air France, not in 1968, but in November 1971 in a short-haul (B2) version with capacity for 281 tourist passengers, there being a longer-range B4 version, both using CF6–50C engines.

Since 1971, there had been constant political pressure on the UK to re-join the Airbus and to purchase a RB211-powered version of it for British Airways. In the middle and later 1970s, there was a determined attempt, at least on the part of BAC, to get together with European partners (first in Europlane – dealt with later – and then with the French and Germans) to agree the specifications of a family of jetliners which could command worldwide markets and which were based on One-Eleven developments and on the A300B. Up to nationalisation, these attempts had foundered because, or so it appeared, there was no section of the market which could not be fully met by some modification of the basic A300B. This led to one member of the BAC engineering team saying that, if the market surveys showed a major requirement for a 25-seater, a scaled-down Airbus proposal to meet it would be on the table by the weekend.

In the end, as already briefly noted, in the autumn of 1978, British Aerospace *did* re-join Airbus Industrie, partly to preserve the lucrative business of building the wings for the B2 and B4 (long-range) models, and partly to obtain a British involvement in the new scaled-down, wide-bodied, 200/220-seater version, the B10, and, hopefully, to lay the foundations of a strong European alternative source of airliner supply to that of the USA. The deal was that BAC would, from 1 January 1979, become a full member of Airbus Industrie, with a share of 20 per cent and voting rights equal to those of the French and German partners. The 'entrance fee' was the immediate payment of 50 million US dollars for the UK share of the net assets of Airbus Industrie, including work in progress on 1 January 1979. BAC was immediately to undertake its share of the development of the A310 (B10). The UK investment, including the initial 50 million dollars, would, it was announced, build up to a peak of £250 million by 1983.

At the time of the signing (October 1978), the Airbus sales of B2 and B4 had reached 117, with forty-eight more on option. The project, although different from the one from which Benn had withdrawn in 1968, was, by 1978/9, at least well-found, even if hardly likely to show a profit to its then main investors, the French and German taxpayers.

Just before the new UK Airbus deal was finalised, British Airways rushed off and ordered narrow-bodied Boeing 757s, the direct competitor with the B10, a move which, understandably, so infuriated the French that discussions with the UK were jeopardised for a time. Freddie Laker did something to heal the breach by ordering some standard B4s, and the British Government made an announcement that if, in the future, British Airways needed wide-bodied aircraft in the 200-seat category, then the B10 would best serve such a need.

With the new British Aerospace (formerly HSA) 146 coming into the 'up-to-100-seat' market, the Airbus wide-bodied B10 jousting with Boeings (narrow-bodied 757 and wide-bodied 767) in the 200-seater category, and with the B2 and B4 established in the 250/270 seat range, the BAe Commercial Aircraft project teams were left to contemplate the best choice of market to go for between 100 and 200 seats. Some of the older hands from BAC could be permitted a cynical smile at the years of effort they had already devoted to both the 250-seat class (the BAC Three-Eleven) and to the 200-seater (BAC Two-Eleven and then Europlane).

Nonetheless, a European civil aircraft industry might well emerge from the turmoil of the sixties and seventies. The opportunity remains. Meanwhile, let us return to the main narrative.

Overlapping the initial Airbus negotiations and following on the demise of the BAC Two-Eleven, came the proposal made to Wedgwood Benn for the BAC Three-Eleven, and it is to that aircraft, and the Ministerial reaction to it, that the BAC story now turns as a matter of continuity rather than of chronology.

24

Three-Eleven

The story of the BAC Three-Eleven was one of the most involved, both politically and financially, in the history of the company. It was also the most important civil project BAC had ever proposed, and arguably the most important civil project which a UK Government had ever had to consider. Its details were tabled at a time when the debate on what Great Britain should do about the world civil market was celebrating its tenth anniversary.

The ingredients of the Three-Eleven saga – for a saga is what it was – were the aeroplane itself; the version of the Rolls-Royce RB211 engine which was needed to power it; BEA, who wanted to buy it; the purchase of English Electric by General Electric, which brought Sir Arnold Weinstock on to the BAC scene; and the proposals for BAC to 'go public' to raise money for the project, to satisfy the controversial views of the Minister of Technology, Anthony Wedgwood Benn. Then, finally, came the 1970 General Election, the Rolls-Royce difficulties, and the consequent lack of enthusiasm in the new Heath Government for almost anything connected with civil aviation.

At all material times in the main history of the Three-Eleven, Wedgwood Benn was the Minister responsible for the industry. His was a remarkably uneven performance which inspired little confidence in the future of British aerospace at home and none abroad. As a Bristol MP, he was a supporter of Concorde, but whether for constituency reasons or from conviction, only he can say. On the other hand, he stood up at the SBAC dinner on 28 June 1967, and said, 'Ministers of Aviation have run off with sums of money that made the Great Train Robbers look like schoolboys pinching pennies from a blind man's tin. Since the War, the Government has spent £5000 million on the aircraft industry – £1500 million of it on research and development – six or seven times as much as the Government expenditure in either the shipbuilding or motor vehicle industries. Successive Ministers of Aviation have secured victory after victory in the battle for the public purse. Some of the most distinguished aerospace leaders have come to me wearing the mantle of Government on their shoulders. "A strong British industry is in the national interest," I am often told. "What the Government must do is to re-organise itself this way or that way in order to safeguard this vital national interest and

BAC One-Eleven Series 200, the original production version, in the livery of British United Airways, then headed by Freddie (now Sir Freddie) Laker. BUA's order was the first to break the BEA/BOAC 'monopoly' by making BUA the first independent British airline to become the initial customer for a completely new type of aircraft.

Blue Water, the highly promising tactical surface-to-surface missile system whose cancellation in August 1962 not only caused 1000 redundancies and the closure of the Luton Guided Weapons factory but 'hung like a pall over Stevenage for years afterwards.'

Thunderbird, the mobile anti-aircraft missile system which was originally developed for the British Army by English Electric, was for many years in head-on competition with the Bristol-developed Bloodhound system ordered by the RAF.

TSR2 – the supersonic, low-level, strike-reconnaissance aircraft which was one of
the main catalysts in the formation of BAC. Its cancellation almost destroyed BAC
two years after the Corporation was formed. But in TSR2 'the British industry
produced probably the finest of all its warplanes.'

Three moments in the life story of TSR2. *Top*, the first flight from Boscombe
Down on 30 September 1964. *Centre*, a hitherto unpublished photograph of the
TSR2 mock-up being burned at Warton only a few weeks after the project's
cancellation. *Bottom*, one of the completed aircraft awaiting destruction as a target
at the Shoeburyness gunnery range – with, beside it, another cancelled BAC
aircraft, the all-steel Type 188.

The Bloodhound surface-to-air missile system, developed by Bristol for the RAF
and later ordered also by Australia, Sweden and Switzerland, is still in service
today. The inset illustration shows an 'unarmed' Bloodhound scoring a direct hit
on its target during trials.

A photographic impression of the BAC Three-Eleven – 'the most important civil project BAC had ever proposed and arguably the most important civil project which a UK Government had ever had to consider.' BAC invested £2 million and hundreds of thousands of man-hours in the Three-Eleven, only to see it die when it was announced, in December 1970, that no Government funds could be made available for it.

Jaguar supersonic tactical strike aircraft of the RAF in typical operating conditions –
at very low level and in bad weather. Jaguar has repeatedly shown that its
Navigation and Weapon-Aiming Sub-System (NAVWASS) enables it to locate
its target in any weather and make one-pass attacks of deadly accuracy.

it must be ready to put this amount of money into this project." But you have to persuade me that any public investment has a real chance of producing an economic pay-off. You must satisfy the taxpayer that this is the best way of deploying the scarce money and manpower which we may have available.'

There was quite a lot more in the same vein in what quickly became known as the 'Train Robbers' speech. At this particular SBAC dinner, the President, Mr R.F. Hunt, was not slow to reply. Having said that the industry's custom of inviting its Minister to speak at the annual dinner had assured it of a different speaker each year, he pointed out that of Mr Benn's 'Train Robbers' £5000 million,' £3500 million had been for the purchase of aircraft for the defence of the country – aircraft which even Mr Benn himself had described as 'superb.' Over the same period, the industry had exported £2000 million worth of aircraft and engines, the majority in dollars, and against world competition. 'Thus, since the War,' said Mr Hunt, 'we have not only provided for the air defence of the country, but have earned almost two thirds of the equivalent amount in foreign currency.'

But, as was predictable, it was not Hunt's reply but the Minister's 'Train Robbers' label which was the one which hit the media, and, in this way, Benn successfully convinced the public that aerospace industry had been featherbedded to the extent of £5000 million in gifts – or, indeed, thefts – from the public purse. The fact that most of that money was simply payment for goods ordered, made and delivered in the normal way was completely lost. The research and development comparison with shipbuilding and motorcars was irrelevant, but doubtless produced the desired political effect among workers in the Midlands and on Clydeside.

It was left to *Flight International*, in a leader, to take the Minister up on another point. 'Why,' it asked, 'should not leaders of industry come to a Minister and suggest ways in which the Government machine should be reformed? Mr Benn implies it is hardly their business. But surely it is? They are the country's professional aviation people. They have more experience of the system than any of the myriad Ministers and Permanent Secretaries who have flitted across the scene over the years.'

It is difficult to over-state the damage which the 'Train Robbers' speech did to the industry – especially overseas. It also created an impression at home of a gang of capitalist crooks who had milked thousands of millions from the public purse for their own private purposes until now, at long last, Mr Benn had arrived on the scene as the people's hero to put a stop to it all. He painted a picture which is still widely accepted, even though, as this book has shown, practically every company in the industry was at that time still struggling merely to survive Mr Benn's Party's own decision of two years before to suspend, at a stroke, all the new British military projects and to spend hundreds of millions on buying US equipment instead – many of those dollars having been hard earned by the very industry which was now being held up to public contumely by its own Minister.

The success of this speech in terms of publicity and its popularity with the militant Left undoubtedly remained in Wedgwood Benn's memory, for, as Industry Minister in 1976, he was once again to use the same basic arguments in support of nationalisation – quoting the total Government business with aerospace as though it represented some kind of subsidy rather than the purchase of ordered equipment, and arguing that as the Government was putting such amounts of public money into an industry then the public had the right, and indeed the duty, to run it.

The 'Train Robbers' speech was in 1967. In 1969, also at the SBAC dinner, Wedgwood Benn was, by contrast, heaping lavish praise on the same men he had insulted two years before. 'Last year,' he said, 'production was £500 million and exports £234 million. This year, production is expected to reach £535 million, with exports of £280 million or 52 per cent. If every industry in the country exported half of its production, we would have no problems at all. Nobody who has anything to do with the aerospace industry can fail to be excited by it or infected by the enthusiasm of those who work in it . . . the industry's remarkable performance reflects great credit on the manufacturers who work in British aerospace . . . we have a common desire to make money by making aircraft or engines or equipment.'

The 'Robber Barons' of 1967 heard all this with rueful, if polite, attention. They had spent their lives trying their best to make money by making aircraft and had precious little help to thank Wedgwood Benn or any Minister for – save for a cancellation list as long as your arm, huge purchases from the USA, and interminable fights for payment and for support for civil ventures mostly doomed from the start by the blindness of Government-owned airlines to the requirements of the world markets. Indeed, it was in this very speech that Wedgwood Benn presented his earlier decision not to support the Two-Eleven (or the A300B), as though this was a positive step towards maintaining the industry's competitive edge. What the Two-Eleven decision actually did, as has been shown, was to re-invent the B727 in the shape of the Trident 3, thus turning that particular wheel full circle.

Bereft of the Two-Eleven, BAC had immediately begun definition work on another airliner, the Three-Eleven, with which it could maintain its hard-won position in the world civil market, and sustain its commercial teams and factories at Weybridge and Hurn. The One-Eleven was wearing thin, and Concorde, as always, was under threat, though it did now have the bonus of the Minister's personal support.

The BAC Three-Eleven was an advanced-technology wide-bodied airliner with a typical all-tourist layout of 245 seats at eight-abreast over a range of some 1450 n.m., and 270 seats at nine-abreast for the Inclusive Tour market. It was designed round two rear-mounted Rolls-Royce RB211 engines developed in the Dash-61 version to over 50,000 lb static thrust, was quiet, and had development potential in both airframe and engines to keep it in the forefront for many years to come. Into the Three-Eleven had gone all the structural integrity and engineering experience which had started with the Viscount and had been extended through the Vanguard, VC10 and One-Eleven. It was aimed at a service date of 1974, was very economical, and had an identified global market potential of at least 1000 aircraft and a sales potential of 250–350 in that market.

Its design incorporated the latest Farnborough-pioneered high-lift wing concepts, and, in the view of many experts, represented the best airliner project which BAC had ever come up with. The mock-up was, at various times, visited by airline engineers from all over the world, and almost without exception they were considerably impressed. As BAC had openly stated that it would not launch the Three-Eleven just on a home order, but would require sufficient starting orders to ensure success in the market, this overseas approval of the project was of key importance.

Such, then, was the airliner which Lord Portal, in December 1968, had spoken of as being necessary to BAC if it was to face the next decade 'competitively armed at all points of our technology.' It was also the airliner which the commercial aircraft side of the company needed to stay established in the transport business, and to which it had turned its full creative attention as soon as the decision on the narrow-bodied BAC Two-Eleven had gone the wrong way.

In November 1969, Sir Reginald Verdon-Smith wrote to Wedgwood Benn, giving details of the Three-Eleven (on the progress of which the Ministry had already been kept fully informed), and said that the Board had decided that the project should go forward subject to financial participation by the Government as set out in an appendix to the letter. The decision, added Sir Reginald, had been endorsed by the three shareholders, The General Electric and English Electric Companies, Vickers Limited, and Rolls-Royce Limited. The history of BAC's success in the civil market was fully set out, and a detailed sales assessment was given. This showed that, of a total world market up to the mid-1980s of 1148 aircraft in the wide cabin twin-jet field, BAC could, on past performance and reputation, expect to sell 241 by 1984 against competition from the USA and the A300B. Of this total BAC already expected starting orders for forty-three aircraft – twenty of them from BEA.

At this stage, BAC had already sounded out the Ministry on two kinds of launching aid. The first was of the conventional kind, which estimated development costs of £150 million, and asked for 50 per cent aid (£75 million) to be recovered by the Government over 250 aircraft on an increasing scale of levies. BAC would also request a Government loan of up to £30 million maximum to cover half the capital employed on production at an interest rate of $5\frac{1}{2}$ per cent. The alternative scheme was on a loan basis to cover 85 per cent of net capital employed, including development and production, up to a maximum of £120 million in the years 1975 and 1976 – the Government to guarantee the loan with recourse to B A C, and the maximum interest rate to be 5½ per cent. The Government was to insure B A C for recovery of 50 per cent of estimated development costs if less than 250 aircraft were sold, with a maximum Government liability of £75 million reducing until 250 aircraft were sold, when Government liability would be nil. This, in fact, would be the same liability for Government as its actual net outlay under the conventional 50 per cent launching aid.

The Minister replied that the proposals would be studied carefully, assumed that B A C could offer full security for the loan, and that its repayment would not be directly dependent on the success of the project itself. He also enquired about B A C's ideas for bringing any other major partners into the venture. These latter, at that time, amounted to a substantial sub-contracting deal with Scottish Aviation and Shorts, and getting the specialist suppliers – as in the U S A – to finance their own research and development and tooling of their share of the project. This was an important new feature of the proposal. There were also talks with Boeing, and investigation into a trade-off of orders against local work with Romania, Poland and Yugoslavia.

There was considerable examination of the position in B A C and with the Ministry throughout the first six months of 1970, it being clear that, in the Government's view, to sustain the Three-Eleven, B A C would need more capital. There was even a brief consideration of a revival of the earlier proposal that the Government should take a minority interest in the company. Eventually, after exhaustive analysis of B A C's forward finances, and many discussions in which Sir Arnold Weinstock was now powerfully involved, a position was arrived at whereby the Ministry would consider increasing the Three-Eleven launching aid to 60 per cent if B A C increased its share capital from £30 million to £50 million and involved the private sector, through the City, in this increase.

There is still little doubt in Sir George Edwards' mind that, if the General Election of June 1970 had not intervened, or had the Labour Party not lost it, then the Three-Eleven would have gone ahead. He believes that Wedgwood Benn would have approved B A C's subsequent proposed financial provisions, including the issue of £12 million Convertible Loan Stock (thus involving the City as well as the Government and B A C in the enterprise) and would have seen the project safely through the Cabinet on that basis.

As it was, from July 1970 onwards, B A C was dealing with the Heath Government, and with a new Minister of Technology, John Davies, and a new Minister of Aviation, Fred Corfield.

The Conservative Min-Tech was informed right away (early July), via the Permanent Secretary, Sir Richard Clarke, that the B A C shareholders were willing to increase their equity holdings in B A C to a total of £40 million through the conversion into capital of their existing advances to BAC and the subscription of new shares. The remaining £10 million (later £12 million) would be raised by the issue of Convertible Subordinated Unsecured Loan Stock. Sir Richard Clarke was also informed by Sir Reginald Verdon-Smith that there was reason to believe the institutions would probably give this issue a fair wind.

With a new Government, however, it was now a new ball game, and BAC was already spending its own money on the Three-Eleven at a rate which looked likely to top the £2 million mark by the early autumn. On 16 July Sir Arnold Weinstock let rip in an internal memorandum which began, 'The continued inertia in the handling of this [Three-Eleven] project has given rise to a situation in which it will either come to a stop or fail commercially as a result of the simple efflux of time.' He then traced the long history of the dealings with Min-Tech and its insistence on the further £10 million of equity, commenting that it was questionable whether the insistence as to the mere form of the subscription (via the City) of this £10 million was all that relevant in a project costing some £160 million. 'I should not have thought,' he added, 'that it could really be the decisive factor.' Sir Arnold went on to say that every day lost made the commercial success of the Three-Eleven more uncertain. BAC was spending £250,000 a month which might be abortive, and the situation was now quite untenable. The problems of Rolls-Royce complicated the Government's position, but the fact was that the Three-Eleven could fly perfectly well with American General Electric engines which could be bought off the shelf. He then called for a decision by 15 August and, failing that, GEC/EE would propose to the BAC Board that the Three-Eleven should then be discontinued.

The Weinstock memorandum, although internally addressed, was mainly meant for external consumption, and it was in fact shown to Mr Heath, whose comment was reported as being simply, 'Oh.'

Despite this warning – to which Sir Arnold was to refer many times in the remaining months of 1970 – the stately dance with Min-Tech went on. BAC, through Lazard's, made all the complicated arrangements for the Convertible Stock issue of £12 million, of which GEC/EE was willing to underwrite £4 million, providing the Government stuck to their 60 per cent of launching costs proposal. Sir Arnold remained very doubtful about going to the City just to get £8 million underwritten and in this he was supported by Lord Poole of Lazards (and Rolls-Royce), who could not believe the scheme would founder at Min-Tech just because £8 million had not been secured. If it was necessary, however, he was satisfied the money could be raised on the market.

There were, however, still strong Ministry indications that City involvement would help the project, and the proposals were duly circulated in the City and the soundings taken on it seemed favourable. John Davies was notified on 29 September that rather over half of the total commitment of £12 million would come from the City and rather under half from General Electric and Vickers. This, in Sir Reginald's view, amply met Government conditions that there should be evidence of private sector support, and that this support should take the form of raising the share capital of BAC to £50 million. Sir Reginald added to the Minister, 'I understand that you may have difficulty in reaching a decision about the RB211–61 [the development of the Rolls-Royce RB211 engine needed for the Three-Eleven]. We hope this engine will go forward as we have always maintained we would choose it in preference to the General Electric's CF6. We should remind you, however, that we have also said we would be prepared to go forward with the BAC Three-Eleven initially fitted with the CF6 if it were not possible for the Government and Rolls-Royce to proceed with the RB211–61.'

As time went by and no decision was made, Sir Reginald wrote to Mr R.T. Armstrong, the Prime Minister's Principal Private Secretary (4 November), calling attention to the delay, to the continuing BAC private-venture expenditure, which, he said, was now only authorised for one more week, and adding that the consequences of abandoning the project were alarming, not only for BAC but nationally.

It was, however, all in vain. On 3 December 1970, Mr (later Sir) Frederick Corfield, Minister of Aviation, announced that there were no funds available for the BAC Three-Eleven nor for UK re-entry into the A300B European Airbus (Rolls-Royce had used them all).

Thus, once again, a General Election had dealt BAC a heavy blow. The Labour victory of 1964 cost the company the TSR2 and nearly put the military side out of business. The Labour defeat of 1970 cost BAC the Three-Eleven and left the commercial aircraft factories with no apparent future. The whole sorry Three-Eleven business had wasted £2 million of BAC money, and had occupied countless thousands of man-hours and the almost exclusive attention of the BAC Board for over a year. 'A tragic and stupid decision which Britain will regret for many a year,' said Sir George, and he is of that view still.

It was, however, not entirely unexpected. Edward Heath had inherited a terrible situation in Rolls-Royce because of the Lockheed contract on the RB211, for which many blamed Wedgwood Benn's optimism as much as they did Rolls-Royce. All the election-time speeches, notably by John Davies of 'No more lame ducks', had had to go out of the window within weeks when the first lame duck proved to be Rolls-Royce, with all its worldwide contracts (including for the MRCA). If the reports coming to BAC of Heath's complete exasperation with any part of aerospace were true, then perhaps it was not to be wondered at. So, once again, Whitehall preoccupation with Rolls-Royce had resulted in a sacrifice of the airframe side, and even though Rolls-Royce was officially bankrupt in February 1971, it perforce had to be re-formed as a nationalised concern (by a Tory Government) and every penny of available cash was needed to settle its problems.

The immediate result at BAC of the Three-Eleven decision was a redundancy on the civil side of some 900 highly qualified people, including some very senior ones, a big economy drive in which Sir Arnold took a strong personal interest, and the start of yet another casting around for possible international partners in the hope that some part of the huge market for a new jetliner could be salvaged for British factories.

This serial story is picked up again later in the book with the history of Europlane and the subsequent formation of the European 'Group of Six.'

25
Guided Weapons' Success

While all the public drama had been centred on aircraft – on the TSR2, Spey-Mirage, AFVG, UKVG, VC10, and BAC Two- and Three-Eleven – and on the long drawn-out merger crisis, the Guided Weapons Division had quietly picked itself up from its flooring by the Blue Water cancellation. Jefferson later called the mid and late sixties, the years of 'progress and problems,' which was true. They were also years of patient consolidation, and the building up of the most inventive and go-ahead guided weapons operation in Europe, with the parallel establishment of the leading Space facility, involving much new technology and the recruitment and training of the men to apply it.

The original Luton site had had to be closed and also the splendid little factory at Cardiff, the apple of Jack Jefferies' eye, which, however, was sold to Bristol Siddeley Engines, virtually complete with a work-force which, in ten years, had never staged a strike and, as Pat Adams records, only one five-minute sit down. Guided Weapons had, after initial production problems, sorted out and made in quantity the former Vickers private-venture infantry anti-tank missile, Vigilant, which had been exported to Finland, Kuwait, Saudi Arabia and Abu Dhabi (total value of £4½ million), as well as the 12,000 rounds sold to the British Army. Vigilant, in which Vickers invested over £1 million, owed its existence and much of its success to Colonel Harry Lacy, Guided Weapons' military adviser, who, when at Vickers, had fought through all the thickets which surround any private-venture weapon which arrives before the Establishment judges carrying the dreadful label 'NIH' – 'not invented here.' Eventually, to break the log-jam, a go-for-broke demonstration was staged at Larkhill to which top Army brass was invited, and at which a splendid Army corporal, fortified by, of all things, a jumbo-sized bottle of orangeade, hit tank after tank from all angles with the small remaining stock of hand-made, hand-wound (Vigilant was wire-guided) rounds. Vigilant was important in the Guided Weapons story because, when it was transferred to Stevenage at the merger, it brought Guided Weapons into the anti-tank field, and gave Stevenage quantity-production experience. This was followed by the deal with Fairey's over Swingfire – a bigger vehicle-mounted, jet-nozzle-controlled, anti-tank missile – and so developed a second string to the then Guided Weapons bow of the major anti-aircraft systems, Bloodhound and Thunderbird.

From 1962 to 1965, Swingfire was developed, tested at Larkhill and Kirkcudbright and modified to production standards, and, by the end of 1965, twenty rounds had been fired. Stevenage did the weapon, while Bristol made the ground control and test equipment and the classroom trainer.

Swingfire gave birth to two derivations, Beeswing, an infantry version, and Hawkswing, a helicopter-mounted adaptation. Both had completed development when they became held up in economy drives in the 1970s, but remained on the shopping list, Beeswing being exported to Egypt in Land-Rover-mounted form. Swingfire itself entered operational service with the Royal Armoured Corps in 1968, and has since been exported to Belgium and Egypt, with, hopefully, more to come.

The centre-piece of Guided Weapons effort, however, from 1964 onwards, became a project first called ET316, and then, in 1966, named as Rapier. Rapier drew much from the PT428 project, cancelled in 1962, which was designed to be a weapons system to combat fast aircraft at heights from 100 to 10,000 feet and was a rival to the American Mauler. PT428 was an all-weather blind-fire weapon, and was very sophisticated indeed. The need for some such system in the face of the development of such low-level attack aircraft as TSR2 and Jaguar was self-evident. Jefferson was, at the time, of the view that both PT428 and Mauler were too ambitious and complicated, and that a start point on such a vital project should be a line-of-sight (i.e. fair-weather) system for which all-weather capability could later be developed. The Government cancelled PT428 in favour of Mauler (and possibly of TSR2 funding), but, as predicted by Jefferson, the all-dancing system proved to be beyond American technology as well, so Mauler fell by the wayside, still leaving the requirement unfilled. Jeff therefore persuaded BAC to fund, to the extent of £250,000, private venture work on a basic system known as Sightline, which kept his 'start simple and then add on' philosophy alive until a design study contract on ET316 came through in March, 1963, and a development contract in March 1964.

From the start of ET316 it was designed so that there could eventually be an add-on of blind-fire. In its origins, however, Rapier was the simplest and most mobile anti-aircraft weapon, which could destroy aircraft by actually hitting them using a light, and therefore highly manoeuvrable, round which could follow an evading target. The essential of Rapier has always been that it is a 'hitt-ile' as opposed to a 'miss-ile' – the former needing only a small payload which penetrates the aeroplane and then explodes, as opposed to a big, heavy warhead which damages by a near-miss, but is much less nimble.

Apart from an ability to hit fast and very low-flying aircraft, Rapier had to be very transportable (including by helicopter), which meant compact ground equipment capable of being towed by a Land-Rover (Rapier has a towed weight of under one ton – a lightweight gun is over seven tons), and it also had to incorporate its own automatic test equipment for ease of field maintenance and the reduction of technical manpower. The operational team also had to be small (five men to the ten needed for an anti-aircraft gun).

The Rapier work was split between Stevenage and Bristol, which did more than anything else to weld these two teams to a common purpose, and other specialist firms had to be brought in to a BAC systems management concept similar to that of Bloodhound. These were, principally, Decca, Cossor, GEC, Coventry Climax, Standard Telephones and Cables, and Barr and Stroud.

Much of the Rapier testing was done in Australia at the Anglo-Australian range at Woomera, 300 miles north-west of Adelaide. Both Bristol and English Electric had test teams established at nearby Salisbury in the 1950s, and a combined operation from 1960 on was regularised in early 1961 by the formation of British Aircraft Corporation (Australia) Pty Limited, which looked after BAC's aircraft and guided weapons affairs, with Alan Millson (ex-Vickers) as Managing Director and a New Zealander, Group Captain C.W.K. Nichols, the English Electric Manager at Salisbury, as Sales Manager (Military Products). A distinguished Australian, Sir Dan McVey, later became Chairman, succeeded in 1968 by the Hon. F.M. Osborne. Jack Warner of Bristol took over Salisbury, with Arthur Stockwell (English Electric) as his Deputy and, as in the UK, two 'warring' factions had to be brought together, which, because they worked and lived side by side, was more quickly done in Australia than in the UK. BAC (Australia) and its Guided Weapons set-up at Salisbury continued to be an important part of BAC's worldwide effort, both in engineering test and sales until they were inherited by the new British Aerospace in 1977.

Rapier was technically a brilliant success. It incorporated its own alarm system, incredibly quick reaction and target acquisition, plus lethal accuracy. It gained a Queen's Award for technological innovation – one of the hardest of accolades to earn.

In 1966, BAC eventually gained official permission to start a study on the blind-fire all-weather and night-time add-on, the Government at the same time placing a research contract on Elliott's for the radar. This system, called DN181, was formally evaluated at Woomera in 1974 and demonstrated with great success at Aberporth in the same year.

There can be little doubt that, at nationalisation, Rapier, in both its line-of-sight and its blind-fire versions, was the finest low-level anti-aircraft system in the western world. This was even admitted by the US technical Press, and there is good reason to believe that, had the Pentagon been allowed the final say in the big US evaluation programme of the early and mid-1970s, Rapier would have been selected for the US Army – the USA having, yet again, failed to produce its own satisfactory comparable weapon. There were, however, other and heavy political considerations in connection with offset costs, and the order eventually went to the Franco-German Roland. This was about the same time that the Australians were also evaluating all-comers, and they, with no other axe to grind, placed a £20 million order for Rapier. Rapier – already in service with the British Army and the Royal Air Force Regiment in NATO – had, by nationalisation, won export orders worth over £600 million. These included the joint development with the then Government of Iran of a self-contained tracked vehicle-mounted version. The Government has already announced that Rapier and its future developments will remain in service with UK Forces until 1992 – a pretty fair tribute to the Jefferson philosophy as advocated (and rejected) in the very early 1960s.

While Swingfire and Rapier were 'in the mill,' Guided Weapons was strengthening its teams and widening its activities. With the departure of Lord Caldecote, Jefferson became both Chairman and Managing Director, and the clear overall and undisputed boss, which command he was to carry with him in 1977 into British Aerospace, when BAC Guided Weapons and Hawker Siddeley Dynamics were merged. His record as an engineer, an administrator, and a hard-headed negotiator and salesman is, as has been noted, in many ways, similar to that of Sir George Edwards. Their personalities, it is true, are superficially very different, but basically they have much in common, which may account for the mutual confidence which always existed between the two men.

Under him, Jefferson had Alec Sanson (ex-Napier) as Sales Director (Taffy Higginson left BAC in 1968). In Sanson, he had an extrovert, enthusiastic and tireless world-roaming emissary, who did so much to make known the qualities of Rapier. David Farrar and Jack Jefferies left Guided Weapons, Bristol, to return to the Filton aircraft side (Farrar subsequently returned to Guided Weapons, but later left the industry, and Jack became Chief Executive at Filton).

Don Rowley at Filton took over a new Guided Weapons offspring, the Electronic and Space Systems Group, which included the Stevenage Product Groups, and Eric Beverley returned to Guided Weapons from Weybridge to become Commercial Director alongside Reg Raff, the Financial Director. J. McG. Sowerby, who had been with Guided Weapons until 1964 and had rejoined it in 1968, re-organised the Engineering Department and became Director of Engineering (later Divisional Technical Director). Tom Slator was appointed Divisional General Manager (later Vice Chairman), and Alan Smith was made General Manager (Bristol). Tom Kent became in charge of production and later Deputy Managing Director, while Rowley later became Assistant Managing Director. It is a reflection of the strength of BAC Guided Weapons Division that – when nationalised and merged in 1977 as British Aerospace Dynamics Group under Jefferson – Jim Sowerby, Alec Sanson, Don Rowley, Reg Raff, Eric Beverley, Tom Slator, Tom

Kent, Hugh Metcalfe (formerly Chief Executive, Stevenage) and John Parkhouse (BAC Guided Weapons Projects Director) all became members of the Group Board, while Tom Kent and Jim Cattanach became the Managing Director and Technical Director of the Group's Stevenage – Bristol Division.

The gradual spreading-out of Guided Weapons Division into Space was inevitable. All the necessary disciplines were already established, and there is an obvious read-across from building and pushing up a missile and controlling it towards the stratosphere, and the extension of the sortie into orbit. Bristol were the first to get a toe in the Space door when, in 1960–62 they did some instrument work for the first Anglo-American research satellites. Those satellites, UK1 and UK2, were built in the USA, though their payloads of experiments came from the UK. Pat Adams in his book quotes Robin Caldecote as saying, 'We fiddled about with Space for two or three years and everyone was very sceptical. I remember a meeting with Jeff and Leslie Bedford when we said "Either we're in this Space business or we wrap it up." We thought it was worth being in, so we put Bedford in charge of Space, and from that day it prospered.'

The first breakthrough was at the end of 1962 when BAC got in on the first all-British satellite, UK3. Things were then a bit at sixes and sevens between Stevenage and Bristol, which had an independent effort on sounding rockets (later to develop into the very successful Skylark programme) and Space electronics, so Doug Fraser was appointed as Divisional Space Executive.

It was already clear that there was going to be a lot more to Space than the technical side. It was from the start a highly political and international business beset by partnerships and consortia, and also by company and national rivalries and distrust. There was soon to be a European Space Research Organisation (ESRO), and also a European Launcher Development Organisation (ELDO), to be followed by many more bewildering sets of initials. The scene was described by Adams as one of 'international skull-duggery' to which could be added a prolonged outburst of French nationalism. Doug Fraser, and later Ray Munday, had for years to be BAC joint guides through this bewilderment, but meanwhile there was UK3 to be done under the technical leadership of RAE, Farnborough.

In January 1964, BAC got a contract for the spacecraft structure, overall integration, and ground check-out equipment, while GEC were to supply the main electronic equipment. The payload was a series of research studies, five in all, mostly to do with radio noise both from Earth and from the galaxy. Every aspect of UK3 – of which five full-sized models were built – had its own troubles, and it was a remarkable achievement that the flight model was sent to California to its launch site on schedule. It was duly and successfully launched on 5 May 1967, and, on achieving orbit was renamed 'Ariel 3.' It was this which prompted

Beverley to send a telex to Bedford quoting from *The Tempest*, 'Ariel, thy charge is exactly performed.' Ariel 3 remained in orbit and sending back data for twelve months beyond the one year which was asked of it.

In 1965 and 1966, the BAC Space team began its important and fruitful association with Hughes Aircraft Company of the USA by calling them in (1966) as consultants to a consortium, of which BAC was a member, on the ESRO Thor–Delta-launched satellite. Leslie Bedford and Jeff Crowder led the BAC team in California, which gained valuable experience. Earlier (1965), a small party of Stevenage engineers had worked with Hughes on Intelsat II, the communications satellite, and a formal ten-year collaboration agreement grew out of these contacts.

As a result, in 1967, another BAC Space team was at Hughes working on the design of Intelsat IV, which led to the construction at Filton of a large-scale Spacecraft assembly facility. BAC were responsible for the design and manufacture of the complete mechanical ground support equipment, which meant that Production and Quality Assurance staff could get deeply involved in a major Space programme. Excellent relationships were established between BAC and Hughes, and a great deal of Intelsat IV work was given to Filton, which had the help of a small Hughes management team to keep an eye on things. To handle the work, the large special Space building was put up at Filton, starting in 1969, and opened in April 1970 by Lord Delacourt Smith, the Minister of State at the Ministry of Technology.

Eight sets of sub-system equipment were delivered to Hughes on time and gave such satisfaction that six more sets for Intelsat IVA were ordered. BAC also erected a complete Intelsat – the first, in fact, to be launched, and in position over the Pacific in time to relay pictures of President Nixon's visit to China. Intelsat IV had twenty colour TV and 12,500 telephone channels.

There then followed four sets of sub-system equipment for the USA's own domestic satellite system, Comstar I, to which BAC was the only overseas contractor. This meant that BAC had supplied sixteen sets of revenue-earning satellite hardwear to Hughes – an achievement unequalled outside North America, and reflecting great credit on the Bristol team under Ray Munday and Reg Astbury.

On the domestic scene, BAC, in early 1969, became prime contractor on the UK4 satellite, which was launched in 1971, and in 1968 it began the structural design and manufacture of X3. This satellite had the distinction of being the only launch (at Woomera in 1971) using the all-British Black Arrow launch vehicle. Then followed UK6, while in the wider European context, BAC provided the altitude measurement system, both sensors and electronics, of the HEOS (Highly Eccentric Orbital Satellite) A2 which went into its eccentric orbit in 1972. BAC had already worked with MBB of Germany on HEOS A1. In 1969, ESRO proposed a scientific satellite, COS-B, to investigate cosmic particles, and, once again, BAC was involved, this time with a consortium called

CESAR, led by MBB, BAC being a major sub-contractor responsible for 25 per cent of the programme. This, too, was successfully launched, in August 1975.

The emergence of applications satellite programmes produced in BAC the technical expertise required for these new fields, and, in 1971, the European consortium of STAR (Satellites for Technology Applications and Research) was formed with BAC as a leader member and Ray Munday as its founder Chairman. This, in turn, led to the winning of the GEOS contract for a synchronous orbit satellite, 22,300 miles above the equator, to probe the Earth's magnetospheric environment. The STAR consortium also became responsibility for ISEE-B, led by Dornier, but with considerable BAC involvement. ISEE-B was for the NASA/ European Space Agency International Sun-Earth Explorer System.

The biggest disappointment of BAC's Space effort was the collapse of UK direct involvement with the American Space Shuttle. The initial Space Shuttle work involved the airframe side of BAC (because of Concorde) as well as the Space team, and, in the manoeuvring for the NASA contracts, nearly all the USA contenders wanted BAC as their UK partner, which was very gratifying. Eventually BAC chose, on Handel Davies' advice after he had made an evaluation sortie to the USA, to ally itself with North American Rockwell – now Rockwell International – because of all their Apollo experience, BAC being interested in the Orbiter vehicle of the Space Shuttle rather than the launcher.

A BAC team spent nearly two years in California and became fully accepted as key members of the Orbiter design effort, taking part in the successful Rockwell 'presentation' to NASA. BAC had hoped to get invaluable experience out of making hardware for the Orbiter and out of the Space side as well, while Rockwell for their part were most anxious that BAC should stay with the project. The British Government, however, decided it could not afford seriously to participate, and the opportunity was snapped up by Germany instead. Considering the potential of the Space Shuttle, and all that it must mean in mankind's next quantum leap forward in understanding of our Universe, for the UK to have pulled out of the Shuttle was akin to turning its back on the invention of the wheel. Rockwell were very upset to see the BAC chaps leave, and so were many people back home – notably David Farrar, who had been Shuttle Project Director and co-ordinator at Filton. Not long afterwards, he left BAC.

The Shuttle apart, BAC had, by the time of nationalisation, built itself into a leading Space firm, with the best facilities and the fullest experience of hardware in orbit in Europe, to say nothing of Skylark launchings.

Space was not Jefferson's only diversification from Guided Weapons. The missile systems remained at the heart of the money-earning, but there were other important and worthwhile spin-offs. These included the electronics side of the Electronic and Space Systems Group (ESS) and this, under Brian Raybould – the leader of the team to Rockwell – came up with original work on telemetry, remote data-acquisition, and all kinds of complex systems for missiles, sounding rockets, satellites, hovercraft and aircraft, as well as valuable work on electronic counter-measures. It was ESS which devised the truly remarkable set of systems for testing the production Concordes, and also the digitally controlled Concorde air-intake control system, as well as all kinds of antennas. The Group also devised Consub – an unmanned, remotely controlled, submersible vehicle for exploring the seabed and inspecting underwater structures by means of television cameras.

The Precision Products Group, based at Stevenage, specialised in gyroscopes and was fathered as long ago as 1951 by John Noble and Roy Hurrell, when they devised a gyro for Thunderbird. This bit of pioneering grew until, in 1960, a special gyro factory was opened at Stevenage. With its super-clean areas and vibration-proof instrument test-plinths projected through a suspended floor from 50 ton concrete blocks in the basement, this was a factory without peer in Europe. A licence tie with Honeywell Inc. for miniature integrated gyros started a happy association with this leading American company, but eventually BAC became so well established in the field that in 1975 it bought out the future royalties. Another BAC licence for a gyro was from Northrop. The machining of beryllium for naval gyros caused a lot of fuss at Stevenage in 1961/2 with local environmental protesters in full cry on the score of air pollution. In the end, it came to nothing when it was shown that the exhaust from the beryllium shop chimneys was cleaner than the natural Stevenage air around it!

The Precision Products Group (PPG) by 1977 employed about 800 people, had a turnover of £7 million a year, and had contributed to the navigational systems of the Royal Navy, and the Jaguar nav-attack system. It had also invented the Precision Indicator of the Meridian for underground work (used in construction of new London Underground lines), a level-measuring instrument called Electrolevel, and even gyro-stabilised binoculors – all this as spin-off from the basic business of providing inertial-quality gyros to the weaponeers.

Another spin-off was the Reinforced Microwave Plastics Group, making nose-cone radomes for Thunderbird, then for TSR2 and later for Concorde, and gaining orders from Electronique Marcel Dassault for the Martel missile, for Exocet, and, in partnership, for Tornado. PPG in 1970 was awarded the Blue Ribbon Merit Award of the Society of Plastic Industries of the US for the Concorde radome, and by 1975 was established as the European leader in its field, with substantial export orders and holding the Queen's Award for Technological Innovation.

An Industrial Products Group was also formed at Stevenage, under ESS, to market spin-off, including and especially Automatic Test Equipment, and reached a £7 million-a-year turnover in 1973.

Finally, and fittingly, back to the main business of the Guided

Weapons Division – guided weapons. With Rapier and Swingfire established, there had to be follow-ons apart from the Swingfire variants already mentioned. For some time, Jefferson had had his eye on the naval requirements side, which hitherto had been the monopoly of Hawker Siddeley Dynamics and Shorts. In 1966, he appointed Captain Duncan Ritchie, RN, as Naval Adviser, and he certainly paved the way for BAC before his sad death from a heart attack in 1975. He lived, however, to see Seawolf and Sea Skua well on their way, and to use the goodwill engendered by BAC's handling of the UK Polaris support contract (1963/4) to get the company accepted in the Admiralty as worthy of Their Lordships' note.

Sea Skua is the western world's only lightweight antiship missile system and, at nationalisation, was in full development for the Royal Navy. It is an airborne system for Lynx helicopters (or other aircraft, for that matter) and is designed to destroy missile-carrying fast patrol boats. Sea Skua can neutralise such craft, and it can also deal a significant blow against larger warships.

Seawolf is a truly remarkable weapon which may yet rival Rapier as a best-seller. It was first talked about back in 1963 as an all-weather anti-missile system and, after a Bristol pre-feasibility study, BAC was, in 1966, chosen as the missile contractor for the project, then called PX430. Later came the Project Definition study (1966) and, thanks to the Zuckerman system, a Development contract was eventually placed in September 1968. Marconi and Vickers were also involved, thus, incidentally, keeping the project within the BAC family. In 1970, BAC was confirmed as prime contractor – the year pre-guidance trials began at Aberporth. Guidance trials started in 1972 and research and development trials were carried out at Woomera from December 1972 to April 1974. In 1973, a Petrel supersonic target, itself only slightly bigger than the Seawolf missile, was fired down-range and successfully intercepted. The damaged and 'shot down' Petrel was brought to London and shown at a number of exhibitions.

After this, the Seawolf system later successfully completed many more tests on land and at sea in HMS Penelope. It is the western world's only naval point-defence missile system with a proven anti-missile capability. Its ability to intercept and destroy small supersonic missile targets has been amply demonstrated, and no other known weapon is effective against such a variety of anti-ship missiles and aircraft. It is no exaggeration to say that Seawolf, by the time it was handed over to British Aerospace, had attracted the attention of all the western world navies.

The many-sided activities of Guided Weapons Division, ranging from the binoculars and radar reflectors, through target drones such as Jindivik, gyros, ATE, and Consub, to the great range of world-leading weapons and to space satellites, has more than justified Sir George's early belief that BAC needed three legs, and that one of those legs had to be

Guided Weapons. By the time of nationalisation, the Division had earned over £300 million in exports and, with the help of its specialist service advisers working under the Military Adviser, Major-General Marshall, and its terrific sales team under Alec Sanson, had laid the foundation of still greater success.

The culminating and possibly most famous sale under BAC's banner was that of Rapier to Iran, during which Alec Sanson made a personal presentation of the weapon's abilities to the Shah. This led to a contract worth nearly £50 million in 1970, to be followed in 1974 by one for the blindfire version, worth some £60 million. Then, in December 1975, came the massive £186 million deal on Tracked Rapier, mounted on M548 vehicles built in California. This development was financed by BAC, and BAC agreed to help Iran set up its own production line for the missile. All this, of course, was long before the 1979 revolution in Iran terminated the contract.

The speed with which Tracked Rapier was evolved shows there is still considerable merit in the private venture system when it can be afforded. 'We didn't have a committee sitting for months on what colour it should be painted,' Sanson is reported as having said. There is little doubt that Sanson's comment came from the heart. Guided Weapons procurement had always been fractured because a weapons system involves so many different parts which have to be separately developed, and by different firms, but all in parallel. Sir Reginald Verdon-Smith has described Guided Weapons as suffering from the worst shortcomings of the embodiment loan system – the vehicle itself, the propulsion unit, the guidance and control usually being provisioned under separate contracts, over which the prime contractor has no control, leading all too often, to lack of co-ordination, both of time-scale and quantities. The establishment by the Government of a Production Executive was a step forward in this complex matter, but many of the difficulties still remain.

But, committees or no, cancellations and slow-downs notwithstanding, BAC Guided Weapons Division products have been bought by fourteen countries, and, in its last BAC year of 1976, the Division's exports were nearly £50 million.

Because of its Space content, this chapter would be incomplete without mention of the remarkable 'Mustard' proposals, although they actually came from the Aircraft side. They were set out in a paper by Mr T. W. Smith of the Preston Division and given to the 6th European Space Symposium at Brighton in May 1966. The paper was entitled *An Approach to Economic Space Transportation*, and it incorporated (with permission) some of the work done by BAC's Preston Division at Warton on a Government study contract.

Mr Smith was the leader of a BAC team, under the general direction of Ray Creasey, Director of Research and Technology at Warton, which had been looking at Space transportation ideas and concepts since the late 1950s. Smith and his small team came to the conclusion that the cheapest system was based on a vertical take-off lifting body. Three of these, basically identical and fixed together so that two would act as boosters to the third, which would go into orbit, could carry good payloads into Space, and would be able to land normally and so be used again. They called this scheme 'Mustard' (Multi-Unit Space Transport And Recovery Device), and it attracted a deal of public attention. Mustard owed something in concept to an earlier Douglas idea of lifting bodies in tandem, i.e., one on top of the other, but the resemblance of the BAC Mustard studies of 1965/6 to the US Space Shuttle of 1972 has often been remarked upon on both sides of the Atlantic.

It was the 1966 argument of the Warton research team that Europe could afford this Space transportation system and had the technology to make it work. Mustard was clearly preferable to one-shot rocket launches of small payloads, which, Warton argued, were a dead-end development on which Europe should not waste resources or cash. All this ended up in the Whitehall filing system, and British access to Space remains 'by courtesy of the USA.'

26

Lord Portal Retires

On the last day of 1968, Marshal of the Royal Air Force the Viscount Portal of Hungerford KG, GCB, OM, DSO, MC, and one of Britain's great men, retired from the chairmanship of BAC, and was succeeded by Sir Reginald Verdon-Smith.

Lord Portal had, from 1960, steered BAC through its many formative problems, and then through the successive crises of TSR2 and the long-drawn-out merger proposals. With the support of BAC's parents he had held firm when the company nearly went out of business as the Government squeezed it and its parents towards compliance and surrender at the end of 1965. When he retired, the future looked brighter and more assured than at any time since TSR2, and, under him, BAC had discovered its corporate entity.

Lord Portal's most obvious characteristic was his ability to create the calm and quiet with which he always seemed to surround himself. It was impossible to imagine him ever being stampeded into a hasty decision by special pleading or by an incomplete presentation of the facts. The man who had remained a pillar of Churchill's Chiefs of Staff for the greater part of the war had already withstood far more pressures than could ever be exerted upon him by politicians and civil servants of stature and abilities far below his own.

The standing and authority of Portal are something which, at this distance in time, are difficult to convey. Denis Richards, in his biography *Portal of Hungerford*, reports the reply of Churchill's military adviser and representative on the Chiefs of Staff Committee, General Ismay, to someone who asked, 'I know it's a very difficult question to answer, but who do you consider to have been the greatest commander on our side during the war?' Ismay said, 'It isn't a difficult question to answer at all. The answer is Peter Portal, . . . quite easily.' This opinion was widely held, not just by British colleagues whatever their Service, but by the top Americans, and, one feels, by Churchill himself.

Sir Reginald Verdon-Smith is quoted in Richards' book as saying, 'Portal felt it his duty to be [in BAC] the independent Chairman of a complex group with elaborate relationships and to see justice done and commonsense prevail, not to get involved in detail . . . he was extremely authoritative and very short on speech. He showed a particular interest in the young and encouraged the apprentices [he founded the Portal Award] and was always ready and willing to go to such events as Works prize-giving.' Short on speech, yes – but if that carries an implication of brusqueness – no, not unless brusqueness was intended. George Edwards was probably nearer the mark when he said, 'Any impression of aloofness came simply from his modesty.' There was shyness there, too – and perhaps a firm control on a sense of irreverent fun which many of his earlier contemporaries remember, and over which, in his later greatness, he probably had to mount guard.

With Portal there was no display of pomp, no parade of underlings on his arrival, often self-driven, at the Pall Mall garage. He carried his own bag, and waited his turn for the lift and, if others drew back, he made light conversation to bring them forward again. A kind man, but one of such clear strength that he never had to do anything to underline it. Richards, in his book, seems to suggest that Portal may well not have known that he carried such an aura, and says that when, at the beginning of the war, he was Commander-in-Chief, Bomber Command, he was the only senior officer in the Royal Air Force who was surprised when he was made Chief of the Air Staff. This, too, was the man who never thought it worth mentioning at home that he had that day been offered, and declined, the post of Minister of Defence. Ruthless he clearly could be if necessary, and those who had ever had the misfortune to receive his telling-off have told Richards that it was something which they would never forget all their remaining days. Yet one doubts if, in so doing, he ever raised his voice beyond its normal quiet and careful delivery.

The fascinating thing from 1960 to 1969 was the relationship between Portal and Sir George. Some have said that GRE 'manipulated' Portal into support for all the Edwardian ideas – which is a ludicrous suggestion. When Portal supported Edwards it was because, on careful analysis, he believed Edwards to be right – just as, when CAS, he had supported Harris and Tedder. He also realised that Edwards was much more than a gifted engineer and designer, but was a man destined to stand out among his fellows in any walk of life he had cared to follow. Portal, of course, had had years of experience in picking out the nub of any problem from a confusion of advice and paperwork. Edwards often appeared to arrive at the same end-point almost by instinct, and to set the evidence round it later. Edwards, in addition, had the gift of the vivid phrase with which he would sum up an argument or a person or a situation; often funny, and suspiciously near to a wisecrack, yet hitting the nail in a throw-away of half a dozen words.

The two men, so dissimilar in background, had much of their thinking and motivation in common. Both were intensely patriotic, both had an honesty of purpose and an integrity which were beyond challenge, both were fighters, and neither had patience with false argument or mere rhetoric.

Both were natural leaders of men, and both, in their different spheres, had once themselves done, and with outstanding success, most of the jobs which their juniors were now doing. It is interesting that, before they came together in BAC, each had asked the same key test-question of a subordinate proposing a course of action. It was simply, 'Are you sure?' It was GRE's habit to keep this question till last, often until whoever it was was actually at the door on his way out, and would have to turn to answer, so meeting GRE's eye-to-eye gaze. If there was then the slightest hesitancy in the reply – or any drop of the eyes – the day was lost. Edwards had one more hurdle to erect. 'All right,' he would say, 'have it your way. But when it goes wrong don't forget I warned you' – pause – and then the Edward's grin, robbing the words of all malice.

Like Portal, Edwards was a kind man. He once said that one of his nightmares was that he was driving down Brooklands Road from the Weybridge factory and the pavements were lined by the work-people all shouting, 'That's him – that's the man that put us all out of work.' On one of the few occasions when he had to move someone sideways from a job which he prized but was not cut out for, it was Edwards who was to say, 'I'd not live through the last five minutes again for any money you'd care to name.' Portal perhaps would have found that side of being the boss easier – but, then, often he had inherited officers who had already been promoted above their ceiling, Sir George, in the main, had chosen his own men, and if one proved not quite up to it, he saw the fault as his.

During the years when they put the parts of BAC together and made it a Corporation, Portal's was the private strength, and GRE's the more public role. It was GRE, as Managing Director, who met the media and appeared on TV – Portal having no taste or inclination in that direction at all. Edwards, with his ready wit and quick-as-a-flash thinking, was good at it. His gift of simplifying complex things, and putting them into everyday language, made him a popular performer. He enjoyed such debate, but only if the questioners gained his respect by asking the 'right questions' – by which he meant the key ones. For commentators and interviewers who dealt just in innuendo or unsupported assertion, he had no time at all, and for them he would save some splendid squelch answer – to be followed by the famous grin – only this time with just a touch of malice in it. On one occasion, when asked to appear in a BBC current affairs programme, he arrived to find the producer screening an introductory film about the industry, and listing British aviation 'disasters,' in which he included the Viscount and the Hunter – two outstanding best-sellers. 'Jolly interesting,' said GRE. 'Before we do or say anything else, will you show me the references from which you scripted that film?' After some argument the reference file was produced, and proved to be a collection of newspaper cuttings, mainly from the (then) *Daily Worker*. 'I thought,' said Sir George, 'I had been asked here to take part in an intelligent discussion. Instead I'd have to spend my time pointing out all the things that are wrong in that film and I don't reckon I'm going to bother.' He turned to Archie Shields, his driver throughout Vickers and BAC days, and said, 'Shields, give me my hat – we're leaving.'

The film was ditched, and the programme, with GRE on top of his form, was subsequently spoken of as one of the best of all current affairs discussions. It led to many further TV invitations, but, after the film incident, Sir George was very selective about those he would accept. He would, within reason, do any programme for Richard Cawston, the distinguished BBC documentary film-maker ('He encourages me to go on talking and when I've finished I always find I've said more than I first intended to – he's good.') Michelmore was another GRE favourite ('Always polite and doesn't set up to know more about my business than I do'), and, later, Michael Charlton ('He asks the right questions, but he lets me answer them'). He would not, however, take part in organised confrontations with campaigning journalists ('Why should I help to build up their importance?'), and, in later years, when Chairman himself, he would only appear when others taking part were of the same rank, either politically or industrially, as himself. During Portal's time, however, Sir George willingly shouldered the task of being the front-man with the media, although even then he kept a careful eye on the dangers of over-exposure.

Both Portal and Edwards had the same quick appreciation of which battlefields to choose, and of the after-effects of a conflict. 'It is no good,' said Sir George, 'having a public up and downer with blood all over the floor if, at the end of it, you know you're going to lose. All you do is to make enemies who will wait for you next time round. Only fight in public if you reckon you can win, and never box the other fellow in so tight that he's no back-way out. All he can do then is to come on forward straight at you, with everything he's got. If you leave him a compromise back-door, the chances are he'll take it.'

That BAC owed much of its success to the Portal-Edwards axis is certain. Portal, who had known so many great men, rated Edwards highly as a leader and as a man; Edwards, for his part, admired Portal to the point of veneration, and he became the third of GRE's heroes – Horatio Nelson and Brunel being the other two. He hated to see him go – but Portal had done his BAC job, and, as in December 1945, when the job was done, he simply went away. The farewell present he chose – under protest – from the BAC (Operating) Board was three water colours of Sussex. A great Englishman.

Lord Portal's farewell message to the Corporation was printed in the Christmas 1968 issue of the BAC newspaper *Airframe*. In it, he said:

> During the eight years of my chairmanship, I have seen BAC develop from a number of previously autonomous units into a unified Corporation which can truly claim to be the most powerful force in European aerospace. I have also watched the start of European collaboration which, if it can survive its infancy and solve the problems inherent in a multi-racial approach, can bring great

prosperity to all concerned. The problems are not unlike those which faced BAC itself in the early years, and I am confident that the course we are steering is a proper one, and that Concorde, Jaguar, and, I hope, MRCA, will lay stable foundations for future success far greater than we would achieve alone. The important thing has been that BAC should achieve real strength, both technically and commercially. We have to be a company worth collaborating with, not only in Europe, but worldwide. This position you have now undoubtedly achieved. Your success, first with the BAC One-Eleven, followed by the big sales of Lightning and developments of the Jet Provost, then with Guided Weapons and, more recently, Space satellites, has been the fruit of your own exertions often in the face of vacillating national policies. I thank you all for that great effort.

One result is that BAC has gained two successional Queen's Awards for export achievement, and today has a backlog of orders approaching the £400 million mark, of which over 60 per cent is for export, and only some 20 per cent is for the account of the Government. This does not include the enormous potential of Concorde or the production of Jaguar. In short, we have emerged into a position of some independence of the changing policies of the Government of the day. Such has been our aim since the cancellation of TSR2 threatened the entire Corporation. It is clear that BAC must never again be at such a risk that one isolated Government decision could menace its whole corporate existence. The present percentage of Government orders gives us about the proper balance for long-term stability.

The talk of imminent mergers and/or nationalisation (which was so unsettling for a long period) is no longer heard, and the way ahead is brighter for BAC than it has ever been. If the current discussions for the MRCA project and for the important BAC Three-Eleven jetliner are successfully concluded, we shall be equipped to face the next decade competitively armed at all points of our technology.

Portal's successor in the BAC Chair was Sir Reginald Verdon-Smith, who was Chairman of The Bristol Aeroplane Company when it became one of BAC's parents, and, now that Bristol had been taken over by Rolls-Royce, was the better able to hold the ring should there be any clash of interest between Vickers and English Electric. Sir Reginald, as a founding father, had been a BAC Board member from the start, and had been involved directly and indirectly in the industry all his adult life. He was a barrister and had City interests in banking and insurance. The appointment of Sir Reginald, though no surprise within BAC, was undoubtedly so for the Government, because Sir Reginald had been under recent attack for an excess profit alleged to have been made by Bristol Siddeley Engines on a Government maintenance contract. This attack was felt by many in the industry to be unfair, partly because of the then system of balances by which a contractor who had lost heavily on one contract, probably through no fault of his own, was allowed some compensating fat on another, simply to enable him to stay in business, and partly because, although he was Chairman of the parent of which BSE was a subsidiary, many thought that such criticism as was deserved should have been aimed elsewhere, although Sir Reginald, as Chairman, never himself sought to take anything other than the full blame. Sir George was later to say, 'Appointing Verdon-Smith to succeed Peter Portal was a mark of our confidence in V-S who had been badly treated and made a scapegoat for others.'

Sir Reginald was, inevitably, a different kind of Chairman from Portal. He had always been involved in the battle rather than above it, and had the overall industrial problems on both the aircraft and the Guided Weapons side at his fingertips. Not surprisingly, he studied those problems with the logic of counsel approaching a brief, and, at all times, he kept a sharp eye on the attitude of the City towards the company and its financial position. All this comes out clearly in his authoritative 1972 Barnwell Lecture on BAC, many extracts from which have been quoted in this book.

Verdon-Smith had a comfortable relationship already established with Sir George, although, according to Richards, he was quite prepared, if GRE in his view was overstating a case, to say, 'Oh, come off it, George!' Yet probably the finest and fullest tribute to Sir George was one given by Verdon-Smith on a private occasion at Pall Mall, when he made a presentation to mark the award to GRE of the Order of Merit. It was a generous and brilliant speech, and will be remembered by all who heard it. In the final paragraph of the Barnwell Lecture, Sir Reginald said, 'BAC inherited a wealth of talent. Lord Portal brought leadership and authority. Many others have played their part. But above all I wish to acknowledge, in terms of unqualified admiration, the work of one man – the man whose natural ability, immense determination, humour and humanity have made him BAC's unquestioned leader. Without Sir George Edward's breadth of vision, BAC might never have been formed. Without his perseverance, it might never have survived. As a result of both, its prospects are surely great.'

27
Further Progress and a Re-Organisation

Lord Portal's last year in the Chair (1968) saw BAC's sales reach £191.4 million, an increase of £33 million over 1967. Exports were £75.7 million, an increase of nearly £24 million – an achievement which, as Lord Portal mentioned in his farewell message, gained BAC another Queen's Award. The profit before tax was £6.257 million and, after tax, £4.235 million. The total dividend for 1968 was £1.7 million, and £2.5 million was transferred to reserves. The actual excess of sales over expenditure for 1968 was £15 million, but 'old account' profit took £4 million, development amortisation £3 million, and interest another £1.6 million. The reserves stood, on 28 December 1968, at £4.105 million, and the share capital remained at £20 million. The average number of employees for the year was 35,879. Lord Portal could, indeed, look back on his eight years of command with considerable satisfaction at the end-result.

It was during 1968 that there was an important change in the name of the main company from British Aircraft Corporation Limited to British Aircraft Corporation (Holdings) Limited, and the old BAC (Operating) Limited became BAC Limited. This change was made on the basis of a note written by Sir George in early January 1968, in which he said that he was now convinced from the Benn statement of December that the Government was resigned to there being no merger and no nationalisation of BAC in the foreseeable future, and that BAC, as Lord Portal had said, would press on as an independent private enterprise company. The five-year forecast, when revised, would show a reasonable picture providing that (a) Concorde continued, (b) One-Eleven sales, helped by devaluation, were maintained ('This will need the toughest selling ever'), and (c) that something was worked out to take up the Preston spare capacity ('likely to be left free by the AFVG fiasco'). The Guided Weapons programme, he assumed, would stay sensibly as known.

The future of BAC, Sir George emphasised, now rested squarely on the shoulders of the executives to design, sell, and efficiently make their various products within the financial limitations imposed by the main Board, which was composed mainly of nominated shareholders' representatives – eight out of a total of twelve. He wanted to see a change in the titles and responsibilities of the two senior Boards (BAC Limited and BAC (Operating) Limited), with the Chairman of the new BAC Limited a full-time Executive. 'If,' he continued, 'I were invited to take up that position, I would regard, as an essential part of my remaining term, the selection and preparation of my successor. I am sure the necessary talent exists in the Operating Board. A secondary advantage of the change is the removal of the present mental barrier which I know a number of the Divisional Directors have about their chances of ever becoming a Director of BAC.'

He then proposed the changes in the Board names, with the proviso that the Chairman of BAC (Holdings) must be of the same stature as the present Chairman (Lord Portal). The senior representatives of the parent companies could, perhaps, take the Chair of the Holdings Board in rotation, changing, say, every two years. The extra burden that this would impose on Lord Nelson, Sir Leslie Rowan, and Sir Reginald Verdon-Smith would probably be eased by the Board meetings being reduced to six a year.

This proposal was considered, agreed, and on 1 August 1968, it was promulgated, Sir George being – as expected – Chairman and Managing Director of the new BAC Limited.

This apparently pointless changing of Board nomenclature was, in fact, far from pointless. Virtually the whole responsibility of running BAC as such now devolved upon the Executive Chairman/Managing Director, and his colleagues on the new BAC Board and in the Divisions – which were all represented on the BAC Board by their Chairmen/Managing Directors. William Masterton became Deputy Chairman, and Tom Pritchard, Financial Director. The Holdings Board still represented the wishes of the shareholders, but the main business of the company was now firmly in the hands of the full-time Executives under GRE, and the central power of the BAC Board was underlined and strengthened.

The Governmental back-down over the nationalisation/ rationalisation/merger issue, although opening the way to the management reforms just described, also landed BAC in 1968 with a renewal of the problem of the 20 per cent shareholding held by Rolls-Royce as a by-product of its purchase of Bristol Aeroplane, one of BAC's original three parents. Rolls-Royce wanted Bristol Siddeley Engines, but it did not want any shares in BAC, and nor did BAC want an engine company as a step-parent: there were bound to be conflicts of interest on both sides. It was one of the founding terms of BAC in 1960 that any shareholder wishing to dispose of his shares must first offer them to the other partners, and Rolls-Royce, having failed to 'sell' their BAC interest to the Government in the proposed big take-over deal, now set about divesting themselves of their 20 per cent to Vickers and/or English Electric, or, failing that to anyone else, including, if need be, the general public.

To be fair to Rolls-Royce under Sir Denning Pearson, they were not pressing hard on the matter, but they did not want to nominate a Director to the Shareholders' Board, and they did want the matter to be progressed towards resolution. Before the shares could be sold to anyone, however, a value had to be placed on them, and this led to a whole series of meetings and calculations as to BAC's worth. The bulk of this burden fell on Willie Masterton and his staff, and was not made any easier by the 'old account/new account' complication, nor by the uncertainties of the future product programmes, notably an AFVG successor at Warton, a BAC One-Eleven successor at Weybridge, and, as always, Concorde.

Among the many sums done during the Rolls-Royce affair was a particularly interesting one dated May 1969 by Willie Masterton which was a summary of BAC's total profits 1961–8 on 'new' and on 'old' account against total shareholders' capital employed, together with the allocations of both to individual shareholders. The total pre-tax profits (after interest on outside borrowings), expressed as a percentage of average total shareholders' capital employed, were:

Year	Capital £ millions	Pre-Tax Profits £ millions	%
1961	54	4.7	$8\frac{1}{2}$
1962	49	4.1	$8\frac{1}{2}$
1963	55	4.8	$8\frac{1}{2}$
1964	70	4.5	$6\frac{1}{2}$
1965	68	7.4	11
1966	55	4.1	$7\frac{1}{2}$
1967	49	5.7	$11\frac{1}{2}$
1968	46	10.3	$22\frac{1}{4}$
	446	45.6	$10\frac{1}{4}$
Average	56	5.7	

Masterton observed that an overall pre-tax of $10\frac{1}{4}$ per cent (net return over 6 per cent) on shareholders' investment after charging for amortisation of VC10 and One-Eleven development must be regarded as satisfactory.

A breakdown between the parents showed that, in the eight years, Bristol had received £7.259 million; English Electric, £26.642 million; and Vickers, £11.682 million. Of this, English Electric had £18.9 million 'old account' profits, and Vickers had written off £10 million of the VC10 losses. Taking the total capital employed by the individual shareholders, including loans and investment in old account, Bristol had an annual percentage return of $13\frac{1}{2}$ per cent, English Electric of 20.4 per cent but Vickers only 4.46 per cent, this resulting from its high capital employed on the VC10 and unamortised development costs.

The discussions, calculations, and re-calculations on the Rolls-Royce issue were to drag on until the Rolls-Royce financial crisis of 1970/71 ended in its dramatic bankruptcy. Sir Reginald Verdon-Smith has since written that it was a cause of great regret to him that Rolls-Royce did not sell their shares in BAC long before disaster overtook them. Sir Reginald has also commented that it was never opportune, as originally intended by the shareholders, to make a public issue of capital, thus reducing the Corporation's dependence on its corporate owners, and also reducing their involvement in BAC's policy-making.

Examination was, of course, made of the possibilities of going public, or at least up to 25 per cent public, during the Rolls-Royce discussions. The problem was, then, and subsequently, the obvious one of lack of certainty as to the future. Although BAC in the late 1960s was doing quite well, and showing good returns on investment, the outlook was not one to attract substantial outside money. Concorde remained a centre of public controversy and covered by question marks; the tri-national MRCA programme, which eventually plugged the AFVG hole at Warton, was not generally regarded as solid until the mid-seventies; and One-Eleven sales were falling off with still no resolution as to its successor. These things were seldom out of the headlines, and it is difficult to see how an offer of BAC shares would have been other than coldly received. After the fall of the Heath Government, the Labour administration had a mandate to nationalise the aircraft and shipbuilding industries, and that effectively ended all plans for making BAC a public company. To round off the matter of the Rolls-Royce 20 per cent shareholding, this was eventually bought from the Rolls-Royce Official Receiver by the remaining two shareholders on a fifty-fifty basis – thus making BAC equally jointly owned by Vickers and by GEC (the successor to English Electric), which is how affairs remained until the end.

GEC came into the BAC picture late in 1968 when GEC took over English Electric, having already bought AEI. As a result, the powerful figure of Sir Arnold Weinstock became the spokesman for a half-owner of BAC and, as with Rolls-Royce, he did so by the 'accident' that English Electric, which was his prime target, happened also to be a principal shareholder in the Corporation. Sir Arnold had no interest whatever at that time in the aircraft industry, save that it was a major customer for his electronic products, notably those of Marconi-Elliott. It was clear from the beginning that he was not overly impressed by what little he knew of BAC, and, with the exception of the Guided Weapons Division, which fitted naturally into his GEC electrical and electronics empire, he was more than willing to get rid of the rest at the best price he could. Later, he personally made a much fuller examination of the military and civil aircraft side, not all of it entirely on a financial basis, but with some regard to the wider national interest, and decided that, if it was carefully monitored, BAC might well be worth holding on to. By the mid-1970s, Weinstock, at first seen at Warton, Weybridge and Filton as the dreaded axe-wielder, had become, behind the scenes, a tower of strength to BAC, and emerged as the leader of the fight – right to the last ditch – against the 1977 nationalisation.

Sir Reginald Verdon-Smith took over the Chair of what was then British Aircraft Corporation (Holdings) Limited on 1 January 1969, and combined it smoothly with his other interests, notably the deputy chairmanship of Lloyds Bank. In his first report, he was able to describe 1969 accurately as one of 'exceptional achievement.' It was in 1969 that the Concorde 001 prototype made its first flight at Toulouse (2 March), that of 002 following at Filton on 9 April. Over a hundred Jet Provost Mark 5 aircraft were ordered for the Royal Air Force (14 January) and the first one was delivered on 4 September; Panavia was formed to build the MRCA (28 March – discussed later); the 200th Skylark sounding rocket was launched by BAC at Woomera (22 April); and the early Jaguars were getting airborne and flying supersonically. The Singapore Government placed a £10 million contract for refurbishing and modification of the ex-RAF Bloodhound installation (3 October) and BAC was chosen as prime contractor and design co-ordinating authority for the new British satellite, UK4 (24 February). Swingfire entered service with the British Army (26 March), Rapier completed its firing trials at Woomera (18 September), and, above all, during the year thirty-eight BAC One-Elevens were delivered, bringing the total in service to 164 with thirty-six operators in fifteen countries. Fifteen further new One-Elevens were ordered, and the cost of development was progressively being amortised over the first 200 deliveries in accordance with the policy laid down in 1965. There was a further substantial order for Vigilants for the Army – making 12,000 missiles to date – and, as a result of the Intelsat IV contract, the new Space Centre was put under way. Export records were broken with £85 million – 46 per cent of BAC's total business – the main contributors being the BAC One-Eleven and the Lightning.

On the overall financial side, the 1969 results were a little below those of 1968. Turnover was down from £191.4 million to £183.9 million, but total trading profit was only £150,000 down at £12.2 million – but this was after charging over £4.5 million to One-Eleven development amortisation as against just over £3 million in 1968. The net profit before tax and after interest was £5.574 million (£6.257 million) – but Corporation Tax was 2½ per cent higher at 45 per cent. The after-tax net profit was £2.793 million (£4.235 million) which, Sir Reginald commented, although lower than the 1968 figure, compared extremely favourably with the out-turn of earlier years (1966 – £198,000; 1967 – £1.53 million). A dividend of £1.7 million was declared, the same as in 1968, and £1 million was transferred to reserves. Sir Reginald also referred to the fact that BAC had, in its ten years, made new investment in capital expenditure on buildings, plant and machinery of £30 million – over £4.5 million of it in 1969.

In the 'Conclusion' to his report, Sir Reginald said, 'At a time when some of the best known elements in the aerospace industry, both in Britain and in the USA, are experiencing particularly intractable problems, both technically and financially, it is encouraging to be able to report that the prospects for BAC are potentially excellent. In the short term, the favourable results of 1968 and 1969 should be followed in 1970 by another satisfactory year's progress. In the longer term, our future success rests on the foundation provided by our wide spread of projects embracing, as they do, those which are in full production and a number under development which rate amongst the most technically advanced in the world.'

During 1969, Dr A.E. Russell, Chairman of the Filton Division, retired from executive responsibilities, but succeeded Sir George as Chairman of the Concorde Airframe Committee of Directors. 'Russ' was truly the father of Concorde, and his outstanding contribution to British aviation over a working lifetime was recognised by an honorary fellowship of the Royal Aeronautical Society, by election as a Fellow of the Royal Society, and later, by a generally applauded knighthood. Geoffrey Knight, who was already Chairman and Managing Director of the Weybridge Division, also became Chairman of the Filton Division on Russell's retirement, having George Gedge as his Managing Director there, and promoting John Ferguson Smith from Deputy Managing Director at Weybridge to Managing Director, which post Knight relinquished. In September 1969, Mr Handel Davies, formerly Deputy Controller (Research and Development) in the Aviation Group of the Ministry of Technology, joined BAC as Technical Director. He came into industry after a distinguished career at Farnborough, Boscombe Down and the Ministry of Defence. Allen Greenwood made a significant change from being Assistant Managing Director of BAC to Deputy Managing Director, but Lord Caldecote left the Corporation and the Holdings Board consequent upon his resignation as a Director of the English Electric Company – which company now belonged to GEC.

In May of 1968, the aircraft industry had to fight yet another battle with the Government which made known its belief that the aircraft industry had not exhibited a favourable growth-rate over the past ten years. It had a good export record, but this was allegedly achieved at too great a cost as the defence and airline needs of the UK could be met much more cheaply by overseas purchase (the old Treasury/Zuckerman argument).

BAC made quick reply that the Government's own formidable record of cancelled British projects was enough to account for a lack of growth – what else did they expect? – and also that such clear expressions of lack of confidence in the industry had a very bad effect on the overseas sales prospects of such British products as had managed to reach fruition. As for the accusation that aviation used up too much of the UK's research and development money, most of this was really part of the procurement cost of aircraft which the Government had at one time or another decided to purchase. The fact that, once the research and development money was spent, the Government often then killed the project was hardly the fault of the industry.

Nothing came of these various Min-Tech papers and questionnaires and policy committees, save to underline the chop-logic and short-term thinking that went on when Ministry officials were seeking to bolster up a case for Britain to abdicate in favour of the USA and France from an industry which was undoubtedly at the spearhead of that very technology for which Min-Tech was supposed to be the Ministry, and which also employed over a quarter of a million of highly qualified people.

In February 1969, the Society of British Aerospace Companies (SBAC) entered the lists and produced a well-publicised document, *Into the Seventies*, which was sub-titled *A Future Plan for Britain's Aerospace Industry*. The principal object of this booklet was yet again to demonstrate to the Government, and, in particular, to the Whitehall mandarins, that the industry was essential to the national well-being and that Government/industry co-operation should be strengthened, not weakened. The SBAC called attention to the fact that, from 1958 to 1967, two-thirds of the UK civil aerospace output went overseas and in 1967 it was 69 per cent. In the two years 1966/7 exports averaged £208 million and, of this, £58 million or 28 per cent went to the USA. No other major British engineering industry had a comparable record. The nearest to aerospace's 28 per cent rate to the USA was the toy industry (21 per cent of output) but its value was only £3.4 million against aerospace's £58 million. In the first nine months of 1968, the aircraft exports going to the dollar market formed 36 per cent of the total. The report also made the point of the high conversion-rate of aerospace products – which represented mainly skills and man-hours and little raw material – but worth £50,000 per ton, compared to £500 a ton for a new car.

These were much the same arguments that Sir George had long been using in speeches and lectures, and the start of one he made in 1970 to the Guild of Air Pilots and Air Navigators (a year after the SBAC report) is worth quoting:

> Last year, the industry exported goods and equipment worth over £350 million. To achieve this, the industry employs 240,000 people, giving an exports-per-employee figure of twice that for the UK manufacturing industries as a whole. An industry earning £1 million per working day is a national asset by any standard. In BAC alone, the investment of public monies of £25 million in 1950–70 [company investment, £122 million] has produced a total benevolent effect on our balance of payments of £733 million.

Returning to the 1969 SBAC document: having established the case for the industry, it went on to forecast total sales of £808 million (excluding Guided Weapons) by 1977, of which £570 million would be for export. (In fact, in 1977, British Aerospace – in effect, just BAC and Hawker – achieved, on their own, sales of £859 million, of which £536 million was exported. This included Guided Weapons but, of course, excluded engines and all the substantial electrical and other equipment sales as well as the contribution of outside concerns such as Westland and Shorts.)

SBAC ended with a plea to the Government to collaborate with industry – British or British-and-European – on a range of new civil projects, military aircraft, weapons and engines, with their associated equipments, and also underlined the future importance of Space. In the military aircraft, weapons, engine, and satellite fields, a number of the SBAC proposals was eventually taken up in one form or another and notably, on the aircraft side, by the MRCA and the Hawk, but a deaf ear continued to be turned to the need for new commercial transports.

28

Variable Geometry

There have been many mentions in previous chapters of variable-geometry aircraft concepts which concerned BAC – notably the AF VG and the MRCA, now named as the Tornado. The variable-geometry, or, more popularly, the swing-wing, idea had in fact been studied, and in some detail, at Weybridge and then at Warton, not only throughout BAC's lifetime, but within Vickers, for all the post-war years.

The basic advantages of variable-geometry wings is that they can be put into the forward or straight position for take-off and for economical, long-range, high-altitude cruise or loiter on patrol, but can be swept back for high-speed supersonic flight, thus giving considerable operational flexibility. Aerodynamicists had talked about the possible advantages of moving the sweep of wings for many years before supersonic flight made such theories of immediate practical value. The UK pioneer of genuine application of the idea was Dr Barnes Wallis (later Sir Barnes) of Vickers, who had come into considerable prominence during the war with his anti-dam and anti-shipping mines and his Tallboy and Grand Slam bombs. Before that he had been responsible for the highly successful R100 airship, and for the subsequent lattice-work geodetic form of structure of the Wellesley and Wellington aircraft.

Wallis began his variable-geometry studies in 1945 and concentrated on doing away with the tailplane and rudder, and producing an aircraft with a very high lift/drag ratio, the variable wings themselves, by changes of sweep and of incidence, providing the control functions. He was aiming at an ultra long-range aircraft, preferably civil, capable of flying non-stop and un-refuelled from London to Sydney. Wallis obtained Ministry backing for a series of model trials under the name 'Wild Goose,' which lasted from 1949 to 1954. First of all, these were hand-launched tests at Weybridge, followed by trolley launches at Thurleigh, Bedfordshire, and then at an old RAF airfield at Predannack in Cornwall. The Ministry of Supply had its eye on a possible very long-range gun-fired anti-aircraft missile, 'Green Lizard,' which deployed flip-out variable-geometry wings, while Wallis was much more concerned with the transport possibilities. The Wild Goose programme, and various offshoots of it, did not progress particularly smoothly, but a good many flights were made, enough to set Wallis working on a follow-up called Swallow. This had an arrow-head delta 'lifting' fore-body and variable-geometry wings, and had (rather surprisingly, if the engine-failure case is considered) engine pods at the long lever arm of the wing tips, the pods themselves swivelling to keep head-on into the airflow as the wings altered their sweep. The wings were ingeniously pivoted at the base of the delta so that, when fully swept, they formed a straight line with the delta forebody.

Swallow, at first Ministry of Supply funded, later became a joint Government/Vickers responsibility, and led to various military submissions, including a bomber. The 1957 Sandys White Paper ended the Government funding, and Wallis was not very keen on a brief-lived further proposal to build a small piloted variable-geometry aircraft with conventional tailplane – regarding the replacement of a tail as a retrograde step. Further, ever since the casualties of the Dambuster raid which upset him deeply, Wallis had been most averse to risking life in experimental aircraft.

With UK funds drying up, he turned for finance to the American Mutual Weapons Development Programme under John Stack, who, with colleagues, visited Weybridge, while a British team, under Wallis, went to NASA at Langley field. The USA had already built a subsonic variable-geometry aircraft, the Bell X-5, in 1951, but the Wallis proposals went well beyond that, and into supersonics where variable geometry really paid off. The Americans were given all the Wallis data in good faith, but, instead of providing the expected financial support for the British programme, they kept the studies back at Langley Field, and applied them, to Wallis's annoyance, to a conventional and purely US military aircraft, eventually giving birth to the concept of the F111. The Wallis tail-less arrowhead had disappeared, but his work had certainly demonstrated to the Americans the engineering practicability of wing pivots which would operate at high speed. This was in 1959, and in that year the new Weybridge Military Project Office took over further variable-geometry responsibility under Maurice Brennan, whose team included Alan Clifton (ex-Supermarine) and N.W. Boorer, who had been Chief Designer (Research and Development) under Wallis. They worked on a variable-geometry solution to a joint Naval/Air Staff Requirement for a very high speed (Mach 3+) interceptor-strike aircraft, OR346, which was presumably to succeed TSR2, itself still only in the design stage. Eventually, experimental research submissions were called for (ER206), and Vickers submitted an up-date of the Wallis tail-less delta fore-body concept, with a whole family of derivatives. The OR346 suffered the usual fate in 1960, but a naval requirement for a Sea Vixen replacement survived. This was pursued by Alan Clifton (Brennan had gone to Folland as Chief Engineer to devise a variable-geometry version of the Gnat) and by Spud Boorer, and, in 1962, the team came up with Type 583, a variable-geometry interceptor with two re-heated Medways with deflected thrust and cross-over jet pipes to meet the engine-out case. In the end, the 583 was superseded by the Hawker 1154 which, in its turn, was also abandoned. At this stage, Vickers and BAC had done a great deal of basic work on variable geometry and, after the Wallis pioneering efforts, had made many engineering studies of pivot structures and mechanism.

In 1964, all variable-geometry work was transferred from Weybridge to Warton, with Boorer supervising the hand-over, and more studies were put in hand on the application of variable geometry to light strike and trainer aircraft, for both of which there appeared to be an opening. Warton put up to the Government a proposal for a multi-role variable-geometry aeroplane, the BAC P45, which could do the STOL fighter job and also meet a known trainer requirement. The P45, which underwent its feasibility studies in 1963 and 1964, would have made a perfect aeroplane on which to introduce practical swing-wings, and BAC pressed the Government to build two prototypes, the first of which could have flown in 1968. What was now needed, Warton argued, was to build an actual variable-geometry aeroplane and to stop all the talk and theory which had now gone on for over twenty years without the UK putting anything into the air except Wallis models. This was immediately post-TSR2, and the choice before Healey at the Ministry of Defence became one between a Franco-British collaborative aeroplane based on the subsonic Breguet B121 ECAT, or an Anglo-French collaboration on the variable-geometry BAC P45. He chose the former, and the Jaguar was evolved on a fixed-wing basis. Alongside the Jaguar, however, Healey had negotiated the AFVG, which was to make use of BAC's variable-geometry knowledge and was to be British-led in design.

The AFVG feasibility study was issued in July 1965. It was to be multi-role, and have a high altitude speed of Mach 2.5. The eventual final version of the AFVG, arrived at after a number of changes in the specification, was for quite a large aeroplane, 60 feet long overall and of $42\frac{1}{2}$ feet unswept span, and a sweep-back to 70 degrees. A full-scale mock-up was built at Warton, and showed the AFVG to have an all-moving tail-plane, and two rear-fuselage M45G engines. As has already been recounted, the AFVG only lasted until June 1967 when the French, who were already doing their own variable-geometry aircraft, the Dassault Mirage G, pulled out of the project, still leaving the UK once again with no swing-wing project, and with an important part of the Warton design team virtually unemployed.

Healey's response, as already recorded, was to send his representatives out to explore the chances of the UK getting in on the European F104 replacement consortium, and, at the same time, to give BAC a holding contract so that its variable-geometry work could continue under the title of the UKVG. Once again BAC pressed hard for permission to build a quick prototype to get some actual flying experience, but once again the answer was 'No.'

Another and little-known attempt to get Warton into the swing-wing business was started in Australia by Jeffrey Quill. He had been trying to sell Jaguar to RAAF as a trainer replacement for their Macchi 326s, but the Australians considered the aircraft to be too large and expensive. The Commonwealth Aircraft Company was also promoting a local aircraft design for the Macchi replacement, but this was too small. Quill suggested to the Australian Controller of Aircraft and Guided Weapons (Fleming) that Australia and BAC could combine jointly to design and build a single-engined, variable-sweep aircraft based on Jaguar which would meet the RAAF requirement and would have good export potential. Back in the UK, Sir George and Freddie Page approved the idea, and four senior Australian designers were sent to Warton to work on the proposal, the combined team being headed by Ray Creasey. The result was the AA107 design, which was supersonic and swing-wing, had good tactical ground attack capability, and was powered by one un-reheated Adour engine. It was, in many ways, a fore-runner of the Hawk, but was unfortunately ahead of its time. The RAF policy of the day was that Jaguar was to be its new advanced trainer, and there was, therefore, no UK requirement for the AA107. An Australian order alone could not justify the research and development expenditure and, after six months or so, the idea was dropped. Afterwards, the RAF turned away from the idea of having the Jaguar as an advanced trainer, and came up with a requirement for a smaller aircraft which the AA107 could well have filled. Both BAC and Hawker Siddeley submitted rather similar fixed-wing designs for this, but the order went to Hawker and the Hawk.

While on the subject of Warton enterprise, an interesting and rather off-beat project of the 1960s was its P35, the so-called 'Jumping Jeep.' This was basically an Armed Reconnaisance Vehicle designed for cross-country work. It incorporated an air-cushion (hovercraft) ability to enable it to cross water and marshland as well as to drive on ordinary roads. Its most striking ability, however, was to be able to leap straight up in the air and then to 'fly' forward, which enabled it to clear most obstacles. The technical details of the P35 are still restricted. The 'Jumping Jeep' could carry a good range of weapons including mortars and anti-tank missiles. The idea was first looked at in 1960, and there was a feasibility study contract from 1962. In November 1966, however, the Ministry of Defence halted the work, and although BAC studied applications of the 'leap' principle, and of a combination of ordinary road-using and hovercraft abilities in commercial vehicles, the project was eventually put aside.

At this stage, Warton was becoming cynical. It had seen TSR2 and the P45 go down the drain; it had seen all the French manoeuvres to ditch the AFVG and, with Healey's massive orders for USA equipment still soaking up the Defence Budget, it had no belief whatever that the UK VG would ever be built. Healey, too, in 1967, had his problems, even if they were all self-inflicted. The F111 – as predicted – was in all kinds of trouble, and its costs were rocketing; the politically clever idea of engining the British Phantoms with Speys had proved to be a financial disaster; the unpopular advisers who had told him that the French only wanted a defence interceptor and would pull out of the dual-role AFVG had proved to be right; and he was facing a shut-down at Warton, the most important military aircraft design centre in the country (if not Europe). His (and Warton's) last hope was that the UK could somehow insert itself into the European F104 replacement programme, even though the British had no F104s to replace. The European consortium was already looking at a number of proposals including a German (NKF) and VSTOL US collaboration aircraft (the AVS, which became very complicated indeed).

Healey, however, was able to get his foot in the door first, as has been stated, with the RAF as 'observers' at discussions between West Germany, Italy, the Netherlands, Belgium and Canada, and later as partners. The British then proceeded to steer the European requirements towards that which the RAF wanted, until, in late 1968, they had the multi-role strike and long-range fighter variable-geometry specification they had set out to obtain from the beginning. In the process (October 1968), they lost Canada, which was re-evaluating its basic defence position *vis à vis* NATO and at the same time, Belgium withdrew, and there was generated a certain amount of resentment, especially in Belgium and the Netherlands. The latter, however, did not finally withdraw until July 1969. Both these countries were much later to meet their simpler needs by the eventual purchase of American F16s – the object of the original consortium having been to avoid just such another round of defence purchase from the USA. West Germany, and, after some havering, Italy supported the UK and, in December 1968, the three Air Staffs – with the Netherlands taking a 'rain-check' – agreed the new aircraft's configuration and an Interim Management Organisation was established. The MRCA swing-wing programme had been launched.

Early in 1969, three-nation joint design teams, with the Dutch still taking an official interest, were formed from BAC, Messerschmitt-Bölkow-Blohm and Fiat, and the basic aeroplane began to be clothed in detail, while cost-sharing, work-sharing and the various standards and procedures were also worked out. The number of aircraft which each country would require was the yardstick by which the apportioning of work and cost would be decided, and, with the F111 now finally off the UK shopping list, the RAF spoke for 385 aircraft, West Germany for 600 and Italy for 200. The Dutch reluctantly backed out, the aeroplane being too complicated and costly for their defence budget.

So, at long last, the UK was to build, or at least to share in the building of, an actual variable-geometry aircraft, even though it was in conventional form and far removed from the Wallis super-range tail-less Delta. Sir Barnes, however, never gave up his advocacy of this format, and continued to study it, and other more advanced and even sub-orbital lob transports until well after his eightieth birthday.

The following timetable of the P45/AFVG/MRCA story gives a potted history of BAC's 'progress' with variable geometry from 1963, until the end of 1969, when the MRCA project could be described as properly launched.

Table 3

1963

30 January	Work started on P45.

1964

19 February	P45 work – Feasibility Study started.
16 May	BAC Assessment of Anglo-French Requirement.
5 August	P45 work – Feasibility Study completed.
12 August	P45 work – Further development started.

1965

17 May	AFVG Memorandum of Understanding.
11 June	First Contract.
2 August to 31 October	Second Contract
1 November 1965 to 31 July 1967	Feasibility Study Contract.

1966

7 November	Ministers' meeting in London between Mr Healey and M. Messmer. (Go ahead deferred).
14 November 1966 to 28 February 1967	Joint Studies Contract.

1967

16 January	Ministry decision to go ahead with AFVG.
21 March	Visit of General Steinhoff and German Party to Warton.
17 April	Ministers' meeting.
5 July	Official withdrawal of French from AFVG.
1 August	Start of UKVG Project Study phase.
25 October	Presentation to German Air Force at Bonn with MOD and Min-Tech.
31 October	Visit of Bundestag Defence Committee to Warton.
November	German firms EWR, VFW and Bölkow formed a working group to implement the first part of the concept phase of a European variable-geometry aircraft.

1968

5 March	Representatives of Belgium, Canada, Hol-

	land, Italy and German Air Forces met at the Luftwaffe headquarters at Porz-Wahn.
17–18 May	Meetings of the Chiefs of Air Staff of Belgium, Canada, Holland, Italy, and West Germany in Rome.
7 June	Presentation of 1 versus 2-engine studies in Bonn.
17 July	Meeting of Air Force representatives from Belgium, Canada, Holland, Italy, West Germany and Great Britain in Bonn.
23 August	Meeting of representatives of BAC, Canadair, EWR, Fokker and SABCA at Amsterdam-Schipol.
5 September	Meeting of representatives of BAC, Canadair, EWR, Fiat, Fokker and SABCA at Munich.
11–12 September	Meeting of BAC, MBB and Fokker.
23 September	Conference of representatives of all six firms at Weybridge.
Second week in October	Meeting of the Chiefs of Air Staff from all six countries. Instructions given to implement a Joint Feasibility Study by the end of December 1968. Canadian representative announced the intention of his Government to withdraw from Consortium until basic political defence and economic questions had been clarified.
11 October	Meeting of the firms of the Consortium at Fiat, Turin. German interim Managing Director named for the industrial consortium.
22–23 October	Meeting of the Consortium at Fokker. Meeting informed of the withdrawal of Canadair from the Consortium.
23–24 October	Unofficial talks between representatives of industry and the Operational Requirements Group at Munich.
25 October	Initial Statement of Work.
30 October	Conference between members of the Consortium and the Requirements Group at Munich. Consortium informed of the withdrawal of Belgium.
29 November	Interim Feasibility Study Report.
19 December	Statement of Work.
1969	
31 January	Final Feasibility Study Report.
14 March	Baseline Configuration Brochure.

26 March	Panavia formed.
1 May	Start of Definition Phase.
6 May	Start of 60-day engine competition between Rolls-Royce and Pratt & Whitney
14 May	MRCA Memorandum of Understanding.
20 May	Revised Statement of Work.
14 July	Engine Proposal.
28 July	Netherlands Defence Minister announced formal withdrawal from Consortium.
26 September	Avionica formed.
30 September	Turbo-Union formed.
1 October	Engine Contract placed.
13 October	Instructions to Proceed and Holding Contract (1 October 1969 to 31 December 1969).
23–27 November	Design Review in Munich.

A fuller history of BAC and variable-geometry work, and of Sir Barnes Wallis's patents, can be studied in Ollie Heath's lecture of January 1970, 'The MRCA Project,' printed in the *Royal Aeronautical Society Journal* for June 1970.

29

The MRCA

The initial announcement of the MRCA Memorandum of Understanding was made in the House of Commons by Dennis Healey after question-time on 14 May 1969. He said:

Four European Governments, West Germany, Italy, Holland and the UK, have been working together over the past year to harmonise their national requirements for a military aircraft which would enter service in the late 1970s. Feasibility studies have shown that these requirements can be met in a multi-role aircraft which could be built to a substantially common design. Representatives of West Germany, Italy and the UK have today signed a Memorandum of Understanding under which they will co-operate on the next phase of project definition which will last about a year, and I hope that within a month or two the Dutch Government will also sign. The countries co-operating are likely to require over 1000 aircraft, of which the RAF stands to take about a third.

It is proposed to introduce it in 1976 in the tactical strike/reconnaissance role and subsequently in the air defence and maritime strike roles. We are thus planning eventually to replace Vulcans, Buccaneers and Phantoms by variants of a single basic design. This will have very substantial advantages in the logistic and training fields. By sharing the cost of developing and producing these aircraft, the European countries concerned will meet their defence needs much more cheaply than any one of them could on its own. Technologically, it can help to provide a solid foundation for the future of the aerospace industry in Europe.

The British Aircraft Corporation, Messerschmitt-Bölkow, Fiat and Fokker have formed the Panavia Company jointly to develop and produce the aircraft. Although the engine and avionics will not be chosen until the project has been more closely defined, importance will be attached to making the project entirely European.

Agreement on this project marks a great step forward in harmonising the operational thinking of the major NATO governments and in demonstrating their conviction that, in the field of defence technology, no less than that of defence, survival depends on unity. For these reasons, it has a political significance for Western Europe extending well beyond the military and industrial needs it will meet.

The Minister, having made that statement, immediately left the Chamber to give one of those unofficial, unattributable Press conferences at which a Minister can hide behind the convention that he is an anonymous Ministry spokesman. He told the Press much more (especially on costs, which subject he had not mentioned in the House) than he had told MPs, for which he landed himself into hot water, and the charges, counter-charges, and denials went on for some time afterwards.

He revealed at the conference that by 1980 he expected the MRCA to provide two-thirds of the RAF's front-line combat strength, that the Managing Director of Panavia would be a 'brilliant young German engineer called Madelung,' the Programme Manager, a Dutchman (General Stockla), and the Production Manager, an Italian (Dr Delmastro). There would be, in effect, two design directors known as 'Systems Engineering Directors'; one was Ollie Heath, head of the BAC Project team at Warton, and the other a 'man from MBB' (Langfelder). The total work in the early stages would be divided in proportion to the then estimate of numbers of aircraft required, the German estimate being 50 per cent higher than that of the British. There would be a competition for the engine between Rolls-Royce and the USA (Pratt & Whitney), and the Minister believed Rolls-Royce 'can win on merit.' The Minister then said that the UK share of the research and development costs would be about £150 million, possibly something under that, and the German share nearly £200 million. The Italian share would be less than that of the UK, and the Dutch very much smaller. The unit-cost per aircraft would be a bit over £1.5 million for the RAF two-seater version (at this stage a single-seater and a two-seater were both proposed). The ball-park requirements seemed to be, from the Healey briefing, Germany 600 aircraft, UK 385 aircraft, and Italy 200 aircraft. If the Netherlands came in, the total initial production would be some 1285 aircraft.

The Minister told the Press that the French, having pulled out of the AFVG, had tried to sell the Mirage-G into every European country, including the UK, but without success. In his view, the French were sceptical about whether the MRCA negotiations would be successful, and that they might be able to pick up some of the pieces. Subsequently, the question of the French joining the MRCA had been touched on, but it appeared that the French had no actual requirement for an aircraft at all. They were quite free to join the consortium, providing they stated a convincing natural requirement for an adequate number of aircraft – otherwise not, and in his view, that ruled the French out.

In the early days of the MRCA, there were, as stated, two versions of the aircraft – the Panavia 100 and 200 – the 100 being a single-seater for the close air support and air superiority roles for Germany and Italy, the

200 being a two-seater for strike, naval strike, and training for the UK, Germany and Italy, the Italians wanting a two-seater only for training. By March 1970, however, there had been a major re-adjustment of the numbers of aircraft which each of the three countries would need, and along with this went a decision by Germany and Italy to take the two-seater as standard. The whole MRCA production programme was thus simplified into building the two-seater, with some UK-only modifications for their particular Air Defence Variant in order to accommodate the radar and associated systems.

The new numbers required were Germany 400, RAF 400 and Italy 100, with airframe research and development total estimates falling from £410 million to £320 million, as there were now only seven instead of an originally planned thirteen prototypes needed, and six pre-production aircraft instead of thirty.

The work-sharing programmes, and the proportion of the shares held in Panavia, necessarily fluctuated to reflect the changes in procurement plans. Initially, the Panavia shareholding had been Germany 49 per cent, UK 34 per cent and Italy 17 per cent. The new division became Germany 42.5 per cent, UK 42.5 per cent and Italy 15 per cent.

As the project progressed there were further changes in procurement as inflation stepped up the costs, and the 'split' eventually became:

UK	385 aircraft (220 Strike and	
		165 Special Air Defence)
Germany	324 aircraft	
Luftwaffe	212	Both Strike
German Navy	112	
Italy	100 aircraft (Standard Strike and Air	
		Superiority)

This gives a total of 809 aircraft, 805 of them 'new,' and four being modified from pre-Series aircraft.

The shareholding in Panavia remained at nationalisation, at least officially, at 42.5 – 42.5,– 15, but in May 1976 Mr William Rodgers of the Ministry of Defence said in Parliament that the UK's share of the total programme was really 47.6 per cent.

Turning now to the MRCA as such, and as it was finally specified, the aeroplane on which the RAF eventually settled for as its main front-line warplane for the 1980s and beyond was no longer just a Canberra replacement, but a replacement for practically its whole combat strength with the exception of the Jaguar and Harrier and the specialist aeroplanes such as maritime reconnaissance, transports, trainers and helicopters.

Up till the application of variable geometry, the long search for a 'miracle' general-purpose aeroplane to fill a number of combat roles had not been very successful. In actual war conditions, the specialist aircraft, fighter or bomber, had historically proved superior to anything which, in trying to be both, was less than the best at either task. By the mid-1960s, however, and with the Royal Air Force no longer having an East-of-Suez role, and having become a wholly European air force, the NATO requirements lay within a narrower span than before. These require-ments were for an aircraft which could not only fulfil, but fulfil in the face of sophisticated Warsaw Pact defences, the following roles:

Close air-to-ground support (battlefield interdiction)
Air superiority
Interdiction strike
Reconnaissance
Naval support strike and reconnaissance
Operational training

To examine the tasks in more detail: for close air support, the new design called for STOL (3000-feet take-off and half that for landing) to obtain quick reaction-time from dispersed sites, a transonic performance at low altitude, good gust-response, high manoeuvre-capability and an adequate lo-lo radius of action on internal fuel alone, carrying a strong and variable weapon-load to match the targets. Air superiority required the same characteristics, plus high supersonic speed, and high rate of climb and manoeuvre at altitude. This altitude performance would automatically follow from the transonic ability at low level.

Interdiction-strike-reconnaissance, over land or sea, called for the same basics as battlefield strike, but with a longer penetration-range and more sophisticated all-weather radar, electronic counter-measures, and nav-attack systems. Put the other way round, the aircraft which could do long-range interdiction strike using wing-tank fuel could also do the shorter range task with 'dry' wings and on internal fuel only. It would be something of a mis-use of the powers of the MRCA to put it on to close support but, since it might well be called upon to help out the Jaguars and Harriers etc., it had to be able to do so, and indeed, Healey spoke of it early on as being available to take over from the Jaguar.

An analysis made of the above requirements by the three Air Staffs showed that, provided the basic aircraft was given a sufficiently healthy margin of power, it was possible to devise one which would accomplish all the missions specified by the three nations by the fitting of the 'black-boxes' appropriate to the interdiction and recce roles and by the provision of the suitable weapon stowage and nav-attack equipment. What made this flexibility technically possible was the choice of variable-geometry wings which, by selecting the correct settings, would enable an MRCA to fulfill all the various requirements without loss of efficiency in any one of them.

There was argument for a time, especially in Italy, about a two-man crew in the air-superiority role, but the ever-increasing complexity of the defence task which, more and more, calls for the operation of avionics and ECMs – a demand which will certainly not decrease with time – showed a clear need to have one man flying the aeroplane and the other concentrating on the avionics.

The result of these deliberations was a Feasibility Study for a two-seater, twin-engined, variable-geometry aircraft with a speed of $M=2+$ at altitude and of $M=1+$ at ground level, with excellent gust-response, and STOL. Two Mauser cannons were to be fitted as standard and provision made for the carriage of all kinds of attack and air-to-air weapons, including the German special requirement for defensive 'Streuwaffen' to counter the Warsaw Pact preponderance of tanks.

Comprehensive all-weather avionics, blind delivery and recce systems were called for from the electronics industry for the interdiction, recce and naval strike versions, while the fact that the final MRCA was to be a two-seater enabled the training requirement easily to be met. The variable-geometry 'plot' was for a straight wing with high-lift devices for STOL, and for very good attack-manoeuvrability over a battlefield. For transonic speeds and for combat manoeuvrability, the wings would be swept to an intermediate position and combat slats and flaps used. For prolonged high speeds and maximum acceleration, the wings would be swept right back.

The Royal Air Force Air Defence requirement, which eventually represented 165 of the total British buy of 385 aircraft, called for something special which was not needed by the Germans and the Italians. The UK Air Defence problem uniquely involves the interception over the sea of raiders and reconnaissance aircraft coming in over the far northern waters, and also those aimed at shipping in our Western Approaches. This is not a dog-fight or a 'Richthofen's Circus' kind of situation, but a long-range outpost battle, fought, on the UK side, by patrolling aircraft which are capable of long loiter and are, in effect, high-altitude and (by sweeping the wings) high-speed launching platforms for the latest air-to-air guided missiles.

For this vital UK and NATO defence task, an adaptation of the standard variable-geometry MRCA provided the perfect vehicle. The RAF's Air Defence Version – the Tornado ADV – is four feet longer than the standard, to contain the extra avionics and some extra fuel. The air-intercept radar will detect targets up to 115 miles, and the Sky Flash missiles, of which it carries four, will engage multiple targets at a distance of over 25 miles. For close combat, there are Sidewinder missiles under the wings and the Mauser 27 mm cannon. The ADV, thus armed, will patrol 300 to 400 miles from its home territory for over two hours at a time, including provision for an interception and ten minutes of combat. Even without air refuelling, the ADV has on board fuel enough to cross a continent the size of Australia. The ADV division of responsibilities is that the pilot controls the attack and weapon delivery, while the navigator looks after target detection, communication with the aircraft's computer, operation of the radar and other sensors, and the overall evaluation of the tactical situation.

Once the aircraft was fully defined and, with it, the thrust required from the two Turbo-Union R B199 engines, which were duly selected as the powerplants, the technical progress on this, Europe's biggest-ever military aircraft project, was remarkably smooth, and, considering the magnitude of the task, and that there were three partners in both airframe and engine, almost without incident and certainly without upheaval. For that, much credit must be given to the organisation of Panavia itself and of the three-nation NATO set-up which was evolved to control and monitor the programme.

30
Panavia

There is little doubt that Panavia represents the best format yet devised for a major multilateral military aircraft undertaking. The company itself had three shareholders, MBB (initially DM60,000), BAC (DM39,600) and Fiat (DM20,400), and was registered under German law at Munich on 28 March 1969. The shareholdings have altered over the years to reflect the changes in procurement already mentioned, and Fiat has become Aeritalia, but principle and principals have remained the same. It might be better to be able to register a European company under some new kind of Common Market law, but a European collaborative enterprise still has to be registered as answerable to the law of one chosen country – in this case, Germany, which had originally spoken of ordering 600 aircraft to the UK's 385.

There were two important new aspects in Panavia which have undoubtedly contributed much to its success. The first was that it was given its own headquarters staff, and the second was that the aircraft it was building was given a NATO designation and put under the control of a tri-national NATO organisation known as NAMMO (NATO MRCA Development and Production Management Organisation) – an organisation officially recognised by the NATO Council.

NAMMO was the top-level Ministerial body, but under it was a day-to-day management agency (NAMMA) to which were attached senior officers and officials of the three nations, and they were housed in the same building on the outskirts of Munich as Panavia. The industrial set-up of Panavia incorporated the lessons BAC had learned from Concorde and Jaguar, and took the evolution of international collaborative enterprise a stage further. Whereas SEPECAT, the Jaguar company, had been, in effect, a 'brass-plate' affair to hold and place contracts, Panavia had a real existence in that it not only had a Board and a Managing Director, but, as already mentioned, also had a staff. True, this staff was on secondment from the three parents, but many of them were wholly transferred to Munich (with benefit of German rates of pay) or commuted there on a regular basis in company executive aircraft. The Managing Director was, as Mr Healey had said, one of the younger and most promising of MBB's engineers, Dr Gero Madelung (later also Professor of Aeronautics at Munich University). Professor Madelung remained in his key Panavia position until 1978, when, with the programme fully established, he was succeeded by Dr C.P. Fichtmüller.

Gero Madelung, a nephew of Willie Messerschmitt, had received part of his engineering education in the USA, and was a remarkably good choice. He spoke excellent English (the official language of Panavia), had a thorough grasp of every aspect of the MRCA programme, and was both liked and respected by all who had the pleasure of working with him. It might have been thought, even in the late sixties, that there could have been tension in meetings chaired by a member of the Messerschmitt family, when one of his functional Directors, the Marketing Director, was the man who had test-flown the Spitfire throughout its operational life, who had fought in the Battle of Britain with the RAF, and who had also fought in the Seafire on attachment to the Royal Navy, Jeffrey Quill. This was far from the case. The two men got on extremely well and, amidst some banter, Quill autographed a photograph of a Spitfire for Gero's famous uncle, and, in return, received an autographed photograph of a Messerschmitt 109. Madelung's Flight Test Director too, was a famous wartime British fighter pilot, Roland Beamont, and he had under him German, Italian and BAC test pilots. It all worked surprisingly well, the younger members of the Panavia team being post-war, and the senior people finding the Germans (mostly Bavarians), most congenial colleagues. Working with the Germans was certainly more straightforward and tranquil than working with the French.

Freddie Page and Allen Greenwood were the leading BAC figures in Panavia, with Mr E. Loveless as Madelung's Deputy and Ollie Heath and Helmut Langfelder as, in effect, co-Chief Designers. Here again, two talented men, Heath and Langfelder, could have found themselves at cross-purposes, but, instead, became firm friends, and their friendship was to last until Langfelder's sad death at the age of forty-nine in a helicopter crash in France in 1978. Langfelder had just been made Chairman of MBB, taking over from Ludwig Bölkow, head of MBB throughout the setting-up and the crucial stages of the MRCA programme.

The initial Panavia Board was Allen Greenwood, with Ludwig Bölkow, F. Forster-Steinberg (MBB), F.W. Page (BAC), and F. Giura and C. Raffagni (Fiat). Greenwood was the first Chairman, and Herr Bölkow and then Signor Giura later occupied that position in rotation. The functional Directors (Managers, really) under Gero Madelung and Loveless (Programme Management) were Heath and Langfelder as joint Directors of Systems Engineering, Herr Klapperich (Finance and Contracts), Signor Delmastro (Production), G. Althusius (a Dutchman, ex-VFW, Procurement) and J.K. Quill (Marketing). Later, Roly Beamont became Director of Flight Test.

There is no doubt that Panavia has, organisationally, been the most successful of European collaborative ventures. From the time it was formed on 26 March 1969, it set about its job in a most workmanlike way. A Programme Management System was evolved by Madelung and Loveless to cover the airframe, the engine and the avionics, and to provide the customer (NAMMO) with a positive central planning, directing and controlling organisation. Initially, the MRCA avionics were by separate contract, thus giving NAMMO three main contractors to deal with – Panavia, Turbo-Union (for the engine) and a three-nation avionics consortium (Avionica). The lessons of TSR2, however, argued against the avionics being out of the control of the main contractor, and in early 1970 Avionica disappeared, and Panavia was made responsible for the development and procurement of the avionics through three sub-contractors, EASAMS in the UK, ESG in West Germany and SIA in Italy. NAMMO and its agency, NAMMA, then had to deal with only two companies, Panavia and Turbo-Union. The latter company was jointly formed by Rolls-Royce, MTU (Man Turbo and Daimler-Benz) in West Germany and Fiat to produce the RB199 engines for the MRCA on a work- and cost-sharing basis similar to that of the airframe.

With a final assembly line to be established in each country, there was no need for actual money to change hands, save for the controversial purchase from the USA of the main radar, which was available from Texas Instruments but would otherwise have had to be expensively designed and developed in Europe to the detriment of the cost of the MRCA and its timetable. This apart, the UK Government paid for the British work on the MRCA in Sterling, and the Germans and Italians acted similarly. This meant that currency-value fluctuations did not affect the programme, as each country was contributing hardware and man-hours paid for in its own currency and in its own country. As with Jaguar and Concorde, there was no duplication. BAC was responsible for all the nose-section and cockpits, rear fuselage (including engine bays) and tail units. MBB had the centre-fuselage and the manufacture of the wing-pivot (to which BAC had contributed much), while Fiat had the design of the wings (Dr Mautino) and the building of them.

The Panavia Programme Management System — PMS – provided a Statement of Work, a Work Breakdown Structure, a Programme Control Centre, a Configuration Management System, a Weapons System Specification Tree, a Data Management System, a flow of Technical Progress Reports, and an integrated Schedule/Cost System. All this information – down to every sub-contracted work package – was fed into Central Control, and into a computer network, along with data from Turbo-Union. The inter-relation of any hold-up or problem on the programme and on the cost could thus be seen immediately and chased up. The PMS was impressive to see, and it was impressive in its results.

The cost-control of the MRCA has been outstanding throughout. The planned programme set up by the Governments through NAMMO was liberally sprinkled with 'milestones' such as the Feasibility Study Phase (April 1969), the Project Definition Phase (to July 1970), the Development Phase (to March 1973), and then the Production Investment Phase (to 1976), and finally the placing of production orders for forty in 1976 and 110 more in May 1977 – a day or two after nationalisation.

At each of these phases, the three Governments reviewed the progress in great detail, and naturally paid particular attention to cost control. In this, Panavia had an excellent record, and it was Madelung's boast that right up to the go-ahead on production, which was given in 1976, there had been no escalation in either the man-hours or the amounts of material required for the programme. 'That,' he said, 'is all we in Panavia can ensure. What has to be paid out for those man-hours and material in Germany, the UK and Italy is something out of our control.'

NAMMA, being in the same building as Panavia, could check continuously and in detail on the progress of the project, as all the key information, covering the two main contractors and all their sub-contractors, was displayed in visual form, plotted against target dates, in the control room. The sub-contracting had to be spread between the three countries in accordance with the basic shareholding, and this complicated procedure was supervised by NAMMA, although the recommendation lists of the best suppliers were put forward by Panavia, together with the tenders as to cost. Mauser were something of an exception in this, as they were given a separate direct contract on the MRCA's gun, but this spend was counter-balanced by compensating work given to the UK and Italy.

All in all, Panavia can claim to have laid down the pattern for major European collaborative projects on cost-efficiency, fairness, and general harmony, and there can be little doubt that the company will continue in the aviation business after the MRCA Tornado which gave it birth. This was emphasised in 1978 by Freddie Page, then Chairman of Panavia, when he said the company would undertake further projects if and when customers agreed their future requirements. He described Panavia as 'a huge step forward in the evolution of European commonality which has important ramifications in many key areas such as finance, tax, and company law, as well as in supply logistics, operation and training. It is therefore inconceivable that this pioneering effort should in future be thrown away and wasted. Indeed we hope it will expand so that Panavia will include other nations.'

In fact, Panavia, while working on the MRCA, has also kept in its hand by working on project studies of future lightweight fighters which may well yet prove to be very useful experience.

It is not the intention of the author to follow the fever chart of the MRCA Development Phase or to catalogue the various Parliamentary and media inquests and protests aimed at the concept, or the costs, and the continual flow of rumours, many of them of USA or French origin, alleging this or that shortcoming, or forecasting imminent and outright cancellation. The people actually concerned with the aeroplane knew that it was coming along very well, and were more certain than they had ever been with such a project that it was fully supported by the respective Governments and that there were no grounds for any cancellation. The requirements held firm and so did the specification of the aeroplane to meet those requirements. Even though the wage and raw material inflation of the early seventies hit the estimates, the rock-bottom basic ingredients of man-hours and materials remained, as Madelung emphasised, constant, which was a considerable tribute to the rigorous NAMMA/NAMMO/Panavia system.

As with Jaguar, much of the public confusion about costs arose from differences between the UK method and the European method of presentation. The Germans quoted the full cost of ownership *and operation* of its MRCAS – what Healey referred to as 'programme costs' – while the UK was more accustomed to publish first the research and development (or non-recurring) cost as a lump sum, and then quote separately the unit manufacturing (or recurring) cost of an aeroplane standing on the tarmac ready for delivery. Normally, in the UK, the cost of providing an RAF airfield and personnel, plus fuel and maintenance for X years of front-line service, was not thrown in, as it often was in Germany and France.

Further, in Germany the costs were naturally given in Deutschmarks and, with Sterling ever weakening, what divisor did one take to convert DM into pounds? In fact the widening gap between DM and Sterling and Lire didn't really enter into the matter (save for the shared cost of the TI radar from the USA) because, as has already been explained, each country paid for its own work in its own currency. What *did* matter was that three nations were getting the aircraft they wanted from a long production-run of 800 aircraft (excluding exports), with virtually no foreign currency involved, and with work provided, via 500 firms, for up to 70,000 Europeans – half of them in the UK.

Eventually, the more responsible Parliamentarians and media in the three countries became reasonably satisfied that to replace the MRCA with a comparable aircraft from the USA (not that there was one) would cost much, much more, and that the MRCA cost-control was being very carefully and successfully monitored. There were some very favourable official comments on this subject in all three countries. In the UK, Mr Brynmor John, then Under Secretary of State for the RAF, said, in 1974, 'It has been a splendid achievement to keep so close to the original estimates of cost and time.' A year later, in June 1975, he observed, 'The MRCA is clearly the most successful international collaboration ever, in which the real escalation of costs has been minimal and has been carefully controlled.' In the same year, Mr William Rodgers, UK Minister of State for Defence, said, 'The cost estimates initially made in 1969 have been kept to remarkably well, allowing for inflation and changes in the exchange rates. It is certainly the case that, to cancel the MRCA and buy a foreign aircraft, the total cost would be greater and the cost across the exchanges would be very great indeed. That would be so, irrespective of any possible earnings from the MRCA.'

There was also technical and military praise for the aeroplane and its performance from the Ministers of Defence and Chiefs of Staff of the collaborating nations and from leading politicians of both the British major parties, while Harold Wilson described it, after the first flights, in these words, 'The MRCA is one of the wonder-birds of aviation and that's agreed not only by us, but by our partners abroad. I believe it is cheaper and better for us than any other alternative plan. MRCA is going on, and we are very proud of it.'

To complete the factual 'milestone' history of the project, in March of 1973 the three Governments cleared the project into the production investment phase, and on 14 August 1974, the first prototype successfully flew at Manching, near Munich, followed on 30 October by the flight of the second prototype at Warton. The pilot on both occasions was Paul Millett, BAC Military Aircraft Division's Chief Test Pilot, along with Nils Meister of MBB at Manching, and Pietro Trevisan of Aeritalia at Warton.

Four more prototypes flew in 1975, including the first Italian-assembled MRCA — the fourth aircraft being fully equipped with the advanced avionics and terrain-following system, all of which functioned very well. In 1976, with all the prototypes and two pre-Series aircraft flying, the first series production contract for forty aircraft was signed and that for a second batch of 110 aircraft on May 1977, including the first three AD V models for the RAF. BAC, in its final report as a separate company, was able to state that, allowing for inflation and other outside influences, the costs of the MRCA had, throughout, been kept very close in real terms to those originally estimated when the project started.

There were, as was only to be expected, some teething troubles, notably in the early flights with the fuel control system, but there was nothing of a vital nature and there was happily no truth whatever in allegations of excess drag as the performance of the aircraft itself subsequently proved. There were some delivery delay problems of engines to the full thrust requirements, but this again was not overly surprising on such an advanced turbo-fan as the RB199.

Some critics predicted that the Tornado — as it had now been named — would never reach M=2 at altitude, but they were answered by flights to well over Mach 1.9 on engines of less than full power. As Freddie Page said with a wry smile at this time (early 1977), 'We will, of course, reach Mach 2 with the proper engines, but in fact it makes no operational difference at all whether the AD V Tornado launches its air-to-air missiles at Mach 1.8 or 1.9 or 2.1.' In fact, Mach 2 was achieved by Paul Millett on prototype 02.

The real story of the Tornado — the production and operational phase — was just starting when BAC handed over to British Aerospace as the UK partner in Panavia. There can be no doubt, however, that all three nations involved will get an aeroplane for service through the eighties and nineties which will be second to none in its allotted tasks and which, as it proves itself in squadron service, can hardly fail to win many millions of pounds in exports.

It will, however, have been a long, long wait for the famous Canberra replacement, the OR 339 of February 1958.

31
A Time of Change

Having followed through the stories of the various variable-geometry proposals leading to the MRCA on the military side, and, in the civil field, having catalogued the grief of the Two-Eleven and then the Three-Eleven projects, we should now return to the overall state of BAC, which was last set out for the year 1969.

The succeeding two years, 1970 and 1971, were to be unhappy ones for the company, and this unhappiness, in all its forms, stemmed from the basic fact that Weybridge Division, so recently the main profit-maker with the One-Eleven, was now, because of two harmful decisions by successive Governments, without a new project and was precious near to being on its uppers.

It will be remembered that GEC had become a 40 per cent shareholder of BAC when it took over English Electric, and Sir Arnold Weinstock, Managing Director of GEC, was, by 1971, most unhappy about the future and, indeed, the very viability of the civil side of the company. At one Vickers/GEC 'parents' meeting (in April 1971), he said that the planned production of the One-Eleven should be firmly cut off at the 215 already committed (fourteen of which were then unsold), and he pressed for plans for the closure of at least one of the three major civil plants at Weybridge, Filton and Hurn. He stated very firmly that GEC could not be expected to agree to the financing of any further civil projects until BAC had re-evaluated the One-Eleven position.

Sir George was not present at this meeting as he was in hospital for a stomach operation which was to keep him out of BAC affairs until the early summer. In truth, the One-Eleven overall financial position was not good. BAC had over £50 million locked up in completed aircraft and the twenty-seven still on the line, of which thirteen were on firm order and fourteen unallocated. There was also, at the end of 1970, a further £17 million at risk from customer lease-deals and debts, which figure was increasing throughout 1971. Against this, there was £37 million to come from the sale of the aircraft under build, and the other liabilities were, to a certain extent, covered by recourse on the aircraft, whose secondhand value, though always a matter of fluctuation, would, hopefully, remain high.

All in all, the Weybridge Division was forecast to have only a £7 million positive cash-flow in 1971, and this would be needed to meet the increased working capital requirements of other Divisions, notably Guided Weapons, although the latter were also expecting a substantial settlement of several millions for their claims on Libya for the cancelled Rapier contract earlier mentioned. There was certainly no money in 1971 for further speculation on unsold One-Elevens and, in the opinion of the bankers and of ECGD, BAC was overstretched on the civil side in relation to the resources of the company.

The whole situation at this time was complicated by the Rolls-Royce bankruptcy of early 1971 which had gravely undermined world confidence in UK aerospace. There was also an obvious further complication for BAC in that the Rolls-Royce Receiver (via Bristol Aircraft (Holdings)) now held 20 per cent of BAC's shares, and had nominated Whitney Straight and Dr Llewellyn Smith to the Holdings Board to watch his interests. In view of all this, and the depressed state of the airliner market generally, Sir Arnold was very firm that BAC should pay no dividend in 1971 but should retain its after-tax profits (eventually £2.4 million). Vickers, through Sir Leslie Rowan and Mr (later Sir) Peter Matthews, were equally definite that BAC should pay a dividend (Vickers had just had to pass up on their own), and Sir Reginald Verdon-Smith said that the BAC Executive shared the Vickers view that, unless a dividend – with Rolls-Royce in mind – was paid, customers could easily take fright and believe that BAC was also headed for the rocks.

Battle lines were thus drawn on the dividend issue, while GEC also maintained that BAC total capital expenditure in 1971 should not exceed the depreciation in that year, and there should be no exceptions to this except for expenditures specifically sponsored and recoverable in full. The same went for any private-venture expenditure.

It was quite clear that Sir Arnold was determined to impose a very strict economy regime over all aspects of BAC, even down to the modest annual contributions to charity. He took the line that if any shareholder's money was to be given away, then the shareholders would do it for themselves. With Sandy Riddell and Lord Nelson, he kept the spotlight on the performance of the civil factories (which had now – spring 1971 – become merged as the Commercial Aircraft Division), pointing out that Concorde, still with a big question-mark against its survival, was the only funded project on the go other than the One-Eleven, which he wanted to wrap up for the reasons stated.

At one time in mid-1971, the situation became so bitter that the GEC members of the Holdings Board deliberately stayed away from meetings, producing a 'no quorum' position and thus, in effect, putting the Holdings Board out of action.

This, in turn, led to a number of alternative financial and organisational plans being drawn up by Willie Masterton on the general theme of buying out GEC (and the Rolls-Royce Receiver) and making BAC a subsidiary of Vickers. Some of these schemes had Guided Weapons 'hived off' to GEC but, as Masterton himself pointed out, any such violent restructuring of BAC, with Vickers as the sole shareholder of a now purely aircraft company, could well meet with objections from creditors who had lent money to a BAC which at the time of lending had included Guided Weapons and which also had had GEC and Rolls-Royce as shareholders.

It is pointless to describe all these various schemes for dividing BAC and raising market money, because none was ever put into effect. Vickers and GEC remained the main shareholders until December 1972, when the Rolls-Royce 20 per cent plus the old Bristol loans were finally bought in for £6¼ million from the Receiver by Vickers and GEC equally – thus making Vickers and GEC the sole and equal owners of BAC. This remained the position until the end.

There can be little doubt that, certainly through 1971 and, in diminishing strength, up to 1973, GEC wanted 'out' of BAC, but it also wanted to end up as owning the Guided Weapons Division, which would have fitted in well with Marconi. The BAC 1970 financial results, as has been said, undoubtedly failed to impress Sir Arnold Weinstock – sales being down to £150.4 million (£183.9 million in 1969). Exports were down to £48.9 million (£85.3 million); profit before tax was £3.8 million (£5.5 million); but profit after tax was £2.2 million – only £500,000 less than in 1969.

The 1971 results were likely to be much the same, and, in the event, this was the case. Sales (£158.9 million), exports (£62.6 million), and profits (£4.2 million before tax), were all slightly up on 1970, but the after-tax profit was still only £2.4 million, on a capital employed of nearly £64 million, of which £46.5 million came from the shareholders at earnings per share of 12 pence. No dividend was declared, Sir Arnold having eventually gained this and, indeed, most of his other points, save that none of the three factories of CAD (as the Commercial Aircraft Division became known) was closed, although there were inevitably heavy redundancies, amounting in the end to nearly 2000 in the Division overall.

The GEC view of BAC had softened a little by 1972. The intake of new orders in 1971 had, for the first time, topped £200 million, and this sign of revival was to be repeated in 1972.

Another improvement, certainly in the eyes of Sir Arnold, was a simplification of the method by which the parents controlled their investment in BAC. From the start of 1972, much more emphasis was placed on the main BAC Board – originally the old BAC (Operating) Board – under Sir George Edwards. Consequentially, the position of the Holdings Board became less important as far as day-to-day matters were concerned, and it was, to a considerable extent, replaced in practical terms, by direct contacts between the top Directors of the parents, including and especially Sir Arnold Weinstock, with Sir George.

Sir Reginald Verdon-Smith, one of the 1960 founding fathers of BAC, relinquished his chairmanship of the Holdings Board in January 1972 and returned to his distinguished career in banking. No further Chairman of the Holdings Board was ever appointed, and Sir George, as Chairman of BAC, was now the only Chairman in the Corporate structure. He relinquished his managing directorship of BAC, but became Managing Director of BAC (Holdings), which made him directly responsible to Lord Robens, as Chairman of Vickers, and Sir Arnold. Later, Vickers were to be content with keeping a watching brief, mainly through Lord Robens and Peter Matthews, and to let Sir Arnold play the larger role in such strategic direction and advice as he thought BAC might need.

The Holdings Board, however, continued to exist. The Receiver's Rolls-Royce representatives dropped out after December 1972, when the share transfer was completed, and, with Sir George, the Board comprised Sir Raymond Brown, Lord Nelson, Sandy Riddell, Sir Peter Matthews and Ronald Yapp. Later (1972–7) there were additions and changes. Messers C.W. Foreman, Allen Greenwood, W.C.P. McKie, Tom Pritchard and J.T. Wiltshire joined; Sir Raymond Brown and Ronald Yapp retired, as, of course, did Sir George Edwards when he left the industry at the end of 1975.

There was also re-organisation inside BAC itself. The joining together in mid-1971 of the civil aircraft factories as the Commercial Aircraft Division under Geoffrey Knight's chairmanship and with John Ferguson Smith as Managing Director has already been mentioned. The Preston/ Warton complex became in name what it had always been in fact, the Military Aircraft Division (always written in full to avoid the unfortunate initials). Freddie Page became its Chairman and Managing Director. BAC thus settled into the three-Divisional format – CAD, Military and Guided Weapons – which it was to retain.

Three days before Christmas 1971, BAC suffered a heavy blow when Willie Masterton, its Deputy Chairman, collapsed and died outside his Pall Mall office. The burden on him as Financial Director and then as Deputy Chairman had been immense and sustained. He had carried the brunt of the complex paper work involved in many financial crises – TSR2, the Government's proposed merger of BAC with Hawker Siddeley, the intended marketing of BAC shares to support the Three-Eleven project, the FCI loan, and, in 1971, all the examinations, submissions and appreciations which stemmed from the apparent GEC-Vickers impasse, as well as the complications which arose from the Rolls-Royce affair. The sudden loss of this brilliant man, whose quiet but thorough, lucid and resourceful analysis of all the options open to the company at each of its major decisions had done so much to keep BAC in being, took from the Corporation a remarkable and veritable tower of strength. A gloom was cast over the Directors and senior executives of BAC and of its parents, the more so as the manner of Masterton's untimely death was a reminder of the toll exacted by long periods of strain and overwork. Thus, in the space of a few days, the former Bristol top-level participation in BAC virtually disappeared: Willie Masterton died, and Sir Reginald Verdon-Smith retired from the chairmanship. Only Tom Pritchard, BAC's Financial Director, and Geoffrey Knight remained in the top councils, Dr (later Sir) Archibald Russell having retired at the end of 1970.

There were a number of other important personnel changes in 1971. Marshal of the Royal Air Force Sir Dermot Boyle, Vice Chairman of the Holdings Board, retired in October, and Mr A.D. Marris also left the Board at the end of the year. At Weybridge, in the restructuring of what was to be CAD, three Directors who were approaching retiring age, Dr Henry Gardner, John Pull, and Bob Handasyde, stood down after a combined 133 years of service to Vickers Aviation and BAC. Later, when CAD was formed, George Gedge, who had been Managing Director of the old Filton Division, became overall BAC Director of Manufacturing, John Ferguson Smith becoming Managing Director, under Knight's chairmanship, of the now combined Filton and Weybridge Divisions.

It was also in this fateful year of 1971 that the nation mourned for Lord Portal, the man whose wise leadership had held BAC together during its earlier years and whose counsel was so often subsequently sought by Sir George, who himself came so near to death when unexpected complications immediately after his first operation required him to undergo a second within the space of a few days. In a remarkable display of his mental and physical resources, Sir George was, by the summer, showing much of his old vigour in the defence of Weybridge and CAD and, if memory serves, also still able to bowl a few overs of his formidable brand of leg-spin, adding a few more to his hundreds of victims before the season was out.

To carry on the BAC internal re-organisation story to its final format, in November 1972, Sir George, while remaining Chairman, gave up his managing directorship of BAC and Allen Greenwood became Deputy Chairman and the openly nominated heir to Sir George. He ceased to be Deputy Managing Director – there now being no BAC Managing Director to be Deputy to. Geoffrey Knight ceased to be Chairman of CAD, and Freddie Page took over command of all BAC's aircraft activities as Managing Director (Aircraft) of BAC and as Chairman of both the Military and Commercial Aircraft Divisions. Harry Baxendale became Managing Director of the Military Aircraft Division. In a matching appointment on the Guided Weapons side, G.R. Jefferson became Managing Director (Guided Weapons) of BAC as well as Chairman and Managing Director of the Division.

In this way, Sir George brought about a situation which he had always had in mind and which he firmly believed to be right: an engineering company run by engineers – himself in the top chair, with the two men who had emerged as dominant in their fields in full overall command of Aircraft and Guided Weapons. He also had an engineer/administrator named as his Deputy and eventual successor.

It is of interest that, on nationalisation, the new British Aerospace was to adopt exactly the same basic format – with the same two people, Page and Jefferson, in command of the Aircraft and Dynamics Groups respectively. The overall Chairman, as was predictable, was, however, not an engineer, but a politician (Lord Beswick), although his Deputy was Allen Greenwood.

Geoffrey Knight remained with BAC as non-executive Vice-Chairman, and in this appointment was free to concentrate on what was his undoubted forte – civil aircraft sales and airline liaison, with especial regard to the Concorde situation. Later, as the Concorde options melted away to just those of British Airways and Air France, and with no successor to the One-Eleven to market, Geoffrey Knight took first part-time, and then full-time appointments in the City, and so, gradually, bowed out of the company.

During 1972, BAC undoubtedly turned the corner. It was able, albeit in two instalments, to pay off the £15 million FCI loan, and so shrugged off a heavy weight of interest. Although sales dropped by £5 million to £153.3 million, exports rose from £62 to £66 million, and profit before tax from £4.2 million to £6.7 million (£3.75 million after tax). A dividend of £1.7 million was paid, and over £2 million transferred to reserves, making them over £12 million. The capital employed dropped to £50 million, and the earnings per share shot up from 12 pence to 18.8 pence. The annual report described these results as 'a significant improvement,' and commented that the encouraging situation could be regarded as a successful outcome of the company's long-term policy of spreading its activities over a wide range of products. The work in hand at the end of 1972 was worth £360 million – an increase of £60 million.

It was during 1972 that the 200th BAC One-Eleven was delivered, and the line was still kept in being while a strong sales drive on the 'small-field' One-Eleven 475 and the 500 Series continued. Europlane (see later) was also formed in yet another attempt to initiate a new civil programme – with Sir Arnold raising his eyebrows in a terse note or two on limiting the unsecured investment.

On the other side of the coin, the Government's public attitude to the Concorde was by now undoubtedly much more favourable. The progress of the flight test programme by the two prototypes was proving to be most impressive, and a third Concorde, the first of the larger pre-production aircraft, had flown in December 1971. The factory and work outlook for the Commercial Aircraft Division, was, however, still gloomy. New designs and projects were no substitute for hardware being built and sold, and the demise of the Three-Eleven had left only the Concorde and the tail end of the One-Eleven programme, plus whatever in-house or outside sub-contracts the energetic Frank Denning, whose unenviable task it was to plan the shop-floor loading, could obtain.

In the Military Aircraft Division, things were much happier. The first production Jaguar had flown in November 1971 – three months after the first flight at Warton of the eighth and final Jaguar prototype. Deliveries to the French Air Force were to start in 1972 and to the Royal Air Force in 1973. The sales of BAC's privately funded Strikemaster variant of the Jet Provost had topped the 100 by the end of 1971, the long-running 'refurbished Canberra' programme had gained a further £4 million contract from Venezuela, and the Guided Weapons Division's Swingfire had been sold to Belgium.

The key event of 1972 was the actual signing in November of Concorde contracts by both BOAC and Air France. BOAC ordered five with three on option, and Air France four with four on option. There were also preliminary purchase agreements by China (two aircraft) and Iran (three aircraft). These orders finally put Concorde on to an undeniable footing and brought the Concorde line up to sixteen aircraft, with permission to buy long-dated materials for six more.

There had also been in June 1972 a demonstration tour by Concorde 002 (the British-assembled prototype) to the Middle and Far East, Japan and Australia and back – a tour about which Sir George had reservations and which, as will be seen from the fuller history of Concorde in a later chapter, was indeed a mixed blessing. The full airline-standard Concorde (02) with significantly reduced smoke emission was only six months away and, with hindsight, it might have been a better vehicle for the first overseas sales sortie to Japan and Australia. Even so, the remarkable serviceability of 002 on such a strenuous tour was undoubtedly most impressive. It was in 1972 that the surprise intensification of the Chinese interest in the VC10 came to a peak but, as has been recounted, nothing could now sensibly be done economically to revive this production.

The military aircraft emphasis moved smoothly from Lightning and Canberra to Jaguar and Tornado, with substantial deliveries continuing of Jet Provosts and Strikemasters. At Guided Weapons, Rapier was nearing operational deployment, with deliveries to the UK Services and to Iran just about to start. The add-on Blindfire version was coming on well, and so were Seawolf and Sea Skua. BAC also took over all the shares in British Aircraft Corporation (Anti-Tank) Limited at the termination of the joint venture with Fairey Engineering.

At the end of the year – about the time of the eventual purchase by Vickers and GEC of the Rolls-Royce 20 per cent of BAC shares – Sir George, looking to the future, said this clearly lay in collaboration and a further strengthening of BAC's established links with Europe. He tempered this, however, by a return to the theme which he maintained throughout his whole BAC career – namely, that markets come first. There was no earthly point in building aeroplanes for their own sake, and for Europe to do so just for political reasons would be economic madness. He voiced a similar view about European mergers, about which there was much political and media talk at the time (even Sir Arnold had wondered if the possibilities might bear examination). Such mergers, Sir George said, were not lightly to be entered into. They had to have a genuine and continuing purpose, and, above all, they had to have real aeroplanes to sell to customers who wanted to buy them. Collaboration within EEC was one thing, and actual marriages might result in the fullness of time, but meanwhile there was no hurry.

In saying this, Sir George was not only keeping his options open, he was also determined that BAC, with its three active Divisions, its proven expertise in all the major branches of aerospace, and its hard-won world standing, was not going to get itself tied into any uncommercial activities, or yet to become sub-contractors to the extent that the UK lost a design ability which, once gone, could never be recaptured. He was a great believer in keeping Britain's powder dry and her technology intact, but he was far from sure that his views were shared by the politicians of either of the major parties.

32

A Strong Platform

The advent of the Heath Government and its almost immediate 1971 pre-occupation with the Rolls-Royce drama almost predictably led to another attempt to push through some kind of BAC-Hawker Siddeley merger. The drive towards this came to its peak in 1973, with Mr Michael Heseltine as Minister of Aviation. Mr Heseltine, at this period, presented a rather dramatic image, with virtually shoulder-length styling for his blonde hair, and suits of somewhat exaggerated fashion. His oratory, too, was on the flamboyant side, and, at one time, he seemed to be advocating not only a unification of British aerospace effort, but simultaneously that of all the EEC, which Britain had voted to join. This he saw as leading to European ventures into civil aircraft, military aircraft and guided weapons/Space, but – in the general interpretation of his rather all-embracing remarks – each under a separate heading and, presumably, a separate organisation.

The general industry view of any BAC-Hawker merger at this time was that it would probably happen one day, but was unlikely with such individualists as Sir Arnold Hall at the head of HSA and Sir George at BAC. Neither company stood in particular need of it, and indeed the Hawker Siddeley Group's involvement in aerospace was now a minority one in that aircraft and weapons accounted for only somewhere between a quarter and a third of its industrial empire.

Sir George's attitude to Ministry pressure and to the media merger speculation was the same he had earlier displayed towards the Benn proposals. He answered the questionnaires, drew attention to the fact that by December 1973 (during the three-day working week) the BAC order book stood at £644 million, of which over £400 million was for export, and let the overall monetary value of BAC sink in with all concerned (£30 million for its real estate alone). To the media enquiries, BAC simply said, 'BAC does not want a merger with Hawker and, as far as it knows, Hawker hold much the same view.'

It is possible that, had the Heath Government not fallen, bringing in a Labour Government with a mandate for nationalisation of aerospace, there might have been a voluntary and freely negotiated merger. Willie Masterton had, back in 1971, said he could make a lot of financial sense out of it, but the stumbling block was a chronic underestimation of the value of BAC, even during the leaner years.

During the 1973 'merger-itis,' Sir Arnold Weinstock once again reverted to thoughts of hiving off the Guided Weapons Division, buying in the complementary Hawker Siddeley Dynamics, and putting them together with his other electronic interests, notably, of course, Marconi. This would have left the purely aircraft sides of BAC and Hawker to get together, and drew from Sir George a comprehensive and detailed paper on the need for inter-dependence between guided weapons and aircraft, and the grave dangers of fragmenting an industry which, more than ever, needed strength right across the aerospace board to be competitive and to survive. Sir Arnold appears to have accepted Sir George's views, although, when the Labour Government was returned in 1974, he had a study done of an outright purchase by GEC of BAC Guided Weapons Division. This, however, would have had no protection if the Government was intent on nationalising the guided weapons business as part of the aircraft industry – and, since the Government was clearly so intending, the GEC/Guided Weapons fragmentation was not pursued.

On the question of European collaboration, which Heseltine appeared to see as merged European international companies, one each covering the three main aerospace disciplines, BAC's views remained those outlined by Sir George and given in the previous chapter. There was, and remains, no doubt that, if the European aerospace companies came together to build military aircraft and weapons jointly specified and funded by the Governments concerned (an expansion of the Panavia principle), and if the same thing happened with transports for the EEC's Government-owned airlines, then such a European aerospace industry could not only rival that of the USA – it could probably surpass it. In short, EEC has the combined technological resources, experience, skills, and supporting home markets to supply all its own needs, and also to be in a competitive position to take a very large slice of the considerable other world markets outside the USA, and, in some cases, actually inside the USA, as has been shown by the One-Eleven, HS125, Harrier and A300.

As Allen Greenwood was often to say during his many later attempts to get some large European aerospace understandings launched, 'all that is really needed is the political will of the EEC Governments.' Future historians may well wonder why so little progress was made towards such obvious and potentially highly profitable goals when the Prime Ministers of Britain, France, Germany, Italy, the Netherlands and Belgium could have virtually settled the matter at any time, owning as they did, directly or indirectly, the basic aerospace factories of Europe, the main defence forces of Europe, and the key airlines. An over-simplistic view could be that the national leaders, so to speak, could lock their military chiefs in one room, and their airline chiefs in another, and say, 'You can come out when you have agreed your joint requirements for 1980 onwards. When we have those requirements, we will ensure they are built in Europe, with a fair division of the funding, design and build, according to how many each country needs of what.'

Such day-dreams, however, are not the stuff of reality. There is, for example, no way yet even of forming a geniune European company as such, there being no such thing as EEC Company Law. Collaborative enterprises – Panavia, Sepecat and Airbus Industrie, for example – have to be registered in one country to that country's laws. Air Forces have different re-equipment schedules and national airlines demand compensation the moment their Government tells them what to buy – even if, as we have seen, it is an aeroplane they initially specified themselves. So VFW-Fokker put the F28 into production and naturally wanted no European competitor. British Aerospace went ahead with its own plans to build the BAe 146; France and Germany, as the main partners, invested vast sums in the A300 and, finally with UK as 20 per cent partners, the A310, while Dassault has always believed it can live alone.

A united Europe, planning and developing its resources to a common plan, is still no *fait accompli* in aerospace as in so many other things. Nationalism still tends to divide. But, if 'political' aeroplanes with no true market do not wreck the factories first, it must eventually come right. Certainly, there are enough men of stature in the relevant countries who, despite setbacks, are working to that end. European space consortia seem to manage; maybe some kind of Panavia with France in it, and now the new Airbus company with the UK in it, both with sensible forward programmes, will yet pave the way.

Back in 1973, however, BAC continued to concentrate on making a success of its separate and privately owned existence. It did so to the extent of its most successful year since its formation. After two successive years of an intake of new orders which had topped the £200 million mark, 1973 new orders rose to £450 million, giving a backlog of £636 million, of which £400 million was for export. The declining trend in sales, which dated back to 1968, was halted, a total of £174.3 million being reached for the year (£153.3 million in 1972). Exports reached over £92 million (£66.7 million), and the 1973 trading profit was the largest in BAC's history at nearly £17 million (£9.7 million). The profit after tax rose to £5.8 million (£3.7 million), and the dividend was £2.5 million, earnings per share going up to 29.2 pence (18.8 pence) on a capital employed of £52.5 million.

The basic position of the company also showed substantial improvement. The FCI loan had been repaid in 1972, and bank borrowings to finance sales were, in 1973, reduced from over £8 million to less than £1 million. Liquidity improved, with a rise in cash balances from £6.7 million to over £12 million, and reserves were up to over £15.5 million. The annual report made the comment, 'The successful outcome of the year's trading can be attributed to the spread of the Group's activities in all main sectors of the aerospace industry and to its achievements in overseas markets.'

Sir Reginald Verdon-Smith, DL, HON. LLD, HON. DSC, MA, BCL, who became
Chairman of BAC on Lord Portal's retirement at the end of 1968, having been a
Director of the Corporation from its formation.

Two of the missile systems which won an international reputation for BAC's Guided Weapons Division. Swingfire (*above*) is a long-range, second-generation, anti-tank weapon system. Seawolf (*below*) was the first shipborne point-defence system with proven ability to intercept missiles as well as attacking aircraft.

Swallow, the Barnes Wallis concept of a tailless variable-geometry aircraft, with 'lifting' forebody and variable-sweep wings. Work on this concept came to an end when the 1957 Sandys White Paper stopped Government funding but it laid the foundation for further BAC research.

This full-scale hinge mechanism for a variable-sweep wing was built as part of BAC's engineering investigations into variable-geometry aircraft, begun at Weybridge before the formation of the Corporation and later transferred to Warton.

Above: An artist's impression of the AFVG – the Anglo-French project for a variable-geometry, multi-role strike fighter put forward at the time of TSR2's cancellation in 1965 but ended two years later by Dassault's unilateral withdrawal. *Below:* The final product of BAC's long advocacy of variable-geometry design – the Anglo-German-Italian MRCA (Multi-Role Combat Aircraft), later named Tornado.

Left: One of the 400 or more successful launchings of the Skylark upper-atmosphere research rocket jointly developed by BAC and the Royal Aircraft Establishment, Farnborough. Skylark has been used for space research by many countries.

Right: A photograph taken from Skylark during an Earth Resources survey in Argentina, showing the spent rocket motor dropping away, shortly before its recovery parachute opened. As an economical means of space research, Skylark has yet to be equalled.

MUSTARD (Multi-Unit Space Transport And Recovery Device), the 1965/6 Warton
study which foreshadowed the US Space Shuttle. The illustrations show the three
'lifting bodies' joined for launch, with two acting as boosters for the third. The
third body would then separate and go into orbit and, on completing its mission,
re-enter the Earth's atmosphere, returning to base, like the boost vehicles, to make
a conventional landing.

Mr A. H. C. Greenwood, CBE, JP, CEng, FRAeS, who became the last Chairman of BAC on the retirement of Sir George Edwards at the end of 1975. He also saw BAC through the process of nationalisation, becoming Deputy Chairman of British Aerospace.

At the time of this annual report, Concorde was undergoing yet another examination in depth by the British and French Governments, and speculation about its future was rife. There had been so much worldwide publicity about this aeroplane over the years that many people, both at home and overseas, had begun to equate the commercial success of Concorde with the viability of BAC. This was particularly annoying because, as Sir George had several times pointed out, although Concorde was a 'headline' product and provided substantial employment for the CAD workforce, it occupied something like a quarter of the company's factory space while only contributing under 5 per cent of the profits. It was, therefore, decided to emphasise this in the 1973 report which recorded the current re-evaluation of the project and said that only 15 per cent of BAC's total orders were for Concorde (against 30 per cent at the end of 1972), and that, if it was cancelled or significantly cut back, it would raise serious problems in relation to the level of employment and the utilisation of the extensive and valuable facilities allocated to it. On the other hand, under the terms of the funding contracts, BAC could expect to be reimbursed for relevant expenditure and, in the meantime, Concorde's contribution to current profits was minimal in relation to the volume of work.

This statement did much to allay outside fears that, if Concorde went, BAC would go with it (although, in the event, the Governments decided to continue with the project). In fact, the upturn in BAC's fortunes was due to the military work and, in particular to the development of BAC's relationship with Saudi Arabia (discussed later). In May of 1973, a Memorandum of Understanding had been signed by the British and Saudi Governments for five years' worth of training and other technical services for the Royal Saudi Air Force, to a value of £315 million. This was an inter-Governmental agreement, but BAC was contracted by the Government to be responsible for the programme, plus the provision of spares, etc., to the value of a further £10–12 million a year.

Also in 1973, the Jaguar entered service with both the French Air Force and the RAF, and work had started on the production investment stage of the Tornado. The Guided Weapons Division was also doing well with Rapier and had landed the contract with Iran. The civil side remained in the doldrums, but One-Eleven sales continued to creep up, 211 of Sir Arnold's 215 having been sold by the end of the year. The 180-seat Europlane venture was halted in this year, but the search for a new civil project – collaborative or a One-Eleven development (discussed later) – continued, as indeed it was destined so to do for the remainder of the Corporation's life.

An interesting flame, already mentioned briefly, which flickered in 1972 and early 1973, only to die, was a Chinese proposal to buy thirty VC10s, if BAC would reconstitute the production line. This BAC was willing to do, and Vickers was willing to sell all its VC10 rights, save for existing 'old account' spares, to BAC for £1.6 million. The price per aeroplane came out at well over £6 million a copy, and though there was also talk of a licence deal, the proposal fell through. The Chinese approach was nonetheless an interesting one. They had been customers of Vickers for Viscounts, and meticulous contractual arrangements for the aircraft servicing and training had been made and scrupulously adhered to on both sides. Vickers had leant over backwards to ensure that the Chinese were satisfied with the integrity of the company they were dealing with, and this unexpected VC10 approach – and also a Concorde option – seemed evidence that those efforts had not been in vain. The Chinese also purchased Tridents from Hawker and if, as seems likely, they continue to regard British aerospace overall in a favourable light, one would like to think that this goodwill stems, at least in part, from the success of the Viscount transaction.

On the assumption that Sir Arnold Weinstock, who was, in effect, supervising BAC on behalf of GEC/Vickers by his direct contacts with Sir George, was satisfied that the 1973 results measured up to his exacting standards of return on investment, then the 1974 figures must have given him even greater pleasure. Sales leaped up from £174 million to £271.8 million, of which a remarkable £173 million was for export. This enormous jump represented the translation into deliveries of the considerable orders, mainly military, received in the previous three years. Even so, 1974 still ended with orders in hand of £815 million (£636 million for 1973), and £600 million of this was also for export. The 1974 order intake was £450 million. Trading profit rose from £16.9 million to £24.4 million, and profit after tax more than doubled from £5.8 million to over £12 million. Earnings per share on an issued capital of £30 million (it had previously been £20.1 million but was increased by capitalising some of the reserves) were 40.1 pence (19.6 pence).

One extraordinary item, not included in the above figures, was for £8 million for the sale to the parents of part of the Weybridge site. This was the land and buildings, some of them dating back to World War I, on the west side of the stream which runs through the middle of historic Brooklands. For some long time prior to 1974, Weybridge had been contracting by moving its rather scattered manufacturing facilities to the east of the river, thus liberating valuable ground for future sale – such possible sale being complicated by a long discussion as to whether a new motorway would or would not be routed through Brooklands. In the event, after all the usual hearings and protests inseparable from proposed new roadways, the approved route just missed Brooklands at the cost of part of the BAC sports field.

The 1974 report, like the 1973 one, in referring to the technical progress on Concorde and a hoped-for in-service date of 1976, emphasised that the project continued to engage some 25 per cent of BAC's manpower and facilities, but represented only 12 per cent of orders in hand, while its contribution to profits remained small.

Although the Military Aircraft and Guided Weapons Divisions

continued to provide the bulk of the company's business (Guided Weapons obtained a double Queen's Award – one for export and one for technical innovation), the report notes a 'welcome upturn' in the demand for new and used One-Elevens. In fact, contracts for all the original 215 aircraft had been signed by the end of the year (213 delivered, four in 1974) and a contract for a further five of the 500 Series had been received from Tarom, the Romanian national airline. A hush-kit to enable earlier One-Elevens to meet the new international requirements on noise levels had also been successfully developed. The decision back in 1971 not to wrap up the One-Eleven was now being justified by events, and this continued to be the case up to and beyond nationalisation.

It was, of course, in 1974, that the Heath Government, following the miners' strike and the three-day week, appealed to the country, and was narrowly beaten to put Labour into a minority Government situation. Nationalisation of the aircraft and shipbuilding industries was part of the Labour Party manifesto, and there was much speculation as to whether this would happen. The Government quickly announced, however, that BAC was included in its nationalisation proposals and that it intended to complete the related legislation 'during the present Parliamentary session.' This statement was included in BAC's 1974 report, and it marked the beginning of three dramatic years, with the issue in doubt almost to the very end.

33
Saudi Arabia

The BAC-Saudi Arabia relationship, which, in large measure, was responsible for the sharp upturn in the company's affairs, dated back to 1962/3/4 and culminated in May 1966 with an order from Britain of a defence system which included Lightning and Strikemaster aircraft, to a value of some £65 million. In retrospect, this was the most important order ever placed with BAC, and, in view of what was to grow from it, it is worth detailing the preliminaries summarised from a well-researched report in *Flight International* at the time.

Britain's recent £100 million-plus order from Saudi Arabia for a complete new air defence system represented the culmination of more than two years of patient negotiation, and a triumph for UK salesmanship in the face of the stiffest American competition up to, and in fact beyond, the eleventh hour. Despite earlier agreement between Britain and the US to make a joint package submission for the Saudi contract, based on British fighters and American missiles, a Lockheed sales team was preparing fresh presentations on the F104 in Riyadh when the British companies concerned received a letter of intent at the beginning of December 1965, accompanied by a 2.5 per cent deposit.

The British sales victory was all the more remarkable in view of US influence in Saudi Arabia, through the long-established Arabian/ American oil company (ARAMCO), plus the USAF Military Aid Advisory Group (USMAAG) which has been operating with and advising the Royal Saudi Air Force for nearly 15 years. Despite this nominal US assistance, however, including the supply of a single squadron of North American F86F Sabre fighter-bombers, the RSAF was little more than a token force among its powerful Middle Eastern neighbours prior to current re-equipment plans.

A forcible reminder of its nominal status, came at the time of Egyptian intervention in the Yemen, when the RSAF proved largely powerless to protect border villages against bombing raids by marauding UAR aircraft. Not only were the handful of Sabres completely inadequate to oppose hordes of Soviet-built MIGs and Il28s, but it also seems that the American donations did not extend to the provision of armament.

Plans were therefore laid down by King Saud and his brother Faisal, who succeeded him on the throne, for a new and completely sophisticated air defence system, including radar early-warning and communications equipment, surface-to-air missiles and supersonic fighters and fighter-bombers. The scope of this potential contract is indicated by the fact that, at that stage, about £100m was allocated for its undertaking, compared with an annual defence budget in Saudi Arabia of about £50m.

In view of the strained relations between Saudi Arabia and Britain in 1963, it appeared that the contract would be wide open for the American industry, but through the efforts of a British businessman, Mr Geoffrey Edwards (a former RAF Group Captain), some of the enquiries for Saudi Defence procurement were diverted to the UK. BAC became involved through the possibility of selling Canberras to Saudi Arabia, but, in November 1963, the interest of the RSAF switched to Lightning interceptors. The necessary information was prepared on the Lightning FMk2, as the then current production version, and BAC were required to put up a case to compete with the Northrop F5, at that time the main American contender with official US backing.

In view of the size of the package contract, many other submissions were received, but only two of the proposers – Northrop, with an F5B, and BAC, with a Lightning F3 – reached the point of local demonstration flights. The Lightning demonstration was flown by BAC Preston Chief Test Pilot Jimmy Dell, in an RAF aircraft which was taken briefly on charge during its return from long-range ferry trials. The Lightning was diverted to Riyadh from Bahrain, and a BAC support team was flown out from the UK in a chartered DC4. Technical support included BAC supplying its own air traffic system at Riyadh, with a portable UHG set. The Farnborough-type demonstration, including a practice 'scramble' initiated by the Defence Minister, Prince Sultan, was a resounding success. Dell planted a 'bang' from 25,000 ft and enjoyed authorised low-level runs over the town. He was also required to demonstrate the manoeuvrability of the Lightning during simulated ground attack approaches.

A month after the Riyadh demonstration, in August 1964, a Saudi Arabian mission led by the chief of the general staff, General Abdullah Al-Mutlaq, visited BAC Preston, AEI International and Airwork Services, to study the overall British package, including radar and electronics, Thunderbird missiles and training support. At the same time, an RSAF Sabre pilot, Lt Hamdan, soloed a Lightning FMk2 after two brief check-flights in a TMk4 trainer from Warton, and reached Mach 2 on his own.

Although he was able to confirm such aspects of the Lightning performance as accelerating from Mach 0.9 to beyond Mach 2 in about three minutes in standard atmosphere, climbing initially at no less than 50,000 ft/min. (254 m/sec.) and spin recovery with ventral

tanks and Firestreaks installed in $2\frac{1}{2}$ seconds, increased competition
was encountered from a Lockheed submission for the F104, also with
US Government support. The US package included electronics and
Raytheon Hawk surface-to-air missiles, and clearance for Lockheed
to sell the Starfighter was the first to be given by the American
Government for the Middle Eastern area.

In 1965, the French Government also intervened for the fighter
contract, with a joint offer by General de Gaulle to Jordan and Saudi
Arabia for the Mirage III, and the Mirage remained competitive with
the Lightning to the end. When it appeared that no single country
would be awarded the entire Saudi contract, the virtues of a combined
Anglo-US deal were pressed by Ministry of Aviation Parliamentary
Secretary John Stonehouse, and this was the proposal eventually
accepted by the Saudi Government.

As it stands, the British portion of the package comprises 34 BAC
Lightning FMk53 single-seat fighter bombers and six TMk55 two-
seat trainers. Although basically an export version of the RAF's
extended-wing Lightning FMk3, the Mk53 will be an even more
advanced version with ground-attack capability for the first time.
This will be conferred by underwing pylons, with 1000 lb (454 kg)
bearing capacity, for various stores, plus two 30 mm Aden cannon
mounted in the forward part of the ventral tank fairing. A prototype
installation is due to fly from Warton within the next few months.
Mission capabilities of the RSAF Lightning FMk53s are stated by BAC
to include Mach 2 interception, with Firestreak or Red Top AAMs; air
superiority; strike; and reconnaissance.

Including the 25 BAC 167 Jet Provosts on order for basic training,
the RSAF Lightning contract will total around £65m, to which will be
added a further £25m for the associated ground environmental radar
defence system by Associated Electrical Industries International.
Technical support and training by Airwork Services Limited will
account for a further £22m, and the Saudi order will mean about
1000 British personnel going into Arabia during the next three years
to assist with completion of the contract. The AEI component includes
provision of the completely new Type 40 surveillance and tactical
radar, similar to that offered for the NADGE electronics contest in
NATO. A modern, high-capacity, nation-wide communications
network is included in the system, to pass information to a central
control.

Other major beneficiaries include Ferranti, with about £3m worth
of Airpass air-to-air interception, target-course computing and
weapon-aiming radar, and Rolls-Royce, with £8.5m for Avon 300-
series turbojets. Bristol Siddeley will build the Viper ASV20s for the
BAC 167s, which are pressurized versions of the standard Jet Provost,
with Martin-Baker ejection seats. The latter company, of course, also
provides the seats for the Lightning. Marconi will produce a major

part of the communications equipment under sub-contract from AEI.

All the companies concerned are forming the Saudi Arabian Air Defence Consortium, of which the main US member will be Raytheon, with its £25m contract for Hawk missiles and support equipment. The Saudi order will also reportedly include a quantity of the Cessna T41A primary trainers, for initial air experience, and it is more than probable that other aircraft procurement will be involved in the eventual overall contract. Even as it stands, however, the present £130m Saudi order will undoubtedly result in the finest air defence system throughout the Middle East by the time it is fully operational within the next five years.

Although the first of the main contracts (that with BAC) between Saudi Arabia and the UK consortium companies (BAC, AEI and Airwork Services, with Jim Adderley of BAC as General Manager) was not signed until May 1966 (the other two were not signed until 1967), a letter of intent, as stated, had been received in December 1965. This also called for a very prompt, and indeed virtually an emergency, supply of six re-conditioned Lightnings with spares, equipment and armament to a value of just over £9 million. The code name of this rush operation was 'Magic Carpet.' It was accepted that there would be little ground control radar, or communications environment in which these six high-performance fighters could sensibly operate, but the main thing was that they should be delivered and should be seen to be flying (ex-RAF Lightning pilots being recruited for the purpose). At the same time, BAC Guided Weapons had to deliver, under separate contract, a Thunderbird ground-to-air missile site (Saudi was already a Vigilant purchaser), which BAC had to install and service for three years until the fuller network of American Hawk missiles could take over.

Jim Adderley recalls that the raids by Egyptian Air Force MIGs on the airfield at Khamis Mushayt and the town of Najran caused such alarm that he and Glen Hobday of Warton had to break off the negotiations for the main contract to deal with the Magic Carpet question:

At the beginning of April, a group of us, including Glen Hobday and myself from BAC, negotiated and signed in one day contracts for almost £20m, covering the supply of two Lightning T4s, six Hunters, and two mobile radars to be supplied by AEI, together with support and certain building work by Airwork. The construction work was largely to make Khamis Mushayt suitable for high-performance aircraft and included the building of a new control tower.

Two or three weeks later, the contract for the remaining four Lightning Mark 2s was also signed, the delay being due to the fact that we originally offered Mark 1s and had to return to the UK to ascertain the availability of Mark 2 aircraft.

The Hunters arrived early in May, followed shortly thereafter by the Lightnings, and the radars were delivered and installed in the south-east of the country at about the same time.

However, as the airfield was still unsuitable because of largely unavoidable delays in the construction work, the Magic Carpet aircraft did not go down to Khamis Mushayt until early in 1967, although, despite this, the deterrent threat of them, even based at Riyadh, was sufficient to stop any further Egyptian incursion.

The contract for the Thunderbird battery was negotiated separately and signed in June or July of that year. It is particularly interesting that the entire battery was shipped from Germany, landed at Jeddah, and then transported in a convoy of over 100 vehicles from Jeddah to Khamis Mushayt over virtually uncharted country. The whole convoy arrived intact, and the Thunderbirds were operational almost immediately. The Thunderbirds were maintained and operated in general by BAC personnel under the command of Saudis, but the final act of pressing the button to fire had to be performed by a Saudi officer.

Magic Carpet was, as reported in *Flight International*, backed up in May 1966 by the main contract which, all told, was to a value of over a further £140 million. AEI (later taken over by GEC) were to supply and install radar and other basic air defence equipment. Airwork were contracted to service BAC and AEI equipment and to train Royal Saudi Air Force personnel to fly the aircraft and to use and service all the installations. Meanwhile, they were to provide pilots and other key technical people. BAC's eventual contract was for forty Lightnings and twenty-five Strikemasters, with spares and armament to a value of nearly £71 million. Each of the three British companies had to guarantee to the Saudi Government the performance of the other two.

In August 1968, a further Saudi contract was signed for the repair of aircraft components and spares to a value of £4 million a year.

As the RSAF Lightnings were required to have a ground attack capability (in the RAF they were purely interceptors), Warton mounted a considerable and successful private-venture development programme to this end. This enabled the Lightnings to carry and deliver underwing stores and also to carry supplementary fuel. The programme went so well that an attempt was made to interest the RAF in this additional potential (the last RAF Lightning was delivered in 1967), but without success. The effectiveness of the ground-attack Lightnings was, however, as has been said, dramatically demonstrated by the RSAF in the early 1970s.

There were, in the late 1960s and early 1970s, problems involving the three-company consortium. Accordingly, in 1972, the Saudi Government expressed a wish to deal with just one firm – BAC. As a result, in May 1973, a Memorandum of Understanding was signed directly between the Saudi Arabian and British Governments, BAC being directly contracted by the British Government to service the British-made aircraft, to train RSAF personnel, and to provide technical and domestic buildings. This new agreement was for five years and was initially to a value of over £250 million, but other tasks were later added which brought it up to £315 million. BAC also agreed to provide spares and equipment to RSAF orders, which contracts ran at £10 to £12 million a year, later doubling to £24 million a year by 1978. The servicing of radar and some other air defence equipment was excluded from this contract and was taken over by Lockheed. Also in 1972, Saudi ordered ten more Mark 80A Strikemasters and the modification of the earlier aircraft to the 80A standard at a value of £5½ million, and this was followed by a £7.8 million contract in 1976 for eleven more Strikemasters, bringing the RSAF complement up to forty.

To bring the Saudi contractual story up to date, in September 1977, HRH Prince Sultan, Minister of Defence and Aviation of the Saudi Government, and Mr Fred Mulley for the UK Government, signed a four-year extension of the 1973 agreement (running from 1978 to 1982), the value of which was stated to be over £500 million. It will thus be seen that, including the original 1966 Magic Carpet contract, total orders to the value of over £1000 million have already been placed in Britain on behalf of the Royal Saudi Air Force.

The tasks for which BAC became responsible in Saudi Arabia were, and are, considerable and diverse, and have never been fully appreciated. In summary, there are ten of them:

1. Technical support of aircraft
2. Flying training at the King Faisal Air Academy at Riyadh and the Lightning Conversion Unit at Dhahran (its task now completed save for refresher training)
3. Training at the Technical Studies Institute, Dhahran
4. On-job training at bases
5. Provision of supply staff to augment RSAF supply personnel
6. Motor vehicle maintenance
7. Armament support
8. Advice on provisioning and procurement, including spares ordered by the RSAF
9. Construction and building maintenance
10. Aero-medical services

The most important of these tasks, and the yardstick by which BAC's overall performance is often measured by the Saudi Government, is the maintenance and support of the Lightning, Strikemaster and Cessna aircraft. This requirement calls for over 60 per cent of these aircraft (65 per cent in the case of the Strikemaster), which are deployed at three bases, to be fully available for flying duties at the start of each day. This target is consistently met and often bettered, and RSAF aircraft

serviceability now compares favourably with that of any other modern
air force.

The King Faisal Air Academy is the RSAF's Cranwell, and is the élite
establishment for the training of officers, pilots, and the future leaders of
the RSAF. A BAC staff of highly qualified and experienced flying
instructors and graduate lecturers are responsible for all aspects of the
professional training of the cadets from *ab initio* flying instruction on the
Cessnas to advanced training on the Strikemasters.

The Technical Studies Institute, which, like the Academy, was
originally set up by Airwork, is rightly considered to be one of the
show-pieces of the Middle East. Some 500 students a year go to the TSI
where they are first taught English and then basic engineering and
specialist trades, of which forty-four are covered. Graduates, who form
the backbone of the RSAF, then continue their training 'on the job' at the
bases. British Aircraft Corporation is still the company responsible for
all this, and for the training of Flight Controllers, examinations,
literature and so forth. It is also responsible for the instruction, tools,
training aids, classroom facilities, publications, and test equipment for
the subsequent on-job training.

The supply and maintenance of aircraft and non-aircraft equipment
and spares covers motor vehicles, cranes, bowsers, crash equipment,
generators, armament stores, medical supplies, on down to text-books,
clothing, and domestic furniture. The orders for this wide range of
equipment and spares are placed by the RSAF on BAC who process all that
cannot be met within the Kingdom back to the Support Department in
the UK, which then ensures the timely delivery of the supplies to the
customer. This task involves many departments at Warton and also
external agencies, generating business for over 750 companies, most of
them British.

The construction and maintenance of technical and domestic facilities
and buildings at all the RSAF bases has been a monumental, and at times
very difficult, task. It has involved 200 new facilities, the provision of
electrical and water services, workshops, barracks, stores, houses and
sports grounds, and, in completing them, first the consortium and then
BAC were much in the hands of outside firms, not all of which were
satisfactory. By 1978, however, all the works called for in the first five-
year contract were completed.

The manpower and back-up needed for such an enormous overseas
undertaking were and are immense. In Saudi Arabia itself, there were,
by nationalisation, over 2000 British BAC employees, most of them
highly qualified – this in addition to a local labour force of nearly 3000.
At Warton there were, in the Saudi Arabia Support Department, some
250 other BAC staff, backed up by 350 more in other sections of the
Warton complex. This Support Department was specially built for the
job and equipped with the latest computerised audio-visual aids to check
stock levels and to monitor and speed supplies by rapid two-way satellite

telex links with Riyadh. It is backed by a shipping department at Samlesbury. The whole project is monitored and managed by a control centre where up-to-the-minute displays show the progress state of every phase of the programme.

The man placed in overall command of this great enterprise in 1977 was Air Chief Marshal Sir Frederick Rosier, formerly Deputy Commander-in-Chief, Allied Forces Central Europe, who had joined the Military Aircraft Division as Military Adviser in November 1973. Alongside him at Riyadh was set up a UK Government team from the Ministry of Defence to take up any Government-to-Government matters which arose and, at the same time, keep an eye on overall programme performance.

BAC's success in gaining and keeping the Saudi contracts, and the experience which was built up over such a wide field of activity, gave it, in effect, a new product to market – Defence Support Services. It soon acquired, because it had to, a civil engineering ability enabling it to construct airfields, runways, roads and major buildings. This, in addition to its existing ability to supply and service military and civil aircraft and defence weapons, put BAC in a very competitive position in what is, beyond doubt, a growth industry within an industry. In 1976, somewhat similar services, but on a smaller scale, were extended by BAC to Oman which, in 1974, had ordered both Rapier and Jaguars in a strengthening of its defence forces. Kuwait (initially, like Saudi, a Vigilant customer) also continued to need support services for the Lightnings it ordered in 1966, and for its twelve Strikemasters – an order, incidentally, received in parallel with that for Saudi Arabia, and worth some £40 million.

The full story of BAC's efforts in Saudi Arabia and the huge back-up organisation at Warton is deserving of a book in itself. Many BAC people at all levels – Sir George, Freddie Page, Lord Caldecote, Sir Dermot Boyle, Allen Greenwood, Jim Charlton, Jim Adderley, Alec Atkin, Harry Baxendale, Roly Beamont, Alan Millson and so many, many more did a terrific team job to turn Geoffrey Edwards' initial 'breakthrough' of 1965 into the success it became. Yet, in the final analysis, it was the BAC people out in the desert whose hard work and professional integrity won the respect of the Saudis, without which the contracts already stretching to 1982 would never have been renewed or extended.

34

Commercial Aircraft Division and Europe

The serial story of the search for a new civil project to augment and then to succeed the One-Eleven has received recurring mentions in a number of the previous chapters. The histories of the Two-Eleven and the Three-Eleven have already been recounted, along with Sir Arnold Weinstock's 1971 opinion that BAC was 'finished' in the airliner field. Naturally, this was not a view which had much support at Weybridge, nor did it accord with the Vickers tradition, despite the financial maulings of the Vanguard and VC10, both of which, it was argued, were due to outside and restrictive pressure on the specifications to the detriment of marketability. Sir George, with Allen Greenwood and a number of the old Weybridge hands, remained convinced that there were still big and profitable opportunities open to BAC on the civil side, providing that the new airliner was, from the start of its design, aimed firmly at a properly researched world demand as to size, performance and timing. Freddie Page was not so sure, and Sir Arnold was unlikely to change his views unless any new project was well covered as to launching costs and initial orders.

CAD, however, possessed the best market analysts in Europe, and they were backed up by very sophisticated computer facilities in which were stored the operational details of every airline in the world, its growth rates, traffic, financial status, city pairs, and all the other factors which would shape its next equipment requirement and the likely timing of it. Technically, therefore, BAC was able to sort out what ought to be built (allowing for the areas already covered by the USA), and there was no doubt that it could then, and on its own, build and market any airliner to engineering and reliability standards as good as or better than those of any competition. The trouble, of course, was launching aid, and BAC realised that no British Government was going to help fund a civil venture unless it was a European one, with other Governments and therefore other manufacturers (and airlines) involved.

For that reason, after the demise of the Three-Eleven, the next attempt by BAC to get a new airliner launched for the 1980s was an all-out European collaborative proposal. It was called the 'Europlane QTOL,' and its emphasis was to be on airfield quietness and very lively airfield performance.

'Europlane' was a joint company first discussed in 1971 and established in February 1972 by BAC, Messerschmitt-Bölkow-Blohm (MBB) of Germany and Saab-Scania of Sweden. Each partner owned a third of the shares, and the first Chairman was Herr Werner Blohm. Geoffrey Knight and John Ferguson Smith were the BAC Board Directors and the Chief Executive was Ken Bentley of BAC, with his colleague John Prothero Thomas as Marketing Director. Herr Herbert Flosdorff of MBB was Technical Director and Mr Jan Hull of Saab, the Finance and Programme Director. Together they formed the Management Committee.

In September 1972, the Spanish aircraft company of CASA joined the consortium, and its Chairman, Enrique Maso, and his colleague, Enrique Guzman, joined the Board, on which Allen Greenwood had now replaced Geoffrey Knight. The other MBB Director was Franz Forster-Steinberg, and Saab-Scania's two top aerospace men, Dr Tore Gullstrand and Mr Tord Lidmalm, represented the Swedish interests.

The new company was a mini-Panavia in organisation, with its operational headquarters at Weybridge. A great deal of preliminary effort went into market surveys, and a number of different sizes and configurations of aeroplane were studied before a basic twin-aisle 180/200-seater was decided upon, and details of it were announced at the Paris Air Show at the end of May 1973.

Europlane was to have a range of 500 miles from runways of 4000 feet and up to 2300 miles from runways of 5580 feet, and its engines were to be two proven RB211 or CF6 type turbo-fans in the 40,000 lb class, which already had an extensive airline background. The choice of these engines had two other considerable advantages. They were quiet, and they had a lot of power stretch in them, which would enable Europlane to grow in size and range as a natural development. The Europlane team also had it in mind that, with very low community noise levels, it might be able to operate round the clock at most airports – a very important consideration for the Inclusive Tour market. On shorter ranges, it could also use the subsidiary strips which were then being talked about to relieve airport congestion by diverting to them aircraft of short take-off and quick climb and descent abilities.

There was much discussion as to the ideal positioning of the engines – underwing or overwing (for noise shielding) or rear-mounted from the fuselage (for maximum shielding by wings, over the intakes, and tailplane, over the effluxes). The model shown at Paris had such high rear-mounted engines. The estimated Europlane total non-recurring launching costs, including tooling, were £180 million.

Presentations of Europlane were made to the four Governments in February 1973 and details were given to substantiate a world market in the Europlane category of some 1350 aircraft by 1985. The aircraft was aimed at a slot below the A300B Airbus and above the proposed French go-it-alone Mercure 200. This latter aeroplane was a paper development of the Dassault Mercure 100, of which only a meagre handful had been sold. The French, however, used the Mercure 200 as a kind of 'blocking' threat to any aeroplane proposed by the UK and as an extension of the French-led options already devised round the basic Airbus.

Europlane, though itself a soundly based concept, and despite energetic promotion and publicity efforts led by Norman Barfield, never quite seemed 'for real,' mainly because MBB were getting more and more financially involved in the A300B, and began leaning away from Europlane which, with its envisaged stretch, could be seen (and was seen in France) as a potential competitor to the A300B at the lower end of its development bracket.

In September 1973, therefore, all the Europlane partners agreed to put the project in abeyance, which effectively marked the end of the venture. Because of the oil crisis, the world economic situation was, at this time, hardly a good one in which to launch a new aeroplane, and Europlane was but one of a number of paper projects which aircraft manufacturers on both sides of the Atlantic were to talk about, but not build, for the next five years.

Throughout 1974, however, Allen Greenwood, who was the then President of the European Association of Aircraft Industries (AECMA), continued to be active in trying to put together some kind of strong alliance on the civil side which would be comparable to Panavia. He was, and had been for a long time, a convinced European, and had been much involved with the Concorde, Jaguar and MRCA programmes and organisation. He had also fathered a BAC tie-up on advanced trainers with Macchi of Italy which, although it came to nothing in the end, was further evidence to Europe of BAC's genuine willingness to collaborate. At this time, Greenwood was also keeping in close touch with EEC through the Commissioner for Industry, Sgr Spinelli, who was also taking a detached look at what Europe might make of itself in the whole aerospace field – given the political will.

By the summer of 1974, after much diplomacy, persuasion, and many tours of Europe, Greenwood had six companies more or less 'on-side.' They were BAC and Hawker (who could both see that they were now likely to be thrown together by nationalisation anyway), plus Aérospatiale, MBB, Dornier and Fokker-VFW. During Farnborough week of 1974, agreement was reached between Greenwood, Sir Peter Fletcher (Hawker), Ludwig Bölkow (MBB), M. Christofini (Aérospatiale), Claudius Dornier (Dornier), and Mr Klapwick (Fokker-VFW), saying that their six companies had agreed, with the knowledge of their Governments, to work together in the civil field to examine what European aircraft ought to be built. In this they would have the co-operation of British Airways, Lufthansa and Air France. In the meanwhile, all the companies would make the most of the existing European transport programme, the Airbus, the BAC One-Eleven, and the F28, and would provide mutual support for that purpose.

By the end of the year there were three working parties of 'the Six,' as this group of companies came to be called. Design, on which BAC was represented by Ken Lawson; Manufacturing (Tony Harvey and Arthur Rowlands of Hawker); and Organisation (Handel Davies). Handel, as Technical Director of BAC, was the senior Britisher engaged in these detailed studies which were prepared for the Executive Board of 'the Six.'

During 1975, the working groups came to the conclusion that the right thing to do was to concentrate on a derivative of an existing design. To start an entirely new aircraft, considering the state of the market, would, they believed, be wrong as this would lead to a high price because the recovery of big development costs would be incurred for relatively small gains in efficiency. This conclusion led to a narrowing of the field to developments of the already well-established One-Eleven, (known as the '800' and the X-Eleven), and the French Mercure 200. Although Aérospatiale were planned to be responsible for the main construction of the Mercure 200, it was clear that Dassault now had to come into the picture, and Aérospatiale were asked to invite M. Vallières to join 'the Six' – which, for some reason, they failed to do. Nonetheless, an approach was eventually made to Dassault by other means, and 'the Six' became 'the Seven.'

Meanwhile, Ken Lawson had, with his colleagues, prepared a broad paper on the Mercure 200/BAC One-Eleven 800, and this formed the basis of an eventual report in April 1976 by the Executive Board to the Principals. This report concentrated its attention on an objective evaluation of European candidate aircraft in the 135–75 seat category, exploiting twin 'ten-tonne' engines, with a view to making recommendations on the options open to the European manufacturers.

The derivative aircraft considered were:

> Mercure 200
> One-Eleven 800
> Trident 5

The Aérospatiale AS 200 project was also evaluated as an example of a new aircraft. The report stressed that a satisfactory assessment could not be made without proper understanding of the influence of market requirements throughout the short/medium range. The report had, therefore, been prepared in the wider context of a comprehensive product policy for Europe.

The report estimated there would be a market for 1200 to 1600 aircraft up to 1990 in the capacity of 135 to 175 seats. The market demand would build up rapidly around 1980, mainly for a small aircraft (135–55 seats), with emphasis shifting to a larger version (155–75 seats) in the mid-eighties. This larger model would be centred in the USA, whereas demand for the smaller one would mainly arise in Europe and the rest of the world.

'The major part of the overall market rests outside the US,' said the report. 'It is a traditional market for the European industry and one which offers a real chance for a successful European programme, having a share of the total world market which can be expected to be between 25% to 35% (assuming US competition).'

It then went on to state that the European objective should be to offer aircraft to cover the full spectrum by developing a family of aircraft, which should be complementary to the A300 programme, both programmes together covering a capacity range from 135 to 335 seats. All members of such a family would have to be competitive with US aircraft in all respects. The market could best be served by offering a small aircraft as soon as possible, followed by a stretched version as soon as the market demand and competitive pressures required it, provided that engines of suitable thrust rating became available (CFM56 and JT10D). The report stressed that this family must be developed, produced, marketed and supported by a credible European organisation, combining all resources, especially in the field of product support. As Airbus Industrie was the only integrated European organisation, and as it was gaining increasing credibility with the airlines, any new and wider organisation should evolve in conjunction with Airbus Industrie.

The conclusions of the report were to recommend that the first member of the new 'European' family should be the smaller aircraft, exploiting twin 'ten-tonne' engines at their initial rating. Provision, however, should be made for development into a larger aircraft, as engines of higher thrust became available.

The working parties and the report were in favour of deriving these aircraft from existing designs 'because,' said the report, 'studies made so far have not shown a compelling case for a completely new aircraft.' It then went on, 'There are two candidate European derivative aircraft (the One-Eleven and Mercure) which offer good prospects for development. On purely technical grounds, the Mercure 200 has some advantages compared to the One-Eleven 800. However, the One-Eleven 800 draws on wide experience, has a good market base, and demonstrates an excellent reliability and maintainability record. Therefore, the final selection of one of these projects will depend upon prior clarification of political, national investment and worksharing issues which may be of over-riding importance and which can only be resolved by the Principals within the framework of an overall European product policy.'

Vallières' attitude to this report when it was presented at a Principals meeting in Bremen in April 1976 was predictable: the chosen aeroplane was to be the Mercure 200, and he was not prepared to listen to any other solution.

In saying this, Vallières doubtless had in mind a statement made at the Paris Air Show of 1975 by the French Minister of Transport, which said that the French Government had unilaterally decided to go ahead with a new airliner project. Anyone could negotiate to join with them in this if they so wished but, in any event, the French were going ahead and that was that. The time limit for discussion was in the autumn.

This virtual ultimatum was seen in Germany and the UK as basically a bluff and, indeed, autumn 1975 came and went with no new announcement. Vallières, however, undoubtedly had official encouragement for establishing the Mercure 200 as the new French project, but it was also known – and indeed he himself stated – that he was seeking American collaboration. It seemed, therefore, that the French Government was not now entirely willing to shoulder all the costs of the aeroplane single-handed, but was still set on it being French in origin.

Greenwood's reply to Vallières was not, as some expected, 'All right: then go off and build it' – but, instead, he made an offer to set aside the One-Eleven pending an intensive and objective study of the Mercure 200. This examination was then put in hand, but it revealed nothing new. The Mercure was a promising design, but it lacked the market base of the established One-Eleven.

Soon after this the French – both Aérospatiale and Dassault – were busy with collaborative discussions with Boeing and McDonnell Douglas, and, in August, the French Government announced agreement had been reached between Dassault and McDonnell Douglas under which McDonnell Douglas was to provide marketing support for the Mercure, and was to accept 10 per cent (later 15 per cent) of the risk of the project. This deal later appeared to die, and with it the Mercure 200.

The British (BAC and Hawker were now fully acting together, with Handel Davies, John Stamper, Michael Goldsmith, Ken Bentley and Arthur Rowlands as the men most closely concerned) were also engaged in dialogues with Boeing and McDonnell Douglas. Boeing, who already had a tentative agreement with Aérospatiale on participation in the then proposed Boeing 7N7 150–60 seater, also offered a deal to the UK whereby BAC/Hawker would undertake the detailed design and manufacture of the wings and their internal fittings plus the engine stubs and undercarriage – the work having to be done to match Boeing prices. This looked a promising proposition in that it gave the UK design work as well as manufacturing, but later Boeing, according to the British delegation, retreated somewhat from this offer, and became difficult to pin down. Collaboration plans with the USA now began to fade, and European projects came again to the fore.

By nationalisation, in April 1977, the whole European venture of 'the Six' was virtually back at square one. Attention was still centred on the 140–65 seat range (the B10 version of the Airbus was looking after the 200-seater market), and it was agreed to take a fresh look at what should be done. Derivatives of the One-Eleven came back into the review, as did the new Aérospatiale design, the AS200.

These comings and goings are mostly outside a history of BAC, as many of them took place after British Aerospace had been formed. There were, both in BAC and in Hawker, and later in British Aerospace, two camps: pro-USA collaboration and pro-European. The American hopes – if that is the right word – virtually went when Boeing announced its own wide-bodied B767 (200-seater) programme to go alongside the 200-seater B757 (ex 7N7), using a narrow-bodied B727 fuselage. Throughout all this, 'the Six' and the European adherents had received but little of the active collaboration and advice from British Airways, Air France, and Lufthansa which had been looked for in the 1974 arrangements, and, in 1978, British Airways having already, with Government permission, ordered nineteen B737s of 115 economy-class seats, followed this by ordering nineteen B757s of 186 seats, which are, however, to be powered by a smaller derivative of the Rolls-Royce RB211, the RB535.

Once again, the Whitehall emphasis had been given to Rolls-Royce at the expense of the airframe industry, even though, as had often been pointed out, engines, while very important, are, in the final analysis, bought-out equipment for an airframe. There could be British and European airframes without Rolls-Royce engines (e.g., the Airbus), but it was unlikely that Rolls-Royce could continue to prosper without British and European airframes.

At the time of the British Airways Boeing 757 announcement, the key European airframe manufacturers were studying what were known as the 'JET' proposals – 'JET 1' being a 130-seater, and 'JET 2' a 150-plus-seater, and the UK was also negotiating to rejoin the Airbus, for which Hawker Siddeley Aviation was still making the wings. Meanwhile the UK was on its own, pressing on with the new and Government-backed BAe146 70–109 seater feeder-liner which had been the centre of much pre-nationalisation controversy, while also continuing reaping the benefit of BAC obstinacy in keeping the One-Eleven line (223 sold) in being. A protocol with Romania on the One-Eleven 475, which had been discussed long before nationalisation, came to fruition immediately afterwards (May 1977), for the local manufacture in whole or in part of some eighty aircraft, which would bring much work to British Aerospace (and also to Rolls-Royce).

Thus, by the autumn of 1978, the One-Eleven, first conceived in 1960/61, was still earning its keep, but plans for a successor were still being bandied back and forth across the Channel, while the British national carrier continued to buy American. It could be said that some progress had been made since 1973 in getting a European policy for future transport aircraft, but some words of Sir George should be mounted and framed and put over the desks of the multi-nation decision-takers: 'To build aeroplanes for political purposes is a short cut to ruin. No airliner should be started unless it clearly meets the needs of the world market-place.'

35

Sir George Hands Over

BAC, as has been seen had, from 1972 to 1974, built up its yearly sales from £153 million to £271 million, its after-tax profits from £3.7 million to £12 million, and its earnings per share from 12.5p to 40.1p. Although these comparative figures are unadjusted for inflation, they remain impressive, the more so when it is remembered that, in 1972, the £15 million FCI loan was repaid, and that orders in hand at the end of 1974 were to a value of £815 million – £600 million of which was for export.

This high export content of BAC's sales throughout its life made nonsense of the 'featherbedding' argument which was much deployed during the nationalisation debates. BAC was nobody's 'weak sister' leaning on the British taxpayer for its livelihood so much that the taxpayer might as well own it. Three-quarters of its income by 1974 was from abroad. Admittedly, its military products owed – or mainly owed – their initial existence to the requirements of British defence forces (though much private-venture work had gone into export developments of both aircraft and weapons), but those defence forces got superlative equipment in return for their money, and they certainly could not have bought comparable aircraft or weapons more cheaply from any other source. This is to say nothing of the effect further huge foreign defence expenditure would have had on the British balance of payments, plus the consequent loss of UK exports and of UK technology and employment.

In 1975, BAC set even higher records and gained two more Queen's Awards. Sales were up £36 million to £307 million, of which two-thirds were now for export. Trading profit was nearly £30 million, profit after tax was over £14 million (£4.2 million distributed), and earnings per share were up to 47.2 pence. Orders still in hand had increased from £815 million to £850 million.

At the end of 1975, the Government introduced the expected Bill for Nationalisation of the Aircraft and Shipbuilding Industries, including BAC, and a month later Sir George Edwards retired from the company and from the industry. These two events were only marginally connected, it being widely known that Sir George had, for some time, been preparing to retire, and to hand over the BAC Chair to Allen

Greenwood. Sir George was now over 67, had had to undergo a second debilitating operation for the tangles in his stomach, but, despite medical advice, was still continuing to work himself regardless of his limits of physical and mental endurance.

Sir George would probably have retired a year or two earlier when the upcurve of BAC's fortunes was firmly established, but both Sir Arnold Weinstock and Lord Robens were keen for him to stay on – providing he didn't 'overdo things.' He did stay on, but it was not in his nature to be anything approaching a part-time Chairman. He was always either fully committed to an enterprise – or out of it altogether. What he did do was to make it very clear, right from the start of the run-up to nationalisation, that he was not a candidate for the chairmanship of whatever organisation was set up for the new British Aerospace. It was his belief that, whoever became the top man in what was still basically a merger of BAC and Hawker ought to hold that position for five years at least in order to shape and weld it – much as Lord Portal had done in BAC. 'I would be in my seventies before I could hand over, and that would be absurd,' he said.

Sir George also made no secret of his views on nationalisation of the aircraft industry. 'It is,' he said in a number of interviews and speeches, 'completely irrelevant to the problems of the industry. A change of shareholders isn't going to sell us any more aeroplanes.' He also foresaw a whole new layer of mainly political decision-taking being super-imposed between top industrial management and the relevant Minis-tries, and this, he believed, could only slow down an already cumbersome system.

Sir George's decision to go at the end of 1975 – a decision taken and made known to the parents and to the Government in the late summer – did, however, owe something to the impending nationalisation. It would give Greenwood a clear run at a time when it seemed no better than even money whether the Government would be able to put such a controversial measure through Parliament, or, indeed, would survive long enough to be able to try.

To the question of what should be the industry's attitude to nationalisation if it came about, Sir George took the line that, although it was, as he had often said, irrelevant, if it did happen then, as far as he was concerned, he would do all he could to see that the resultant organisation was one which could be made to work.

This was falsely interpreted by some commentators as being a kind of back-handed blessing on nationalisation and Sir George had to use several subsequent public occasions to put the record straight. 'I am completely opposed to nationalisation,' he said. 'I have already described it as utterly irrelevant to our problems and as a waste of public money. But, if it is to be, then, after forty years in the industry, I am concerned to see that the new set-up is as sensible and efficient as any advice from me can make it.'

The departure of George Edwards was deeply felt throughout all of BAC. His had been the guiding hand and influence from its inception, and by 1975 he was the dominating figure in all British aerospace. He had first come to Weybridge as a draughtsman in 1936, having turned down one previous offer of a job there because he wanted five shillings a week more than Vickers were willing to pay. By 1939, his ability and personality had so impressed the formidable Rex Pierson, the Chief Designer, that he was appointed to the then key position of Experimental Manager, one of his first contributions being the anti-magnetic mine version of the Wellington. By the end of the war, he was Chief Designer, and had been awarded the MBE. This was followed in 1952 by the CBE and the Royal Aeronautical Society's Gold Medal. The next year, he became, first, General Manager and Chief Engineer of Vickers Armstrongs (Aircraft) and then, Managing Director. He had already been responsible, first under Pierson and then heading his own team, for the Viking, its military variants, the Viscount, the Valiant, and the aborted V1000, and was to play a major role in the Vanguard, VC10 and One-Eleven. He was knighted in his presidential year of the RAeS, and it was a matter of the greatest pride to him that the knighthood came through the service to which he had dedicated himself throughout all his professional life – the Royal Air Force.

By the time BAC was formed, Edwards was fully armed at all points of the aircraft industry compass. To his engineering reputation, he had added triumphs of salesmanship with the Viscount and was the shrewdest observer of the Whitehall and Westminster scene in the business. Honorary degrees, awards and medals (including the FRS) came to him in profusion from both sides of the Atlantic, culminating, in 1971, with that most prestigious of all British honours, the Order of Merit.

Prince Philip wrote of him in the supplement to *Airframe* which marked Sir George's retirement, 'Sir George Edwards is one of those exceptional men who have stamped their genius on the course of human events. His achievements have earned him a place among the great company of pioneers and innovators in world aviation.'

Sir George handed over to Allen Greenwood a BAC whose all-round financial and industrial strength had put it at the pinnacle of European aerospace. It was a strength which was based not on the passing whims of the Treasury mandarins, but on orders from abroad – a tap which Whitehall could not turn off. Again – as Lord Portal had done as Chief of the Air Staff at the end of the war, and later as Chairman of BAC – GRE simply and firmly bowed out. He resigned all Board memberships and devoted himself to his pro-chancellorship of Surrey University, to Surrey County Cricket Club, of which he was eventually to become President, and to the foundation of a Hospice. 'If I keep an official connection with BAC,' he said, 'then any of the senior chaps who don't hold with something or other that AG [Greenwood] might want to do, will show up moaning on my doorstep. I'm not going to have any of that, and that's why my break is going to be complete and final.'

For Greenwood, the task of succeeding GRE was doubly formidable. Not only was he taking over from one of the country's truly great men, whom he had served from the days when he was technical assitant to Edwards in the old Vickers drawing office, but he was doing so with Anthony Wedgwood Benn stretching out his hands to take over the company and establish in it his undefined but highly publicised worker's democracy. As far as Greenwood could see, he could just be a caretaker Chairman for a year – or, depending on the sick-parade vagaries of voting numbers in Westminster, be secure in his command for a normal span. In this ambiguous situation, there was only one thing he could do – carry on the business of BAC regardless of nationalisation, and this, with the help of Page on the Aircraft side and Jefferson at Guided Weapons, he duly did.

Greenwood made no attempt to be a second GRE. The two men, though always close, were entirely dissimilar in method, and Greenwood's background of command had not been as extensive – nor could it have been – as GRE's. Edwards had held posts which, in their different ways, had given him an almost unchallengeable authority since 1940. He was not, either by nature, or by his thirty-five years of command experience, much given to consultation, save that which was forced upon him by his owners – that is, by Vickers Chairmen until 1960 and then by the parents of BAC. Internally, in BAC itself, his method was to ascertain facts, integrate them with what he knew of the Whitehall intentions of the day, and then issue decisions. It was a kind of benevolent autocracy – benevolent in that a Department head could always gain access in order to raise an objection or to advance an idea. But if such objection was ill-founded, or the idea ill-thought through, then GRE could be fairly terse. He once said of his method of command, 'If any of the chaps feel strongly enough about something, then they'll be round quickly enough. They all know where I live, and they know I'll listen to what they say. If it makes sense, I'll back them up.'

Allen Greenwood, by contrast, did all his consulting prior to a decision and, in case of conflict, patiently sought a compromise if, in his view, a sensible middle course was obtainable. He had always been blessed with almost old-fashioned good manners and courtesy, which went along with a sense of humour that was not always immediately apparent to the slower witted of his colleagues. AG's capacity for hard work, and for keeping on top of the piles of paper which inevitably flooded into his in-tray was prodigious. Yet he combined this tidy-minded administration with constant travel round all the BAC sites, and tireless visits abroad in his seeking for the European solution of the long-term problems of the industry, of which he had been for so long the leading advocate. Throughout his sixteen months of chairmanship, with all the domestic burden which the nationalisation saga imposed upon him, Greenwood still regularly met with the leaders of the French, Italian, German and Dutch industries, consulted the officials of the EEC in Brussels, presided over the meetings in Washington which led to the broadening of BAC (USA) Inc., into a joint company with Rolls-Royce, and its re-establishment on a new site near Dulles Airport. Yet still, at the end of each week, he left very few letters or memos unanswered or telephone calls un-returned. If, towards the end, when British Aerospace was being shaped under Lord Beswick, he was showing some signs of weariness, the wonder was that he was not on a sick-bed. Earlier – just after he retired – Sir George permitted himself the comment, 'AG is doing the job I always knew he would do. He is being Chairman of BAC. I was never really the Chairman, whatever it said on my door. I was always the Managing Director, and that's the difference between the two of us.'

The final year of BAC – 1976 – showed, under Greenwood's chairmanship, by far the best results in its sixteen years' existence. Total sales reached a remarkable £483.4 million, a jump of no less than 57 per cent, the export content of these sales reaching over £270 million, an increase of some £70 million. The profit after tax was £19.1 million (£14.1 million), and earning per share went up from 47.2p to 64 pence. This last of the annual reports included this paragraph:

The Directors wish to record the growth and prosperity of the Group activity under private ownership since 1964, which was the first full year in which the businesses merged in 1960 were effectively consolidated in their present form:

	1964 £ million	1976 £ million
Sales	116.7	483.4
Pre-tax profits	1.0	39.9
Outstanding orders at year end	361.0	1031.0

To which figures, the report added this comment:

The aerospace industry was referred to as a prime candidate for nationalisation in Labour's Programme for 1973, and this concept was promoted by a Joint Working Party from the Labour Party, the Trades Union Congress, and the Confederation of Shipbuilding and Engineering Unions in a statement in July 1974 approved by the National Executive of the Labour Party. At that time, and since that time, no evidence was or has been offered or made available to show why and how the aerospace industry's operations would be thus improved for its own or the national good. Those responsible in Parliament for bringing about this change in ownership for doctrinaire political reasons will have created additional and unnecessary burdens for the management of the recently established British

Aerospace, burdens which can only be successfully borne by professional managers with ingenuity and resourcefulness of the highest order. It is to be hoped that they will not only be able to master these new problems but will maintain or even better the progress made in the world's highly competitive markets by the industry under private ownership.

In the same report, there was this general summary of the last year of BAC:

The continued growth in the volume of new orders over the past four years has once again produced record levels of sales and profits in the year under review. Orders in hand amounting to £1031 million at the end of the year have passed the 'billion pound' mark for the first time and compare with £850 million at the end of the previous year. Exports, mainly of military products and associated services, have again made a substantial contribution to total sales and profits and constitute some 75 per cent of current orders.

The Military Aircraft Division has had a particularly successful year with a high level of profitability. The British, German and Italian Governments have maintained their support for the Tornado (formerly MRCA) project and the signing in 1976 of the first production contracts for this aircraft is of major significance for the future of the Division.

The Guided Weapons Division has again achieved most encouraging results, derived mainly from the Rapier and Swingfire missiles. This Division has also been able to strengthen its future prospects following the signing of a major contract with Iran for development and production of a tracked version of Rapier and the execution of a licence agreement for the manufacture of the European Milan missile, both of which are expected to produce substantial future sales.

In Commercial Aircraft Division, Concorde has demonstrated in its first full year of commercial service, outstanding reliability and passenger appeal on its main routes to Washington and South America but the continued refusal of the New York Authorities to admit the aircraft to that city has been a major obstacle to the securing of further orders and to the continuation of a satisfactory production programme. Further orders have been obtained for the BAC One-Eleven and manufacture and development are being maintained. The Division is also undertaking a substantial amount of sub-contract work. However, due to the run-down in the Concorde programme, it is not possible to continue to utilise fully its manpower and facilities with the result that it was regrettably necessary to announce early in 1977 a corresponding reduction in manpower and rationalisation of facilities.

Average employment in the UK decreased by approximately 1250 to 34,528 and, by the end of the year, total manning had fallen by 2200 to 33,750. These reductions occurred mainly in Commercial Aircraft Division while employment in the two military divisions remained relatively stable. In addition, overseas employment has been maintained at more than 2000, of which the largest proportion is in Saudi Arabia and other Middle Eastern countries.

36
Concorde

References to Concorde have already been allowed to thread their way, with no detailed explanation, through many of the chapters of this book. This should have caused no great perplexity. Readers of an aviation history can be expected already to be aware of the generalities of the Concorde story, and most will be familiar with much of its detail. BAC existed for seventeen years and the Supersonic Transport Project which eventually became Concorde was with it from start to finish. This was a distinction the SST shared with only one other product – the Jet Provost and its development, the Strikemaster, though it can be argued that the One-Eleven concept came half-formed into the original British Aircraft Corporation as the Hunting 107. No other pre-1960 aircraft or weapon project stayed the full course, though spares and re-furbishings for several such were still a good source of income in 1977 and look like remaining so through the 1980s. The Britannia, Viscount, Vanguard, VC10, Canberra and Lightning are obvious examples of the longevity of service which has gone hand in hand with the increasing capital costs of all major civil and military equipment.

In approaching an account of Concorde from SST project to entry into service, the author is faced with a bewilderment of choices. He can follow the day-to-day fever chart of rows in Parliament, of political rows with the French, of battles with the protest groups at home, in the USA, and many other places, and of the continual fight against a unilateral British withdrawal. He can also follow, in parallel, the many technical crises of design, of range and of payload, of production, and above all, of mounting costs. There is drama a-plenty to be found, with the aeroplane, with the two Governments, with the airlines, and between the major contractors. To produce a sensationalised account of Concorde would be relatively easy; it could certainly be titillating in terms of who said what to whom, and when, but, in this author's view, it would also be unforgivably petty.

Whatever the strategic and commercial rights and wrongs of the decision to start, and then to continue with, a twice-the-speed-of-sound airliner, the fact is that Concorde was created, was put into regular service, and was designed, built, tested and certificated by the British and the French to a timetable which would not have disgraced any major conventional subsonic transport.

Technically, Concorde was a triumph which can stand alongside the US and USSR space programmes, and way above the Soviet attempt to emulate it. When British SST projects were·first publicly set out in March 1959, the novelty had hardly yet worn off the realisation that fighter aircraft were regularly flying faster than sound. The thought that the UK, which had, by then, produced only one such supersonic fighter, the Lightning, nevertheless had the technology to design and build a reliable, certificated, fare-paying, passenger-carrying aeroplane for everyday use seemed to belong to science fiction. Yet, in December 1967, the prototype of an Anglo-French SST was rolled out, and on 2 March 1969, it flew, ten years almost to the day after a British Supersonic Transport Committee had reported to the Ministry of Aviation that such an aeroplane was feasible.

The immensity of the Concorde achievement is still not really appreciated outside the limited circle of those who are in the business of aviation. The problems which faced the designers were mountainous. A supersonic airliner not only had to cruise beyond the speed of sound, it had, for aerodynamic reasons affecting range and economy, to cruise at twice that speed, i.e., at Mach 2. It also had to produce this performance not for the ten-minute dash of a fighter (which was then pampered by a maintenance crew until its next short flight, maybe several days later) but for three or four continuous hours per sortie, with at least two such flights a day up to 2800 hours to 3000 hours a year. The comfort of the conditions inside the passenger cabin had to be indistinguishable from those inside any conventional jetliner; the safety, reliability, handling, and the ability to face engine failure at take-off or *en route*, plus docility at lower speeds round the airfield, had to be in conformity with the highest standards of British and American Certificates of Airworthiness. The engine intakes and airflow had to function, by variable geometry, equally well at low speeds at ground level as at Mach 2 at over 60,000 feet, and the whole aircraft had to be able to operate anywhere in the world and to go on doing so, without excessive maintenance costs, for ten years or more.

In achieving all these things, each of which was at the frontiers of the state of the art, Concorde had also to meet its operational specification: an ability to carry 20,000–25,000 lb of payload for 4000 miles – amounting to a hundred first-class passengers either way across the North Atlantic between New York and Paris and London with reserves. If it accomplished this, Concorde would represent the biggest single advance ever in the speed of air transportation by being over twice as fast as any jetliner currently in operation. It would be an aeroplane which would halve the journey-time on any route on which it flew and which could link any two major cities of the world in half a day.

That all this was eventually done, and done by an unlikely seeming combination of French and British engineers where both the USA and the USSR failed, should be a matter of intense national pride, and such opinion polls as have been sampled on the subject indicate that, in fact, it so is. It is beyond doubt that Britain's share of Concorde raised the standing of this country in the eyes of many other nations in a way which only those who saw the crowds which greeted it overseas and heard their applause will fully credit.

The first positive moves towards what was to become Concorde were made when Mr (later Sir) Morien Morgan, Deputy Director of RAE, and his Supersonic Transport Committee reported in 1959, after three years of study, that a 100-seat aircraft with a speed of Mach 1.2 and a range of 1500 miles could be developed, and also a 150-seater with a speed of Mach 1.8 and a trans-Atlantic range. The latter proposal made much more sense; the medium-range type was put on the shelf (the French later revived it), and joint feasibility studies were given to Hawker and Bristol. These were to be based on brilliant Farnborough work on arrow-head, slender-delta wings by Dietrich Kuchemann in the mid-late 1950s. The Bristol team, under Dr Russell, supported by his Chief Engineer, Dr Bill Strang, and by Mick Wilde, produced the Bristol 198 proposal, powered by six Olympus jets mounted under the wing. This was a 132-seater with a maximum take-off weight of 380,000 lb, which was considered to be too heavy. It was modified to a 100-seater, the Bristol 223, with a take-off weight of 250,000 lb, but also with a trans-Atlantic range.

This was an all-British effort, and a contract for a design study was awarded to what was by now British Aircraft Corporation in 1960, but on the condition that BAC should try to find an international partner to share the risks and the cost. The USA was already turning its thoughts to a big Mach 3, steel-and-titanium entrant, and showed no interest in a mere Mach 2, but the French took up the offer through Sud Aviation, builders of the Caravelle. Sud, a nationalised company then under Georges Hereil, also wanted to do an SST, but with a 1500-mile medium range, which it called the Super Caravelle. Dr Russell maintained that it was only on an oversea sector length such as Paris–New York that the time-saving advantages of an SST would really pay off while avoiding sonic boom problems. There were some lively meetings between Russ and his team, and his French opposite numbers, Pierre Satre and Lucien Servanty. Neither side would give way, and, at the Paris Air Show of June 1961, Sud, to underline their attitude, showed a Super Caravelle SST model on their stand. The difficulties dragged on through the rest of 1961 and most of 1962, with the UK Ministers, Peter Thorneycroft and later Julian Amery, putting on pressure for an Anglo-French accord to be reached in the political interests of European, and hopefully EEC, collaboration. In early 1962, the powerful Georges Hereil left Sud to become Chairman of Simca, and his place was taken by General André Puget, former Commander of the Free French Bomber Squadrons based in the UK. Puget knew and liked the British and formed an immediate rapport with George Edwards who, to oil the wheels of collaboration, placed VC10 sub-contract work into Sud's factories at

Toulouse. In the end, it was decided to carry on with both the SST proposals, the medium-range French one, and the long-range British version – a model of what was in effect the latter having been shown by way of riposte at Farnborough in September 1962.

Eventually – and despite American attempts to dissuade the British Government – on 29 November 1962, a treaty was signed in London by Minister of Supply Amery and the French Ambassador M. de Courcel. The UK was to have the engine 'lead' as it had long been agreed to use the supersonic Bristol Siddeley Olympus, but the French nationalised engine company, SNECMA was to be responsible for the nozzle. In return, the French were to 'lead' on the airframe, and to have 60 per cent of the work to balance the pro-British engine 'split.' BAC was to be responsible for fuselage nose, droop snoot, forward and rear fuselage, fin, rudder, and nacelles, including the air intakes and the engine bays. The French were to be responsible for the wings, centre section, elevons, and under-carriage. There were to be two assembly lines, Toulouse and Filton, but no duplication of manufacture. The total estimated development costs were put at between £150 and £170 million, half of which was to be borne by each country.

There were a number of basic things wrong with this Anglo-French SST set-up. First of all, it was seen at the time, and especially by Russell, Strang and Mick Wilde, as very wrong and most wasteful to process two projects (the French medium-range and the British long-range ver-sions). The Super Caravelle, however, was to continue to cloud the overall Concorde issue until 1965, when what both sides now agree was commonsense finally prevailed.

The second major error was the 'organisation' of the Anglo-French effort. There were two management teams – one for the engine and one for the airframe. The engine one was not much bother, but that for the airframe, basically because of the French dislike of the UK long-range proposal and the British dislike of the Super Caravelle idea, was soon in trouble. It needed all the skills and authority and mutual regard of General Puget – the first Chairman – and of his 'Deputy,' Sir George Edwards, to keep the arguments within bounds. The chairmanship of the Airframe Committee alternated yearly between Sud and BAC, so there was never a permanent boss.

At lower level, no senior Englishman really regarded himself as 'deputy' to a Frenchman, or vice-versa, so nearly every technical proposal had to be fought out several times. There was really no such thing as a 'lead team' and no Chief Designer or Chief Engineer. Over the top of this difficult Airframe Committee, there was a standing Committee of Government officials, the Concorde Directing Commit-tee which monitored on behalf of the French and British taxpayers what was a 'costs plus' operation (BAC having refused to get financially involved on a private-venture basis). Later, the very top-level, and therefore very busy, men on this CDC found it too time-consuming and delegated responsibility to a Concorde Management Board.

It was a most cumbersome and unwieldy system, productive of long, and in many cases, indecisive meetings, and yet, in many ways, the final design was to benefit from them. Sir George, who played the major BAC role in the early and most difficult days, and who had a great deal to do with the initial technical shaping of the project, came later to believe that much good stemmed from what, at the time, seemed to be the endless arguments. He maintained that, together with the very comprehensive ground testing of every part of the aircraft, the exhaustive nature of all the discussions resulted in an aeroplane which had a most remarkably smooth flight development programme. It also has to be remembered that this first essay in major Anglo-French collaboration had no precedent and was pioneering not least in the most ambitious transport aeroplane ever attempted, but also in the management structure of such a huge international undertaking. The Sepecat Jaguar and the Panavia MRCA were later to benefit hugely from the lessons of the shapeless administration of Concorde.

One of the good things about the Concorde agreement was that it was a Treaty. Julian Amery had made it so, and had made it one without a break clause so that the French could not withdraw from it unilaterally without heavy recompense. This feature of the Agreement was, in 1964, paradoxically, to work the other way round. It was the new Labour Government which wanted to kill off Concorde (as well as the UK military aircraft programmes) but, to its fury, found that it could not do so without risking heavy penalties.

The SST's name of Concorde (with an 'e') was decided not long after the Treaty signing. Mr F.G. Clark, the Publicity Manager at Filton, submitted the name to the author during a telephone call – giving credit for the idea to his son, then an undergraduate at Cambridge. The author laid it before Sir George, who liked it, but said – 'With or without an "e"?' The author thought it looked better and more attractive to the eye with an 'e', and Sir George said, 'It will also give pleasure to André [Puget].' He thereupon suggested it to Sud, and it was accepted. There has since been built up quite a mythology about the name (and its final 'e') being forced on the British by French chauvinism, but the above is the simple and plain fact of the matter. The final 'e' was put in 'Concorde' by BAC merely because it looked right – and it still does. Young Clark was publicly presented with a Concorde model by André Puget, and treated by Sud to a week's 'all found' holiday in Paris – the extent of the meaning 'all found' not being closely probed by his father. As far as the author knows, the name was not submitted to any Government Committees, and Julian Amery protested strongly at not being consulted.

After Macmillan's Common Market rebuff by de Gaulle, a verbal Government order to BAC was issued, via the author, that BAC was, in all its literature, to drop the 'e' forthwith, and that, as far as the Government was concerned, the aircraft was now to be called 'Concord.' Sir George, having entered into a personal agreement with Puget, predictably wouldn't break it – and so there was a ridiculous situation (which lasted until December 1967), when all BAC public information on Concorde used the 'e' and all that from the Government did not. It was not until the prototype roll-out ceremony that Wedgwood Benn, in his speech, officially restored the 'e' on behalf of the Government to mark a great milestone in Anglo-French collaboration.

It became clear in quite early days that the longer-range Concorde was still not going to be big enough (and therefore heavy enough) to be trans-Atlantic with any payload. Russ had never departed from his original 1960 estimate of 385,000 lb all-up weight, and he regarded talk of 250,000 lb or even 350,000 lb as a waste of time. It was also clear that the initial estimate of £150 to £170 million for the development costs was also going to bear little relation to reality. For several years, Russ had a grubby, folded piece of paper in his wallet which he would produce at the drop of a hat and show to anyone (Press representatives included). It said, 'All-up weight, 385,000 lb – total development costs, £1000 million.' He proved to be almost exactly right on development cost (£500 million to each country) and the in-service maximum all-up weight of Concorde was 400,000 lb.

For the range/payload (and therefore weight) reasons mentioned, Concorde had virtually to be re-designed. The fuselage was in 1964 lengthened by 14 feet and the wing area increased by 15 per cent. The weight went up to 367,000 lb, with a re-designed and more powerful Olympus 593 engine to match. A year later, another $6\frac{1}{2}$ feet was added to the fuselage, the wing aerodynamics were improved, and the rear bulkhead pulled back even further to increase the passenger-cabin length to 129 feet to accommodate, at need, up to 140 economy-class seats. The Olympus now needed to be a 40,000 lb thrust engine – and this it duly became.

These two re-designs, which could only be done when the long-range Concorde had been accepted as common policy, put up the cost considerably, but they did make the Concorde into the aeroplane which Russ had advocated from the start. It was these delays and consequent cost-escalation which led him to say many times afterwards that the UK could have done Concorde (as it finally emerged) much more quickly and more cheaply on its own than by going in with the French on a fifty-fifty basis. Maybe. But, of course, a 'go-it-alone' British Concorde, unprotected by the Anglo-French Treaty and the threat of French recourse to the International Court at the Hague, would have been axed in December 1964. In fact, without an international partner, it would never have been started at all, and the only international partner on offer was France.

The Americans, it will be recalled, had set their sights on a big Mach 3 transport built in titanium and steel. This obsession ruled them out of partnership with the UK, despite all the force of persuasion Sir George could bring to bear on Washington and the West Coast. It was, in the end, also to put them out of the first-generation SST business completely.

Concorde was designed for a more modest speed of $M = 2$ – if 'modest' is an applicable word to such a great venture. This was on the basis that the skin-friction temperatures would then be low enough to enable the airframe to be built of aluminium alloys, about whose fatigue and manufacturing properties a great deal was known. It also avoided opening up many problems connected with plastics, oil and other basics, whose properties, when exposed for long periods to extremes of temperature, appeared doubtful and would certainly need a lot of expensive research.

Sir George would probably have preferred, for market and finance reasons, to have had an Anglo-US SST, but once the die was cast and after he had ascertained that America was still determined on Mach 3, he was considerably relieved. 'There are,' he said in 1962, 'only yet a few minutes of world experience of level flight at Mach 3, and that hardly seems a sensible basis on which to build a big airliner in which you can sell seats to Mr Jones of Wigan. As for building in steel – we [BAC] are the only company in the world that has tried it [T188] and we can tell them how difficult it is. Let them get on with it, because in my view it isn't on.'

Sir George's view, which was a hard technical appraisal, was not shared by many of the commentators of the day, who credited the Americans with an almost superhuman ability in aeronautics, and who forecast that Concorde would be outdated by the US competitor – bigger, faster, cheaper – almost before it flew. Sir George, too, had a healthy respect for the American industry, and his fear was of a different kind. He was frightened that the USA would quickly realise the technical and economic facts of life of a Mach 3 transport, and would switch to a Mach 2 competitor in aluminium. But they didn't. After spending vast sums, the project – which had eventually been awarded to Boeing, after stern competition with Lockheed – was killed off by the Senate. At one time, Boeing had added the complication of swing-wings to their design but, after the contract had been awarded, they reverted to a more conventional Concorde-like delta with a cruise speed of Mach 2.7.

What the cost of this American SST would have really been is anyone's guess, but the anti-pollution lobby, a day or so before the Senate vote, came out with their dramatic ozone-destruction allegations, and have always since claimed that it was they who killed the project. This is doubtful: the cost was the more probable cause – that and the fact that Boeing did not seem to put up much more than a token fight. Some Boeing people were later to say they were glad to see the back of the thing, having already realised that, if the job could be done at all, it could only be at such huge expense that it would be bound to be axed before completion. Whatever the truth, the Americans, who had been fading from the SST scene throughout 1970, finally left it in March 1971, by

which time they were already seven years behind Concorde, which had
had two prototypes flying supersonically since late 1969. The Americans
had, by 1971, already spent $1000 million *not* to have an sst – which was
more than the uk had spent to bring Concorde well into the flight test
and pre-production stage.

The Concorde prototypes, 001 and 002, had not been altered during
the re-designs of the production models (their build was too far
advanced), and were some 19 feet shorter. Aerodynamically, however,
they were more or less the same, and were used by Brian Trubshaw and
André Turcat and their teams in Britain and France respectively to break
the back of the test programme. They were followed by two pre-
production aircraft (01 and 02) before the first 'proper' airline-standard
aeroplane was rolled out.

The full story of Concorde cannot possibly be told within the
compass of this book – save by doubling its length. There are already
many volumes devoted to the subject, some of which are given in the
bibliography. Geoffrey Knight's *Concorde – the Inside Story* tells of all the
negotiations with the airlines, of the American purchase-options and
their eventual cancellations, and of the many cost investigations which
were held by successive Governments in both the uk and in France. The
Clark/Gibson book is a wonderfully illustrated and detailed story of the
aeroplane as such. Both are recommended reading.

The eventual cost of the development of the joint project over some
fourteen years was nearly £1000 million – £500 million of which was
paid by the British, which works out at under a relatively modest £40
million a year. This, however, was a far cry from the £150/£170 million
total estimate of November 1962. Something like half of the £830
million increase went in straightforward inflation and exchange-rate
alterations, which still left over £400 million (£200 millions in each
country) which has to be set against re-designs and just 'getting the sums
wrong.'

For example, at the end of 1964 – two years after the signing of the
Treaty – a detailed paper had to be presented to, and approved by, the
Treasury as a prerequisite to the execution in 1965 of the main
development contract between the Government and bac. This paper
had to cover, among other things, the cost-effectiveness of the project,
its potential market, and the effect on such market of the (then) proposed
us competition. It was written by Tom Pritchard, who had the help of
Professor Tress, who held the Chair of Economics at Bristol University.
It was a very coherent and closely argued document, and one which,
looking back after his retirement at the end of 1977, Pritchard regarded
as among the most important of the many major bac papers for which,
over the years, he had been responsible. In it, the total direct
development costs (1965 prices) of Concorde to 1970 were estimated at
£280 million and the production cost per aircraft, on the basis of a
hundred Concordes, was put at £4.2 millions. These figures, two years

into the overall programme, were most carefully researched in the knowledge that they were for the scrutiny of Treasury experts whose antagonism to aerospace and its investment monies had not changed since long before TSR2 (and for that matter, was still being publicly voiced – or leaked – in 1979).

Yet even the critical Treasury accepted 1965 Concorde estimates which, only a few years later, would not have covered the development and tooling for a conventional medium-class subsonic transport based on virtually standard engineering.

The point of the above is that the cost of this daunting and complex technological achievement was seriously under-estimated from the start. Such grave under-estimates, as has been pointed out earlier, are by no means confined to aviation. Comparable percentages have been recorded in such apparently straightforward things as motorways, bridges and high-rise buildings, and have occurred all over the world. In the case of Concorde, which was breaking entirely new ground, it can now be realised that there was no yardstick by which its eventual cost could be measured. A fully honest answer to cash questions both at Concorde's inception and during its earlier development would probably have been 'Don't know,' which would hardly have been acceptable to Parliament or the people. Even Russ's famous bit of paper with £1000 million scribbled on it could hardly have been more than an inspired guess. To the people most deeply concerned at the time £1000 million seemed ridiculous – until, in the end, it wasn't.

During the lifetime of Concorde, the BAC top team remained more or less constant, save that Russ semi-retired in 1968 after the back of the job had been broken. Sud, however, underwent many changes, including being merged with Nord into Aérospatiale, and had four successive leaders – Georges Hereil, Puget (whose sudden posting in 1964 as French Ambassador to Sweden as a punishment for escalating costs infuriated Sir George), Maurice Papon, a former Paris Prefect of Police, and then, in 1968, BAC's old colleague of Air France and Jaguar days, Henri Ziegler. By the time Ziegler retired (and there were then two more Presidents of Aérospatiale in quick succession) the Concorde work was virtually over.

At the beginning of the collaboration there had been a great deal of nationalism evident of the 'the French are trying to do us down and claim Concorde as their own' kind in the UK, and 'perfide Albion' in France. Some of it was to be found in various personal relationships but, as 001 and 002 began to fly and as later, with 01 and 02, they made many visits and gave many rides all over the world, including the USA, this edginess had worn off. As Sir George said on that memorable day in 1969 when both 001 and 002 flew together at the Paris Air Show (002 joining the Le Bourget circuit from BAC's test field at Fairford), 'If anyone starts niggling about the British and the French again, I'll just remind them of what they've seen today.'

It was, as far as the author recollects, at that Paris Air Show of 1969, that the Tupolevs – father and son – surprisingly visited the BAC Chalet to take wine with Sir George and Russ, presumably to talk about their Tu144 'Concordski' which had flown the previous year. There was an interpreter present, and, after the usual courtesies, the elder Tupolev turned to GRE (who had met him on various UK missions to the USSR and said, 'Do you have any problems with your air intakes?' 'No – they are working fine' was the reply. There was then a long pause. 'And your intakes – they are all right?' asked Sir George. 'Yes – fine, fine,' replied Tupolev, and, after handshakes, he and his entourage left without another word. When they had gone, Sir George turned to Russ and said, 'They've got problems with their intakes' – which, as later became apparent, was no less than the truth.

One of the things about Concorde which was particularly irritating to BAC was that all the publicity about it, which went on for practically the whole life of the Corporation, gave many people the impression that BAC stood or fell on Concorde. It was in truth, as has been shown, never more than a minor contributor to the profits, but it did occupy a wholly disproportionate share of the factory space at Filton and Weybridge, and of the time of many of the top executives. As a result, whenever the impending cancellation of Concorde was in the headlines, which was pretty often, a great deal of reassuring had to go on all round the world that BAC was not, as a result, going to go bankrupt.

On the plus side of the ledger, BAC gained an enormous amount of unique high technology (and prestige) from Concorde, and so did many others of a large network of sub-contract firms all over the British Isles. Hugh Conway, then Managing Director of the Rolls-Royce Bristol factory, once replied on TV to the standard complaint that Concorde's money would have better been spent on new schools, hospitals, and social services by saying, 'This country has to make and sell things first. It is only when it has sold enough that it can afford hospitals and school milk in the first place.'

It is true that by the time BAC was nationalised the once high sales hopes of Concorde had dwindled to the handful for British Airways and Air France. As an aeroplane, Concorde met the specification and performance laid down for it, and it had proved its dramatic time-saving advantages all over the world. The trouble was that it was bereft of routes on which to fly. This was particularly true for British Airways. South Africa was ruled out because no intermediate refuelling stop was politically possible in Black Africa. The Australian service was held up by problems with Malaysia and Singapore, and Tokyo's new airport could not even be opened for its own conventional traffic because of protesting students. Until the US barrier was finally broken down, British Airways could only run Concorde between London and Bahrain. Then, after the years of public and private battling against the US environmental lobby ('We stopped our SST and we're going to stop yours'), and the US Governmental hearings – most fairly and ably conducted – came the year of trial service to and from Washington International at Dulles in 1976, to be followed, in 1977, by regular scheduled operations into Kennedy Airport, New York. Even so, the annual utilisation rate of each of British Airways' five Concordes was only a few hundred hours, instead of the 2500 to 3000 hours that are needed to make the aeroplane profitable.

As a result of these early limitations on Concorde, it has been widely labelled as a money-loser. Basically, however, it is a profitable aircraft and, at current fare rates and payloads, which have – as expected – remained very high, Concorde can make a lot of money once its utilisation rate can be worked up to normal levels. What the early years of trans-Atlantic service have proved is that Concorde is no threat to anybody's environment. The ozone myth has been exposed, the boom bogey has been shown to be no threat to populated areas, and take-off noise is no worse than that of most other jets and is over in a shorter time. It is the author's belief that one by one new Concorde routes will open up and that, one day, it will appear on the services where its impact can be most dramatic of all – over the Pacific.

Back in 1958, in a famous Presidential lecture to the Royal Aeronautical Society, Sir George Edwards pointed out that once two places were brought within a twelve-hour journey circle of each other, then traffic between those two places shot up to the roof. This was, he proved, a fundamental truth, and had remained good for all forms of transport over all kinds of journey-distances from the stage coach to the jetliner. It would, he argued, also remain valid for an SST which he was even then foreseeing as coming into the realms of the possible for the 1970s. Concorde cannot quite bring Australia and London within twelve hours of each other – but near enough. And the same is true of trans-Pacific. It is there particularly that the 'shoot up to the roof' traffic growth has never yet had a chance to happen (as it did on the Atlantic when jets came in). Concorde can bring that service to the Pacific and it can generate there that 'twelve-hour journey circle' traffic-leap which, beyond doubt, is there to be stimulated. Some operator will do it sooner or later. There can surely be no valid Concorde objections now left to worry San Francisco or Tokyo.

Whatever happens to Concorde as such, it is self-evident that supersonic travel is not now going to disappear. There will eventually be a new SST (only one model probably, the aviation world can hardly afford to develop and sell two in competition). It will be bigger than Concorde, although Concorde's 100 first-class seats have been shown to be right for the first generation of SSTs. It will have longer range and be quieter, and every long-haul airline in the world will have to buy it. It is then that the UK's investment in Concorde will surely pay off. Only two manufacturers in the world have the unique and invaluable knowledge which comes from having built, flown and certificated an actual SST –

British Aerospace, as it now is, and Aérospatiale. That knowledge – whether pooled with the USA and its big home market or not – must eventually be at a premium.

37
Nationalisation

The nationalisation of BAC was, unhappily, a long drawn-out process. It was disruptive of stability, unsettling to management, workers, customers, and international partners, and productive only of politically motivated division and uncertainty. As has been stated, and after much Left Wing talk about nationalising most of Britain's key industries, including aerospace, shipbuilding, banks, insurance companies, ICI, and many others, a positive move was made against aerospace in 1973. It was then referred to by the Labour Party as a 'prime candidate,' and in 1974 its nationalisation was approved by the National Executive and was in the manifesto on which the Labour Party was returned to power in 1974 as a minority Government, both in terms of MPs and, as usual, of votes cast.

As a result of this election, nationalisation became central to the thoughts and activities of BAC and of its two parents for three full years. The uncertainty lasted from the spring of 1974 until 1977 – that is to say, during the last twenty-one months of Sir George Edwards' chairmanship, and the whole of the sixteen months' span under Allen Greenwood. BAC was finally nationalised at the end of April 1977, being joined with Hawker Siddeley Aviation, Hawker Siddeley Dynamics (the separate Hawker Siddeley guided weapons company) and, presumably for Scottish employment, and therefore local political considerations, Scottish Aviation. This company, which marketed the Bulldog trainer and the ex-Handley Page Jetstream and also operated as a general engineering sub-contractor, was having a very difficult time and, unless nationalised, had a doubtful future.

In the spring and summer of 1974, however, there was considerable uncertainty as to the future structure of the industry. It was not known what priority the new Government would give to any legislation on aerospace nationalisation, what would be its scope, or indeed, in view of the Labour Party's minority situation, whether such a controversial measure would be brought forward at all. There was also always the possibility that the Government would not survive long enough to implement much of its considerable programme of Socialisation. Nonetheless, BAC's parents had to assume that they would soon have to surrender control of one of their important assets to the Government, and to make arrangements accordingly.

From the point of view of Vickers and GEC, this was clearly going to be a tightrope-walking exercise. On one hand, they had to ensure that BAC remained not only actually viable during any twilight zone between private and possible public ownership, but also demonstrably viable in the eyes of the banks, customers, and foreign governments. On the other hand, they had a duty to their own shareholders to see that no more of their monies were put at risk in BAC unless there was Government cover. No one knew what the compensation terms would be, when and how compensation would be paid, or on what basis. There was also, apart from the actual shares, a tangle of loans and 'old account' business to tidy up, including the £8 million from the sale by BAC to the parents of the surplus land at Weybridge west of the river Wey. The temptation to share out BAC's cash reserves before the blow fell must have been considerable, but to have done so, although legal, would have weakened the company and would probably have produced strong protest from the BAC Directors. In the end, all that happened before nationalisation was that £15 million of advances to BAC from the parents (£7.5 million each) were repaid. A dividend of £4.2 million was declared for 1975 and the maximum legal dividend was declared on the last year of private trading (£3.4 million, or 17 per cent of the available profits in 1976).

Both parents did take yet another look at hiving off the Guided Weapons Division and turning it into a separate company (as with Hawker Siddeley Dynamics) in case the Government decided either to exclude Guided Weapons from their embrace, or could be put in a position whereby they had to enact special legislation so as to include it. After much study, and as it became clear that Guided Weapons was going to be treated as part of the aircraft industry for the purposes of the new Bill, no further action was taken.

The first official Parliamentary step towards nationalisation was made on 29 October 1974, when, in the Queen's Speech, it was announced that legislation would be introduced in that session to bring the aircraft industry into public ownership as part of the Government's general industrial strategy. To some, it was a surprise that nationalisation of the aircraft industry was to be pressed forward so quickly and with such a slender mandate as, in the view certainly of the Opposition, to be no mandate at all. To others, including Sir George, it was no surprise at all. The Left-Wing Ministerial staffing at the Department of Industry, with Wedgwood Benn as Secretary of State and Eric Heffer as Minister of State (Lord Beswick was the other Minister), had put the writing on the wall. Benn and Heffer would assuredly hold out for the public ownership of aircraft and shipbuilding as a top priority, and it seemed pretty obvious that Frank Beswick was only in the Department of Industry prior to being named as the head of the new aerospace set-up as and when it was formed.

A few days after the Queen's Speech, Sir George, who was on holiday in Cornwall, sent a handwritten note to Wedgwood Benn about the industry – '. . . in which I have spent almost forty years.'

'Whatever views I might have about the desirability of nationalising BAC,' he went on, 'this letter is to say that I am determined to do what I can to make the industry in its new form a success.'

This part of the letter was later quoted by Benn at the Press conference when he tabled a Consultative Document prior to the Shipbuilding and Aircraft Bill. The result was that in some sections of the industry and of the Conservative Party, Sir George was labelled a 'collaborationist' – the word being used in the sense that it was a synonym for 'traitor.'

In fact Sir George had consistently taken the same line throughout the summer of 1974 and had said openly to the Press and on T V, as already recorded, that nationalisation was irrelevant to the problems of the industry but, if it was going to be nationalised, then he saw it as his duty to the industry, to which he had devoted a lifetime's work, to do all he could to ensure that the new organisation was as sensible in structure as his influence could make it. Indeed, within a few days of the election, Sir George had had luncheon with Sir Kenneth Keith, Chairman of Rolls-Royce, to agree with him that they would oppose any National Enterprise Board between the nationalised companies and the Government, and also that neither wanted the airframe and engine sides joined together, but would press for one engine company and one airframe-guided weapons–helicopter company.

From the time of the election, Sir George was privately convinced that Benn would push through nationalisation early in the new Government's life, and that it would become law. It was, in his view, not a subject on which the public felt deeply and certainly not one which would bring people out in a procession of banners down Whitehall. He did not believe that the Liberals or any of the other minority parties would combine to precipitate an early new election which would probably cost them their jobs, and in any event the Conservative alternative, if Heseltine's seeming views were to prevail, was to split the UK industry into three separate lumps and Europeanise it in some unspecified way with the British components as the only profitable ones. Of two bad proposals, Sir George preferred Benn's which he believed could be made to work if it was given the right management structure with the ability to run its business as a business. Hence the Cornwall letter.

The pre-Bill Consultative Document of January 1975 relied heavily, in setting out its reasons for nationalisation, on the old argument that the public should own aerospace because the Government supported it so heavily. Figures of £650 million for military Research and Development and civil support plus £800 million for Government military purchases since 1966 were quoted and, it was claimed, an industry which was so dependent on public expenditure should be owned by the public. Only by nationalisation would the industry be put into good shape to make the most of its international opportunities. It was news to BAC that it needed to be put into 'good shape' since, on the day the document was published, its firm order book was for well over £800 million and the firm export orders, which, by definition, were not being paid for by the Government, were for £500 million.

There was a great deal in the document about industrial democracy and the need for the workers to participate in decision-making 'at all levels,' but the general organisation of the new Corporation would, in the main, and subject to the Secretary of State for Industry and Parliament, be left to the Corporation to work out. Nothing was said about compensation, save that it would be 'fair,' the Corporation would be free to diversify, and (good news) it would not be answerable in any way to the National Enterprise Board. After the Second Reading of the Bill, an Organising Committee would be set up, consisting of the Chairman-designate of the new Corporation plus a nucleus of other members of what eventually would be a kind of Holdings Board.

At the Press conference on the Document, and notably in a TV interview with Michael Charlton, Wedgwood Benn was much pressed to define 'industrial democracy' and 'worker participation,' to all of which the Minister replied that he could not impose these things from above, but they had to develop from the wishes of the workers themselves. He did stress that by 'workers' he included management and professional employees as well as those who worked by 'hand.' After nationalisation, however, there was considerable and immediate controversy inside the industry because some took the line that only members of Trade Unions could be recognised for negotiating purposes, thus excluding from consultation getting on for half of the Corporation's employees. This problem of who is a 'worker' and what is 'democracy' is, however, beyond the scope of this book.

At this stage (January 1975), there was no mention of Scottish Aviation, nor, more importantly, of Westland Helicopters, which company remained in the private sector and whose workers had been at some pains to say they preferred it that way. No reason was ever given as to why two such disparate industries as aerospace and shipbuilding should be lumped together in the one Bill – the one industry desperately ill, and the other not.

The industry and interested parties were given only something like three weeks to make comments on the Consultative Document – such comments being, presumably, the 'Consultation.' Lord Nelson replied on behalf of the parents (Vickers concurring) on 11 February, and made the points that there was no case for public ownership, that the industry was efficient and healthy, and no argument had ever been advanced that nationalisation would make it more so. It was illogical to argue that, because the Government was a major customer and a source of support for advanced development, this justified taking the industry into public ownership. Such vertical integration, even under favourable conditions, had not been universally successful, and, in practice, a purchaser was in a stronger position if not financially involved in the ownership of the suppliers. The existence of private financial involvement in the suppliers was an important protection for the Government and the tax-payer, in that purchasing policies were closely monitored and responsibly executed. The repeated proposal on wide freedom to diversify would cause considerable uncertainty and confusion to other manufacturers and workers.

The BAC response (12 February) followed the same lines, only in much greater detail, paragraph by paragraph. It set the record straight on the health of the company (there was some 'lame duck' suggestion in Benn's document), and commented pointedly on the lack of definition of most of the proposals. It was stressed that any proposal that all the workers should share in all the decisions at all levels could only lead to long delays in getting any decision at all – and this in an industry whose overseas trade depended so much on quick response to customer requirement and demand.

About this time (19 February), Lord Robens wrote to the Foreign Secretary, James Callaghan, pointing out the unease in Saudi Arabia about nationalisation and asking him to reassure Saudi Arabia that they would still be dealing with the same people they were used to, and that it was safe to place further aerospace orders with Britain – about which they were in some doubt. This was but the first of many similar reassurances that were to be called for over the next two years.

With the preliminary skirmishes over, meetings between the Department of Industry and the industry began to take place, BAC being represented by Sir George, Greenwood, Page, Jefferson, Pritchard and Cookson. The Department of Industry was represented at one meeting by Mr de le B. Jones, Mr K. Warrington, and Mr R. Mountfield, and at another both Wedgwood Benn and Lord Beswick were present. The discussions, as far as they went, were sweetly reasonable, and many of BAC's detailed points were apparently accepted (including the clumsiness of Wedgwood Benn's proposed name for the new Corporation 'The Aircraft Corporation of Great Britain').

There were also political meetings of various kinds with Conservative spokesmen, notably one held by SBAC with Heseltine and his anti-nationalisation team. The Conservative view was that the Labour Party intended to follow aerospace by the nationalisation of electronic and equipment firms, and that the Cabinet was not interested in the defence of Europe or the UK. It was, they said, pursuing a calculated strategy of destroying the defence of the country, and the nationalisation of aerospace was only one element in this strategy. Companies should be urged to inform their labour forces of the possible consequences of nationalisation.

BAC, however, neither under Edwards nor Greenwood, never indulged in much overt tub-thumping on the issues. There was no attempt by management to instruct, warn, frighten or otherwise influence the employees. Such political action within its factories would have been counter-productive, and was not in keeping with the traditions of BAC. In any event, the work-force was kept fully aware of what was going on through the exhaustive coverage by the media, especially T V. From time to time, Sir George or Allen Greenwood used an existing public speaking engagement to reiterate their opposition to the proposals and to ask in what way the performance of the industry could conceivably be improved by the transfer, at great expense, of the shares of BAC from the present owners to the Government. This, they argued, was surely the key question, and, to date, no single advantage has been brought forward. The disadvantages, however, as far as competitive edge was concerned, of 'working for the Government' were only too well known from the track records of previous nationalisation ventures.

A small BAC working party was set up under Greenwood to answer questions from individual and constituency-interested MPs of all parties, and to provide facts and figures to any who sought them. Much of the emphasis here was to show that BAC was nobody's 'lame duck' – this inference having been widely drawn overseas where the competition was saying that both BAC and Hawker were being nationalised to save them from a Rolls-Royce type bankruptcy. Benn, too, tried to scotch this one, but not with overmuch emphasis as his own Consultative Document had itself sown the first seeds of this particular and damaging falsehood.

Conservative politicians were somewhat critical of BAC at this stage because they felt the Chairman and the Board should be barnstorming the country and the factories, and joining openly with the Opposition in vociferous and political protest. That the BAC Board did not do this was because, from where they sat, it seemed a waste of effort. The issue was going to be decided by Parliament, and it was unlikely that all the speeches in the world were going to change the direction of one pair of voting shoes from the 'Aye' to the 'No' lobby, come the Second Reading. It was, in BAC's view, much more sensible to devote its energies behind the scenes to getting the Bill adjusted here and there by quiet persuasion at the Department of Industry itself, with the ultimate objective of having a workable set-up at the end of it. If, in the unpredictable way of politics in such a closely matched House, the Government fell for other reasons before the Bill became an Act, then so be it.

On 17 March 1975, the Minister made a statement on compensation, which was both complicated and vague. The compensation was to be calculated by reference to the average Stock Exchange quotation during the six months ending 29 February 1974, and the value of unquoted securities was to be determined 'as if they had been quoted during the same period.' Both BAC and HSA were, of course, unquoted companies – BAC being wholly owned by GEC/Vickers, and HSA (and HSD) being wholly owned by the Hawker Siddeley Group.

The BAC Board was quick to point out that the price at which a security is quoted on the Stock Exchange is influenced as much by external factors as by the situation of the particular company concerned. It was, therefore, totally unclear how compensation would be calculated for an unquoted company such as BAC, particularly bearing in mind that the six months chosen by the Minister as the yardstick included the October 1973 war in the Middle East, the three-day week, the oil crisis, and the run-up to a general election. It was noted, however, that there were provisions for arbitration. In the same 17 March statement, Wedgwood Benn added Scottish Aviation to his shopping list. He also strictly controlled distribution of profits. Tom Pritchard immediately observed that this meant the parents could no longer reasonably be expected to provide funds or to undertake guarantees or other commitments when they could see no return, either by way of distributable profit or enhanced compensation. The Banks and other outside sources of finance were in the same negative position.

On 1 May, the Bill itself was published. At almost every point, it gave such direct powers to the Minister that he could involve himself at will in all the day-to-day activities of the new Corporation (now named as British Aerospace). At the same time, it placed upon British Aerospace the clear responsibility to undertake its tasks in the most efficient and economical way possible – a charge which it was quite impossible to fulfil in the light of the Minister's over-riding powers over every decision the Corporation would take. There was also – and for the first time in legislation – a statutory obligation on the Corporation to introduce industrial democracy without, however, defining such 'industrial democracy' in any way.

It was a very bad Bill, so clumsily worded in some of its clauses that even senior civil servants at the Department of Industry were unable to tell industry what the words were supposed to mean.

Vickers and GEC, on 5 May, issued a press release roundly attacking the Bill as not being in the best interests of the country or the industry, or of the people working in it. It dwelt on the success of the BAC merger, and its order book of £800 million, of which £600 million was for export, and asserted that all past experience had shown that under nationalisation decision-making would be slowed down, costs would rise, competitiveness would be reduced, and job security would eventually be diminished.

There was one other part of the Bill which caused considerable unrest, both inside and outside aerospace, and that was the granting to the Corporation of 'very wide powers,' subject to the Secretary of State's consent, 'to diversify and to acquire other companies by agreement.' This meant, or was interpreted as meaning, that the Wedgwood Benn/Heffer combination could, through British Aerospace, take over almost any company they wished without further legislation, subject to whatever was meant by the words 'by agreement.'

By this time, the spectacle of Wedgwood Benn, sitting as he did in the seat of power over all British industry, and holding the views he did (and does), was giving rise to growing alarm, not only at home but overseas. Whether for this reason or not, Harold Wilson moved Benn from the Department of Industry in the early summer of 1975 and transferred him to Energy and North Sea oil, bringing in Eric Varley to the Department of Industry; later, when Eric Heffer left, he also added Gerald Kaufman, a member of Wilson's so-called 'Kitchen Cabinet,' to the Department of Industry Ministerial team.

It had now become clear that, for timetable reasons, the Bill was not going to get its Second Reading in the current session of Parliament, and that BAC and Hawker were going to be left in operational and financial limbo under, as it were, 'suspended sentence.' The Government still did not possess legal powers to provide finance for on-going work, but, with the publication of the Bill, the parents and banks no longer had any incentive to fill the gaps for the reasons already stated.

It would be wearisome indeed to go through all the detailed discussions on the Bill which took place between BAC and the Department of Industry during the summer and autumn of 1975 – most of the points being aimed at giving to the new Corporation the right to run its affairs free of day-to-day detailed control by the Minister, and ensuring that proper levels of finance would be available to progress work in hand and to support new projects. The Ministry kept making reassuring noises that the Minister would, in fact, only intervene on major matters of public interest (as defined by him) and maintaining that the proposed funding in the Bill was adequate (which it certainly was not).

In the event, the new Bill under Varley turned out to be very little different from the Wedgwood Benn one, and this was made clear in the first week of September to a deputation from SBAC which had gone to the Ministry to point out the damage that was being done by all the delays and uncertainties.

On 19 November 1975, in the Queen's Speech, notice was again given that the Bill would be re-introduced early in the session, and, as far as could be discovered, it was now hoped to have vesting day (the day the shares in BAC, Hawker, and Scottish Aviation were handed over to the Government) some time in July 1976 (the original date had been 1 January 1976).

The Aircraft and Shipbuilding Industries Bill was given its formal first reading on 20 September 1975, and the Second Reading debate was on 2 December. It was the predictable hotch-potch of shipbuilding speeches and aircraft speeches and, although there had been speculation that the Government could well be defeated, as the Liberals were against nationalisation, it was not to be. The Ayes had it by 280 votes to 275.

With the Second Reading out of the way, and any hopes the industry had that it might bring about the downfall of the Government dashed, the Minister was now legally able to appoint his interim Organising Committee for British Aerospace – this Committee to become the Aerospace Board when the Corporation was duly vested in the July. He began on 4 December by naming – as expected – Lord Beswick as Chairman of the Organising Committee and Chairman-designate of British Aerospace. Lord Beswick thereupon left the Department of Industry and was succeeded there by the promotion to Ministerial rank of Gerald Kaufman. It was not until 13 April, however, that Lord Beswick was able to announce any further members of his Committee. The reason was that some of the key top men in the industry itself either wanted nothing to do with a nationalised Corporation or were very reluctant to commit themselves. Sir George had already retired and was never a candidate, while Sir Arnold Hall had also made it quite clear that he was staying with that substantial part of the Hawker Siddeley Group which was outside aviation. Sir John Lidbury had also opted out, as had Sir Harry Broadhurst. Allen Greenwood, now Chairman of BAC, was very much in two minds as what to do. He had recently made several strong speeches against nationalisation, but in the end, after consultation and a lot of private heart-searching (he was in receipt of other and tempting offers), he agreed to serve as a member of the team.

The other original members of the Organising Committee were Mr L. W. Buck, President of the Confederation of Shipbuilding and Engineering Unions, and General Secretary of the Sheet Metal Workers Union; Mr (later Sir) G. R. Jefferson, Chairman and Managing Director of BAC's Guided Weapons Division; Dr (later Sir) A. W. Pearce, Chairman of Esso; Mr Eric Rubython, General Manager of HSA; and Mr John Stamper, Technical Director of HSA. Greenwood was named as Deputy Chairman-designate of British Aerospace and all the other members were full time save Dr Pearce. Later appointees were Sir Frederick Page, Air Chief Marshal Sir Peter Fletcher and Mr B.E. Friend as full-time members and Mr D.O. Gladwin as part-time member. Dr G.H. Hough was a member for some eight months in 1977 and resigned at the end of October 1977.

The Committee stage of the Bill lasted for a record fifty-eight meetings until 13 May 1976, the Government holding on to all its main points, but on 25 May, Mr Maxwell Hyslop, a Conservative MP, threw a major spanner into the procedural works when he claimed that the whole Bill was hybrid. He pointed out that it excluded from nationalisation the Marathon Shipyard in keeping with a promise given by the Labour Government to the Texas owners of the yard when they purchased it. All relevant companies in the same line of business in the UK were not, therefore, being treated alike which, he said, made the Bill hybrid, a view, which if sustained, would put the Bill back to square one. The Maxwell Hyslop point was in fact sustained, the Speaker ruling there was a *prima facie* case, and the examiners later confirmed hybridity.

It so happened that 24/25 May were the dates of the first British Airways Concorde service to and from Washington, and therefore 'to' (24 May) and 'from' (25 May) the USA – a notable occasion. On the Washington–London flight, Gerald Kaufman said jocularly to the author, 'When we get to Heathrow, I'll have to rush away to the House to see through the next step to getting you safely nationalised in time for Farnborough.' Little did he know what uproar he would find awaiting him in the Chamber.

It is not proposed to follow here all the heated Parliamentary debates, and the procedural moves which went on through the rest of 1976, or the many amendments passed in Lords and referred back to Commons. The key point is that the industry was *not* nationalised by Farnborough, and the entire fate of the Bill hung in the balance for the rest of 1976. It was, indeed, no better than even money that the Bill would ever become law as, at one time, it looked as if the House of Lords might be able to keep it, as it were, 'in play' until the end of the session, when, yet again, it would have to be re-introduced anew – assuming that the Government decided to re-introduce it at all in view of their greatly upset timetable and also assuming they were still the Government. A Lords-versus-Commons confrontation was very much on the cards, and, during all this, the aerospace industry continued in the limbo which had begun back in early 1974.

The working relationships which had been set up by BAC and HSA, particularly on the civil side (both were members of the 'Group of Six') continued, but were under some strain. The truth was that BAC deep down believed that, in the end, nationalisation would somehow come about, whereas Hawker Siddeley did not. There was, therefore, a natural 'holding back' at top level, especially as there was doubt as to the actual status (if any) of Lord Beswick's Organising Committee. It was a very bad time for all those involved. No one was sure where affairs stood (including the Government); overseas customers had continually to be reassured that, whatever happened, their interests would be safeguarded, and the competition exploited the shambles by harping on the bankruptcy theme. Some of the more extreme Left Wing speeches in the many debates were given the widest circulation as evidence that British Aerospace was about to be controlled by a 'workers' Soviet' which would eventually 'black' all deliveries of products and spares to any country of whose government of the day they did not approve.

The Parliamentary chaos was eventually sorted out when the Government agreed to remove twelve ship-repairing companies from the Bill. The Lords did not precipitate a Lords-versus-Commons confrontation over their rejected amendments and, by agreement, Varley was able to announce on 2 March 1977, that the Bill would now move through its final stages and on to the Royal Assent stage. This duly happened, and Vesting Day, initially planned for 1 January 1976, was finally 29 April 1977.

The Organising Committee then became the British Aerospace Board, with Lord Beswick as Chairman, and Allen Greenwood as Deputy Chairman. After all the delays and frustrations, it was almost with a sigh of relief that BAC heard the news. Almost anything, it was now felt, was preferable to the uncertainties of the past three years.

As expected, British Aerospace was internally divided into two Groups – the Aircraft Group under an engineer, Freddie Page, (now Sir Frederick), as Chairman and Chief Executive, and the Dynamics Group, also under an engineer, George Jefferson (later Sir George), as its Chairman and Chief Executive. Jeff's job of organising the amalgam of BAC Guided Weapons Division and Hawker Siddeley Dynamics was comparatively straightforward. The products were complementary rather than competitive, and the main factories of Hatfield and Stevenage were conveniently close together. Freddie Page had a more complicated task and ended with six Divisions to Dynamics' two.

Although not strictly relevant to this book, the British Aerospace organisational charts are appended at the state at which they were actually implemented on 1 January 1978. (Jefferson left British Aerospace in 1980 for British Telecom.)

BAC provided the new set-up with its senior main Board professional (Greenwood); with both the Group Chairmen and Chief Executives (Page and Jefferson); with the main Board Secretary and Legal Advisor (Cookson) and its Treasurer (John Hanson). The Military Aircraft Managing Director (Atkin) and both the Aircraft Group and Dynamics Group Commercial and Financial Directors came from BAC (Baxendale and Sawyer, the late Eric Beverley and Raff). The other Group directorates were more or less evenly divided between BAC and HSA, with all the Divisional managing directorships going to men who had either held that position before nationalisation or had been in a senior post with the previous owners.

On the whole, the British Aerospace operational organisation, as finalised by Page and Jefferson, could be said to meet Sir George's originally stated hope of 1974, that it would be 'a workable set up.' It was still basically in force, with Sir Austin Pearce as the Chairman after Frank Beswick, when British Aerospace went semi-private by going semi-public in February 1981, under the Labour threat of re-nationalisation without compensation. British Aerospace, however, put half of its £100 million of 50p shares on the market at 150p per share, the Government retaining the other 50 per cent. The order book of the day showed an estimated £1551 million for military aircraft, £519 million for civil aircraft, and £1345 million for guided weapons and Space – a total, with other odds and ends, well in excess of £3400 million.

Envoi

This book began with some account of the embarrassing number of aircraft design firms operating in Great Britain at the start of the post-war period. Gradually, most of those companies were, under Government pressure, absorbed either into BAC or HSA, until the SBAC became popularly known as the 'Society of Both Aircraft Constructors.' This was an unfair jest as SBAC represents not only the major air frame groups, but also Rolls-Royce, Westland and Shorts, one or two smaller units, and particularly the many companies whose electronic, ancillary and specialised equipment products, materials and skills provide an overall aerospace ability which is still unmatched anywhere in Europe and is equalled only in the USA and the USSR.

The process of the merging of the major companies which went on in the fifties and sixties was as inevitable as has been the still growing collaboration with the European industry – our main bulwark against American domination of the Old World's high technology. It is, however, fitting that this history should end with a reminder of the great pioneer companies whose names and achievements, some dating back to before World War I, are still remembered with pride, and which today, some still on their original sites, are now incorporated in British Aerospace.

Airspeed	Gloster Aircraft
Armstrong Whitworth	Hawker Aircraft
Avro	Hawker Siddeley Aircraft
British Aircraft Corporation	Hawker Siddeley Dynamics
Blackburn Aircraft	Hunting Aircraft
Bristol Aeroplane	Percival Aircraft
Coventry Ordnance	Scottish Aviation
de Havilland	Sopwith Aircraft
English Electric	Vickers-Armstrongs (Aircraft)
Folland Aircraft	Vickers-Supermarine
General Aircraft	

It is a great heritage, and to it has to be added the considerable Guided Weapons and Space facilities which BAC and HSD and their former parents created in more recent years. It can truly be claimed for British Aerospace that it began its life in 1977 with the most comprehensive range of skills and experience in military and civil aircraft, weapons, and Space, of any single company in the world. From BAC alone, it inherited an order book worth £2000 million. This unique Corporate combination of technical and trading strength is something which British Aerospace must now trumpet abroad. The opportunities are almost boundless.

But, as one hopes this book has done something to show, this strength and these opportunities would not exist but for the determination which, for its seventeen years of life, BAC showed in the face of many adversities, many of them the direct result of bad national planning and a continual failure in Whitehall to realise that Great Britain's aerospace heritage was as much a potential economic saviour in peacetime as it had been our actual saviour in war. The debt the nation owes to men like Mitchell, Pierson, Joe Smith, George Edwards, Lord Portal, Sidney Camm, Roy Dobson, Roy Chadwick, Sir Reginald Vernon-Smith, and the de Havillands, and their colleagues in the companies which became BAC and HSA, is truly enormous. British Aerospace still has engineers of achievement and stature comparable to the great ones of the past, and a 1980 worldwide order book of nearly £3500 million is a token of that.

Appendices

Appendix 1

British Aircraft Corporation
Financial Achievement

In this short table, the last years of BAC are contrasted with the earnings of 1961 and 1964/5/6. In 1961 BAC made a trading profit of £567,000 and a profit after tax of £132,000 which, after various deductions, became £90,000, and no dividend was declared. In 1964, total sales were £116.7 million, pre-tax profits were £1 million, outstanding orders £361 million and, again, there was no dividend. In 1965, the profit after tax was down to £104,000, and in 1966 it was little better at £201,000. The key details of 1968–76, however, make it interesting reading.

In 1971, new orders exceeded the £200 million mark for the first time, and this was repeated in 1972. After that, the 'outstanding order' book position at the end of each year was:

Year	Total	Export content
	£ million	*£ million*
1973	636	400
1974	815	600
1975	850	600
1976	1031	760

At nationalisation, with the Saudi and other contracts at finalisation, BAC's order book had reached £2000 million, over three-quarters of which was for export.

The number of employees in BAC varied in the brackets between 36,000 and 33,000, the total at the end of 1976 being 34,528, with a wages bill of £132 million. (In 1966, the wages bill for 35,879 employees was £45.2 million.)

	1968 £ million	1969 £ million	1970 £ million	1971 £ million	1972 £ million	1973 £ million	1974 £ million	1975 £ million	1976 £ million
Sales									
UK	115.7	98.6	101.5	96.3	86.6	82.3	98.8	107.5	213.3
Export	75.7	85.3	49.0	62.6	66.7	92.1	173.0	199.6	270.1
Total	191.4	183.9	150.5	158.9	153.3	174.4	271.8	307.1	483.4
Trading profit	12.0	10.6	7.7	8.6	9.8	16.9	24.4	26.9	33.8
Net profit after tax	4.2	2.8	2.2	2.4	3.8	5.9	12.0	14.2	19.2
Dividend	1.7	1.7	0.5	NIL	1.7	2.5	4.5[1]	4.2	3.4[2]
Earnings per share	21.2p	14.0p	11.1p	12.0p	18.8p	29.2p	40.1p	47.2p	64.0p

[1] Plus £15 million repaid loans to shareholders.
[2] Limited by statute.
NB Share capital until June 1974 was £20 million, after which it was increased to £30 million.

Appendix 2

British Aircraft Corporation and BAC (Holdings) Limited Main Board Members 1960–77

1960

Marshal of the Royal Air Force Viscount Portal of Hungerford, KG, GCB, OM, DSO, MC (Chairman)

Major General Sir Charles Dunphie, CB, CBE, DSO

Hon. George Nelson, MA, Hon.DSC, CEng, MICE, MIMechE

Mr R.P.H. Yapp

Sir Reginald Verdon-Smith, LLD, BCL, MA, FIEE, FRAeS

Sir George Edwards, CBE, BSC (Eng), CEng, Hon.DSC, Hon.FRAeS, Hon.FAIAA

Rt Hon. Viscount Caldecote, DSC, MA, CEng, MIMechE, FIEE, FRAeS

Mr W. Masterton, CA

Mr G.A. Riddell, BCom, CA

Marshal of the Royal Air Force Sir Dermot Boyle, GCB, KCVO, KBE, AFC

Mr A.D. Marris, CMG

1961/2

Sir Charles Dunphie retired from the Board and was replaced by Sir Leslie Rowan, KCB, CVO. Mr A.W.E. Houghton joined as Production Director. The Hon. George Nelson succeeded to his father's title of Lord Nelson of Stafford and, with Sir Leslie Rowan, became Joint Deputy Chairman. Sir Dermot Boyle became Vice Chairman. Sir George Edwards was appointed Managing Director; Lord Caldecote, Deputy Managing Director; and Mr Masterton, Financial Director.

1963/8

Unchanged, save for the retirement in August 1967 of Mr Houghton. In January 1964, BAC (Operating) Limited was formed, with Sir George Edwards as Chairman and Managing Director. In August 1968, the name of the main company was changed from British Aircraft Corporation to BAC (Holdings) Limited, and BAC (Operating) Limited became British Aircraft Corporation.

1969

Sir Reginald Verdon-Smith succeeded Lord Portal as Chairman of the Holdings Board. Lord Caldecote retired.

1970/71

Sir Raymond Brown, OBE, and Mr N.C. Macdiarmid joined the Board mid-year but Mr Macdiarmid retired at the end of the year. Mr R.H. Grierson was a Director between January and March 1971. Sir Dermot Boyle and Sir Leslie Rowan retired at the end of 1970 and Mr W.W. Straight, CBE, MC, DFC, FRIM, FRSA, FRGS, FRAeS, and Dr F. Llewellyn Smith, CBE, MSC, DPhil, CEng, FEMechE, were appointed. Mr Masterton died in December 1971.

1972

Sir Reginald Verdon-Smith, Mr A.D. Marris, Mr W.W. Straight and Dr F. Llewellyn Smith retired at the end of the year. In a re-arrangement of emphasis as between the Holdings Board and its principal operating subsidiary, BAC, the Holdings Board was reduced in numbers to Sir George Edwards (Managing Director), Sir Raymond Brown, Mr P.A. Mathews, Lord Nelson, Mr Riddell and Mr Yapp.

1973

Mr C.W. Foreman, CA, Mr W.C.P. McKie, and Mr J.T. Wiltshire, MA, joined the Holdings Board.

1974

Sir Raymond Brown retired and Mr R. Telford, CBE, MA, CEng, FIEE, FIProdE, FBIM, FRSA, was appointed.

1975

Sir George Edwards retired at the end of 1975. Mr A.H.C. Greenwood, CBE, JP, CEng, FRAeS, and Mr T. Pritchard, FCA, joined the Holdings Board; and Mr Greenwood succeeded Sir George as Chairman of BAC.

1976

Mr R.P.H. Yapp retired mid-year – having served on the Board since its formation.

1977

BAC nationalised. Lord Nelson and Mr G.A. Riddell had served as Board members throughout the active lifetime of BAC. Messrs B. Cookson and B.E. Friend joined Mr T.B. Pritchard on the British Aircraft Corporation (Holdings) Board which continued to exist as a subsidiary of British Aerospace.

Appendix 3

British Aircraft Corporation (Operating) Limited
and British Aircraft Corporation

From 1960 to 28 December 1963, British Aircraft Corporation Limited Reports and Accounts consolidated those of Bristol Aircraft Limited, English Electric Aviation Limited, Vickers-Armstrongs (Aircraft) Limited, Hunting Aircraft Limited (BAC interest, 70 per cent of share capital), BAC (Australia) Pty, Limited (from March 1961), BAC (USA) Inc. (from April 1961), British Scandinavian Aviation AB (from June 1962 – BAC interest, 60 per cent of share capital), British Aircraft Corporation (AT) Limited (from January 1962 – BAC interest, 50 per cent of share capital).

On 28 December 1963, the Corporation formed a new wholly owned subsidiary company, British Aircraft Corporation (Operating) Limited, to which was transferred the whole of the business previously carried on by its four operating subsidiaries – Bristol Aircraft Limited, English Electric Aviation Limited, Hunting Aircraft Limited, and Vickers-Armstrongs (Aircraft) Limited. The Guided Weapons interests of Bristol Aircraft and English Electric Aviation had already been integrated in 1963. British Aircraft Corporation (Operating) Limited thus comprised the following operating Divisions:

British Aircraft Corporation (Filton)
British Aircraft Corporation (Luton) (now wholly owned)
British Aircraft Corporation (Preston)
British Aircraft Corporation (Weybridge)
British Aircraft Corporation (Guided Weapons)

Over the years, the above five Divisions were reduced to three – Military Aircraft Division, Commercial Aircraft Division and Guided Weapons Division.

The initial BAC (Operating) Board comprised:

Sir George Edwards	(Chairman and Managing Director)
Lord Caldecote	(Deputy to Sir George)
James Harper	(Filton)
A. W. E. Houghton	(Weybridge and Preston)
W. A. Summers	(Luton and Hurn)
F. W. Page	(Preston)

W. Masterton	(Financial Director)
G.E. Knight	(Civil Sales)
A.H.C. Greenwood	(Military Sales and all after-sales service)
J.E. Armitage	(Financial Controller)

In 1968, BAC (Operating) Limited became British Aircraft Corporation Limited and, after the retirements of Lord Caldecote and Mr Houghton, and the death of James Harper (succeeded as Filton Chairman by Dr A.E. Russell), the first BAC Board was:

Sir George Edwards	(Chairman and Managing Director)
W. Masterton	(Deputy Chairman)
A.H.C. Greenwood	(Assistant Managing Director)
J.E. Armitage	(Commercial Director)
E.G. Barber	(Director of Personnel and Training)
T.B. Pritchard	(Financial Director)
Dr A.E. Russell	(Chairman, Filton Division)
G.T. Gedge	(Managing Director, Filton Division)
G.R. Jefferson	(Chairman and Managing Director, Guided Weapons Division)
G.E. Knight	(Chairman and Managing Director, Weybridge Division)
F.W. Page	(Chairman and Managing Director, Preston Division)
B. Cookson	(Secretary, also Secretary to BAC (Holdings) Limited)

1969

Mr Handel Davies joined the Board as Technical Director, and Mr J. Ferguson Smith joined on his appointment as Managing Director (Weybridge Division).

1970

Dr Russell retired from the Board.

1971/2

Mr H.R. Baxendale joined the Board on becoming Deputy Chairman and Managing Director of the Military Aircraft Division. Mr Greenwood became Deputy Chairman; Mr G.E. Knight, Vice Chairman; Mr F.W. Page, Managing Director (Aircraft) of BAC; and Mr Jefferson, Managing Director (Guided Weapons) of BAC. Mr J.D. Hanson became Treasurer.

1974

Mr Cookson joined the Board as Director of Contracts, and Mr A.C. Buckley became Secretary.

1975/6/7

Sir George Edwards retired at the end of 1975, and Mr Greenwood became Chairman of BAC. Mr Barber retired from the company, and Mr A.T. Slator was appointed to replace him. Later, when Mr Pritchard retired just before nationalisation, his place was taken by Mr D. Wynne.

A number of the most senior officials of British Aircraft Corporation (Operating) and then of British Aircraft Corporation were, over the years, given the rank of 'Special Director' but were not members of the Board. This procedure of giving what amounted to honorary director status and privileges to senior executives was also followed in the Divisions.

Appendix 4

Divisional Boards

Each of the Divisions of British Aircraft Corporation, at first five in number, and later reduced to three, had its own Chairman, Managing Director, and Directors. There were also BAC Directors on the various international Boards such as Sepecat, Panavia and Europlane, and subsidiary companies such as BAC (Australia) and BAC (USA), the latter companies also having local Directors. There were also qualified subsidiaries such as BAC (Insurance Brokers) Limited.

It is not proposed to list all those Divisional and subsidiary company appointments over the seventeen years, but only to give the three Divisional Boards as set out in the final BAC Report which was for its last full year of trading – 1976.

Commercial Aircraft Division

F.W. Page, CBE, MA, CEng, FRAeS (Chairman)
J. Ferguson Smith, FCA (Deputy Chairman and Managing Director)
M.G. Wilde, OBE, BSC, DipAe, CEng, FRAeS (Deputy Managing Director)
K. Bentley, MA, CEng, MRAeS
W.R. Coomber, CEng, FRAeS
G. Hanby, FCA, FCMA
J.T. Jefferies, CEng, FIProdE
E.E. Marshall, CBE, CEng, FRAeS
L.J. Rogers, MA
H. Smith, FCA
Dr W.J. Strang, CBE, FRS, BSC, PhD, CEng, FRAeS
E.B. Trubshaw, CBE, MVO, FRAeS

Military Aircraft Division

H.R. Baxendale, OBE, DL, ACMA (Chairman)
A.F. Atkin, OBE, BSC, DipAe, CEng, FIMechI, FRAeS (Managing Director)
R.P. Beamont, CBE, DSO, DFC, FRAeS
R. Dickson, MA, CEng, FRAeS
S. Gillibrand, MSC, CEng, MRAeS, AMBIM
P. Grocock
B.O. Heath, BSC, DIC, CEng, MRAeS

F.W. Page, CBE, MA, CEng, FRAeS
F.E. Roe, DIC, BSC, CEng, ACGI, FRAeS
Air Chief Marshal Sir Frederick Rosier, GCB, CBE, DSO
R.H. Sawyer, FCA, FCMA, JDipMA
T.O. Williams, MA, CEng, FIMechE, MIEE
I.R. Yates, BEng, CEng, FRAeS, MIMechE

Guided Weapons Division

G.R. Jefferson, CBE, BSC, CEng, MIMechE, FRAeS (Chairman)
T.G. Kent, CEng, MIMechE, MRAeS (Managing Director)
D. Rowley, MA, CEng, FRAeS (Assistant Managing Director, Electronic
   & Space Systems)
E.L. Beverley, DFC, CEng, FRAeS
J. Cattanach, BSc, CEng, MIEE
K. Dixon
Lt Col. H. Lacy, MBE, BSC
Maj. Gen. R.S. Marshall, CB, OBE, MC, MM
J.A. Leitch, MSc, CEng
H. Metcalfe, OBE, BSC, ARCS, CEng, FRAeS
R.J. Parkhouse, MSC, BSC, CEng, FIProdE, MRAeS
R.J. Raff, FCA, ACMA
L.A. Sanson, OBE
R.N. Settle, BSC, CEng, MIEE, MInstP, AssocIMechE, MBIM
S.A. Smith, JP, MA, CEng, MRAeS
J. McG. Sowerby, OBE, BA, CEng, FIEE, SMIEEE
I.D. Woodhead, MBE

Appendix 5

British Aerospace

The following key British Aerospace directorates were awarded to former members of British Aircraft Corporation.

Corporation Board Members

Deputy Chairman of BAe	A.H.C. GREENWOOD
Chairman and Chief Executive, Aircraft Group	F.W. PAGE (now Sir Frederick)
Chairman and Chief Executive, Dynamics Group	G.R. JEFFERSON
Secretary and Legal Adviser	B. COOKSON

Aircraft Group Board Members

Chairman and Chief Executive	F.W. PAGE
Managing Director (Military) of Aircraft Group and Divisional Chairman of Warton Division, Kingston/Brough Division and Manchester Division	A.F. ATKIN
Commercial Director	H.R. BAXENDALE
Deputy Managing Director (Civil) and Marketing Director (Civil), Aircraft Group	J. FERGUSON SMITH
Resources Director	F.E. ROE
Financial Director	R.H. SAWYER
Divisional Managing Director, Weybridge/Bristol Division	M.G. WILDE
Divisional Managing Director, Warton Division	I.R. YATES

Dynamics Group Board Members

Chairman and Chief Executive	G.R. JEFFERSON
Commercial Director	E.L. BEVERLEY
Marketing Director	L.A. SANSON
Technical Director	J. McG. SOWERBY

Financial Director	R.J. RAFF
Director (Army Weapons)	R.J. PARKHOUSE
Director (Naval Weapons)	H. METCALFE
Director and General Manager	T.G. KENT
Administration Director	A.T. SLATOR
Director	D. ROWLEY

Key Bibliography

Good Company, A.R. Adams, British Aircraft Corporation, Stevenage

The Labour Government 1964–1972, Harold Wilson, Weidenfeld & Nicolson and Michael Joseph

TSR2, Stephen Hastings, Macdonald

Portal of Hungerford, Denis Richards, Heinemann

Project Cancelled, Derek Wood, Macdonald & Jane's

Billion Dollar Battle, Harold Mansfield, David McKay

Rolls-Royce from the Wings, R.W. Harker, Oxford Illustrated Press

Concorde – the Inside Story, Geoffrey Knight, Weidenfeld & Nicolson

The Battle for Concorde, John Costello and Terry Hughes, Compton Press

Concorde, F.G. Clark and Arthur Gibson, Phoebus Publishing and BPC Publishing Limited

Concorde – the Story, Facts and Figures, T.E. Blackall, G.T Foulis

Vickers – a History, J.D. Scott, Weidenfeld & Nicolson

Bristol Aircraft Since 1910, C.H. Barnes, Putnam

Phoenix into Ashes, R.P. Beamont, William Kimber & Co.

Inside Story, H. Chapman Pincher, Sidgwick & Jackson

Vickers against the Odds, 1956–1977, Sir Harold Evans, Hodder & Stoughton

Index